SECRET SISTERS

SECRET SISTERS

STORIES OF BEING LESBIAN AND BISEXUAL IN A COLLEGE SORORITY

**Edited by Shane L. Windmeyer
& Pamela W. Freeman**

alyson books
los angeles | new york

MANUFACTURED IN THE UNITED STATES OF AMERICA.

THIS TRADE PAPERBACK ORIGINAL IS PUBLISHED BY
ALYSON PUBLICATIONS,
P.O. BOX 4371, LOS ANGELES, CA 90078-4371.
DISTRIBUTION IN THE UNITED KINGDOM BY
TURNAROUND PUBLISHER SERVICES LTD.,
UNIT 3, OLYMPIA TRADING ESTATE, COBURG ROAD, WOOD GREEN,
LONDON N22 6TZ ENGLAND.

FIRST EDITION: APRIL 2001

01 02 03 04 05 a 10 9 8 7 6 5 4 3 2 1

ISBN 1-55583-588-0

COVER PHOTO COURTESY OF NANCY HAVER.
COVER DESIGN BY MATT SAMS.

Sometimes, when you beat your head against a wall, your heart takes the punishment.

—Dinah Shore, Alpha Epsilon Phi

Dedicated to all the secret sisters out there.
You are not alone.

Contents

Sisterly Love and Friendship

Out and Proud

Straight Sisters' Perspectives

Interventions and Resources

Editors' Note:
Quotation marks around contributor names indicate the use of a pseudonym. All other authors' names are the actual names of the individuals writing the stories.

Acknowledgments

The 11th letter of the Greek alphabet, the lambda, represents synergy. In its greatest form, synergy produces the power of many to come together and produce positive change. Over the six years since we started the Lambda 10 Project and our first book, *Out on Fraternity Row: Personal Accounts of Being Gay in a College Fraternity,* many people have helped us create this synergy. Likewise, with this second book we have been fortunate to have many more people and organizations help us keep the synergy alive.

First and foremost, we thank the women who were willing to write their stories and give voice to being lesbian or bisexual in a college sorority. We recognize your courage and especially appreciate those who we were not able to include in the anthology. All of your voices are what made this book possible, and you are at the heart of our efforts. We would also like to thank the staff of Alyson Publications, especially Angela Brown, Dan Cullinane, and Greg Constante, for believing in us again. Together, the stories in this anthology will build even more synergy and will produce the positive change necessary to educate further on issues of sexual orientation among college Greeks.

Countless organizations and individuals assisted with general support of the Lambda 10 Project and helped us reach contributors for the book. Several of these organizations deserve special recognition: Chi Epsilon; American College Personnel Association; Association of College Unions International; National Association for Student Personnel Administrators; Association of Fraternity Advisors; Human Rights Campaign; National Gay and Lesbian Task Force; *The Washington Blade;* and the Center for the Study of the College Fraternity. Several individuals also deserve special recognition: Richard McKaig, Douglas Bauder, Douglas

N. Case, Janis Singletary, Elizabeth Couch, Jennifer Windmeyer, Nick Geimer, Jim Doherty, Annie Stevens, Kim Howard, Lisa Korn, Mark Guthier, Teri Hall, Regina Young Hyatt, Marcia Kennard Kiessling, Michael Esposito, Mindy Sides-Walsh, Jennifer Bonacci, Wayne Maikranz, Claudia Brogan, Dale Masterson, Jim Johnson, Barry Magee, Tyvola, Carol Fischer, Rueben Perez, Georgia Burgueno, Alice Wolfson, Sylvia Edgar, Gabriel Grabarek, Stan Sweeney, Connie Glen, Debbie Melloan-Ruiz, Darrell Ann Stone, Eloiza Domingo, Lynn Freeman, Ross Freeman, Kate Boyle, Gerald Olson, Bill Shipton, Sheila James Kuehl, Carol Wallisch, and Candace Gingrich. We thank these organizations and individuals for their professional and personal support of our efforts.

It would not be right if we did not give special recognition to someone who is always behind the scenes, Nita Allgood, administrative secretary in the Office of Student Ethics and Antiharassment Programs at Indiana University. Nita is very special and is the glue that holds everything together within the Lambda 10 Project. Her generosity of time, talent, and good humor qualify her for sainthood in our eyes, and we sincerely thank her again for her hard work. Similar acknowledgment is extended to the entire staff of the Office of Student Ethics and Antiharassment Programs for housing the Lambda 10 Project and our ongoing efforts. Without their support, the Lambda 10 Project would not be possible.

In addition, we cannot forget our families, specifically our respective partners Thomas A. Feldman and Douglas K. Freeman. We appreciate your tremendous support, hard work, and dedication to help us complete this second anthology. Finally, we thank all of you who have been a part of the Lambda 10 Project along the way. You believe in what we are doing, and that's what makes all the difference. Thank you.

Editors' Note

Too often in history, the voices of women have not been heard. As student affairs professionals on college campuses, we did not want the story about Greek life for gays, lesbians, and bisexuals to be only half told. *Secret Sisters: Stories of Being Lesbian and Bisexual in a College Sorority* marks the first time gay women's voices have been shared, just as our first book, *Out on Fraternity Row: Personal Accounts of Being Gay in a College Fraternity* shared the voices of gay men for the first time. Over the last six years while we edited both books, we have been sincerely committed to educating people on issues of sexual orientation within the Greek community. Both of us, through our personal and professional experiences, acknowledge the value of a healthy Greek system and the benefits of diversity. *Secret Sisters* provides one more outlet for dialogue to support the ideals of the college Greek system and to create an environment free of homophobia.

While compiling this anthology we hoped to discover the true story, whether positive or negative, about being lesbian or bisexual in a sorority. This book can be useful to women seeking membership in a sorority, women who are currently in a sorority, staff members and alumnae who work with sororities in an advisory or educational capacity, and those who simply wish to learn as much as possible about either sorority life or the lives of lesbian and bisexual women.

The use of pseudonyms by some of the writers shows that homophobia exists in women's Greek letter organizations. Whether or not these women chose to use pseudonyms, their stories unveil the secrecy that has kept the experiences of lesbian and bisexual women hidden for too long.

With the help of the Lambda 10 Project, we launched a national "Call for Writers" via the Internet, through the use of computerized distribution lists, in newsletters of professional associations, in publications written for lesbian and bisexual women, by distributing fliers at national and regional programs and conferences, and through personal contact with potential contributors. The response was enthusiastic, even though fewer writers responded than for our first book. The stories that we received were well written and sincere. We asked each lesbian or bisexual woman to describe her experiences in a sorority, including her stage of coming out while an active sorority member, and to provide information about significant individuals. A straight sister also could write about her experiences in having a lesbian or bisexual sorority sister. During the editing process, we tried to preserve the original style of the writers. We also honored their use of the term sorority, instead of fraternity, in describing their organizations, even though there has been some effort on the national level to use "women's fraternities" as a way to symbolize equality with men's groups.

We grouped stories into five parts according to each writer's stage of development and range of experiences. These sections include "Questioning," "Anger, Fear, and Rejection," "Sisterly Love and Friendship," "Out and Proud," and "Straight Sister's Perspective." To help us show the complexity of women's identity development and to provide a theoretical context for understanding the stories, we invited Nancy J. Evans to write the introduction, based on her scholarly work on sexuality and the experiences of college students. In the closing section on interventions and resources, other practitioners were identified to develop educational tools specifically tailored to the awareness needs of sororities, as identified in our conclusion.

We attained our goal of including a minimum of 25 stories for final publication, but not without difficulty. In fact, we had to extend our deadlines for contributors, since at least a third were unsure about whether they should include their stories in the anthology. More than one contributor withdrew her story because she had second thoughts, and several delayed submitting revisions. This was dramatically different from the response we received from men while collecting stories for *Out on Fraternity Row*. Whether the reluctance of women was related to characteristics associated with gender, such as discomfort with taking risks, or whether it was related to the nature of sororities, we do not know. Perhaps the reason can be found at least partially in the following message that was sent to all members of one sorority after our call for writers was released.

Date: Thu, 14 Jan 1999 19:39:57 -0500
Subject: Request
Happy New Year!
I have been indunated [sic] with E-mails on a message posted on the
listserv. Would you be willing to post my response please?
Appreciate it! [initials of president]

----------Special Message From the President--------

*For those of you who may be interested in responding to the Lambda 10
Project and assisting with their anthology or are asked to answer this or any
other any [sic] assessments or survey's [sic] concerning [name of sorority],
your involvement in [name of sorority], chapter life and so on, it is [name
of sorority] policy that the National President must give permission to do so.
Any public use of [name of sorority]'s name must be approved by an Area
Officer or a member of the National Council. This consistency protects the
privacy of individual members as well as the positive image of our fraternity's name in the public venue. There are also sections in the [name of soror-
ity]'s by-laws on representing [name of sorority] in any form.*

*While sexual orientation is a privacy issue, in this case, if a member
responded and identified her chapter and [name of sorority], another organization, Lambda 10 would be profiting publically [sic] from our name.
[Name of sorority] would be linked in a publication which will be sold and
marketed nationwide. Individual members and chapters do not "own" the
name [name of sorority] and should not on their own authority allow others to profit from the [name of sorority] name. [Name of sorority] is a reg-
istered mark owned by the Fraternity. [Name of sorority] will on occasion
enter into licensing agreements and in this manner our name is protected
and income derived benefits our Fraternity.*

*Additionally should you respond to this or other surveys, you have no con-
trol nor knowledge how that information could be used now or in the future.*

*Lastly, I am confident that each member strives to uphold the promises
made upon joining [name of sorority]. You take pride in yourself, of other
member's, chapter's and our organization's achievements. Please allow each of
us to be proud of each other and uphold the prestige of the Fraternity.*

—*[name]*
National President

The effect of such a directive for lesbian and bisexual sisters could only have been a chilling one, especially if they happened to be closeted. If other sororities sent similar directives, this action may account for much of the reluctance of some sisters to submit their stories. While we could debate the president's interpretation of the Lambda 10 Project, legal issues, and ownership rights, the primary question we would like to ask is this: Would this same tactic have been applied if our invitation for submissions had asked for sisters who have become scientists, lawyers, or physicians to submit their success stories? Receiving a copy of this directive only reinforced our commitment to provide a forum in which lesbian and bisexual sisters could share their stories. We are proud that both the Lambda 10 Project, as a clearinghouse for information about being gay, lesbian, or bisexual in the Greek system, and this book can help counter the silence imposed on "secret sisters."

Our primary intent in presenting these stories is to provide a qualitative description of being lesbian or bisexual in a college sorority. Readers should be aware that the extent to which conclusions derived from the descriptive information can be applied is limited, as the information was collected neither scientifically nor for the purpose of research.

Another limitation of this collection is the diversity of organizations represented. Nearly all of the sororities represented in the book, under real and assumed names, are member organizations of the National Panhellenic Conference. We tried persistently to attract writers from member chapters of the National Pan-Hellenic Council and other multicultural Greek organizations, specifically the historically African-American and historically Latina organizations, but we were not successful. The collection does include a story about Lambda Delta Lambda, a sorority designed specifically for supporting women of all sexual orientations. Many of the women described in the book and those who wrote stories represent a variety of groups in terms of era of sorority membership, geographical home, religion, ethnicity, and college or university. The writers also represent different stages of the coming-out process and sexual identity. In fact, we adapted our title to include both *lesbian* and *bisexual* after discovering that a significant number of stories came from bisexual women. This was in sharp contrast to our first book, where we had a few bisexual men, but assigned one descriptor, *gay*, to all of them.

Finally, we recognize that there may be bias in the perspectives of the women who submitted their stories and in our own views. It is possible that only those women who especially cherished the sisterhood experience bothered to write about it, leaving out those who felt totally negative about their experiences with sororities. Also, since the editors already had considered the Greek experience for gay men and are actively involved with students in fraternities and sororities on their campuses, we may have approached *Secret Sisters* with preconceived ideas about the importance of sisterhood (and brotherhood) in the college experience.

We intended our title, *Secret Sisters: Personal Accounts of Being Lesbian and Bisexual in a College Sorority,* to have a dual meaning. It conveys the fact that many women believe they must keep their sexual identities secret. Secrecy also is linked to sisterhood bonding activities in which there is actually a "secret sister" whose identity is unknown and may be revealed to everyone later. There are many "secret sisters" in this anthology who are finally revealing who they are and who represent the ideals of the college sorority.

We have chosen to highlight one "secret sister," whose accomplishments are many and whose story epitomizes the spirit of this book. Sheila James Kuehl's foreword, "Sorority 'Girl,'" dramatically represents what sororities strive to be but what can happen if support for truth and honesty in the sisterhood does not exist. She tells about the importance of this book from her own perspective, and she ends with a challenge to the entire sorority system. Sheila and the women in this book raise their voices to make sure that lesbian and bisexual women are no longer silenced. We invite you to listen to the voices of "secret sisters" and to begin doing your part to lift the veil of secrecy.

About the Lambda 10 Project

Developed in fall 1995, the Lambda 10 Project National Clearinghouse for Gay, Lesbian, & Bisexual Greek Issues provides support, education, and visibility for gay, lesbian, and bisexual members of college fraternities and sororities. Several initiatives, resources, and educational materials related to sexual orientation and the fraternity/sorority experience can be found online and are specifically tailored to the Greek community. Lambda 10, through its educational efforts, works to create a stronger Greek community based on the founding principles of fraternal life, free of homophobia, and open to anyone regardless of sexual orientation.

Lambda 10 Project
National Clearinghouse for Gay, Lesbian, Bisexual Greek Issues
Office of Student Ethics and Anti-Harassment Programs
Indiana University
705 E. Seventh St.
Bloomington, IN 47408
Phone: (812) 855-4463
Fax: (812) 855-4465
E-mail: info@lambda10.org
http://www.lambda10.org

Inter/National Sorority Chapter Listing

Alpha Delta Pi
Alpha Epsilon Phi
Alpha Gamma Delta
Alpha Kappa Alpha
Alpha Omicron Pi
Alpha Phi
Alpha Rho Lambda
Alpha Sigma Alpha
Alpha Sigma Tau
Alpha Xi Delta
Chi Omega
Chi Upsilon Sigma
Delta Delta Delta
Delta Gamma
Delta Phi Epsilon
Delta Sigma Theta
Delta Zeta
Gamma Phi Beta
Gamma Phi Omega
Hermandad de Sigma Iota Alpha
Kappa Alpha Theta
Kappa Delta
Kappa Delta Chi
Kappa Kappa Gamma
Lambda Delta Lambda
Lambda Theta Alpha
Lambda Theta Nu

Omega Phi Beta
Phi Mu
Phi Sigma Sigma
Pi Beta Phi
Sigma Delta Tau
Sigma Gamma Rho
Sigma Kappa
Sigma Lambda Gamma
Sigma Lambda Sigma Hermandad Latina
Sigma Lambda Upsilon
Sigma Sigma Sigma
Theta Phi Alpha
Zeta Phi Beta
Zeta Tau Alpha

Uppercase Greek Alphabet

Alpha	A
Beta	B
Gamma	Γ
Delta	Δ
Epsilon	E
Zeta	Z
Eta	H
Theta	Θ
Iota	I
Kappa	K
Lambda	Λ
Mu	M
Nu	N
Xi	Ξ
Omicron	O
Pi	Π
Rho	P
Sigma	Σ
Tau	T
Upsilon	Y
Phi	Φ
Chi	X
Psi	Ψ
Omega	Ω

Foreword
Sorority "Girl"
by Sheila James Kuehl

What makes the Greek system so fundamentally homophobic? Does the system, at its core, base its existence, its very survival, on the separation of genders, not only in housing but also in soul? Does it depend on two gender camps forever lined up against opposite walls, thinking only of choosing one from the opposing line, and maintaining some mystery or mastery over the other? Good fences make good neighbors? Do I have your attention?

I was a sorority "girl," and I am a lesbian, and out of that dissonant experience, on which I have reflected now for more than 40 years, I decided to accept the challenge given to me by the editors of this book and write this foreword. The stories in this book differ in detail, but the heightened combination of expectation, pain, and joy are familiar to me; and since I plan, by the end of this opening, to offer some conclusions about the importance of this volume and the meaning of all this, I think the reader has a right to know my own story.

It was 1957, and I was about to enter my freshman (that's what they still called it then) year at the University of California, Los Angeles. I was the first in my family to attend college. I had not belonged to any social clubs in my public high school in Los Angeles, nor did I think I wanted to. But I was 16, a bit younger than most entering college, and I thought belonging to a sorority would help construct an instant body of friends and render the big campus a bit friendlier. I went through rush, pledged Phi Mu, a house filled with the funny, the witty, the plain, the musical, and everything but the gorgeous and most popular. Perfect. Of course, since I did not yet understand that I was a lesbian, nor in those days did you hear the word in public conversation, I had no way of knowing that backdoor rumors were circulating through the house (mainly untrue) that there were lesbians in the membership.

I loved it: the camaraderie, the sisterhood, the songs, the pledge ditch, the sports, the friendship, the support; it was a place to retreat, a base for my run for freshman vice president. And I had a boyfriend. In my sophomore year I was elected pledge trainer, then to student council. In the summer between my sophomore and junior years, however, it all fell apart. I fell in love with a woman, a student from another college. I met her at Unicamp, UCLA's camp for "underprivileged" kids, and I fell hard. This was like nothing I had ever known or felt, and it was definitely, for the first time, the real thing.

The summer ended, but we were still very much in love. We went back to our respective cities and wrote each other every single day. I missed her so much, but I couldn't talk to anyone about it—not my friends, not my folks, and certainly not my sorority sisters. For the first time, I felt truly outside, scared, and alienated. My sorority sisters were all falling in love and talking their heads off about it. I was silent, dammed up. I carefully saved her letters, stacking them in the bottom of the bottom drawer of my dresser in the sorority house; and when I left the house for the next summer vacation, unbeknownst to me, a few were left behind, having fallen out of the back of the drawer.

The woman who was to be sorority president the next year found the letters and read them. When I returned to the house in the fall, the entire alumnae council was waiting for me in the den. I shall never, never forget it. I walked in the front door, filled with joy to be back, and everyone was solemn and staring. I was ushered to the den with my suitcase in hand, and there on the table were my letters, spread out. They asked for my pin, and that was it—no chance to say good-bye to anyone, just out the door. Even now, my eyes fill up to think of it.

In an instant, my world was shattered, I was vulnerable, and I could not even appear to be in turmoil. My friends outside the house thought I was still a member. Every Monday night, when the house had its meetings, I left my parents' apartment, having moved back in (I no longer wanted to live in the sorority house, I said), and sat for two and a half hours at Ship's, a coffee shop in Westwood, so I could go home and pretend I had been at the meetings, as always. I "forgot" to tell my dad about father-daughter day, and on and on. It was devastating.

In the '60s the sorority failed and closed, like so many others. My star was rising and, with only a tiny bit of hubris, I thought it was poetic justice. Imagine my surprise, then, when I received a formal invitation late in the next decade to be a sponsor of the reopening of the house. Ha! No one could remember that I had been kicked out. I was successful, a public official, an attorney, a perfect alumna. I was tempted, and I had even come out by then, but I declined.

Instead I became a key alumna adviser to the new lesbian sorority at UCLA. A friend who had known of my turmoil as a student was currently the Panhellenic adviser and called me one day. "You are an alum without a sorority," she said, "and I've got a sorority without any alums." It was fun and very gratifying.

Still, time heals all wounds, and I am back in touch with all my sisters, though my life in the California state assembly has kept me from joining them for the reunions, so far. And, as well, time wounds all heels, as the woman who read my letters and initiated my pain is not part of that reunion group, nor are any of the alumnae who kicked me out.

So, what's the point?

This volume is important because it teaches, in the most intimate way, the complex lessons of the embrace and rejection of sisters. Lesbians do not want to be "accepted." We want to be, and to have, sisters. As with all love, the greatest enemy of that goal is fear. Homophobia is so powerful that it creates fear in all but the most mature and secure sisters that they too will be thought to be lesbian and that such a suspicion will cause disapprobation to descend on the house. Many of my straight sisters wanted to be brave. They simply did not know how to talk about it to one another or to me. And they certainly did not know how to stand up to the alumnae.

If sororities are going to thrive and not simply survive, however, they will have to reinvent themselves; and the task must be accomplished by those who are currently members. I saw it happen to the Junior League here in California. They went from evincing an almost constitutional fear of the discussion of anything relevant to becoming a vibrant, involved, committed organization, working to combat domestic violence, child abuse, and other critical social problems. The structure is the same, but the fear is gone.

The same must become uniformly true of sororities' treatment of their lesbian sisters. Members who are out are a real credit to their houses—active, involved leaders, campus organizers, women of conscience.

They have been fired in a crucible of hate, distrust, and fear, and have come out the other side. Straight sisters who have stood up to the homophobia are, themselves, rendered proud and strong. When this aspect of diversity is seen as a strengthening and not a weakening element, all sororities will benefit.

I saw this happen to major law firms in the late '70s and early '80s. Early on, they refused to recruit and hire women, convinced their reputation would suffer. Instead these firms learned that having allowed their competitors to hire the best and the brightest, they were being left behind.

The same is true of a sorority. The vibrancy of the membership is the basis of the reputation of the house. Let us hope sororities learn that valuable lesson before they sacrifice another thousand lives to hatred.

Sheila James Kuehl served three terms in the California state assembly, where she chaired the assembly judiciary committee, and in 2000 she was elected to the state senate. During the 1997-98 legislative session, she was the first woman in California history to be named speaker pro tempore of that body. She also is the first openly gay or lesbian person to be elected to the California legislature. Ms. Kuehl graduated in 1978 from Harvard Law School, where she was the second woman in the school's history to win the Moot Court competition. She is now a member of the Harvard University Board of Overseers.

Introduction
Challenging the Image of Sororities
by Nancy J. Evans

Nancy J. Evans preparing for
her sorority initiation
banquet, Dec. 1968

The editors of this book asked me to provide an introduction for their collection of stories written by lesbian and bisexual women and their allies about their experiences in college sororities. In this opening chapter I attempt to provide a context for the narratives you will read in this collection. I draw on research concerning the experiences of women in sororities as well as theory and research concerning women's development and the development of lesbian and bisexual identities. Throughout this introduction, I relate this literature to comments made by this book's contributors, for it is their stories that bring to life the abstract concepts presented by scholars. To begin this discussion, I share with you my story, for along with the literature, it shapes the comments I make later in the chapter.

Fall 1967: I was a sophomore at the State University of New York at Potsdam, in northern New York State. I had survived a rather difficult first year, living with two women with whom I could not have had less in common. I was a first-generation college student from a small rural town in the northern Catskills where few high school graduates went on to college. I came from a single-parent household; my father died when I was 13. And I'd had polio when I was 4 years old and used braces and crutches to get around. I was able to attend college because the New York State Department of Vocational Rehabilitation paid my way. To compensate for my physical limitations, I plunged into academics. I had been valedictorian of my high school graduating class and wanted to do well in college. Although I tried to make friends, I was not very successful. My roommates were pretty typical suburban women, interested in boys and social life. They had little time for me and shut me out of their activities and conversations.

During fall semester of my sophomore year, I decided to go through sorority rush. Potsdam had five local sororities; the New York State higher education system did not allow national Greek letter organizations on any of their campuses at that time. I had never felt I "belonged" in high school and did not feel I belonged in college. I felt I was viewed as an oddity—a crippled woman who studied all the time and did not fit in. It was so important to belong, to do what other students did in college, to be "normal." One way I saw to do this was to be part of the Greek system. As I read the stories that appear in this collection, I related to the desire of many of the women to be part of a community—in the words of Leanna Heritage, to experience a "close-as-family feeling."

When the sorority of my choice did not accept me, I was devastated. I recall sitting on the steps in my residence hall with my resident assistant, crying my heart out, saying over and over, "It's not fair." She responded, "Sometimes life just isn't fair and you have to make the most of it anyway." Those words have stayed with me throughout my life. At that time, they led me to accept the invitation to join another sorority—one that turned out to be a much better match for me. It was not made up of the most popular or attractive women. Rather, it was a collection of interesting, caring, and intelligent women for whom reputation on campus was secondary. They appreciated me for the person I was and what I had to offer the organization.

My experiences in my sorority, Zeta Gamma Sigma, led to improved self-esteem and were stepping stones to my active involvement on campus and eventually to the presidency of student government. This involvement led me to select student affairs as a career. I am now a faculty member at a major research university and program coordinator for a nationally recognized graduate program in higher education. I have published a number of books on student development as well as lesbian, gay, bisexual, and transgender issues on college campuses, and was recently elected president-elect of the American College Personnel Association, a national professional student affairs association. My experiences in Zeta contributed in positive ways to my professional success.

My experiences in the sorority, however, were not all positive. I recall my discomfort at fraternity parties, where I was always concerned about my appearance and what guys would think of me. I never had a boyfriend in college, and finding someone with whom to attend the annual sorority formal was always agony. I certainly relate to the stories in this anthology that tell of similar experiences at such events. Their circumstances might have been different, but the awkwardness and anxiety were the same.

I was never a leader in my house; the highest office I held was that of alumnae secretary. I never lived in my house either; it was much more convenient, given my disability, to live on campus. But the bonds of sisterhood I sought when I rushed became a reality for me in Zeta. One of my fondest memories of college is that of having one of my sorority sisters elected Ice Carnival Queen. A Zeta had never before won this honor, and we all worked so hard to accomplish this goal. I learned that success can happen even in the face of long odds if people pull together, persevere, and have faith. This is another belief that has guided me throughout my life.

As with my experience and the experience of many of the women who contributed to this book, research has demonstrated that sorority life has positive and negative aspects. Certainly, debate has swirled around the legitimacy and value of Greek life since the establishment of these organizations on college campuses.[1,2] On the positive side, students in Greek letter organizations exhibit higher levels of involvement in other campus activities.[3] Individuals who were members of sororities and fraternities in college also report being more satisfied than non-Greeks with their social development in college. In addition, Greek involvement seems to lead to positive outcomes after college. Greek alumni are more likely to engage in civic and volunteer activities. They are also more likely to donate money to charitable causes.

On the negative side, Greek letter organizations have been criticized as sexist and exclusionary and for not living up to the values of the institutions of higher education of which they are a part.[4] Whipple and Sullivan note that many institutions have conducted extensive reviews of their Greek systems and recommended either their elimination or significant changes in how they relate to the larger campus.[5] Greek letter organizations also have been criticized for failing to contribute in a positive way to either the personal or academic development of their members. Areas of particular concern with regard to sororities include alcohol abuse, eating disorders, gender roles, sexual coercion, insensitivity to diversity, and cognitive development.

Alcohol abuse in both fraternities and sororities has been well documented.[6] Both men and women in Greek letter organizations engage in binge drinking to a much greater extent than other college students.[7] In a multicampus study, more than 80% of sorority women were identified as binge drinkers.[8] The amount that women drink also increases greatly after they join a sorority. Sorority women report that drinking is an important part of socializing and that heavy alcohol consumption is associated with most social events.[9]

Sororities also have been criticized for contributing to the development of eating disorders among their members.[10] Women in sororities report more symptoms associated with bulimia than nonsorority women. Experiencing pressure to be thin and knowing others who are bulimic are contributing factors.

Perhaps the pressure sorority women feel in regard to appearance stems from their adherence to traditional gender roles. Two studies found that women in sororities hold more stereotypical views of women's roles than do women who are not members.[11,12]

The extent to which sorority women report sexually coercive experiences, including unwanted sexual advances, attempted rape, and rape, has often been found to be higher than for non-Greek women.[13] In a contradictory study, Sawyer, Schulken, and Pinciaro note that while the level of sexual coercion of some form reported by sorority women is lower than that for women in general, it is still 50%.[14] Copenhaver and Grauerholz note that more than half of the sexually abusive experiences sorority women reported occurred in fraternity houses.[15] In addition, sorority women indicate that sexual permissiveness is encouraged by their peers.[16]

Lack of diversity is pervasive in Greek letter organizations. Historically white Greek chapters continue to be overwhelmingly homogenous with regard to race, ethnicity, socioeconomic class, and values.[17] The rush system perpetuates similarity among members by stressing the importance of finding women who will "fit in" and allowing members to blackball individuals without stating their reasons.[18] Greek members are also less likely to participate in educational programs to increase their awareness and sensitivity to diversity.[19] Rather than experiencing growth in this area, they see their openness to diversity decrease during their first year in college.

Concerns also have been raised about the academic performance of individuals in Greek letter organizations. A national study found that joining a Greek letter organization is related to negative effects on cognitive development. Women in sororities scored lower with regard to reading comprehension and overall achievement than women who did not join sororities.[20] Randall and Grady suggest that because of their homogeneity, Greek letter organizations inhibit critical thinking, since exposure to different types of people and to diverse ideas is limited.[21] In addition, in a study conducted by McCabe and Bowers, high levels of cheating were reported by sorority women (82%) when compared to non-Greek women (67%).[22]

Reflecting on the factors that have contributed to the negative reputations of Greek letter organizations on campus, Baier and Whipple suggest that "educators have been unable to find any evidence that [Greek letter organizations] contribute to the positive moral, ethical, and intellectual development of their members."[23] A resounding indictment, indeed.

Who joins Greek letter organizations? Atlas and Morier report that women who go through sorority rush are more physically attractive, come from wealthier families, use alcohol more, have a higher need for exhibitionism, and are more likely to put themselves in social situations where they might not fit in than are women who choose not to rush.[24] In a study of the values and attitudes of students who join Greek letter organizations, Baier and Whipple note that "the Greek system appears to provide a 'safe harbor' for those who seek conformity, family dependence, social apathy, and extensive involvement in extracurricular activities. The Greek system also provides a 'legitimate' campus subculture for students to associate with others who are affluent, have relatively undefined academic and vocational plans, and place a higher priority on social life than intellectual pursuits."[25]

Given the characteristics of women who typically join sororities, along with the previously presented evidence that members of sororities tend to hold traditional views of the roles of women and devalue diversity, why would a lesbian or bisexual woman consider joining such an organization? First, it is important to recognize that lesbian and bisexual women are influenced by many of the same factors as heterosexual women. Like contributor Jennifer Smith and me, many are looking for close friendships; they want to be part of a group of women with whom they can share their experiences. Women often have a strong need for connection.[26,27] Relationships with others greatly influence how they see themselves and relate to their world. Miller suggests that "women's sense of self becomes very much organized around being able to make and then to maintain affiliations and relationships."[28]

Often, a need to fit in and be accepted draws young lesbians to sororities. "The desire to belong, to be loved, to fit in consumed me during my freshman year in college," Jennifer Smith writes. "I ached to become a part of the Greek organization. The women were beautiful, respected, energetic, involved, but most of all uniform…. I could be unique, once I had the security that I belonged."

Others, however, may join sororities because they seek validation that they are not really lesbian or bisexual. In the early stages of homosexual identity development, according to Cass, individuals may reject indications that they are gay, lesbian, or bisexual by doing everything in their power to prove they are heterosexual.[29] Joining sororities, organizations noted for reinforcing traditional gender roles and behaviors, can be one strategy. Contributor Kelly Steelman's reflections illustrate this dynamic: "While I was excited to finally leave home and be myself, I still could not bear the thought of being a lesbian. I thought if I were more social and dressed a bit more feminine, I could feel straight and find a guy, any guy, that I could be attracted to. After all, IIT was the perfect school for me to achieve this. There were three men for every woman; certainly there had to be one for me." Kelly joined the only prominent sorority on campus to enhance her social life and avoid dealing with the internal struggle she was experiencing over her identity.

In other cases, a woman may have acknowledged to herself that she is lesbian or bisexual, but she may not be ready to share this with others. In their model of lesbian identity formation, McCarn and Fassinger distinguish between individual sexual identity and group membership identity.[30] Often a person is quite sure about her identity as a lesbian or bisexual woman but is not ready to identify with the lesbian and bisexual women's community or to be out publicly. Many women may join a sorority as a way to hide one's identity while also meeting one's needs for affiliation. Several of the women whose stories appear in this book appear to have been in this position. For example, Lindsay Hey was convinced she could never be open about her lesbian identity at her university, and she knew there was "no room for queers" in the Greek system. But, she "wanted the friendships" she saw within the Greek system. "I had already discovered sorority membership was synonymous with a shoulder to cry on, an ear to vent to, and a family to help me grow individually," she writes.

Many women had no intention of joining a sorority but decided to rush because of their friendship with or attraction to another woman in the organization. Kristin H. Griffith had no intention of joining until encountering her soccer teammates at a rush party. Nancy Haver determined she had to join Theta the day she met a member to whom she was immediately and overwhelmingly attracted. Neither Kristin nor Nancy considered the implications of her decision, particularly what it would mean to be a lesbian in a sorority.

At the time they joined a sorority, most of the women whose stories appear in this book wanted to keep their sexual identity secret and believed they could. As time passed, however, the need to come out and be more authentic with their sisters grew stronger. Cass suggests that as individuals become more comfortable and secure with their sexual identity, the desire to become more open increases.[31] In addition, in most cases, women in sororities become close friends. The strain of deceiving their sisters by hiding an important part of who they are becomes extremely difficult for lesbian and bisexual women. But the fear of disclosure resulting from rejection is equally strong. Given the importance of relationships in the lives of women,[32] this conflict between wanting to disclose and fear of disclosing can be agonizing. Michelle Fouts explains, "It was not that I was scared to 'come out' because I did not consider my sisters my friends, because I did…. For a while I was convinced that if any of them found out I was gay, I would be kicked out of the sorority and shunned. I had recurring nightmares of standing in front of the Formal Standards Committee and being told that I was unfit to wear the sacred pin of Alpha Delta Pi."

In some cases, protecting the sorority from the stigma of having a lesbian member is a factor in a woman's decision about whether to come out. For example, "Marie Baker" writes: "What I had trouble dealing with was that I might hurt the sorority in some way by coming out. It was unacceptable to me that some members might no longer want to be in the sorority or that new members might think twice about joining because of me." Carol Gilligan suggests that many women sacrifice their own needs to take care of the needs of others.[33] Certainly Marie's reasoning supports this pattern.

While Marie eventually decided to trust the women in her sorority and found support when she came out, a few of the contributors in this book never did reveal their identities. Many of them chose to withdraw

from their sorority instead, some officially and others by mentally separating themselves from their sorority and not participating in activities.

Research indicates that women often take longer to come out than do
men; they are often older when they come out, and the age at which they
come out varies more.[34,35] Rust reports that for the women in a study she
conducted, the first questioning of heterosexual identity occurred at age
17 and lesbian identification occurred at age 21.[36] Bisexual women were
even older when they began questioning their identity (age 20) and first
identified as bisexual (25). Henderson suggests two reasons why women
often come out later than men: (1) Sexual orientation may be fluid for
women and more tied to the relationships in which they find themselves;
or (2) Women are more influenced by societal norms that expect that all
women are heterosexual and therefore work harder to live up to these
expectations for heterosexual behavior and identification.[37] For whatever
reason, then, women often do not come out to themselves and others
until college or later.[38]

Also, women often experience periods of time during which they are
ambivalent about their sexual identity and switch back and forth.[39] Social
context plays a role in this process. Many of the stories in this book suggest that sexual identity is somewhat fluid, and this clearly influences
how many women present themselves. Sexual identification seems particularly difficult for bisexual women.[40] Mollie Monahan notes, for example, that throughout high school and college she "always seemed to have
a boyfriend" because in those settings "it was just easier to have a
boyfriend than to not have one." She continues, "I really was (and still
am) attracted to men; I always had someone to take to date parties; and
no one ever questioned my sexuality—sometimes not even me."

Like Mollie, several of the women in this book identify as bisexual.
While bisexuality was once viewed as a transition phase people went
through prior to accepting themselves as gay or lesbian, it is now recognized as a distinct sexual orientation.[41] Getting others to acknowledge one's
bisexual identity, however, often is not easy. Mollie writes, "No one ever
seems to believe my sexual orientation. As if it weren't difficult enough for
me to just come out of the closet, I have to constantly justify my sexual orientation to the straight world *and* the gay world. The gay world thinks I'm
in some sort of transitional stage and that one day I'll realize I'm really
gay.... The straight world thinks I'm in some sort of experimental phase,
that one day I'll wake up and realize I'm really straight."

Development of a bisexual identity is often complex, since different patterns of homosexual and heterosexual attractions are involved over time. Fox notes that "no single pattern of homosexual and heterosexual attractions, behavior, and relationships characterizes self-identified bisexual men and women."[42] Because of the lack of societal support for this identity, confusion and uncertainty about the implications of being attracted to both men and women and about how to create a lifestyle and identity that reconcile their feelings are common among bisexual people.[43] Again, Mollie's struggle throughout college and into graduate school concerning whom to date and how to present herself provides a good example.

While some notable exceptions exist, for the most part, when the lesbian and bisexual women in this book did come out to their sorority sisters, reactions were positive and supportive. Kristin H. Griffith reports that her friend Laura hugged her and told her it would be OK. Elana Mendelson quotes the reaction of one of her sisters: "Congratulations! Thank God! I'm just glad you're not asexual!" Many times other sorority members had already figured out a sister was lesbian. Kelly Steelman writes, "I spent nearly two years worrying what they would think, only to find out that most of them already knew and did not care."

In general, researchers have found that heterosexual women are less homophobic than heterosexual men.[44,45,46] Stereotypical gender roles and negative attitudes toward members of racial and ethnic minority groups, however, are correlated with negative attitudes toward gays and lesbians.[47] Since many sorority members exhibit such tendencies, the extent of acceptance of the women in this book by their sorority sisters may be somewhat surprising. But studies also have shown consistently that students who know someone who is lesbian or gay tend to have less homophobic attitudes than those who do not.[48,49] As most of these women came out only after having been in their sororities for some time, it seems the individual became primary and her sexual orientation became secondary in how other sorority members viewed her.

So far, I have examined why lesbians and bisexual women join sororities and their experiences in coming out to their sorority sisters. What happens after they come out? For the woman herself, the process is generally uncomfortable at first but eventually leads to greater self-acceptance and a sense of relief. For most of the women in this book, as research suggests, coming out is associated with improved self-esteem.[50]

Lindsay Hey's response is typical: "My appearance had not changed out-wardly, but I felt that I had a new glow to my face and a new confidence in my step. My coming out gave me a brand new sense of freedom...."

But as the women moved along in the identity development process and, especially, if they became more active in the lesbian, gay, and bisex-ual community, value differences between themselves and their more tra-ditional sorority sisters became more apparent, causing strain. For exam-ple, E. Plemons notes: "My politics were becoming more radical than they had been in the past, and I was frustrated with the way the sorori-ty—an organization that was supposed to be about helping women suc-ceed—was so obviously hypocritical and, in fact, acted to hinder women." Because of these value differences, Plemons chose to deactivate, became active in the lesbian, gay, bisexual, and transgender student orga-nization, and became a vocal critic of the Greek system. And while valu-ing the friendships and acceptance she found in Tri Zeta, after becoming involved in LGBT activism, Elana Mendelson found she "could not bridge the gap between gay life and Greek life" and chose to immerse her-self in the LGBT community.

Other feminist women, including E. Guzik, stayed in their chapters while working within the LGBT community. Guzik reflects, however, on her disappointment that sororities often do not live up to their potential or stated purpose to assist women in developing leadership skills and self-confidence: "I continue to believe that sororities, more so than coeduca-tional environments, can provide the kind of woman-only space in which women can develop leadership and confidence skills. In some ways, soror-ities can introduce these resources to women who are alienated from or uncomfortable with the resources provided by women's studies depart-ments or women's centers.... Unfortunately, it seems, more often than not, most sororities do not prioritize such strengths but, in fact, perpetu-ate the problems women face with alcohol, eating disorders, and sexism."

Another issue faced by women in sororities comes not from the soror-ity but from the lesbian, gay, and bisexual community. Erin Anne Lawson was one of the women who questioned her decision to remain in the Greek system. She writes, "I struggled with...whether I was being hypocritical to remain a part of a heterosexist institution such as the Greek system." E. Guzik also felt caught between the two worlds of Greek life and the LGBT community while working to remain loyal to friends in both groups.

When a member comes out, some Greek letter organizations think only about the reputation of their chapter. Ali Cannon's experience of being put "on trial" for "behavior unbecoming a member of the fraternity that causes embarrassment to the house or chapter members" provides a harrowing example. In other sororities, such as E. Guzik's, it is the national rather than the local chapter that cannot accept a lesbian member.

Many sororities, however, are powerfully affected by the presence of a lesbian or bisexual member. Getting to know a lesbian or bisexual woman raises the awareness of others in the sorority to the injustices faced by nonheterosexual individuals in our society, and many become active in addressing these injustices. For example, Leanna Heritage writes about her sorority's efforts to establish a lesbian, gay, bisexual, and transgender resource center on campus and their influence in getting other sororities and fraternities involved. "Jessi Opynth" describes herself as a passive activist in her sorority. Because of the presence of Jessi and her girlfriend Meg, her sorority evolved into a different type of organization, one that accepted and appreciated their relationship and valued its diverse sisterhood. The positive impact lesbian and bisexual women can have on sororities is best expressed in Jessi's words: "Meg and I have touched a number of lives, and I would have never predicted such acceptance.... I am amazed at the changes I have seen. I am reassured about moving through the rest of my life holding on to the experiences Meg and I had with this diverse group of women."

What conclusions can we draw from the research and from the narratives of the women in this book? Yes, as Whipple and Sullivan argued, there are many issues facing sororities today.[51] The stories presented in *Secret Sisters* certainly do not portray sorority life as flawless. Alcohol use is prevalent; sexual coercion occurs too often; gender role stereotypes and heterosexist assumptions are rampant in the activities and belief systems of the young women in these organizations. And certainly the experiences these lesbian and bisexual women faced in their sororities were not all positive. Too many report rejection and discomfort in being who they truly were. In addition, the negative attitudes and behaviors exhibited by the LGBT community toward women in sororities demonstrate that intolerance is not just a problem among heterosexuals. Yet one is also reassured. Many women report receiving personal support when they came out, and many feel that their presence in their sororities had a profound effect on other members' belief systems and behaviors. Having a sorority advocate for a LGBT resource center is a sign that good things can happen when young women have the courage to reveal their identities and live authentic lives.

The stories in *Secret Sisters* suggest that sororities are becoming more accepting of women with different sexual orientations and that they are benefiting from the presence of lesbian and bisexual members who come out. Several women were open about their identities when they rushed, and most came out by the time they graduated. The majority were accepted by their sisters, and many served as officers of their organizations. As with any form of diversity, the challenges presented in learning about and coming to appreciate those with different sexual orientations and value systems can lead to greater cognitive complexity and increased sensitivity that carry over into other aspects of a person's life. As such, many of the stereotypes of sorority women being narrow-minded, heterosexist, and self-focused are challenged. Having openly lesbian and bisexual members who are valued by their chapters sends a more positive message about the environment of sororities and the type of women who join them than the one too frequently presented in the media and even in the scholarly literature discussed earlier.

If lesbian and bisexual members are good for sororities, is sorority membership good for lesbian and bisexual women? Ultimately, lesbian and bisexual women must decide whether sorority life might be a valuable addition to their college experience and the extent to which they could be comfortable being open about their identities within a Greek letter organization. It is hard to deny that many aspects of Greek life are uncomfortable if one is not heterosexual. Clearly, the focus is often on heterosexual dating, physical attractiveness, popularity with fraternities, etc. And the danger always exists that members will react negatively to disclosure of a bisexual or lesbian sexual orientation. Yet sorority life is also about the formation of close friendships, support, and caring about one's sisters. For many lesbian and bisexual women, the acceptance and appreciation they receive from their heterosexual sisters can be powerfully affirming. Acceptance from others can lead to greater self-acceptance that enables women to be more open in other settings and to grow in other areas of their identity.

A caveat is in order, lest I be considered a Pollyanna. Of course, many ᵔorities more than live up to their negative stereotypes, and I would not ᵔmend them to any woman, let alone a lesbian or bisexual woman.
ᵔlieve every lesbian and bisexual woman would find fulfillment

in a Greek letter organization. But rather than dwell on negatives, I choose to stress the potential I see in sororities to make a difference in society by providing leadership with regard to appreciation of differences and helping women achieve their life goals. Looking back on my own experiences as a disabled person in a sorority, I know in my heart that much learning takes place when people are willing to move beyond societal perceptions and accept one another for who they really are.

Nancy J. Evans is associate professor and coordinator of the higher education program in the Department of Educational Leadership and Policy Studies at Iowa State University. She holds a Ph.D. in counseling psychology from the University of Missouri-Columbia. Dr. Evans's research focuses on the impact of the campus environment on the development of gay, lesbian, bisexual, and transgendered students. She is coeditor with Vernon Wall of Beyond Tolerance: Gays, Lesbians and Bisexuals on Campus *(1991) and* Toward Acceptance: Sexual Orientation Issues on Campus *(2000). She is an alumna member of Zeta Gamma Sigma sorority at the State University of New York, College at Potsdam.*

NOTES

1. E.G. Whipple, "Student Activities," in *Student Affairs Practice in Higher Education* by A.L. Rentz and Associates (Springfield, Ill.: Charles C. Thomas, 1996), 298–333.

2. E.G. Whipple and E.G. Sullivan, "Greek Letter Organizations: Communities of Learners?" in *New Challenges for Greek Letter Organizations: Transforming Fraternities and Sororities into Learning Communities,* (New Directions for Student Services, no.81), edited by E.G. Whipple (San Francisco: Jossey-Bass, 1998), 7–17.

3. E. Thorsen, *The Impact of Greek Affiliation on College and Life Experiences* (Columbia, Mo.: Center for the Advancement of Social Research, University of Missouri, 1997).

4. J.M. Maisel, "Social Fraternities and Sororities are Not Conducive to the Educational Process," *NASPA Journal* 28, Fall 1990: 8–12.

5. See note 2 above.

6. B.G. Riordan and R.Q. Dana, "Greek Letter Organizations and Alcohol: Problems, Policies, and Programs," in Whipple, 49–59.

7. Henry Wechsler, George Kuh, and A.E. Davenport, "Fraternities, Sororities and Binge Drinking: Results from a National Study of American Colleges," *NASPA Journal* 33, Summer 1996: 260–79.

8. Henry Wechsler, "Alcohol and the American College Campus: A Report from the Harvard School of Public Health," *Change* 28, July-August 1996: 20–60.

9. P. Nurius, J. Norris, L.A. Dimeff, and T.L. Graham, "Expectations Regarding Acquaintance Sexual Aggression Among Sorority and Fraternity Members," *Sex Roles* 35, October 1996: 427–44.

10. S. Kashubeck, N. Marchand-Martella, C. Neal, and C. Larsen, "Sorority Membership, Campus Pressures, and Bulimic Symptomatology in College Women: A Preliminary Investigation," *Journal of College Student Development* 38, January-February 1997: 40–48.

11. L. Kalof and T. Cargill, "Fraternity and Sorority Membership and Gender Dominance Attitudes," *Sex Roles* 25, October 1991: 417–24.

12. B. Kamm and A.L. Rentz, "Sorority Officers' and Members' Attitudes Toward Women," *College Student Journal* 28, September 1994: 303–13.

13. D.M. Worth, P.A. Matthews, and W.R. Coleman, "Sex Role, Group Affiliation, Family Background, and Courtship Violence in College Students," *Journal of College Student Development* 31, May 1990: 250–54.

14. R.G. Sawyer, E.D. Schulken, and P.J. Pinciaro, "A Survey of Sexual Victimization in Sorority Women," *College Student Journal* 31, September 1997: 387–95.

15. S. Copenhaver and E. Grauerholz, "Sexual Victimization Among Sorority Women: Exploring the Link Between Sexual Violence and Institutional Practices," *Sex Roles* 24, January 1991: 31–41.

16. I. L. Lottes and P. J. Kuriloff, "Sexual Socialization Differences by Gender, Greek Membership, Ethnicity, and Religious Background," *Psychology of Women Quarterly* 18 Jun 1994: 203-19.

17. P.M. King, "The Obligations of Privilege," *About Campus* 1 (2), May-June 1996: 2–3.

18. S. Schmitz and S.A. Forbes, "Choices in a No-Choice System: Motives and Biases in Sorority Segregation," *Journal of College Student Development* 35, March 1994: 103–108.

19. Ernest T. Pascarella, M. Edison, Elizabeth J. Whitt, A. Nora, L.S. Hagedorn, and P.T. Terenzini, "Cognitive Effects of Greek Affiliation During the First Year of College," *NASPA Journal* 33, Summer 1996: 242–59.

20. Ibid.

21. K. Randall and D.L. Grady, "The Greek Experiences and Critical-Thinking Skills," in Whipple, 29–37.

22. D.L. McCabe and W.J. Bowers, "The Relationship Between Student Cheating and College Fraternity or Sorority Membership," *NASPA Journal* 33, Summer 1996: 280–91.

23. J.L. Baier and E.G. Whipple, "Greek Values and Attitudes: A Comparison with Independents," *NASPA Journal* 28, Fall 1990: 43–53.

24. G. Atlas and D. Morier, "The Sorority Rush Process: Self-Selection, Acceptance Criteria, and the Effect of Rejection," *Journal of College Student Development* 35, September 1994: 346–53.

25. Baier and Whipple, 52.

26. Carol Gilligan, "In a Different Voice: Women's Conceptions of Self and Morality," *Harvard Educational Review* 47, November 1977: 481–517.

27. J.B. Miller, *Toward a New Psychology of Women* (Boston: Beacon, 1976).

28. Ibid, 83.

29. V.C. Cass, "Homosexual Identity Formation: A Theoretical Model," *Journal of Homosexuality* 4, Spring 1979: 219–35.

30. S.R. McCarn and R.E. Fassinger, "Revisioning Sexual Minority Identity Formation: A New Model of Lesbian Identity and Its Implications for Counseling and Research," *Counseling Psychologist* 24, July 1996: 508–34.

31. See note 29 above.

32. See note 27 above.

33. See note 26 above.

34. A.E. Moses and R.O. Hawkins, *Counseling Lesbian Women and Gay Men: A Life Issues Approach* (Columbus, Ohio: Merrill, 1986).

35. R.R. Troiden, "Homosexual Identity Development," *Journal of Adolescent Health Care* 9 (2), March 1988: 105–13.

36. P.C. Rust, "'Coming Out' in the Age of Social Constructionism: Sexual Identity Formation Among Lesbians and Bisexual Women," *Gender and Society* 7, March 1993: 50–77.

37. A.F. Henderson, "Homosexuality in the College Years: Development Differences Between Men and Women," *Journal of American College Health* 32, April 1984: 216–19.

38. R.C. Savin-Williams, *Gay and Lesbian Youth: Expressions of Identity* (Washington, D.C.: Hemisphere, 1990).

39. See note 36 above.

40. C. Mathieson and L. Endicott, "Lesbian and Bisexual Identity: Discourse of Difference," *Atlantis* 23, Fall 1998: 38–47.

41. R.C. Fox, "Bisexual Identities," in *Lesbian, Gay, and Bisexual Identities Over the Lifespan,* edited by A.R. D'Augelli and C.J. Patterson (New York City: Oxford, 1995), 48–86.

42. Ibid., 75.

43. M.S. Weinberg, C.J. Williams, and D.W. Pryor, *Dual Attraction: Understanding Bisexuality* (New York City: Oxford, 1994).

44. A.R . D'Augelli, "Lesbian and Gay Male Undergraduates' Experiences of Harassment and Fear on Campus," *Journal of Interpersonal Violence* 7, September 1992: 383–95.

45. G. D. Malaney, E. A. Williams, and W. W. Geller, "Assessing Campus Climate for Gays, Lesbians, and Bisexuals at Two Institutions," *Journal of College Student Development* 38 Jul-Aug 1997: 365-75.

46. R.C. Qualls, M.B. Cox, and T.L. Schehr, "Racial Attitudes on Campus: Are There Gender Differences?" *Journal of College Student Development* 33, Nov ember1992: 524–29.

47. Ibid.

48. See note 44 above.

49. See note 45 above.

50. K.M. Cohen and R.C. Savin-Williams, "Developmental Perspectives on Coming Out to Self and Others," in *The Lives of Lesbians, Gays, and Bisexuals: Children to Adults,* edited by R.C. Savin-Williams and K.M. Cohen (Fort Worth, Tex: Harcourt Brace, 1996), 113–151.

51. See note 2 above.

Questioning

I feel there is something unexplored about woman that only a woman can explore. —Georgia O'Keefe, Kappa Delta

In Your Eyes
by Kristin H. Griffith

Kristin H. Griffith (right) with her new sorority sister and best friend, Natasha, at a bid dropping for Kappa Alpha Theta, Washington University, 1993

In my room, my mind was consumed with thoughts of "What if I'm gay?" "How do I meet other gay people?" "All lesbians are butch diesel dykes and I'm not like that, so can I still be gay?"

All sorority girls were rich, stuck-up social butterflies, so I thought. I never imagined I would fit in with a sorority and never in a million years expected to participate in sorority rush. But Ashley, a good friend who lived on my dormitory floor my freshman year, convinced me to rush with her. "Come on, Kristin, just try it. You don't have to join if you don't like it," she'd said. Ashley's mom was in a sorority, and Ashley had always known she wanted to be in a sorority. I, on the other hand, had always known I wouldn't be in one. In fact, I would have preferred to go to a college that had no Greek system at all. But I reluctantly agreed to go through sorority rush, more out of curiosity than anything else.

Sorority rush in January 1992 at a selective private Midwestern university consisted of being whisked from party to party, complete with colorful and elaborate decorations, talking, singing, and smiling. After a day of parties my voice grew hoarse from so much talking and my cheeks sore from so much smiling. Most of the parties were the same. A random sorority girl would ask, "Where's your hometown?"

I'd reply, "I'm from Austin, Texas, but I only lived there my senior year in high school. I lived in Nashville before that."

Then she'd ask, "What's your major?"

"I don't really have any idea yet," I'd usually answer. "Luckily, I don't have to decide until the end of sophomore year."

She'd then ask, "What dorm do you live in?"

"Brown, the freshman dorm. I love it so far."

And then, "What classes are you taking this semester?"

"Calculus II, psychology, philosophy, art history, and women's studies."

With the exception of the Theta parties, the questions and the conversations were mostly the same from house to house.

I was surprised and thrilled to see two of the women on my intramural soccer team at a Theta party. One of them, Kelly, approached me. "Hey, Kristin, how's it going? What do you think of rush so far?"

"Not what I expected. It's tiring, but I've met a lot of people, and it's pretty fun. And all the free cookies and drinks make it totally worth it."

Nadine, my other soccer friend, asked, "Your knee still hurt from the game last week?"

"Not much, but I'm sporting a pretty cool Peanuts Band-Aid!"

My two soccer buddies introduced me to other Thetas and during the night, they often waved to me from across the room. My conversations with the Theta women seemed more real, not as scripted as the ones I'd had with members of other sororities. I immediately felt as if I was part of a family. I loved Theta from the first party and wanted to be a part of it. A thousand miles from my home in Austin, I wanted to be part of a "family," although I still didn't feel "sororitylike" and had no idea whether I would be invited to join. In fact, I may have been the only girl rushing (out of 350) who didn't wear a skirt for the second round of parties. To this day I hate wearing skirts, but by the last round, I forced myself to wear one. But by then all the other girls were wearing formal dresses! Despite my disdain for skirts, on bid-dropping day I received a bid from Theta and immediately joined the 1992 pledge class with about 35 other girls.

After the bid-dropping ceremony, we were all herded into the sorority suite in the women's building. In the suite, the actives welcomed us with singing and pledge T-shirts. "Do you want a cookie, anything to drink?" asked a Theta as nearly 100 others chatted on the couches in the suite. "OK, it's time to go to Chuck E. Cheese's, play video games, and pig out on pizza!" the rush chair said. "All pledges will ride with one of the actives, and we should be back by about 9 P.M. I have directions if any drivers need them. See everyone there!" We all had a great time that night, and I got to meet and talk with many of the new pledges.

I soon became an active member of Theta, one of the largest national sororities in the country, and spent much of my freshman year studying at the library, partying and drinking, and attending fraternity mixers with my sorority sisters. I often spent lunch in the sorority suite with other Thetas. One day Lauren, a junior, said, "Hey, everybody listen up. Everyone, including new initiates—you need to all go to the pub this Thursday night at 9. A bunch of Thetas meet there every Thursday to drink and hang out before the band starts at 10:30. You should all come. It's a lot of fun."

I went to the pub, the on-campus bar, on Thursday night with two women from my pledge class. Robin and Pam dropped by my dorm room, and we each did two shots of rum before walking over. We wound up spending many a Thursday night hanging out in the pub, drinking and playing quarters, listening to a band, then dancing at a frat party afterward. Needless to say, Friday morning classes were pretty rough.

Who would have known that in this conservative heterosexual atmosphere I would, only two short years later, come out as a lesbian and bring my first girlfriend to our sorority formal?

My troubles and confusion started the beginning of my sophomore year. During freshman year, I dated a guy named Paul who lived on my dorm floor. When he came back the following fall, he came out to me. My first response was, "What will my sorority sisters think about my dating a gay guy?" Probably not the reaction Paul was hoping for.

Paul was the first gay person I'd known—or the first I actually knew was gay. Until Paul came out to me, I hadn't realized gay people actually existed in modern society. I suppose I thought they existed only in ancient stories or old movies, not in real life. I guess I lived a pretty sheltered life.

So, a few weeks after Paul came out, I started to "freak out," as he called it. I remember one night in particular. I was lying on my hard dorm bed in the dark with Paul in the room. "Paul, I'm really freaked out," I said. "I think I might like women. What the hell? I can't like women. This is horrible. But I can't get the idea out of my head. What the hell am I going to do? I can't stop thinking about it."

"Don't worry. You're just freaking out because of what I told you. It'll go away."

"I hope so. I just wish I could stop thinking about it. That's all I've been thinking about since you told me you were gay."

Paul was wrong. I never lost those feelings.

During my sophomore year I spent a lot of time sitting in the window seat of my 10th-floor dorm room reading any gay material Paul got his hands on, including *Out* and *Deneuve*, gay and lesbian magazines. Unfortunately, all the articles seemed to be about gay people who were really "out" and comfortable with their sexuality. Their lives seemed far removed from what I was going through. Reading about them just made me feel more alone.

My mind reeled with thoughts of "What if I'm gay?" "How do I meet other gay people?" "All lesbians are butch diesel dykes and I'm not like that, so can I still be gay?" "I'm not attracted to dykes with all of their body parts pierced, unshaved legs and armpits, leather jackets, and motorcycles, so will I ever find a girlfriend?" "Will women even be attracted to me?" I had a hard time concentrating on my schoolwork that year, and my grades suffered. Thoughts of the possibility of my being gay swam through my head day and night. My identity as a heterosexual woman was being shaken to its foundation, and I couldn't stop it.

I talked only to Paul about my feelings, but even with him I didn't feel entirely comfortable. I felt like he thought my feelings weren't real, that I was just reacting to his news of being gay. Maybe I was; I didn't know. I'd never even kissed a woman, so how could I know? I felt so alone and confused. During the day I lived one life with my sorority sisters and friends, going to parties and dating guys, but when I came back to my claustrophobic dorm room at night, thoughts raced through my head about who I was. Really, I just wanted my concerns about liking women to vanish into thin air. I kept hoping.

During sophomore year spring break, I went to Florida with three of my sorority sisters. We stayed at my friend's parents' beach house, and it was the year a major hurricane blew through Florida. One night all four of us were watching the movie *Twin Peaks* in the living room with all the lights turned off when lightning flashed and thunder shook the house. The TV flickered out, and my friends screamed and hurried into the hallway. I followed them, and we all sat down, one friend with her arms and body clutching my leg and with her head in my lap—scared, I suppose. She was very close at the moment—and cute at that. I felt a surge of nervous energy rush through my body, from my toes up through my fingertips. God, what would she think if she knew I was attracted to her?

That vacation was also filled with evenings relaxing in front of the television with my friends painting their fingernails and toenails.

"Aren't you going to paint your nails?" Tracy asked me one night.

"Well, I'm not very good at it."

"I can do it after I finish mine. What color do you want?"

"Oh, I don't really care. That dark red is fine," I said.

I wasn't really into makeup or nail polish, but I never protested when they offered to do my nails, and I definitely enjoyed getting them done.

Later that week, when we were at Epcot waiting in line, I asked Tracy, "So, how are things with you and Greg?"

"Oh, OK, I guess," she said. "We're still theoretically allowed to date other people. I heard Greg is going out with some Alpha bimbo. Whatever. But I am kind of annoyed. After all, I'm not seeing anyone else. Are you hanging out with anyone now?"

"Not really. I'm not really into anyone. Sometimes I hang out with Rich, but I'm not really that into it."

Over time, I felt more and more distant from my sorority sisters, since I couldn't share what I was thinking and feeling about my sexual orientation. Often I was showing one side of myself, a facade, but was feeling and thinking something else. I was still pseudo-dating guys, but all I thought about was women. I was living a lie.

By the end of sophomore year, I was attracted to women more and more, and thoughts of being gay still consumed my thoughts, but I still hadn't kissed a woman. I felt confused and was stressed out. At that point, only Paul and Patricia, my roommate and best friend in my sorority, knew what I was going through. I think Patricia felt a little awkward at first, but she didn't seem particularly bothered by my revelation.

At the height of my stress and confusion, my sorority threw a huge party at a frat house one Sunday night. Corks were flying out of champagne bottles, spraying champagne over the masses of people. We were chugging beer and doing shots of vodka and Cuervo; we were wet and sticky with champagne and covered with spilled beer from our beer slides on the dance floor. Everyone was drunk and pressed against one another, shouting and dancing to the loud music. I remember kissing three different guys on the dance floor.

Our sorority president noticed I was drunk and out of control, so she asked Laura, one of the "sober sisters," to take me home.

"Are you OK? Is something wrong?" Laura asked.

"I don't know."

But something was wrong, and I wasn't OK. I hadn't been OK all year. I wished I could stop thinking about women and go back to feeling OK about dating men—not thrilled, but OK. I wanted to say that, but instead I said, "I don't know."

Laura asked me to take a walk with her, and I agreed. We walked out into the cool night and sat near the tennis courts in front of fraternity row. All the frat houses, except for the one hosting our party, were quiet and still. We could see the houses but were far enough from them that we felt alone.

"Are you sure there's nothing wrong?" Laura asked. "Do you want to talk about it?" She knew it wasn't like me to get that drunk and crazy, dancing and kissing guys.

"I've really been stressed about some stuff lately…but I'm not really sure if I can talk about it," I said. "I probably need to, though. It's really getting to me."

I was terrified to tell her what was wrong, but I was having a hard time holding it all inside. I hated feeling so distant from my sorority sisters because of what I was hiding.

If I hadn't been so drunk that night, I probably wouldn't have said anything. Still, I couldn't face her, and as I was looking at my feet while I sat next to her, I stammered, "I…I think…I think I might like women." I sped through those last few words and cringed after saying them. I didn't look up because I was afraid of the expression she might have on her face, afraid of what she would do or say next.

But Laura just gave me a big hug and said, "It'll be OK."

I was so relieved. That's all I remember saying that night; the rest was a blur. Today, I still wonder what that night at the party was all about—whether I was trying to prove to myself that I was straight and that I liked men, whether I was trying to prove it to others when I was doubting it myself, or whether I just needed to get drunk in hopes of drowning out my confused thoughts.

Laura was the first person in my sorority I told, besides Patricia, and I'll never forget her heartfelt reaction. I was so glad she said it would be OK and hugged me that night. I needed someone to tell me that, because I often wondered if things would ever be normal again.

At the end of my sophomore year, Paul said he had met a lesbian on campus and that he could introduce me to her. I was both excited and scared. I was going to meet my first real live lesbian! Soon after, he introduced me to Margaret, and I was so nervous that all I could say was, "Uh, hi." She was short, cute, had a blond bob haircut, and gave me a firm handshake that took me by surprise. Most college students I knew weren't in the habit of shaking hands. I found out she was in my abnormal psychology class of 150 people. I sat in the middle of the class surrounded by my sorority sisters and a few frat guys we knew, but she sat off to the side of the huge lecture hall with her roommate. After I met her that one time, I'd always notice her in class, but I never said hello to her, although she did sometimes. I felt too nervous and thought my friends might know she was gay and suspect something. Only later did I realize my fears were unfounded and that my sorority sisters had no clue.

Finally I decided I had to talk to her, since I desperately needed a lesbian to talk to—someone who might understand. I got her phone number from the campus operator and had the number for about a week before I mustered the courage to call her.

"Hi. This is Kristin…Paul's friend," I began.

"Yeah, hi. How's it going?" Margaret said.

"Um, OK. Paul gave me your number," I murmured. "Yeah, um…I was kind of wondering…uh, well…if maybe we could talk. I've sort of been stressing about…well…whether I might not be…uh…um…straight, maybe. And Paul said you might be someone good to talk to."

She paused, as if she were waiting for more, then replied, "Yeah, sure…no problem. We can talk." I let out a sigh of relief.

"Do you want to meet somewhere and talk?"

"Yeah. That'd be cool."

"What about tomorrow after our abnormal psychology class? We could meet after class and go somewhere."

I hesitated and then said quickly, "Sure, that sounds fine. Great. Uh, thanks."

"Sure, no problem. I'll see you tomorrow then."

After the phone call, my heart was pounding, and my palms were sweaty. I was nervous already and had no idea what I'd say to Margaret when we met. The next day, my stomach was in knots, and my nervous energy made it impossible to concentrate. I sat in class with my sorority sisters and spotted Margaret out of the corner of my eye. I was so nervous about meeting her after class because of my fear that my sisters might think I was gay if they saw me with her. So after class, I covertly slipped out with Margaret. We walked to a deli bar on campus. It was somewhat dark and deserted inside.

Margaret initiated the conversation once we sat down. "So, you think you might be gay?"

"Kind of. I'm not really sure. I mean, I've never been with a woman."

"Do you date guys?"

"Yeah, but I'm not really into it."

"What do you mean? Are you attracted to guys?"

"Well, they're OK, I guess. I mean, I'm just kind of confused."

"How do you feel about women?"

"Well, I don't know exactly. I get nervous just thinking about them. I'm just really freaked out that I might not be straight."

The rest of the meeting was mostly a blur, since I was so nervous. But it was comforting to talk to Margaret. We talked a few times after that, and she helped me work through some of my thoughts and answer some difficult questions. Over time I developed a crush on her, but she already had a girlfriend—not that I would have known what to do even if she had been interested.

A month into my junior year, I was drinking a few beers with some of my sorority sisters when I saw Margaret for the first time that year. The dark, smoke-filled bar was crowded with drunk and rowdy undergrads. I walked out of the bar to get a drink of water when I ran into her. I told her I wanted to talk to her. Then I got up enough nerve to get out the words, "I've always been really attracted to you."

We talked for a while, then she asked, "Do you want to go back to my dorm room and hang out?"

Excited but scared about what might happen, I agreed and we walked on the long pathway to her dorm and up to the fourth floor. I was nervous as hell and didn't know what to expect once we got to her room. Her bed was near the ceiling; a black futon sat on the floor below. A desk and chair stood across from her futon in the cramped room.

Margaret sat on the futon and patted the space next to her for me to sit down. I was way too nervous for that, even with the beer buzz, and instead sat in the chair.

"Come on, sit beside me," she said.

I sat next to her, and I felt the tension for an hour as we talked and sat very close. Then she surprised me when she said, "We shouldn't do this. My girlfriend is abroad in England this year, and I'd feel guilty. Let me walk you home."

I sighed. Nothing ever happened between us.

Paul found out about the gay, lesbian, and bisexual group on campus, and we started attending meetings. It met on Friday nights from 7 to 9 in the basement of the apartments behind fraternity row. To get to it, we had to walk in front of fraternity row, down a long staircase, and knock loudly on the door. You couldn't get in unless you lived there and had a key. We waited nervously outside, in the sight of frat boys coming in and out of their houses, until someone let us in. Inside were two ratty '60s-style couches that had been, no doubt, discarded by students. Most people had to sit on the lime-green carpet. When the group started, it was just three guys, but over a few years it had grown to about 15 people.

At the time, I was living with Patricia and two of my sorority sisters who didn't know I was gay. I'd lie about where I was going on Friday nights. Group members sat around and talked about gay stuff and socialized. I didn't say much, though, and didn't feel like I fit in, especially since the members always seemed to make negative comments about the Greek system. Great. Sororities and fraternities hate gay people, and gay people hate sorority and fraternity members. Where did that leave me? No other members of the Greek community were in the group, and everyone seemed to have dated lots of people of the same sex and to be out to a lot of people. I wasn't sure if I should even be there. Maybe I wasn't gay. But although I felt awkward at first, I eventually felt more comfortable, and these people later became some of my closest friends. Only a few women attended the meetings—I'd heard they went to a group called LBQ (lesbian, bisexual, questioning) that met at the Women's Resource Center. I went a few times, but the group, filled with women's studies majors—women full of piercings, some radical-feminist separatists, and all avid haters of sorority and fraternity members—didn't make me feel comfortable.

During one meeting in late October of my junior year, a cute new freshman named Liz arrived. I immediately felt a rush of adrenaline when I talked with her. She was pre-med, Jewish, from upstate New York, and on the swim team. After that meeting, I couldn't get her out of my mind. She showed up at a GLB dance that next weekend in khaki pants and a red silk blouse, and my heart skipped a beat. She would become my first girlfriend.

I was so smitten that one day I picked out a huge yellow sunflower and got two of my sorority sisters who knew I was gay to take the flower to Liz's dorm room and give it to her while singing the words to "You Are My Sunshine" and "You Light Up My life" while I waited downstairs. Liz loved it but was embarrassed when people who lived on her floor crowded around the door listening. One of my sorority sisters said, "She was totally blushing the whole time! She loved it!" Soon after we started dating, Liz's friends asked about the flower. She said it was from a "friend."

In December, my sorority held a dance called "Jailbreak" in a dark basement of a dorm with low ceilings, concrete floors, dark gray walls, a dance floor caged in with a black fence, black lights, and fluorescent decorations. We handed out handcuffs as party favors. The music blared while colored lights bounced off the fence, walls, and dancing masses. Each sorority sister could bring three people, and two of my friends and my girlfriend came. That night was unlike any other sorority parties I'd been to. I felt uncomfortable dancing even a few feet away from Liz, fearing people might notice we were dancing too close. I was even paranoid about how we looked at each other, scared that people might notice our more-than-friendly looks. Other couples were all over each other, but I couldn't touch Liz.

Peter Gabriel's "In Your Eyes," one of my favorite songs, came on. I wanted to dance with Liz so much. I wanted to hold her in my arms and feel her body against mine, cheek to cheek.

"I want to dance, but I just can't," I told Liz. "Let's go."

We immediately left the party. Dancing to "In Your Eyes" would have been way more than I could handle, and it saddened me to see other couples dancing close, looking into each other's eyes, and kissing.

My sorority and another sorority threw a pajama party in the spring. Again, we could each invite three people, and again I invited Liz and two other friends. Before the party, about 15 of us met in my suite, drinking Long Island iced teas, mind erasers, and upside-down margaritas. A little toasty upon our arrival, we joined the dancing crowd of pajama wearers. This time, I felt a little more comfortable with Liz and not as self-conscious. A few slow songs played and everyone was dancing, but not us. A little later, I went up to the DJ, who happened to be my ex-boyfriend Rich, and requested, "In Your Eyes."

"Liz, do you want to dance?" I asked when the song came on.

"OK, but are you sure?"

"Let's go," I said.

I braced myself for something horrible, and Liz and I began to slow-dance with everyone else. I felt the stares and hard looks so much that I couldn't enjoy myself at all. No one said anything, but heads were turned. We danced to the entire song; all the while I was thinking I wasn't going to leave until the end of the song no matter how uncomfortable I felt. After the song we made a beeline outside. Even though I wasn't a smoker, I smoked a few cigarettes, which I'd brought along in case I felt stressed. We went home after that, and I felt elated. I had slow-danced with my girlfriend at a sorority party! Interestingly, no one said anything to me about that dance, ever.

When my sorority spring formal rolled around that year, Liz and I were still dating and I asked her to come with me. I couldn't imagine taking a guy when I really wanted to spend the evening with Liz. By this time a few more of my sorority sisters knew I was gay, and it didn't seem to bother any of them, so I felt I had some support even if some people were offended. The formal took place at a fancy hotel an hour away, and we were staying in a room with a friend of mine and her boyfriend who knew about Liz and me. That night I was wearing a black dress with white polka dots, and black hose and heels. Liz wore a tuxedo top, white shirt, black vest, black skirt, black heels, and hose. Nervous as hell, we stepped into the plush red-velvet hotel elevator with some drunk guys in tuxedos. One drunk guy, seeing that we were holding hands, looked us up and down from our hands to our faces. Looking puzzled, he stammered, "Wow, uh, yeah, that's cool…uh, yeah."

The formal, which had a Mardi Gras theme, took place in the Seabreeze Room, which was filled with round tables with black sheen tablecloths, large crystal vases with bouquets of red and white roses, and green, yellow, and purple confetti sprinkled over the tables. A large centerpiece with green, black, and purple masks and white carnations was set in the middle of each table. Tuxes and dresses, '80s and '90s music, and multicolored balloons filled the room. Hors d'oeuvres of cheese, fruit, chilled shrimp, and little desserts filled tables. I introduced Liz to some of my sorority sisters who'd heard all about her but had never met her. A lot of them were excited to meet her, since I'd talked about her incessantly. One sister, Stacy, said, "You guys look so cute together," which we did, I had to admit! The cameraman obviously agreed with Stacy. He just couldn't keep his camera off us, snapping our pictures all night long. I guess lesbian couples are a novelty at sorority functions. Big surprise! We didn't really mind, though, because he was pretty funny and cool. I still have one photo of Liz and me standing near the hors d'oeuvres table while I playfully feed her a piece of honeydew. To me, that picture is priceless.

That night we danced to both fast and slow songs. We danced close, arms around each other, kissing sometimes, just like other couples. We stayed all night, and often we felt uncomfortable—so many people stared at us during the slow songs—but we weren't scared off like the other times. Still, I didn't hear any negative comments. Mostly, my friends came up and said we looked cute together. It was exhilarating to be able to dance among so many of my friends with the woman I loved. For so long, I'd felt like I'd been living two separate lives—one in the sorority and one with my gay friends and girlfriend, and it was a relief to bring them together. I'd spent so much time hanging out with my sisters while they were saying things like:

"Oh, my God, I met the greatest guy and we danced all night!"

"Did you see that guy at that party last night?"

"I had the best date last night!"

I'd remain silent, unable to share my excitement about Liz. But over time, as I came out to certain people, I shared my excitement with them, just as they shared theirs with me.

The summer after my junior year, I piled into a burgundy Oldsmobile with four of my friends from the campus gay group and drove 17 hours to New York City for the Stonewall 25th anniversary parade. We met other friends from the group there, and we all squished into a cramped hotel room with one bed, three of us sleeping on the floor.

I'd never seen so many gay people in my life. In the hotel, in the streets, in restaurants, in gay bars—everywhere! We walked in the march that beautiful sunny day following a mile-long rainbow flag surrounded by several hundred thousand queers. All around us were drag queens in pink feather boas and platform heels, dykes with shaved heads in leather jackets on motorcycles, preppy frat-looking guys in polos, gay men on Rollerblades in tight shorts with their buff bodies glistening in the sun, lipstick lesbians with long hair and painted fingernails, and older men and women as well as the young. Joy filled me; as far as my eye could see,

I was surrounded by thousands of gay people and supporters of all types. Among so many gays and lesbians from all walks of life, I no longer felt alone or that I didn't belong.

At the start of my senior year, I felt more confident about my sexuality. The campus gay group had started programs for students in the dorms about homosexuality, and I joined in. Usually, three to four out gay people from the group took part in a panel format, and we'd each discuss our experience being gay on campus, answer questions, generate discussion about gay issues, and serve as a resource for closeted gay undergraduates. In addition to participating in these programs on campus, I spoke at a Parents, Families, and Friends of Lesbians and Gays meeting with some other members of the gay group and even spoke at a gay conference at our school. For National Coming Out Day, our group got a "perspectives" page in the student newspaper, and four of us wrote articles about being gay. Even though I knew just about everyone on campus read this paper, I decided to write an article about being a lesbian in a sorority. By this time, all of my good friends knew I was a lesbian anyway, and many, though not all, of my sorority sisters knew. Still, some sisters evidently hadn't seen Liz and me dancing at the formal, and I didn't know many of the new freshman and sophomore sisters. How would people react? I had no idea what to expect, but what I did not expect is what happened.

It started the day the article came out. Women from my sorority whom I knew well or even not at all came up to me and said things like, "It's great that you wrote that article. It must've taken a lot of guts. I'm so glad you did it," and "I wanted to congratulate you on your article. It's wonderful." Dozens of my sorority sisters reacted the same way. Boy, was I shocked! The president of our sorority asked if she could put the article in our sorority suite for everyone to read, because she thought it was great. I reluctantly agreed. Later, my president told me the subject of my article came up at a weekly sorority presidents meeting. Someone asked, "Does anyone know what sorority this woman is in?" My president said she was proud to say it was hers. Interestingly, after my article appeared in the paper, two women in my sorority confided in me about being bisexual.

By the second semester of my senior year, I was president and facilitator of the campus gay group. It felt good to be able to help other undergraduates deal with issues pertaining to their sexuality. I know how much I needed guidance and support from gay people, and I couldn't have made it without them.

Today I attend graduate school in Texas and have recently started GLBT, a group for gay, lesbian, bisexual, and transgendered graduate students, faculty, and staff. Still, whenever I hear "In Your Eyes," I remember leaving the dance floor with Liz at the "Jailbreak" party and feeling the stares at the pajama party. I have a picture of Laura, me, and another sorority sister from a visit to Laura's parents' house in Boston a year after graduation—me holding a lobster above a boiling pot of water, and them with their arms around me. When I look at the picture, I always remember that night outside fraternity row when Laura hugged me and said it would be OK. She was right; it was OK. I'll never forget all those lonely nights I spent in my dorm room during my sophomore year or the excitement I felt when first meeting Liz. Sometimes I still wear my old faded pledge shirt to bed, the one I received when I joined my sorority. It brings back painful memories of my fears of being rejected by my sorority sisters and feeling alone and distant from others, but it also reminds me of when my sorority sisters said, "You and Liz look so cute together" and all the congrats I received on my article. That faded T-shirt also reminds me of something my friend Helen, the social chair of my sorority, said when announcing a sorority function during the spring of my senior year. I was pretty close with her, and she reminded people about the event by saying, "And you need to put your date's name on the list in the suite so they can get into the party. So, everyone remember to give the guy's name—" she then looked at me, smiled, and said, "—or the woman's name on that sheet. I hope to see everyone there!" Helen was great.

Two and a half years after I graduated, I went back to my old college city to visit some friends on New Year's Eve. At a party I was introduced to a lesbian who worked at the campus Jewish student center. As we talked, something she said struck me. "There's this freshman woman who comes to the Jewish student center every so often, and she confided in me that she's a lesbian and just joined a sorority," the woman said. "She's pretty stressed out about her situation and not being out to people in the sorority, although she's out to her other friends. She said she heard about some lesbian who went to school here a while ago who was also in a sorority. This woman actually brought her girlfriend to her sorority formal one year, and it turned out OK." I told my new lesbian friend that, in fact, that woman was me.

I sincerely hope this freshman and others in sororities find the right path for themselves and, just like me, find out that it will be OK.

Never, Never Land
by Elana Mendelson

My best friends from home had boyfriends, and I found myself either constantly jealous or not understanding why they'd want to spend their time with these "boys." I wanted to spend all my time with women. I wondered why they didn't too.

Sorority Woman *n.* 1. One who is female and is part of a social group of other women. 2. Bonds with fellow sisters. 3. Goes to fraternity parties. 4. Rushes other women to join her group. 5. Learns valuable leadership experience. 6. Lesbian.

Which one of these doesn't fit? Of course, it's the definition of a sorority woman as a lesbian; but if we are defining me, well…that was the best description of my place in the national sorority Tri Zeta in the mid 1990s. My story is about my college experience in a social sorority and how a lesbian might go about finding "self" in a very heterosexual community.

I joined a national sorority at a large university in Massachusetts in spring 1995 for the same reasons anyone becomes involved in Greek life. I was a college freshman looking for a social group that would connect me to different people. The only thing that differentiated me from other college freshmen was that I thought I might be gay. The question "Am I gay?" had popped into my head at the end of my first year of high school, but I shrugged it off. There was no way I could be. I arrived on campus in September 1994 having no idea what the next four years had in store for me.

I came back from winter break after an uneventful fall semester. I had had a long, frustrating month at home, where I experienced a dream about a same-sex encounter and even had a close male friend come out to me. It was an awkward month, and I looked forward to going back to my freshman lifestyle of drinking and hanging out with a bunch of "normal" straight people. But when I walked up to my dorm room I saw only my name on the door. I learned my roommate had moved off campus, and there I was, 18 years old and living by myself in a tiny square room.

That night I pushed the two twin beds together, lay down in the dark, and cried. I kept asking myself what was wrong with me. *There's just no way I could be gay!* I told myself over and over. Depression was setting in, and I couldn't figure out where to turn.

My older sisters had told me they thought it would have been cool to rush a sorority when they went to college, so I decided to register for formal rush. It didn't feel so "cool," though, when I got through the entire process only to learn that I didn't receive a third-round invitation to the sorority of my choice. I was heartbroken. But one phone conversation changed everything.

I received a call from Monica, the rush director. I had met her and the sisters of Tri Zeta the preceding semester. They seemed like genuine, down-to-earth people. Monica was wondering if I had accepted a bid, and if not, she wanted to invite me to her chapter's rush party. I gleefully accepted. The next week I received my bid to jump into sorority life, and I immediately became active in Tri Zeta, attending Panhellenic meetings as an assistant representative while still a new member.

In spring 1995, right after initiation, I was asked to join the board as the official Panhellenic representative. I was excited, not only for the chance to take a leadership position, but also to be fully immersed in Greek life. Then again, that summer, I realized more and more that I wasn't into guys. My best friends from home had boyfriends, and I found myself either constantly jealous or not understanding why they'd want to spend their time with these "boys." I wanted to spend all my time with women. I wondered why they didn't too.

At the end of summer our chapter president held a weekend board retreat at the apartment of an older sister. I stayed in my big sister Emily's room, as she was still home in Hawaii for summer break. Emily had a roommate, Kelly, who was vice president of our chapter. I had become close to Kelly during the new member period, during which she helped me feel comfortable in my group. Kelly had a great sense of humor and a good heart, and I knew I could trust her. We sat up and talked late that first night of the retreat, and I hesitantly shared with her that I thought I might be gay but, most importantly, wasn't sure. I felt as if I had to tell her it was a big "maybe" so as not to scare her. She simply listened and supported me. Kelly was one of the first people I told and the very first in the sorority. She promised not to tell anyone, and that was the last time we talked about it.

During the next year, fraternity hookups frequently occurred. They were never more than make-out sessions, and there were lots of talks with sorority sisters about guys. We'd play games relating to sexual activities. A popular one was "I Never," the object of which was to drink to every event in which you had participated. For instance, if someone asked the group if they had ever kissed a guy, and you had, you'd take a sip of your drink. It didn't have to be sexual, but it ended up being pretty raunchy. Usually, if you were drunk by the end, you had quite a sexual history. If sober, you were as virginal as Mary herself. Not only was I always sober, but I seemed to be the only one. It got to the point where I received a special award at the end of the year: a "free pass" to "I Never, Never Land," since I couldn't physically get there myself.

I never dressed up to attract men, not because I didn't know how but because I wasn't interested. I had that gay thing in the back of my head the entire time, but I denied it because maybe, just maybe, I hadn't found the right guy. Once in a while I'd think I really was attracted to a guy. I'd pursue, get him, and then not want to talk to him the next day or ever again. After those experiences, I had to hide behind a lot of trees to avoid running into the guys again. I especially dreaded the formals, because I could always pretend to be into finding a man, but I couldn't attend a formal alone unless I wanted to sit out every slow dance. To my first formal, I brought my male friend who had come out to me a few months before. It was a perfect disguise. No one would discover my secret.

In fall 1995, I was elected president of the Gamma Chapter of Tri Zeta national sorority. I was only a sophomore, young to be president. It was a pretty rough first semester for my board, dealing with things none of us had thought would arise. A sexual assault on campus made national headlines and tore apart our Greek community, and several assaults went unmentioned. We were directly involved, along with a few other chapters on campus, but it made the entire Greek system look bad. Non-Greeks, mostly women and lesbians, hated us as a system and demonstrated on campus. There I was at a protest against sexual assault on campus, particularly pointed at the Greeks, and I watched in silence. It wasn't that I wanted to be on the other side yelling about how horrible fraternities were, but I wanted to be with those strong women who compassionately fought for something they believed. There were about 10 men there and 100 women. It was an odd place for me to be, in the middle like that, wanting to support my Greek system but also wanting to be part of that large female group. It was about conflicting ideals—women's rights and sorority rites. My denial was still strong, but I knew I wanted to be on the "other side."

After that, everything got to be too much for me: holding a leadership position, talking to private investigators, constantly speaking to national representatives, issuing statements, trying to keep up morale, and harboring the biggest secret of my life. One rainy and cold Wednesday that spring, I was eating my brown-bag lunch in the student union, and halfway through my sandwich, I lost it…completely lost it. Tears streamed down my face. Confusion and frustration with my life set in. I stood up, went straight to my car, and drove two hours in ferocious rain, without the company of the usually loved radio, in absolute silence, to where my older sister Karen worked. I called her from a downstairs phone.

"Karen?"

"Hey, there! I was just thinking about you. What's going on?"

My voice broke. "I'm downstairs."

We sat for an hour in a Barnes & Noble coffee shop and talked about the things that were stressing me out. I didn't mention my sexuality, which I can say now was the reason for my temporary insanity. We talked mostly about whether I should resign as sorority president since I didn't know if I could handle the pressure. I can't remember much about the conversation, but it made me feel better, perhaps saner than I'd felt in several weeks. We decided I had a meltdown, period. I stayed at Karen's house for three days, getting some unconditional tender loving care from my little nephews.

I returned to school and finished the year. I knew what was happening inside me, and it drove me crazy. I wanted to run from all of it, so I decided to retreat for the summer to Cape Cod, where no one knew me. This turned out to be a big mistake. My plan didn't work, and my secret hit me squarely between the eyes.

In Cape Cod I picked up a job in a retail store, and everything seemed

OK until I found out that my boss was a lesbian. Before this, I had never knowingly talked to a lesbian. I freaked out again and spent the following weekend shut away in a small cabin, writing poetry and crying my eyes out. I decided I'd confront my problem at some point during the summer, maybe at the end after I got more acclimated. But my safe haven fell apart that Monday morning. During a cigarette break my boss came into the break room and was talking about a customer when boom, she asked the question that changed my life. A question that would never make it a secret again. A question I can still hear as clear as a bell to this day: "Are you a lesbian?" My world as I knew it fell apart. All the guards I'd put up over the years came tumbling down. I broke into uncontrollable sobs. But my boss consoled me and made me feel like a normal human being. She helped me throughout that entire summer. I can never thank her enough for bringing me out of the closet.

But I still had many more obstacles to jump. I was known to the world as straight, and I couldn't be quiet about who I was. I was still an active board member and president of Tri Zeta. I wondered what it would do to my sorority.

My first real coming out was telling Jana, a fellow board member. We were the same age, but I was an older sister because I was initiated a semester before her. Jana and some other sisters had planned a weekend visit to a fellow sister in Nantucket. Jana, however, missed the boat and ended up spending the night with me. I was going to go to a lesbian bar that night and decided I'd just take her with me and tell her. On the way to the bar, I said, "I have to tell you about this bar we're going to. It's gay."

She looked at me and said, "OK."

I felt that was a pretty good reaction, so I continued. "I have something else to tell you. I'm gay."

She laughed, threw her arms around me, and said, "Congratulations! Thank God! I'm just glad you're not asexual!"

I told my sorority sisters one by one that what I had feared about my sexuality was true, but I was no longer ashamed. I think I radiated my happiness everywhere.

Still, my coming out was difficult at first. Some people didn't know exactly how to deal with my talking about weekend adventures to gay bars or the really cute girl from one of my classes. I tried to think of a way they could understand what I needed from them without saying, "I need to talk about this, and I need your support because this is hard." I checked out some campus resources and found out about a panel of speakers on campus called the GLBT Speakers' Bureau, which talked to groups on campus about their experiences being gay, lesbian, bisexual, or transgendered. They came to a program I set up and even allowed me to share my coming-out experience with my sisters. A couple of my sisters even talked about their experiences with gay people. The event was successful, and I think we all came to an understanding with one another that night.

Today, I still keep in touch with my sorority sisters via E-mail since we're spread out across the country and internationally. I meet them once in a while for special occasions or just to have a drink to catch up. Justine and I go out about once a month, and she complains about her boyfriend while I share my latest female tragedy. I visited Jenn in San Francisco once, and she even took me to a lesbian bar.

I corresponded with Kelly not too long ago, and she retold the story of what happened in her bedroom during the board retreat, over four years ago, when I halfheartedly came out to her. She wrote, "I think it took forever for you to tell me that night and with good reason. You had no idea how I was going to react, even though we were/are friends. After you finally told me, I remember you telling me who else knew in the sorority. I was the only one, but I promised not to tell…and I never did. I also recall you asking if I had felt any differently about you. I asked you, 'Were you a lesbian when I first met you?' and, of course, you said 'yes.' Then I said, 'Then what's so different? You're the same friend I met a year ago.' The only difference that happened was that you were happier. I actually felt honored that you could trust me with a part of your life that was such a secret at that time." Thank you, Kelly.

My active life in Tri Zeta saved me from something I wasn't yet ready to deal with in my late teenage years. I still wonder what would have happened to me if Monica had not called to invite me to the Tri Zeta rush party that night. We all hear of sororities being these stereotypical, stuck-up organizations, but our chapter of Tri Zeta did not fit in that peg hole. I have nothing bad to say about my sorority sisters. They accepted me for who I was and continued to support me. After that semester as president, however, I went to the "other" side, and I was one of those strong women I so wanted to be, throwing myself into GLBT activism and socializing. Unfortunately, at that time I couldn't bridge the gap between gay life and Greek life. I wanted to be a part of both worlds, but chose to immerse myself in the gay community. I felt I had missed out on so much, finally realizing who I was and where I belonged. I still kept in touch with the sisters of Tri Zeta that last year, but found it too difficult to remain an active member. All in all, I hold a legacy that my relatives can take advantage of, and I sincerely hope they do. I will always and forever be a proud Tri Zeta.

Anchor of Denial
by K.P. Brown

A recent modeling shot of
K.P. Brown

Had I had the courage to come out in college, I might have chipped away at some of the prejudices of my sisters who liked and respected me and would have had to examine their unfounded biases against gays. Maybe even Angie would have reconsidered her pious Christian condemnation for the faceless homosexuals out there.

I rushed Delta Gamma in 1981 because I was unknowingly in love with my hall mate, Angela, who was also rushing DG. I longed to be bonded to Angela in a formal and permanent way, and I longed for the ideal of being pledged to a circle of friends who were likewise pledged to me: I my sister's "champion in her absence and her friend always" and she mine. Sorority membership offered me the promise of security and a family of friends that I yearned for.

Delta Gamma was the newest sorority in the Greek system at James Madison University, and I was full of hopes for our nascent sisterhood. We could make the sorority whatever we wanted. There was no stereotype attached to the sorority, such as housewives, snobs, or weirdos. Because there were no DG alumnae at JMU to rush us, DG sisters from two neighboring universities and local alumnae and officers from the national office came to our campus to conduct interviews. It was sort of like a job interview but with more personal questions, such as "Why did you choose journalism as your major?" or "What do your parents do for a living?"

I came from a typical middle-class family in northern Virginia, just outside Washington, D.C. I had an older brother by two years, Stephen, whom I adored and counted as my most trusted friend. My dad was a supervisor at Western Electric, and my mom served as an executive assistant to a high-ranking U.S. Department of Labor official. Stephen and I were first-generation latchkey kids and took care of each other when Mom and Dad weren't around. Although both of my parents worked, which caused a few raised eyebrows among the Delta Gamma alumnae panel, the Brown clan lived a textbook, middle-class suburban family life. We had a station wagon, road-tripped to Ocean City for summer vacations, belonged to the local swim and tennis club, had barbecues with neighbors, and went to our grandparents' house for Sunday dinners. Mom shopped and played bridge with the ladies; Dad fished and played poker with the men; Stephen was a Boy Scout and Little Leaguer, and I was a Barbie collector and ballerina.

I got decent grades in high school, was on the gymnastics and tennis teams, and dated the class president, David, who in my freshman college year was still my boyfriend and attending his first year at the University of Virginia. My background passed as acceptable to the interviewers, and I was invited to become a Delta Gamma.

Including my hall mate Angie and me, 51 girls, mostly freshmen, were selected for the pledge class of the Epsilon Nu chapter of DG. Angie became the junior Panhellenic officer, and I became editor of the chapter newsletter, which I cleverly named (if I say so myself) *The Epsilon Nus*. During my tenure as a Delta Gamma leader, I felt I was well liked and respected, but I later wondered whether my sisters would hold me in the same esteem if they discovered I was gay. The answer came only after I discovered for myself that I was gay and then only after I learned to be true to myself.

They say college is a time of growth and self-discovery, but little did I know how much would unfold over the next few years. It all started with my friendship with Angela, or Angie, as I called her. She was a highly intellectual girl who let me read her English essays, and I was in awe of her expansive vocabulary, her wit, the perfection of her sentences, the clarity of her thought, the originality of her ideas. Occasionally she wrote me a note or a card for my birthday, when I made a good grade on an important test, or when we were away from each other on vacation breaks, and I read them over and over for their alliteration and intricacy, and sometimes simply to comprehend them.

But despite her peerless cerebral powers, Angie was self-conscious about her appearance. She was slightly overweight and sometimes awkward in social situations, and I figured that was why she liked me. To her I seemed a bouncy blond coed who had it all. I ate mountains of food daily at the D-hall and never gained the "freshman 10." I had a great wardrobe of preppy wide-wale cords, wool sweaters with decorative yokes, and button-down oxford shirts in every color (remember, this was the early '80s), and I was outgoing and active in campus life.

Even though my friends regarded me as someone who possessed too much energy for the safety and comfort of others around me, they genuinely liked me. I enjoyed a busy social life, and most of all I was active in my sorority. Being a member of the Greek system made me feel like an integral part of the student body, giving me a feeling of security and belonging. At JMU, if you were not in a sorority or fraternity, you were a GDI—G** Damn Independent—and usually considered a nerd or social deviant.

When I joined DG, I was unsure what sorority life would offer, but the idea of instant friends and a plethora of social options on weekends appealed to me. Subconsciously, I thought sorority sisterhood would bring me even closer to Angie. When all the DG sisters joined hands to form a circle at the end of each meeting and recited the "Oath of Friendship," I was really making a vow to Angie. I remember the resonance in the words: "I will be her champion in her absence and her friend always." I would have done anything for Angie.

I soon noticed my feelings were more than those of just a friend. I wanted to be close to her all the time. I studied with her in her room or at the library, met up with her between classes to walk with her to her next class, and ate all my meals with her. When the weekend came, we'd hit the grain-drain and midnight madness parties or brother dates together. To get ready on party nights, we played loud music, modeled outfits for each other, and pretended to be rock stars as we played air guitar on our imaginary six-strings and jumped on the beds—our stage. Those were great times for me. I remember one night of party prep with particular fondness. It was before a midnight madness all-nighter, and the rest of the crew had headed to the party. Only Angie and I were left on the dorm wing, primping and picking out our outfits.

"How do I look?" she asked.

I knew she was concerned that her new red V-neck shirt was too low-cut.

"You look pretty. That shirt reveals just enough," I assured her.

She looked back at me with a twinkle in her eye and kissed me on the lips. A quick, light kiss, affectionate more than romantic. I was momentarily dumbstruck.

"Why'd you do that?" I asked.

"Because you looked so cute," she replied innocently.

Then, as if to change the subject and mood, she bounded across the hall to finish getting ready. As I was oblivious to the idea of same-sex attraction at this point in my life, I merely enjoyed the attention she had bestowed on me with her friendly kiss. I was floating with glee. I loved these fun times and my new best friend.

Every night at bedtime, I went into her darkened room and we talked. One night she asked me to rub her back, which eventually became a ritual. I'd rub her back and we'd talk until she fell asleep. Then I'd tiptoe out of her room into mine across the hall.

Once, when she drank too much at a frat party, she asked me to hold her hand to stop the bed from spinning. I held her hand the entire night as I lay on the edge of her bed with her, which caused some gossip in our hall. One of my sorority sisters told me that if I didn't have a boyfriend, she would "wonder" about Angie and me. The fact that I had posters of Olivia Newton-John, whom I worshiped, on every wall in my dorm room was a further indictment.

Even though Angie and I continued to share an intimate friendship, we began to argue frequently. She said I was demanding too much of her time and attention. One night I was going into her room for our nightly back-rub session when I overheard her on the phone talking about me to her mother.

"I feel like she's pushing me to be her best friend. Like she's smothering me. Friendship should warm you like an ember, not consume you like a flame," she said tearfully.

However poetic, the words hurt.

"Except for her, I don't have any real friends here," she sobbed. "Everyone's so superficial. I feel like an outcast. I want to come home."

I crept away from her door and went to my room and quietly cried myself to sleep. I didn't go to Angie that night, and she didn't call for me. The next day, she told me she had made a decision about her future—the news I dreaded. She would not return to JMU next fall. I could tell by her resolve that pleading with her was futile. I was heartbroken.

Shortly after, the sorority went on a camping retreat. When we passed a candle around the bonfire and told "what it means to be a sister," I made a tearful dedication extolling the importance of always loving your sisters "whether they were near or far." I was already grieving over Angie's impending departure, and I bore a lot of guilt about her dropping out. I've always thought that our intense relationship had frightened her and brought up feelings she didn't want to acknowledge, and that I was a part of her reason for leaving.

That summer, I lamented being away from Angie. I dated David, went to the beach a few times, and hung out with my buddy and future room-mate, Mo, with whom I was planning to go to an Olivia Newton-John concert later that summer. Nothing, however, excited me more than a call or letter from Angie. But despite her promise to keep in touch every week, her communications began to dwindle. Occasionally a long-await-ed communiqué would arrive. It would be full of the usual greetings and niceties, and also scolding, which simultaneously worried me about dis-appointing her and made me giddy over her interest in the intricacies of my personality. She'd chide me for being demanding and tenacious, call me a "tigress in conversation," then warn that "caution was the key" because she was "willing to give freely."

On a lighthearted note, she'd tease me about being an Olivia Newton-John groupie, imagining me wearing crotchless black lace panties and "writhing in orgiastic excitement" at my idol's concert. She'd gibe, "I know, that was out of line. It's not my business with whom, I mean how, you get your thrills."

In retrospect, it seemed Angie must have known, on some subcon-scious level, about my proclivities. All the innuendo about Olivia, even if disguised as ribbing, was on the mark.

She would also counsel me about my relationships. "Be nice to Mo, the only person who really accepts you as a composite. And David, are you still leading him on? Do yourself a favor and get your shit straight on that score. Send him my 'agape' love; the weak shall inherit the earth, or had you forgotten...." And at last, she ended the letters with the heartening "Love You Always."

Despite an incredibly eventful summer, including my meeting Olivia Newton-John backstage at her concert, I focused primarily on Angie. I was particularly thrilled by the prospect of visiting her at her parents' home, where, she said, she was lonely and bored. But as the summer wore on, she had little time for me on the phone, and her letters became fewer. I clung to her words when she wrote even the shortest missive.

She would write about how much she cherished my letters and calls, lament how she missed me, and promise to write or call every week. As ever, she couldn't resist kidding me about Olivia: "I'm glad that you met Olivia, except for now I'm not your idol anymore (ha! Yet I do have to flatter myself sometimes). Try not to forget me. Your fan, Angie."

Despite her seeming enthusiasm for me, her cards continued to become more and more brief. She hardly called, even though I wrote and called frequently.

My brother, Stephen, and I were both living at home, and I talked to him a lot about my feelings. He told me just to make other friends; and he said I was a great girl, and if Angie didn't want to be my friend, it was her loss. My boyfriend, David, didn't understand my "obsession" with Angie and said I shouldn't be so upset because, after all, he was my true best friend. In many ways he was, but Angie's attentions meant more to me than anything.

Fall semester of my sophomore year came, and I started classes, without Angie. I lived in the sorority house and was elected senior Panhellenic officer, but I was depressed without Angie. My loss of her as a special sister was a wound that wouldn't heal. I didn't feel like socializing with my sisters or anyone else. I broke up with David and stopped going to parties. I became what we in DG referred to as a "phantom sister," someone who never goes to extracurricular sorority events but shows up for the weekly all-sorority meeting. I signed up for 21 hours of classes a week and got more involved in campus activities. I left the sorority house at first light and didn't return again until bedtime. My sisters tried to be friendly and invited me to join them for meals or parties, but I feigned a headache or said I had to study. After a while, they grew tired of my refusals and left without me.

I didn't fully realize I was depressed. I'd never been to counseling or therapy, which I thought was for really messed-up people, like suicidal teens from broken homes, so I struggled alone in my funk. I forced myself to go to classes and immersed myself in my studies. I made an effort to maintain my memberships in various campus groups, which I think helped improve my condition and gradually got me out of the depression. As time passed, I slowly began to reenter life and get used to college life without Angie.

My roommate in the sorority house, Mo, was a great supporter. She was my favorite hall mate from my freshman dorm, and she became one of my closest friends. Like me, she had a silly, immature sense of humor, and we'd snicker and pass notes at sorority meetings. When the sisters were singing the maudlin song "Anchor in Your Eye" about our revered sorority symbol, we tugged at our eyes as if we had a huge barnacled anchor pulling at our lower lids. We hitched our ceremonial robes into miniskirts during formal ceremonies, and during the sacrosanct candle-light rite, as a candle was passed around the circle of sisters until one blew it out—revealing she had gotten "pinned" (going steady), "lavaliered" (it's serious), or engaged (oh, my God) to a fraternity brother—Mo and I giggled and hid our lapels and our ring fingers, pretending we were the honorees. We were class clowns, to the annoyance of some of the serious sisters and to the amusement of the cool ones. Mo was what a sorority sister was supposed to be: a true friend, supportive and nonjudgmental.

Meanwhile, I still missed Angie. I continued to call and write, but I was frustrated by her sporadic responses. One time I called her and complained that I was the one who always had to make the expensive long distance calls. In response, she sent me $20 to cover the phone bill and wrote that she "had been hinting at the dissolution of our friendship for a long time. Now it is over." I was devastated. She had coldly ended the most important friendship in my life.

None of my sisters understood my despondency, except for Mo, who I think had figured out my orientation long before I did. She consoled me and said I would get over this "crush." I realized the term fit, even though she meant it in a generic, nonsexual way. I worried that my feelings for Angie were unnatural. I heard through the gossip mill that some of the sisters were questioning my sexual orientation because of my infatuation with Angie. And, of course, my Olivia paraphernalia only led to more suspicion.

I freaked out. I took down all the posters. I started dating David again. I became a prominent member of the Panhellenic Council. I took on English as a second major. I applied myself 200% to my studies and activities, earning a 4.0 GPA and a place on the President's List and Mortar

Board. I became a classic overachiever. I showed such verve and passion for sorority life for the next year and a half that my sisters assumed I would be DG president my senior year. Instead, I opted to run for vice president of scholarship, and my good friend Suzanne ran for president. We won our respective offices and became a great leadership team.

Suzanne was one of the most wholesome and naïve girls I had ever met. Like me, she was still a virgin at 21, and we both had steady boyfriends who'd been our high school sweethearts. We became terrific pals, working out and studying together and double-dating.

I realized sorority life was all about heterosexual pairing. The candlelight ceremony was just one example of how boy-girl coupling was rewarded. The most anticipated events of the year were brother dates, sister dates, and the formal dances. Delta Gamma even had "anchor men," who acted as big brothers to the sorority and stood in if, heaven forbid, a sister didn't have a date for an event. For most sisters, the sorority served mainly to facilitate introductions to the opposite sex. Many sisters shamelessly said they came to college only to get their advanced degree, "MRS," implying that marriage was their ultimate goal. Not to say they didn't enjoy the company of their sisters, but the crucial question when planning a party was "What frat can we invite?" The sisters never considered getting together just for each other's company.

We were a pretty homogenous crowd, not very open to outsiders or those who were different. When the topic of homosexuality came up in the sorority, the attitude was one of intolerance. When a feature article in the campus newspaper, *The Breeze*, detailed the life of a closeted gay student on campus, it resulted in vituperative letters to the editor critical of the paper for "endorsing an immoral lifestyle." The topic dominated discussions everywhere on campus. One night when a group of DG sisters gathered in the sorority house living room and the subject came up, their prejudices were typical of the general student body.

"They don't have to broadcast it and force it on everyone else," said one.

"Yeah, why can't they just keep it to themselves? It's sick," said another.

Then came an unexpected response from Suzanne's roommate, Kristen: "I think some people just experiment with their sexuality in college." Kristen's liberal attitude garnered obvious looks of disapproval and suspicion from the rest of the girls in the room. I kept quiet.

Then there was the issue of the fraternity Lambda Lambda Lambda, a gay social club that had petitioned for a charter at JMU. The Greeks and several campus religious organizations protested loudly, saying the university should not give any resources, such as meeting rooms or funds, to support a perverted lifestyle that was offensive to other groups. The guys of Lambda Chi were particularly up in arms, because their members were starting to get mocked by the other frats because of the similarity of their name. The atmosphere of intolerance was so great that the petitioners for Lambda Lambda Lambda asked the University Program Board to keep its members' names secret because they feared harassment.

On the subject of Lambda Lambda Lambda, I said very little to my sisters. I wondered myself why anyone needed such a club and what the members would do at meetings. Talk about homosexual sex acts? Make out? As I'd never been the member of any minority group in my life, I had no appreciation of the need for a support group.

As they say, "When in Rome, do as the Romans do" (Roman, Greeks, same idea), so I went about my college life as a dutiful sorority sister and student at large. In fact, I became a pillar of Greek society. I kept up a hectic pace. I started writing for the school newspaper and taught aerobics classes for the recreation department. My aerobics class became a phenomenon of sorts, attracting up to 600 people per class in the university's gym, and it also became a meeting place for gay men on campus. Through the class I befriended Aaron, a flamboyant queen who, I learned, was the anonymous gay man in *The Breeze*'s controversial article and one of the petitioners for Lambda Lambda Lambda. He was an unending source of entertainment as he and his equally fey friends cruised and swooned over the jocks in my aerobics class. Even though I felt comfortable around Aaron, I still felt uneasy talking about lesbians. He told me a cute lesbian in the class was dying to meet me, and I blurted out a definitive, "No, thanks!"

"Why such a reaction, dearie? I see you walking around campus all the time with a lesbian."

I was shocked, and intrigued.

"Who? I don't know any lesbians."

"Well, if you don't know, I'm certainly not going to rat her out. She'll tell you if she wants you to know."

I was frustrated by this mystery, but I respected Aaron's stance. I still couldn't resist sleuthing and suspecting, so I gossiped with my best buddy, Suzanne. We narrowed the list of suspects down to Kristen, her roommate of three years.

"Oh, my God. I don't want to think about it. I've undressed in front of her," Suzanne said in shock.

Even if Kristen had been gay, I knew Suzanne loved her as a friend and wouldn't have abandoned her. It turned out that Kristen was not a lesbian, and has now been happily married for more than 10 years.

About the time of the "Kristen Inquisition," out of the blue I received a long letter from Angie. She had become a born-again Christian and had found her way at last, and she wanted me to see the light too. She admonished me about the wicked ways of the world that would leave me hungry and dissatisfied and willing to be seduced by any mundane philosophy. She cautioned me to not be snared by this evil. She opined that I was a beautiful person capable of great depths of feeling and insight, and she pleaded with me not to let evil poison the wellsprings of my being. "The way of the world is *death*," she warned.

My reply letter, congratulating her on the peace and contentment she had found in her faith, remained unanswered. But I didn't think of Angie much anymore. I was busy with my sorority life and weekend trips to visit David at UVA. He was a good-looking, all-American guy, well liked by everyone. We enjoyed each other's company, and although he clearly loved me far more than I could love him, I stayed with him because of our terrific friendship. The social acceptance our relationship gave me was also affirming and stabilizing. He and I had decided to wait until we were married to have sex, so the pressure was off to go all the way with him. Things were going pretty well, and I had escaped having to deal with the issue of my sexual orientation until one day when the issue hit home, literally.

My brother called me in tears. Dad had kicked him out of the house because of the company he was keeping. He never said the word *gay*, but I knew he was. The truth was, Stephen had no choice in the matter. He had been gay since childhood, since the time my parents had taken him to a child psychologist when he was 5 because he preferred "girl" toys. It was who he was and he knew it, and now I knew it. I told him to be strong and that I loved him no matter what. I was proud of him. He had the guts to face his fears and accept who he was. I admired him for that, more than he could know.

The next time someone said anything derogatory about gay people, I was a fierce defender. And when the controversy of Lambda Lambda Lambda's charter request was revived and became front-page news in *The Breeze,* I drafted a letter to the editor encouraging the objectors to rise above their intolerance and ignorance. Yet I avoided looking inwardly at my own sexual confusion until one of my courses, a senior seminar on Antony and Cleopatra, made me examine the matter. That was when the Queen of the Nile forced me to see I was the Queen of Denial.

My professor philosophized that in the ideal society, everyone would be bisexual, as in Cleopatra's harem. I was intrigued with the idea, so I discussed it with one of my classmates, Claudette. She was a disheveled hippie-type who lived in a group house off campus and wore Salvation Army clothes. We had become casual friends through the class, and we shared rides home to northern Virginia on weekends and holidays. She seemed cool and open-minded, so on the way home on one such trip, I brought up the subject of bisexuality.

"Yeah," she said, "I think everyone is bisexual to a degree. I know I have bisexual tendencies."

Yikes! I was in the car with a bisexual woman, and I still had an hour's worth of driving left. Suddenly I took a special interest in the road ahead and said little the rest of the trip.

All that weekend, I was preoccupied with what Claudette had said. When we convened for our next Antony and Cleopatra class, I was nervous about seeing her. After class, I surprised myself by asking her out to dinner. We became fast friends, but neither of us broached the subject of bisexuality. She came to my aerobics classes, we studied together, we went off campus for dinners, and we attended "not required" Sunday Shakespeare classes together.

One day after class, I gave her a note in which I mimicked the style of Cleopatra in a verse we had just studied. Cleopatra wanted to tell Antony she loved him, but she was so confused by her feelings that she couldn't think of the right words.

Dear Claudette,

Dear friend, one word. You and I are very close, but that's not it. We are great companions, but that's not it. That you know well. Something it is I would—O, my oblivion is a very Claudette, and I am all forgotten. —K

In my cryptic way, I told her what I was afraid to say straight out, even to myself—that I had a crush on her. Being an astute English major, she got the point.

We both had boyfriends, and neither of us had had a sexual experience with a woman, so we proceeded slowly. A week later, after pulling an all-nighter in my dorm room, we fell asleep on my bed. I woke up in the early morning and felt her close beside me. I moved closer and spooned her body. She moved closer to me. We were both nervous and awkward, so we didn't go any further. From then on we slept together, exploring each other a little more each time. After a few nights, Claudette felt it was time to go all the way. To embolden ourselves, we drank several glasses of wine, then finally made love.

I was aglow with love. My energy level soared in everything I did. I wore out my aerobics students, my professors saw a more involved and interested pupil, and my sorority sisters remarked that I seemed to always be in a great mood. I couldn't tell anyone why I was the happiest I'd been in years. I couldn't even admit it myself.

Though I was intimately involved with Claudette—sexually, emotionally, and romantically—I refused to acknowledge my homosexual feelings. I rationalized that our affair was an experiment. I was dabbling in bisexuality, and when I was done, I would return to my heterosexual life with David. I wasn't gay like my brother, who was born that way. I couldn't be a lesbian. I had a boyfriend. I was feminine and didn't like sports. I wore makeup and dresses. My fling would run its course and no one would know—not David, not my sorority sisters, not even my brother. Meanwhile, I would enjoy my secret affair.

I was so excited about my newfound joy that I decided to call Angie, to whom I hadn't spoken since sophomore year. Without revealing the nature of my relationship with Claudette, I told Angie all about her. How delighted I was to have found this new intelligent and witty friend. I also told her that I had recently learned that my brother was gay. Her response was a joke. "You know what 'GAY' stands for? Got AIDS Yet!" When I said good-bye to Angie after that conversation, it was for good.

Eventually, I brought Claudette to the Delta Gamma house. Claudette obviously didn't fit the Junior League mold with her ragged clothes and shaggy hair, so some of my sorority sisters gave her a double take. Claudette looked at them with equal curiosity. She believed the Greek system was elitist and ridiculous, but she relished the opportunity to sneak inside for a close look at Greek life. She remarked that visiting the sorority house was a cultural experience for her. Although I dressed and looked like my sisters for the most part, Claudette said I was different because I was "real." And although she and I were different on the surface, I identified with her feelings of being an outsider.

Claudette was most thoroughly entertained with Greek life when she accompanied me to the annual Greek Sing, a night of musical competition between fraternities and sororities as well as an awards ceremony. It was an event of great anticipation because at the end of the night, they would announce the names of a select few who had been tapped into Order of Omega, an honor society for individuals who have made outstanding contributions to Greek life. My sisters squealed with pride when my name was called, and they buoyed me to the stage. Claudette could not decide which was more entertaining, the histrionics on stage or in the audience.

When Claudette and I started hanging out on a regular basis, I began to disengage from my sorority sisters. My best buddy, Suzanne, got a little jealous that I was spending all my time with Claudette. I desperately wanted to tell her about my wonderful new relationship, but I remembered her reaction to the possibility of Kristen being a lesbian, and I realized that even with my best friend I didn't feel safe to share my secret.

For the few remaining weeks of school, Claudette and I slept together and shared an intense, exhilarating, and all-consuming secret love. In her enthusiasm, Claudette told her boyfriend, Gene, about us. Unlike many men who simply find the idea of two women together to be an erotic fantasy, Gene was worldly enough to know that Claudette's relationship with me posed a threat to him, and he demanded that we stop seeing each other. After a heartbreaking night of wine and tears, we made love for the last time, and she vowed to be faithful to Gene. I went back to my heterosexual life.

I departed JMU and celebrated the culmination of a successful college career. I was leaving behind not only my school, my sorority sisters, and my life of the past four years, but also the love of my life. Soon after graduation, I told David about my relationship with Claudette. He accepted my bisexuality, which I told him was behind me now, and I committed myself to being his faithful girlfriend. Soon we got engaged, and after many fits and starts, in a beautiful evening ceremony with Suzanne as my maid of honor, we were married.

Despite everything David offered, and despite my deep love for him,

I felt restless in my marriage. He suffered because I was unable to fully commit to him while questioning my sexual orientation. After all, I had never had a true relationship with a woman, only a few dalliances and brief affairs. I felt marriage had shut the door on my self-exploration. David and I spent many tearful nights as I pledged, like an alcoholic, to shed the feelings that pulled me away from him, and he struggled to be strong and patient. But the torment proved too much for us, and we separated.

Soon after, I came out to my parents, who were devastated. In a six-page letter, I told them I was gay and that David and I were separating. They didn't call or see me for a few days after I gave them the letter, but my brother, Stephen, finally convinced them to talk to me. Dad called to say they were terribly saddened by the news, and that they feared I would lead an unhappy life.

After two years of separation, David and I divorced. My brother Stephen was my Rock of Gibraltar through my divorce and coming-out process. We supported each other with love and encouragement as we experienced the pain, rejection, relief, and joy of living our lives as out gay people. Ironically, it was I, the neophyte gay person, who convinced him to get more involved in the gay community, and together we joined the crew of a gay cable TV show. We fancied ourselves a gay Donny and Marie team of sorts, as he operated the camera and I interviewed gay celebrities, artists, and activists.

I owe much of my strength and confidence to Stephen. He showed me by example that persistence and faith pay off. He risked rejection and disfavor by pushing the limits of my parents' comfort level with gayness. Thanks to his determination, Mom and Dad gradually came to accept us as who we are. When my beloved brother was diagnosed with pancreatic cancer in June 1998, my father told him that both he and his lover, Sid, were welcome to live with my parents in the home from which Steve had once been banished, so he could get the best care possible. Sid kept vigil with our family at Stephen's bedside, and when my brother passed away that September, my parents asked Sid to deliver his eulogy. My father's last words to Stephen were "You're the best son in the whole world."

The loss of Stephen has created a void that never will be filled, but I have been brought forward in my life's journey through his untimely death. Now I am more committed than ever to live truthfully and choose true love and fulfillment in my life.

Had I had the courage to come out in college, I might have chipped away at some of the prejudices of my sisters who liked and respected me, forcing them to examine their unfounded biases against gays. Maybe even Angie would have reconsidered her pious Christian condemnation for the faceless homosexuals out there.

Through the years, I lost touch with my DG sisters. I even lost track of Suzanne, who moved to the Midwest somewhere with her husband, Kurtis, and their two daughters. I never had the opportunity to come out to them. Probably a few DG sisters, like Mo, would laugh and say "I told you so." If I were to see them today, I'd be proud to tell them about my life.

I'd introduce them to my partner, Janice, with whom I've built a life in Santa Monica, Calif. I'd tell them about my job as an entertainment publicist at a firm where I'm openly gay among my coworkers. I'd tell them about how I produced a national gay television series, *One in Ten People*. I'd tell them about my wonderfully supportive mom and dad and my extended family of friends, gay and straight, who know all about me and love me for who I am. And I'd tell them I miss my brother each day, but that I carry with me his memory and the most cherished lesson he taught me by example: "To thine own self be true."

Mistaken Identity
by Nancy Haver

*Together we made fun of a woman in the sorority we thought might be
a lesbian. I was caught in the dilemma of knowing what I was but being
unwilling to own the name.*

From the moment I learned where Kate lived, I was determined to
become a Kappa Alpha Theta. I saw her for the first time in our advanced
drawing class. That bright September afternoon in 1973, my first day of
college, everything was exquisitely vivid. Maples burned against the clear
blue Hoosier sky. Strains of the marching band and smells of ripe per-
simmons and beer hung in the air. I found a seat in the drawing studio
and looked up to see her across the room. She was lovely. I recall waiting
to hear the sound of her voice. Because I was an accomplished young
artist, she soon noticed me and asked me about my work.

One day our teacher asked us to break into small encounter groups
and to say what we thought when we looked at each other. I told Kate she
reminded me of a dove, because I saw someone warm and soft whom I
wanted to stroke; she thought this hilarious. She was everything new and
exciting, everything I longed to be. She was outrageously funny, with her
own vocabulary and inventive nicknames. She was warm, spontaneous,
honest, and serious about her work. I madly loved everything about her.
On our walk after class, I found out that she lived in the Theta sorority

house, so I changed my route from the dorm to intersect hers as quickly as possible. Sorority rush soon became a passionate concern for me.

Certainly I knew and had known for years that I was a lesbian. I realized it the excruciating moment a friend called our second-grade student teacher and told the young woman that I had a crush on her. I learned the meaning of *lesbian* from the dictionary, after first seeing it in an ad for XXX-rated movies. To me, the word's connotations made it a foreign and distasteful label that I was hard-pressed to use to describe myself. Reconciling myself to the fact that I *was* a lesbian became an obsessive concern through adolescence and beyond. I never considered telling anyone or being "out." In my freshman dorm there were two women whom we suspected were lesbians; we laughed at them and thought they were freakish. Anyone I knew to be gay I saw as a misfit. I didn't know how I could live with these feelings and still be a part of the life and friends that I knew. Invariably, the women I fell in love with were straight. My world was straight, and joining a sorority seemed a reasonable option for me. All of my peers from high school joined sororities, so I didn't consider doing anything different. My friends and I spent hours in the dorm discussing the attributes and reputations of the various sororities.

As blustery fall turned to winter, my fear that I would not see Kate again intensified. My world revolved around seeing her those two long afternoons a week. We talked more after class on the way home. I can't imagine I said much, enraptured as I was by any contact with her.

I was encouraged by the succession of calls and invitations I received for rush parties and get-togethers with women from the Theta house. In my quiet way, I tried to make myself visible to anyone remotely connected with the sorority. Late in the year, the week of final sorority rush parties took place. No matter how many invitations we received, we were allowed to go to only two parties. In a dream come true, I received an invitation to the Theta house. I spent several hours changing clothes. We waited outside, 25 or so women, and were greeted by the group of sorority sisters. The house was aglow with candles. Kate found me when I stepped inside the house; she was my host for the evening. I floated downstairs with her, with the group talking and laughing. Somewhere amid the underwater motif decorations we found our table and sat and talked with two other women. I was enchanted by the way Kate cut her cake, impressed by the way her fork gracefully passed from plate to mouth. I had to hide my trembling hand. A couple of times her knees touched mine; I wasn't sure if I'd be able to stand. There was more singing, and we filed out onto the street through the aisles of women and dazzling lights overhead. As I made my way down the front walk, I had a curiously strong feeling that my life was about to change. This party took place at an important junction, and the Theta house was to become my familiar place. I skipped the second party at another sorority and spent a sleepless night waiting to hear if I had been chosen.

Later I learned Kate had told her sisters they *had* to take me in, that she loved this woman—me. Soon after, I was accepted, and I enjoyed the flurry of rituals that followed. I was tickled to have my name engraved on the wall in our dark chapter room, linked to the many other women who had been there. It was exciting to sip the special drink and recite solemn pledges with Kate and other friends in that candlelit room. Strangely loyal to that time, I'm still reluctant to reveal the details of the ritual. Different as Kate and I were, we were close, and she watched over me at all of these events. My sisters and I spent Friday afternoons at Harry's Chocolate Shop and many evenings at quirky local bars. I both admired and enjoyed being with these women. Among them were many bright, creative, fun-loving, caring people. That spring, though I had not moved into the house, I often spent time there.

One night we studied for an art history test late into the night. Kate lay down and fell asleep next to me on the television room sofa. Quietly, so she would not be aware of it, I sat awake for hours with my hand touching her hair. But the most thrilling moment of my young life was yet to come.

During my semester as a pledge, I spent the night at the house after evening events, and several times a month I had wake-up call duty at 6:15 the next morning. The bunk room held beds for the 70 or so women living in the house. It was always dark, quiet, and cold. In wintertime, flurries blew through the half-open windows. I found it a peaceful and restful place. We pledges stood quietly at the head of each bunk and whispered, "Good morning. Good morning. This is your first call." It was a thrill to awaken Kate. She was a sound sleeper, so I had time to look at her while she was asleep. When I slept at the house, I slept in Kate's bed while she slept in her shared study. Her bed was right in front of the door to the bunk room, and I got used to the *whoosh* of the door, the hall light, the quiet sounds of a room full of 70 sleeping women.

One night I went with a group of these friends to a keg party at a nearby fraternity house. I came back to bed early and scrambled into the top bunk as usual. I held on while the room spun; then it stopped, and I fell fast asleep. Surfacing from a deep sleep, I felt a warm, soft face against mine. I awakened with a bolt. My God, it was Kate, and she had known all along how passionately I loved her. Feelings of relief and release came in a torrent. I pulled her firmly against me, tried to lift her off the floor with my arms. We kissed deeply and urgently in front of that door, and I couldn't stop. This feverish touching and kissing went on for 15 minutes, and then I heard "Kate?" My heart dropped. I hadn't been kissing Kate, but her boyfriend who mistook me for her. I loudly whispered, "No!" At the same time Kate's boyfriend had wondered why she was so incredibly excited, and I wondered why Kate was wearing glasses. The most ecstatic moment of my life to that point turned into a bad dream. Kate's boyfriend ran out the door.

I dreaded meeting my sorority sisters the next morning. Fortunately they, including Kate, found this incident hilariously funny. I worried they would brand me as a nymphomaniac or, even worse, realize my feelings for Kate. My quickly concocted alibi was that I thought this guy was someone I had met at the party that evening, an explanation they seemed to accept. I did hint at the truth with my roommate, a longtime friend who was beginning to wonder about me. Luckily, no one pressed me on it, and it became a longstanding joke. Kate's boyfriend's fraternity came up with my nickname, "Wrong Rack Haver."

Finally our pledge class reached initiation night. We 13 pledges were sent alone to different rooms upstairs, where we were to compose a speech, song, or poem to present to the entire house. I sat in a room frantically grasping for inspiration, sure I'd break down in front of everyone. After 20 minutes I was led downstairs in my short white gown. My heart pounding in my throat, I sat frozen in terror while my pledge sisters delivered their thoughtful words. Finally, it was my turn. I stepped up on my chair, then onto the tabletop. Stepping out, I did a little disco dance step and shouted the lyrics of a Top 40 hit, substituting "theta" for the lyrics. The room exploded in laughter and applause, and I nearly collapsed in relief.

Perhaps the most sustaining friendship of my life began the first year in the Theta house following initiation. Within a week of meeting, my sorority sister Lynn and I were inseparable. Her father had recently died, and talking about his death brought us close very quickly. I tagged after her, and soon she expected me to be with her constantly. I don't think we spent a day apart during the next 3½ years. Our Theta sisters were puzzled by our friendship, yet they encouraged it. Lynn shared everything with me, though we avoided directly talking about my lesbianism. Together we made fun of a woman in the sorority we thought might be a lesbian. I was caught in the dilemma of knowing what I was but being unwilling to own the name. I can't imagine what I would have done without Lynn; having her there transformed my world. When I was distraught over another woman during our junior year abroad, she consoled me one night. I'd told the woman I was attracted to her, and the next day she stopped speaking to me. I spent what seemed like hours trying to broach the subject with Lynn, but I finally did. I can still see the garish pattern of the carpet and Lynn nervously twirling her ring with her thumb as she tried to figure out how to respond. Finally, she said she didn't want to lose me and our time together and that she didn't want me to get hurt. Lynn avenged this woman's rejection of me by stealing her beloved cowboy boots and throwing them on top of a roof.

By our senior year, Lynn and I spent less time with other friends and felt estranged from the house. Though we participated in all of the events, we missed the older women who had graduated, and we didn't make new friends. We spent many nights drinking bottles of Colt 45 and eating snacks behind the bushes in the front of the house. We went to thrift stores and outfitted ourselves with gowns, put them on, and went to gardens and monuments on campus to take Pre-Raphaelite-like photographs of each other for my art class. The years immediately after leaving college were lonely for me; I missed my friends and Lynn desperately.

As I reflect on my relationships while I was active in the sorority, I recall one summer when I picked up a copy of the new book *Our Bodies, Ourselves*. For the first time outside of fiction and biography, I read about lesbians living openly, and I realized I was not alone with my disorientation and dreams. But what I was looking for, an open lesbian relationship, didn't exist in the vocabulary of the sorority house. There may have been crushes and kisses, but no one was willing to claim that name or identity for herself or use it to describe anyone else living there. I remember a time when I walked into a dance and Kate came over and slowly kissed me on the forehead. No one but me thought a thing of it.

Certainly I lacked the strength and integrity to come out to my sorority sisters. Coming out at that time is still unimaginable to me. The revulsion I saw among my sisters in regard to homosexuality made certain I could never reveal myself as a lesbian and stay in that living arrangement. Since I had no real model of a relationship and thought I never would have one, I wondered if I was even entitled to that identity. Those college years are part of a past life I know was mine yet find difficult to claim. I see now that Kate and I had different interpretations of our relationship. For me, that intense love and fantasy endured nearly 10 years. More than 25 years after graduation, Lynn and I remain the best of friends, and she still hears all of my secrets first.

Recently, I received a Theta alumnae magazine in the mail, somehow making its way across the rift of time and place. I leafed through the magazine, looking closely for some sign—a lesbian alumnae group?—that the Thetas have left behind that rigid fear of nonconformity and their strict image of the ideal woman. None was there; the issue could have been from my time, the early '70s. I imagine that many women segregate themselves in this small world because they want an elite lifestyle and a predictable group of companions. I wish my former friends knew that I'm a lesbian: I see coming out on an individual basis as the only real way to foster love through understanding and to celebrate our differences. I feel deepest gratitude for the lesbians and gay men who speak up under truly difficult circumstances and to heterosexual friends who meet them with grace and support. Being born a lesbian has helped me try to become a better person. I know the way I want to be: From an early age, before I was able to do it, I saw that telling the truth is the most important thing we do in our lives.

I Have a Sister
by Liz Garibay and Sandie Bass

*Liz Garibay (top) and sorority
sister Bridget horsing around*

*Looking back, I know sorority life could never have filled that void;
instead I needed only to be true to myself. I was never with a woman while
I was in college, but deep down I knew I wanted to be. Chad and I had a
good relationship, but there was always something missing.*

Sandie Bass's Story

When I joined Alpha Phi in 1992, I was pretty much in denial. Being
extremely feminine, I thought my feelings toward women were just a
passing phase, simply because I was so feminine. But by my junior year,
after trying to suppress my feelings, I decided I had to be honest with
myself.

I found myself in a strange situation. Here I was, rush director of my
house in a world built around the Greek system, and the gay community seemed so far away. I wasn't sure if I felt locked out of the gay community or imprisoned by my "sorority girl" identity. Having no idea how
to become a part of the gay community, I scoured the university newspaper for some kind of event to attend. I found a social and support
group that met on Wednesday nights in a church about half a block from
my house—almost too convenient.

The night I went, I was terrified that someone from my house would
see me walk into the church and know exactly where I was going (as

irrational as that seems). Before walking into the room, I tucked my Alpha Phi lavaliere under my sweater, not wanting to have to deal with another type of discrimination.

I didn't expect to know anyone at the meeting, so I was shocked to see Chad, my sorority sister Liz's ex-boyfriend, walk through the door. Immediately after the meeting, he and I found each other, and practically the first thing out of both of our mouths was, "Don't tell Liz!"

After that meeting I started getting to know the members of the University of Illinois's gay community, going to the gay bar and dating women. I kept my "other" life a secret for the most part, but hinted at it by telling some of my Alpha Phi friends that I was hanging out at the gay bar because "it's the best place to dance in town."

The hardest part was being unable to talk to my close friends about what was happening in my life. One time, I was really excited about a date I had with a woman with a gender-ambiguous name. I told everyone I was going out with "Chris" and had people loaning me clothes and jewelry for my big date. The night of our date, I sat outside on the front steps of the house waiting for her car to pull into the driveway. I certainly didn't want her ringing the doorbell and asking for me. As it turned out, Chris got lost trying to find my house and left a message on my machine in my room (which I shared with two close friends) letting me know she'd be late. By the time Chris mentioned that she had left a message (midway through our date that night), I knew it was too late—one of my roommates had certainly heard it.

I was terrified to sit down with my roommate and tell her Chris was really a woman. But being one of my closest sisters, she was really cool with it. She was the only sister I told until after I graduated.

Liz Garibay's Story

I met my first intimate friend, Barb, in high school. Our friendship had escalated from being friends to being lovers—a first for us both. But we didn't think we were gay. We just thought we were so close that this was a natural evolution for our relationship. It was a very troubling time, as we hid our feelings for each other while going through all the crap a teenager goes through during junior and senior year. In the end, Barb couldn't handle it, and while we ended up attending college together, we parted and went our separate ways. The funny thing was that as much as we tried to hide our relationship, I have now come to learn that most people knew we were, as one friend puts it, "a bit different."

Alpha Phi was an adventure. I joined in my sophomore year to experience a different aspect of college life. Freshman year had been full of great fun with a group of people whom I'd met in my dorms. The only time we didn't spend together was when they were at their sorority functions or when I was with my boyfriend, Chad. I felt that while I was doing well, I had a void somewhere within me that sorority life could fill.

Looking back, I know sorority life could never have filled that void; instead I needed only to be true to myself. I was never with a woman while I was in college, but deep down I knew I wanted to be. Chad and I had a good relationship, but there was always something missing. After three years, we broke up and hardly spoke to each other. When we came out to each other two years later, I realized just how meaningful our relationship was; and in that moment our kinship instantly became even more special. Today, even though we live in different parts of the country, we remain the best of friends and communicate often.

I spent my senior year frolicking around campus, partying and drinking with my sorority sisters. One drunken evening, I slipped and told my friend Bridget I wanted to kiss her, and our friendship was never the same after that. While I never quite understood why my friendships with some sisters went south, I knew there was something awry. One day my friend Amy kindly reminded me of what had happened many nights ago. I didn't know what to do or say, so of course I denied everything. I just told my sisters they were crazy and that I hadn't meant anything by it. But as much as I tried, it didn't help. Erica, my own pledge daughter, thought I was the devil incarnate, and Tracy pointedly reminded me how disappointed she was, even through letters she sent while studying abroad in Ireland. While I was hurt, I was nonetheless fortunate enough to have friends like Sue, Amy, and Kari to always lend a helping hand.

The following year was different for me. I'd lost some of my friends, but more important, I'd lost my mother. After she died, I questioned every aspect of my life. Coming out to myself was not easy; I fought it with everything inside me. Then I remembered something my mom had always told me: "Just be happy." And with those three words, the rest of my life would change.

My best friend, Sue, was the first sorority sister I came out to. I knew she would be supportive, and I will never, ever forget her response: "Yeah!" Again, Sue just wanted to make sure I was happy. After coming out to my family, who were all supportive, I decided to tell some of my sorority sisters who had been involved in the mess the year before. As I told them, I could see that some didn't understand, some couldn't understand, and others didn't want to understand. And while many of my friendships ended, my sense of self-worth was boosted by those who didn't have to understand and knew that no matter what, I was still just Liz.

In the years since then, I haven't seen many of those people. While some have remained ignorant and foolish, many have come around and have tried to accept me for who I am. Sue will always be my best friend, and Amy and Kari will always be pals to count on. Thinking about my experiences at Alpha Phi makes me smile. It was a great time in my life, and I met some wonderful people. I don't know why some of my friends behaved the way they did. While in my mind I try to blame our society as well as the Greek system for encouraging such attitudes toward homosexuals, I know that individuals are responsible for their own actions. My straight friends have all been raised in the same society as everyone else, so why are they so tolerant? Perhaps the answer is in their environment and upbringing. While Kari is probably the most conservative, suburban sorority girl alive, she's still one of the most caring, understanding, and compassionate women I know. Of course, she still thinks I'm a bit "out there," but she knows that I'm the same person I've always been. She respects who I am, even though she may not understand me, and, more important, she calls me a friend. And if I've been able to bring a bit of diversity into someone's life and help her to better comprehend this world we live in, then in the end, it's all worth it.

Then We Met—"Susie Sorority" and Me

Sandie and I came to know each other as pledge sisters when we joined Alpha Phi. We were never close friends, just your average sorority sisters running into each other at house meetings and functions. We knew that because of our involvement in A Phi, we were somehow a part of each other's lives. It wasn't until later that she'd play a significant role in my life, and much later that we would become important to each other.

During my senior year in college, I discovered Sandie was dating an acquaintance of mine—a woman. This acquaintance had made it clear that Sandie was still very much in the closet and would in no way be coming out anytime soon. I kept my mouth shut to everyone, but I noticed myself watching her closely. I couldn't believe it was true. How come I'd never guessed? How did she hide it so well? To me, Sandie Bass was the epitome of "Susie Sorority." Knowing there was someone in the house who was gay, especially someone like Sandie, aided my own coming out. In a way, she'd made a silent statement to me that it was OK to be gay. After my coming out, my ex-boyfriend, Chad (who also happened to be gay), confirmed Sandie's homosexuality by telling me he had seen her at a gay support group. Even after that, I was still in shock.

Soon after, our paths crossed again when we saw each other at a gay club on campus. While we both hesitantly came out to each other, it was a defining moment. A short while later, I bumped into Sandie on a train in Chicago. We exchanged numbers and decided to go out for a night on the town. And so we went, and just like sorority sisters, we bonded. We visited what seemed like all of Chicago's gay bars in one night. I introduced her to some of my friends, while she did the same for me. We talked for hours about our gay experiences, our time at Alpha Phi, including the good and bad. It was then that we realized how much we really were "sisters."

Better Late Than Never
by Kristine L. Abney

The thought never occurred to me that I might be bisexual or lesbian. Whether I even knew these words, I can't recall. I did know, however, that same-gender sex was not a "Panhellenic value."

In 1965 I traveled 3,000 miles from home to attend Purdue University. I was heady with newfound freedom and ecstatic to be away from the overprotective shadow of my parents. I was soon learning to smoke, drink, and pull all-nighters with the best of them.

In my freshman year I was chosen to pledge a sorority, and in Zeta Tau Alpha I felt I finally "belonged." As an only child, I had longed for siblings, so living in a house with 60 bright, attractive coeds filled a huge void. These Zetas were the "sisters" I had always wanted. Captivated by their good looks and accomplishments, I excelled so as to earn the sisters' admiration and was voted Best Pledge.

In my junior year, my soon-to-be first love returned to the Zeta house from her year abroad. One year my senior, D.V. was witty and worldly, if not a bit butch. Our attraction was immediate, and we were soon spending every available moment in passionate embrace in the hidden nooks and crannies of ZTA. My newly discovered sexual passion and attraction for D.V. consumed me.

I didn't wonder about my sexual orientation. Although I continued to date fraternity men to make a good "showing," I secretly lusted for D.V. The thought never occurred to me that I might be bisexual or lesbian. Whether I even knew these words, I can't recall. I did know, however, that same-gender sex was not a "Panhellenic value." So D.V. and I were careful to hide our mutual lustiness from others, including Mom W., our ever-vigilant housemother.

Despite our best efforts, word of our liaison reached my parents, the good Captain and His Wife. Upon returning home for summer vacation, I was greeted with their somber ultimatum, "Never see this D.V. person again, or you'll be forbidden to return to Purdue!" Shocked by my outing, I collapsed emotionally, capitulated to their demands, and spent the summer in abject misery. Meanwhile, the Captain and His Wife spoke little and looked horribly overwrought. It was my summer from hell, but we never spoke of the "matter" again.

When I returned to college for my senior year, I immediately resumed seeing D.V. as much as possible. By then she was in graduate school—an eight-hour drive from Purdue. We continued a long-distance relationship through my senior year and her ultimate return home to Germany. I was crushed by her departure, especially when I learned she had returned to her former lover. I never heard from D.V. again, but will always remember her fondly as my first love.

After graduation, I fell in love with a work colleague, J.H., a woman 11 years my senior. I still had no label for my same-gender attraction, but wondered how anything that felt so right could be wrong. Two years later, when J.H. ended the relationship because she wanted to marry and have a family, I was profoundly disappointed again.

After this, I gave up the idea of finding happiness with a woman and spent the next 20 years in arid marriages. I numbed the pain in more and more alcohol until an arrest for drunken driving landed me in rehab and my first Alcoholics Anonymous meeting on Independence Day 1987. I had hit bottom, but it was also the beginning of a journey that led to sobriety and, eventually, coming out as a lesbian at age 46. Today, I am grateful for 12 years of sober living and finding the woman of my dreams, but I dream of the day when all sororities are affirming places for young women to find their own truth, regardless of sexual orientation.

Anger, Fear, and Rejection

If you banish fear, nothing terribly bad can happen to you.
—Margaret Bourke-White, Alpha Omicron Pi

The Club
by Jane Barnes

We both ended up at the same shelf, and Alice picked up a book called
Inverts in History. *She scanned a few pages, then gave it to me and I leafed
through it. Oh, dear, it was about homosexuals. It made my chest pound,
because it really looked like a terrible subject, and no one should really read
about it.*

The bus station in Portland, Ore., lost my trunk with all of my new
clothes, so I dressed the first few weeks of college in 1961 in what soon
felt like sweaty rags. I met almost no one, lost my dinner pass, and twisted my ankle crossing the street. If this was adulthood, I was ready to go
back to Northern California to Mrs. Haggerty's home economics class,
even if I had to sew red rickrack on yellow half-aprons for a thousand
years. What's more, my roommate, Violet, was consumed with purchasing the right device for curling her eyelashes (they were long) and struggled every morning about whether to wear the padded or the underwire
push-up bra. I might have cared less, but her very simplemindedness was
so foreign to me that I listened to the debate with great fascination. I
found myself arriving at opinions like, "Yes, wear the purple blouse,"
when really I wanted to ask her if she knew who Fidel Castro was. I'm
sure she wanted to ask me if I ever wore anything but the same green
mohair cardigan.

Finally I met Alice. She was as plain as Violet was pretty and lumbered
down the hall in outsize khakis with a stack of books balanced on one
hefty hip, apt to turn to me in the elevator as we descended for breakfast
and ask if I had read Molière. Had I gone on a peace march? Did I believe
in equal rights for the Negroes? Did I like Patsy Cline? James Baldwin?

She had a Texas accent and a difficult rash on her face, and her hair looked greasy even when clean, but her puzzled frown hid the gentleness of a nun and an abundance of wit, I could tell.

Violet asked me if I was going to rush. "Why rush?" I asked her—I could not resist—"I've plenty of time to get to class."

"No, no," she said, "are you going to rush a sorority?" Ah, I thought, those snobby clubs that are featured in *Seventeen* magazine with a picture of Sally O'Cutie, leaning against a beech tree in a pink sweater, a new member of Delta Delta Delta. What was the point of a club like that? Violet showed me a pamphlet: good fellowship, good service, and Christian values. I had been a cheerleader in high school, attended a 6 A.M. prayer group religiously, and had once put away a half pint of whiskey in a car overlooking the ocean at midnight. I had already joined everything I knew how. The point of it all, it was clear to me, was to make friends with the girls.

I had never seen the point of that, though I myself had had several such friends. Though somehow when girls sidled up to each other, I moved away and stood facing them. I could not have put it that way, but it was true. It didn't feel like a battle, exactly, though I felt something I might have called opposition, especially with the pretty ones.

Why could Alice not put her brain with Violet's body? That way Alice's boyishness might be combined with Violet's overblown lacy feeling. I wanted to stand in the strange area between the two, but I couldn't find it. I made do with checking out Molière's *The School for Wives* from the college library at Alice's suggestion and purchasing a frost-free make-up mirror for Violet. Both friends seemed pleased, and I tried to be.

After classes one day, Violet welcomed me into our room with a warmth that was a little unnerving. I found it rather difficult to sit on her bed. She fairly demanded that I rifle through a pile of tangled panties to find a pair her boyfriend would like.

Doggedly, I held up a cream-colored silk pair with beige lace trim. *The School for Wives*, I noticed, had fallen to the floor beside my tidy bed.

"Now you're talking, Jeanie, my dear," said Violet, winking at me in arch coconspiracy.

When my trunk finally arrived and I took out all the clothes, I realized I had bought suits and blouses—things for an office—when everyone else wore (save for Violet and Alice) plaid skirts and little red sweaters, little gold pins, and bouffant hairdos. The hair, at least, looked not unlike what Molière's 18th-century ladies were probably wont to wear.

I went into Alice's room more often than I cared to think about, reassured by her redheaded roommate, Dora, who usually lay sprawled on Alice's bed with her. I couldn't tell if she was the chaperone or I, but they were always together, finishing each other's sentences and patting each other on the spine as though on-off switches had been installed there. Sometimes they turned on the radio to "The Twist" and danced together. Once I thought I saw them kind of kissing when I went in, but they must have been adjusting Dora's contacts; at least that was what they said. They also opened psychology books and asked me if I had read Jung.

And who is Jung? I asked myself.

"And do you have dreams?" they asked.

"Well, no." But yes—I was lying, of course.

Once I dreamed that Violet came to me in a pair of khakis, riding a horse bareback, and asked me to get on behind. I wrapped my arms around her, and we leapt out the window. She had worn the push-up bra for the getaway—a perfect selection, I thought—and the panties I so liked. Just as I got to the pavement outside, Alice leaned out the window, her face dripping with makeup. She shouted in French (I knew it was French, but I heard it as English, if you know what I mean), "You stupid bitches, get back here. She's not Princess Margaret's, she's mine." (England's dowdy Princess Margaret had just married a society photographer, a handsome but lowly plebian.)

I could hardly tell Alice about this dream, and what was more, I had not realized until the dream that she had a fondness for Violet, which took me aback, since she often made fun of Violet's mud-mask routine or her habit of running to the bathroom in a short black slip. "At least you wear a proper bathrobe, Jeanie," she said. I was wearing it at the time, and I pulled the belt a little tighter. "What did you do that for?" said Alice. "You think I'm going to bite? You think I'm Sappho?" Dora laughed, and her blouse fell open at the neck. Alice looked and then looked at me. I was glad I was not like Dora.

But was I really?

The next night, when everyone crowded into the rec room to watch that square-jawed man John Kennedy on TV, Alice and I went for a walk. Dora declined; she had to study for a chemistry midterm. I felt edgy going alone with Alice, but maybe it was the wind. We dropped by a used bookstore. I had never been in one in my life. "I'm looking for psychology," she told me, but I too was curious about humans, so I followed her to a back room where labels like JUNG, FREUD, and ABNORMAL PSYCHOLOGY announced various subdivisions. I started to hallucinate, as if in some charmed atmosphere. I felt things changing, the way someone has a premonition of a heart attack.

We ended up at the same shelf, and Alice picked up a book called *Inverts in History*. She scanned a few pages, then gave it to me, and I leafed through it. Oh, dear, it was about homosexuals. It made my chest pound, because it really looked like a terrible subject, and no one should really read about it. I looked at the pages blindly, noticing "female pervert" and "two women together" and other terrible phrases—just words, since none of them actually applied to me. I perspired, but the room was so hot, my mouth went dry.

"Looks pretty interesting," said Alice.

"Umm," I said, expecting the police to arrive, or Jesus, brandishing a cross to push me away from the words. Or my gym teacher in high school, who scowled in a suspiciously intense way when we snapped one another on the naked bottom with towels.

"Do you think it's good?" asked Alice.

"Well, it's certainly…" My words left me for the first time in my life.

"I know," said Alice, and I didn't want to know "what" or "how." I was not like "that," and she could just keep her wide-hipped opinion to herself. "I think I'll buy this, but you should get this." She held up a thin book by an author called Sappho.

"Who's he?" I said.

"She, dummy! She's a famous lady. Her poetry is beautiful. You've got to get it."

I picked it up and read, "We shall enjoy it / as for him who finds / fault, may silliness / and sorrow take him!"

Alice was reading over my shoulder. "Doesn't she have balls?"

"Er…my father," I said timidly, "would call that a poor attitude." I paused. Alice studied my face. I looked at her. "So that settles it. I better get it."

I did. And felt rather glad.

We walked back to the dorm, saying we thought one day we could be psychologists or at least teachers. Her shoulder bumped mine as we walked up the hill. I liked it a little, though I didn't like her thick shoes or her orange ski cap and the way it was so tight on her head that it pulled her eyebrows back. Or maybe she just looked like that because…well, because she kind of got too close.

Alice and I said good-bye in the corridor. I dashed off, remembering the sorority rush party scheduled for that night. I went up to lay out my clothes. Violet, taking off her nylons as I came in, held up one leg so I could see all the way up. I saw blue panties this time, and that her words were a little slurred.

"Will you?" she said, and held out a toe. I pulled off the silk stocking, and for me, a girl who grew up by the sea, imagined I was shelling a giant shrimp. Her leg, slick and pink, was finished off with wiggling painted toes.

"Why do you like that mannish woman?" she asked me. "She's got to do something with that hair…."

I thought, *And you ought to get something done to your head*, but instead I just shrugged and wondered if her boyfriend, Gunnar, ever got bored with her.

"I'm going to go out for that sorority I told you about, Jeanie. Are you coming? It's tonight."

"I am. You know, Edith Hamilton is quite good," I said, going over to my bed and picking up a book about myth.

"Is she in Beta Kappa? I know! She's that gorgeous blond over in McCalister Hall. Oh, to be a blond."

I thought I'd rather die than join a sorority that Violet belonged to. But Alice belonged to the ski club and I had joined it, though I was afraid of heights and sliding and the snow on Mount Hood. How much worse could a "songfest" be?

"Where is this thing?" I said to Violet, making a stack of books by my bed. She gave me the particulars and went on to plan her outfit, which included a bright red sweater. She held it up to herself for my approval. Her breasts stood out like raspberry snow cones. Why bother, I thought, since no men would be there.

Violet took her shower first and dressed before me. She looked sensational in that advertisement girl way. She would surely be picked, but not I, because I read too much and still ran around with Alice. But I could be as social as they. Sometimes I read while the other girls chattered in their bathrobes in the downstairs lounge about boys, boys, boys. I hadn't had a single one since I'd gone to the freshman social with Phil

and promptly got drunk and threw up in the front garden of the president's house, perhaps a plus. At least Cynthia Harris, on the selection
committee of this sorority, had asked me all about it. Perhaps that boring escapade translated as daring. I didn't mind.

My first thought when entering the common room of Pickworth
Dorm: *I'm in Giovanni's Oceanside Funeral Home, judging by the shades
of moss.* Our invitations said this event would help the "members to judge
our appearance, moral character, personality, and interests"—no doubt
easily accomplished in 15 minutes while we politely ate corn curls and
drank Hawaiian punch. After at least three sorority piranhas grilled all of
us, they scrambled off to write secret ballots for or against us. Meanwhile,
we were herded into a side room to sing at a piano "The hills are alive
with the sound of music..." or "Moon River" while the double doors
were closed and the regulars decided our fates.

There I stood, pretending to sing alto in a bright blue taffeta
sheath dress bought for my cousin's wedding—the marriage had
already fallen apart—with my good heels and a stomach flattened by
a Junior Playtex girdle—just for some girls. Violet came up, looking
like a dark Marilyn Monroe in a white skirt and raspberry sweater, her
heels wobbling precariously in the thick green shag carpet. Around us
pretty coeds jockeyed for attention from the officers, who wore rose-
buds on their collars, stuck there with pins. Squeals of delight merged
with the wholesome but catatonic sound of Peter, Paul, and Mary,
singing out from the dorm's one hi-fi, built into a cabinet of beige
cloth and fake teak.

"Hi!" squeaked Daisy Kornblatt, whose specialties included being
"bouncy," and certainly she bounced through the house, the ever-present
specter behind her of her father, an officer of the John Birch Society.
There she was, wearing a yellow dotted dress. "Aren't you the poet? I saw
your poem in *The Voyager*. Was that not yours? A poem about suicide?
Now, that was a very deep poem. Almost too deep." *Yes,* I thought, *you'd
find a level surface deep, my dear.*

"Well," she said. "Oh, gosh, I'm about to get a visitor. Um, the voting's
almost finished. I know who I picked! You girls wait here," and she
flounced out while I, smashed against the side of the piano by girls three
or four times my femininity index, looked over the shoulder of a fat
woman in black glasses who leafed through a book of Rodgers and
Hammerstein favorites. She started pounding the opening of "I'm just a

girl who can't say no" while the double doors stayed shut behind us. I watched the pledges smile and mouth words they didn't know.

More waiting and talk of the new movie about Israel called *Exodus* and whether Elizabeth Taylor had gotten fat again. Then the accordion doors roared back into the wall on their plastic wheels, and everyone shouted things like Brenda, honey! Sandy, Sandy, Sandy! Where is Mary Sue Gonix? Has anyone seen Mary Sue Gonix? Confused, we candidates didn't know whether to wait and hear or go up to our rooms. Clumps of girls stood in the doorway, and a little pretty one burst into tears, blotting mascara with a handkerchief without much success since her long nails kept stabbing at her cheeks. She was smiling.

She'd been chosen.

"Hey, Jeanie!" said Violet, rushing up to me. "I got in, but they couldn't pick everyone tonight, so they're going to hang cute little notes on your doorknobs. You'll know in the morning, honey. Where did you get that scarf? I mean, it's a little busy, if you know what I mean."

It was. She was right. It was something about me. My scarf. Or writing poetry. Or the way I looked around a room as if I were hanging from the ceiling in a harness. People looked over at me in a nervous way when I did that, but it was my favorite thing to do. I sneaked up the stairs toward Sappho, the latest translation of which Alice had loaned me, but the others stayed to pretend to want to get to know one another. I went in my room and dressed in a long nightgown. Soon Violet would arrive; already a black negligee lay draped over her pillow. I buttoned my gown up to my neck, got in bed with Sappho, and began to read.

Fortunately, that was the night Violet decided to go "all the way" with Gunnar; she stayed out illegally and all night. I read the whole of my new copy of Sappho, and read her again. Like me, she had grown up by the ocean, loved hard and not well. But did she write this poem here to a woman? Or that to a man? There was something unsettled and unsettling about this. Perhaps they had translated it wrong. After all, the introduction had explained they had found her poems on bandages used to wrap the dead. They had cut the scrolls in half like cinnamon rolls, so sometimes eons later—she had lived in 600 B.C.—they had only found beginnings, middles, or endings of her poems.

I thought about how the sorority had gotten my beginnings but not my middles or ends. Where could I find a club like that, where I could be a poet and curl my hair and wear jeans? Nowhere that I knew of.

I heard someone rustling at the door. When the person had gone, I went out and took the envelope off my door knob. I recognized Cynthia Harris's infantile penmanship and the little telltale hearts she used to dot her i's.

"Dear Jeanie," she wrote. "The girls decided you would like something more for the brainy set, like the Book Study Club, so I have given your name to Hyacinth Gravestone. She will call you to tell you which room they meet in, in the library. All of the best. Cynthia." It would be a cold day in hell before I went to meet girls who couldn't read unless they met in hordes.

I pulled open my Sappho and read number 68: "That was different / My girlhood then / was in full bloom / and you." Suddenly I missed Alice. I got up and went out into the corridor. Everyone was finally asleep. I heard a soft sound like a pipe banging and a little wind.

As I turned toward Alice's room I saw her sitting outside her door in a navy blue bathrobe with her legs crossed, wearing slippers made to look like brown puppies. She was wiping her eyes with her hands. I sat down beside her, deliberately, so our shoulders touched, and waited until she was done. Even sad, she remembered to ask me. "Did you get in?"

"Nope," I said. "Why are you crying?"

"I was rubbing my eyes. Dora's mad at me."

"Oh," I said. "Did she lock you out?"

"No!" said Alice, almost laughing. "Did you want to get in?"

"Of course not," I said. "Did you?"

"Oh, she's always like this before her period," she said. "Want a Mars bar? I got two."

I nodded, and she pulled them out, and we sat in the hall, peeled them, and ate them gravely.

"They didn't like you? A nice girl like you?" said Alice.

"No. I'm too bookish."

"You're barely bookish enough!" said Alice.

I smiled. "Gee, thanks."

"They'd never take me."

"How come?"

"I look like a guy."

"No, you don't."
"Yes, I do."
"Well, I like you."
"I like you."
Then the door opened, and Dora let us in.

One Heart, One Way
by Mollie M. Monahan

I couldn't handle their rejection, especially since I was on my way to becoming president of the chapter. The next year I'd be elected vice president of rush for the Panhellenic Council. During my senior year I'd be chosen BGSU homecoming queen. My whole life was Sigma Kappa. Almost my entire social network was Greek. It was too painful to think about the ostracism I might go through if I came out to my sisters.

Putting this all in print scares the hell out of me. None of my sisters know. My parents don't even know. So here it is. I hope I get to all of them before this is published.

My whole family is Greek. My mom is a Delta Gamma, my grandma is an Alpha Chi, Grampie is a Delta Chi. We have SAEs, Sigma Chis, Delts, Kappas, Thetas…you name it, and we've got 'em. I'm the only Sigma Kappa, as far as I know. Except for maybe one of my second cousins. And the only one (as far as I know) to be attracted to both men and women…besides my uncle, the Delt. They say being gay runs through your mother's side of the family. I'm not sure how universal that is, but it's certainly true for me. Uncle Rob was Mom's brother, and he was gay. And Greek. I wish he were still around to talk to. AIDS took him from us in the '80s. But that's a different story entirely.

So I'm not exactly gay. But I'm not straight either. In kindergarten I had an equally strong crush on Penny as I had on Jeremy. I think most young kids have bisexual tendencies, but our society teaches them to focus only on the impulses they have toward the opposite sex. I learned at an early age to suppress my feelings toward other little girls. No one ever came right out and forbade me from loving other little girls the way

I was supposed to start loving little boys. The idea was just out there. I thought everyone had bisexual tendencies but just didn't act on them. Part of me still thinks that's the case. The reality is that I cannot ignore the feelings.

I was pretty actively bisexual in middle school. I had crushes on both boys and girls, and I even kissed a girl once. My friend Penny was a big part of that. I think if I could find her now, she'd either be gay or bi. We were both the kind of kids who knew their sexuality at an early age, and we knew it was not the norm, so we hid it. In high school I allowed my feelings toward other girls to go into some sort of remission, as if it were a disease. Those feelings never went away, but there were boys who caught my eye, and that was certainly more acceptable. I suppose I was just happy to be accepted.

I did a lot of things in high school to make sure I fit in. I don't think there's a single soul alive who didn't do things just to fit in during high school. I went to parties; I drank; I did drugs; I had sex…with boys. I was a pretty normal kid as far as all the other kids were concerned. Still, I never really completely shook this thing I had for girls.

Growing up, I was an avid figure skater. I never got to be very good (I only just began working on double jumps my senior year of high school), although it was a huge part of my life. I spent every day at the ice arena, where I made some lifelong friends. One day after skating practice my friend Rebecca and I were hanging out in her bedroom. It was a hot summer day, and we were just sitting around in shorts and bikini tops. She was sitting at the head of her bed and I at the foot. We were just sitting there not talking, and suddenly she told me to stop staring at her breasts. I hadn't even realized I was doing it. I was so embarrassed! I wondered how often I'd been caught doing the exact same thing and just no one had the guts to confront me the way Rebecca did. We never spoke of what happened again.

Eventually I went to college. I chose Bowling Green State University because it had a precision ice skating team, and I wanted to continue skating. I think my mother encouraged me to attend BGSU because it had a great DG chapter. But much to her chagrin, I chose not to rush my first year. I wanted to join student activities on campus, but I didn't want to "buy my friends," the great non-Greek misconception. I thought Greeks were snobs, and I didn't want to be associated with that.

During my first year in college I joined several clubs and organizations. I was a floor representative in hall government and, second semester, was elected president of the hall. I joined the publications committee in the University Activities Organization, and I was (of course) a bright shining new member of the Falconettes Precision Ice Skating Team. My boyfriend from high school decided to attend BG with me, and our relationship was strong and stable.

My mother finally convinced me to rush at the beginning of my sophomore year. Even though I told myself I wouldn't join, I signed up anyway to appease her. At that time I was working at a "head shop" (selling Grateful Dead T-shirts, tie-dyes, batik dresses, Fimo jewelry, incense, and so forth), listening to a little-known band called "Phish," reading feminist literature, and intellectually exploring ideas of culture and sexual orientation. I was broadening my views of the world and myself. The last thing I wanted to do was restrict my identity by joining a Greek organization.

Much to my surprise (and my mother's delight) I enjoyed rush. I found almost all of the women to be down-to-earth and interesting— women whom I could see as my sisters. I was invited back to the maximum number of chapters every day of rush. It was an exhilarating feeling.

At the end of rush week, I decided to join a one-year-old chapter on campus called Sigma Kappa. The women were excited to break new ground and develop their own kind of sisterhood, one that was different from that of other sororities. I thought that was pretty cool, and I thought that the fact that they loved my individuality was cool too. Because I chose not to pledge Delta Gamma, however, my mother mourned for months, literally. The DGs are probably thankful I didn't pledge with them now that my story is coming out. Goodness only knows what the Sigma Kappas are thinking.

During sophomore year I also met Rick, who still has a strong hold on my heart. He introduced me to vegetarianism, activism, and guitar. We fell in love hard and fast, and our relationship lasted almost two years. He bought me my first guitar and taught me my first Indigo Girls song. All my sisters loved him and thought we were forever. We were the strangest misfits at all of the Sigma Kappa functions: Rick with his long hair and beat-up Converse high-tops and me with my long skirts, hairy legs, and no makeup. In 1992 that stuff was pretty radical in northern Ohio. Interestingly, though, everyone loved us. Now, in hindsight, it makes sense. We were a part of their heterosexual norm.

One note I should make here is that I always seemed to have a boyfriend. It wasn't really a conscious thing on my part, but it kept me from exploring my attraction to women. From my senior year in high school to college graduation, I constantly had a boyfriend. All my relationships were long, and almost every guy was immediately replaced after we broke up. The only one I was ever fully emotionally committed to was Rick; I was extremely aloof with the rest. Being a student leader in five campus organizations at the time (including my chapter) was always more important to me than a romantic relationship. It was just easier to have a boyfriend than not to have one. I really was (and still am) attracted to men. I always had someone to take to date parties, and no one ever questioned my sexuality—sometimes not even me. And that's the way I liked it.

I feel I should make another point here about bisexuality. No one ever seems to believe that is my sexual orientation. As if it weren't difficult enough for me to just come out of the closet, I have to constantly justify my sexual orientation to the straight world *and* the gay world. The gay world thinks I'm in some sort of transitional stage and that one day I'll realize I'm really gay. Well, it's been one hell of a long stage. A 27-year-long stage, to be exact. And the straight world thinks I'm in some sort of experimental phase, that one day I'll wake up and realize I'm really straight. I have news for all of you. I am bisexual. That's the way it is, and it's never going to change. You all need to start believing me. One day I'll find one person and settle down (I hope). I'm not sure at this point whether that person will be male or female. Only time can tell. All I know is that bisexuality is my capital T Truth (to quote a Robert J. Nash term).

The summer between my sophomore and junior years I attended the gay pride march in Columbus, Ohio, with my friends Joe, Scot, and Eric. I recall seeing a woman who had a big sticker on her back reading SORORITY DYKES UNITE! I asked her which chapter she was affiliated with, and she said she was not actually Greek at all. She ended up giving me the sticker, and I wore it all day. I was not out to myself yet, so for me wearing that sticker was pretty extreme. I was ready to just be what I was. I didn't want to have to intellectualize it. I just wanted to exist. And I wasn't being fully honest in wearing the label of "dyke" either. I loved men then and still do. I just happen to have an equally strong attraction to women.

The end of my junior year was hell. My relationship with Rick was deteriorating. I had feelings for one particular woman that I could not ignore, and Rick needed space for his own reasons. We broke up in an ugly, hateful way. I came out to him; he objectified it by saying he would like to be involved in a threesome with me (which is often the straight man's response, and I will get to *that* later); I got pissed off; he didn't care; and it was over. His version of the story might be very different, but this is how I remember it. Because he'd been a resident assistant, I thought he'd be more understanding. But I see now that he was the wrong person to go to for support. He didn't have any energy left to give me, and I'm no longer angry at him for not being able to give. Our relationship had been over for a long time, and it took that little episode to finalize things. And it opened me up to addressing my sexuality in a way I had not allowed myself for a long time.

As for the straight man's objectification of female bisexuality, I can only *strongly* encourage you guys to stop it. It hurts. Plain and simple. Cut it out. Do you not think women go through enough objectification in this society? Do you think you need to add a little more pain to top it all off? I haven't chosen this lifestyle to become more mysterious, intriguing, or attractive to men. My attraction to women doesn't have anything to do with men. To my straight male friends: Please try harder in your efforts to not objectify me. To straight male strangers: the same. One of my sorority sisters and I used to hold hands at fraternity parties to keep the guys away (she was straight, and I wasn't out to her), but it never worked. They always propositioned us for a piece of the action. All I wanted was to be able to go to a party without being objectified. My bisexuality only made it worse.

The fall of my first senior year (I had two senior years) I had my first experience with a woman, Josie, whom I'd had my eye on for quite some time. She was so beautiful and had amazing sexual energy. She was a women's studies major, president of Womyn for Womyn, and one of the most outspoken radical feminists on campus. She was also the most beautiful person I had ever laid my eyes on. She was brilliant, candid, well-read, and had the most amazing eyes—and body.

So I asked her out. I think I surprised her because she knew I was in a sorority. Nonetheless, it was one of the easiest things I've ever done. We went out and had an amazing time. We stayed up all night talking and kissing and exploring each other's body. I had never experienced anything like it. I think that all women, even straight women, should try kissing another woman at some point in their lives. It's really great. Really soft. Surprisingly soft after kissing men for so many years. Men are so rough with all their facial hair…which I love too, but for different reasons.

I was living in the sorority house then, with my little sister, Bethany. I wasn't out to her, but she probably would have been pretty cool with it. Beth was all around pretty cool. Josie called a lot and sometimes stopped by, which made me nervous. I was one of the most respected members of my chapter and held one of the highest ranking executive board offices as vice president of membership (rush). I was scared to death that my sisters would see me looking at Josie and know how much I was attracted to her. I wanted desperately to kiss her when we were hanging out in my room alone, but I never did. I was too frightened.

Some of my sisters often made gay jokes. People frequently don't understand that when they tell gay jokes there may be a gay person in their immediate presence whom they are harming. Even more disturbing, however, was their reaction to one of our educational programs.

For a while, I was participating in "sexuality panels" through the university's lesbian and gay association. They'd gather a group of students together, all with differing sexual orientations, and open them up to questions. They always wanted to have a "straight" voice, and I was a willing participant. I wasn't ready to be out about my sexuality, but I was ready to be the best ally possible.

We (the executive board of Sigma Kappa) decided to use one of these panels as one of our educational programs. But we didn't tell the membership the topic of the program for fear that they wouldn't attend. The rest of the executive board had no idea about my sexual orientation. When I brought up the idea of having a sexual orientation panel as a program, they all said it was a great idea. Most of them admitted they were pretty unfamiliar with gay issues and that they could stand to learn a little more. I sat on the panel and, as usual, labeled myself straight. Even so, many of the sisters were extremely angry because the topic of the program had been kept a secret and they had been *forced* to attend the event. One sister even said that if she had known the topic of the program, she wouldn't have chosen a seat in the front row so close to *those* people. I was heartbroken. At that moment I felt I could never be out to my entire chapter. All of the support the executive board had unknowingly shown me was lost by a few homophobic statements like that one.

As a result, my relationship with Josie was short-lived, and I ended up breaking up with her in a really heartless way. I got scared and just stopped returning her calls. I had witnessed what my sisters were capable of when they decided someone didn't fit their mold. They could be loyal or cruel, depending on where you stood with them. I couldn't handle their rejection, especially since I was on my way to becoming president of the chapter. The next year I would be elected vice president of rush for the Panhellenic Council. During my senior year I'd be chosen BGSU homecoming queen. My whole life was Sigma Kappa. Almost my entire social network was Greek. It was too painful to think about the ostracism I might go through if I came out.

I still think about Josie, wondering how she is and where she is. I wish I could find her now, because I'm so much more confident in my sexuality. I wish I could have her in my life again. She was so amazing. My friend Cameron, a gay man, encouraged me to come out in college, but I was scared to death. He wanted me to find the solace he had found in the gay community, but I thought I had too much to lose.

I ended up getting into a relationship with probably the most masculine fraternity man on campus. Jim ("Big Jim" was his nickname) was 6 foot 6 and a bouncer at one of the local bars. We dated for two years, and he tried to lavaliere me, but I refused him. He told me he wanted to marry me, and I just blew it off. My sisters told me I was crazy to treat him as I did. They also thought we made the cutest couple, that we'd last forever. Despite my behavior, I did love him and was attracted to him. We had an amazing sexual relationship, but he wasn't "the one."

Today I attend graduate school at the University of Vermont and am finally coming to terms with my sexual orientation in public ways. I'm working on my master's degree in higher education and student affairs administration. As part of my graduate assistantship, I work with student leaders in the Living/Learning Center on campus. I advise Order of Omega and Phi Delta Theta in my free time. I play guitar and sing at coffeehouses and benefits. I speak openly to students, staff, and fellow classmates about my sexuality. I'm proud of undergraduate students who are confident enough to be out on campus, especially since I wasn't able to do the same. I live in the Living/Learning Center with 600 undergraduate students and actively serve as a role model to them as an out graduate student. I've been asked to play at gay coffee hours and the annual GLBTA Speak-Out. My picture was even in the Vermont gay paper, *Out in the Mountains,* as a local bisexual folk artist. As the graduate adviser to Phi Delta Theta, I wear my freedom rings to the Phi Delt house from time to time. While some of the members have a long way to go in resolving their homophobia, most of them fully accept me. One of the members is out to the brotherhood as well, proving how comfortable many of the brothers are with issues of sexual orientation. I can only keep trying with the rest.

Being openly bisexual is tough, though. I've lost lovers and friends who couldn't deal with it. The injustice breaks my heart, but I have to live truthfully, and my truth is my bisexuality.

I'm a proud alumna member of Sigma Kappa, and wouldn't change my experience for the world. I only wish I'd had the strength to be out in college. Being president of a large, highly respected chapter on campus, homecoming queen, Outstanding Greek Woman, *and* being openly bisexual would really have been something to be proud of. In reality, though, I'm not sure if it would have happened. BGSU was ready for a vegetarian, feminist, hairy-legged, no-makeup homecoming queen, but a bisexual one?

I acquired critical leadership skills and did a lot of soul searching as a result of my sorority membership. I started a chapter of the first feminist organization for sorority women at BG called emPOWER (Panhellenic Office of Women's Empowerment). I couldn't have achieved half of what I did without the support of my sisters. I wish I could go back and at least give them the benefit of the doubt. I think most of them would have supported me.

Being a member of a sorority and at the same time loving women makes a lot of sense. I'm drawn to female-centered activities, and as a feminist, I'm proud to know that my founding sisters were the first women to be allowed entrance to a New England college (Colby College in Maine, 1874). I hold my head high knowing I continue to be a part of their struggle.

If any of my sisters are reading this right now and want to know how you can better support those of us who sometimes feel we're fighting this battle alone, I invite your empathy. You don't have to slap a rainbow sticker on your car or march in a pride parade. You just have to love each of us through all of our differences. The national motto of Sigma Kappa is "One Heart, One Way." As one heart bonds us, one sisterhood shows us the way through peace and love. Keep each sister's struggle close to your heart, as it is also your own. And please remember, I'm still the same hardworking, dedicated, loyal sister I've always been. I'm still me.

Nightmare of a National Officer
by *"Carolyn"*

As in most national sororities, our nondiscrimination clause doesn't say anything about sexual orientation. It's a private organization, and I could be dismissed from my duties. I don't honestly think that will happen. Still, I am afraid of exposing myself and allowing me to be me, wholly and completely.

Imagine sitting at a business meeting at the national convention of your sorority, waiting for the slate of candidates to be introduced. Excitement hangs in the air, and the unmistakable feeling of sisterhood surrounds you. After all, this is the national convention, a time of celebration and joy. Now imagine one of your sisters who's running for the national council as she begins her speech about how she has donated so much time and energy, ensuring that the sisterhood you enjoy right now is enriched and deepened. As the carefully prepared words about all the dreams and aspirations she has for your sorority spill from her mouth, a quiet buzz drifts throughout the room. You look around, trying to understand what your sisters are saying. Finally, you make out their words. Your sister, who sincerely wants to make a difference in the future of the sorority, speaks the words she has prepared for the past six months, but with less confidence as she scans the room. And then you hear it. *Lesbian.* The speaker finally understands what they're saying about her, and she knows she's been discovered.

Welcome to my nightmare.

Would they vote for me if they knew? Would they vote for me if they didn't? Would anyone care? Would I be accepted or ostracized? Would they understand that I was the same person that I was 2½ minutes before they found out? How would the older alumnae feel? Would the sisters from my own chapter even speak to me again? Would I be banned from the position I held within the national organization?

The above scenario didn't occur, but I'm certainly afraid of being "outed" to my sorority sisters before I'm ready and even more afraid of being outed publicly without my consent. Coming out to people, no matter who, can be a difficult process. I'm never quite sure what to say or how each new person will react. Unfortunately, today's society, although more tolerant than past generations, is still largely intolerant of gays, lesbians, and bisexuals. We see it all the time as news stories, often tragic, appear across the country. Sororities are no exception; there are a ton of stereotypes that go along with being a "sorority woman" and lead to acts of intolerance.

I hold my sorority near and dear to my heart. We've been through so much together. I currently volunteer for the national organization, in a position I truly love. I smile when I think about a sister somewhere in this country enjoying the things that other national officers and I develop. I enjoy making a difference in people's lives. It's a dream of mine to run for national council someday, but then the nightmare reminds me that I'm probably crazy. Would I be able to truly be myself? If many sorority sisters found out about my orientation, could I deal with the stigma attached to being the first openly lesbian national officer? That, in and of itself, would be a huge role for me to play, not only for the other lesbian and bisexual women in the sorority but also for the heterosexual women who may not be so accepting. Would I alone shoulder the burden of educating the sorority about diversity?

Traditionally I've been an overachiever, at least to most people who know me. Throughout grammar school and high school, I received straight A's. I was never late, never received detention, and was involved in numerous activities, both on and off campus. I participated in my church and sports. Like many other gay and lesbian adolescents, I strove to be the "perfect girl" and worked hard to be successful. When I felt discouraged, my mother reminded me, "You know you can do anything if you set your mind to it." She was right. I often felt that the popular saying "Shoot for the moon—even if you miss you'll be among the stars" was off base. Instead, my motto was "Shoot for the moon and land on the moon. Missing isn't an option."

When college rolled around, I decided to attend a school where I received numerous scholarships. My high school boyfriend and I went to different colleges in the same town, so we saw each other often. Our relationship was so strong that we thought we would eventually get married. He was a great guy, but I never really felt connected to him. I was miserable at school and miserable in my relationship while hiding behind a sunny disposition and a happy smile. I had no idea what was wrong with me. I had a terrific boyfriend, went to a great college, got good grades, and had a loving family and many friends. I had everything I could possibly need, didn't I? For some reason, though, I was completely dissatisfied with my life. I needed something more, so I did two life-changing things: I broke up with my boyfriend and pledged a sorority.

I threw myself into the sorority with everything I had. I made sure I was the best pledge—I was the first in my pledge class to know all my sorority history and songs, and I often studied with my pledge sisters to make sure they knew as much as I did. I knew everything, did everything, went to every activity, and learned as much as I could. After all, this was going to be the new me. I would become a sorority woman and receive all the benefits that came along with it. Then my life would be all right. Once initiated, I was only one of two in my pledge class to hold a position in the chapter. I often hung out with the chapter president, because I knew someday that would be me…it had to be.

The next three years of my college career were centered on the sorority. To me, it was absolutely amazing; the sorority allowed me to be more myself. What a feeling to know that all these women would be standing behind me if I needed them. This was *exactly* what I needed. I went to every function my chapter and the sorority held, including national convention. I couldn't get enough; I felt as if I had found something magical, almost spiritual. I had this bond with women in my chapter and with women across the country. Wow! Imagine the feeling of standing in a room at national convention, seeing everyone wearing the same pin as you, taking the same oath you have taken, and celebrating sisterhood in every sense of the word.

Except for one small difference.

I remember attending various parties and mixers with my sisters. Often I felt I was doing something wrong, even when I wasn't. Sometimes various sisters were drunk and hung all over me, spouting phrases of sisterhood, and other times they dragged me into a single-stall bathroom to talk about some random issue while they "went." I just wrote it off as my being "conservative"; after all, these were my sisters. If it didn't bother them, why should it bother me? And didn't I have an obligation to them if they needed me? Deep down I knew they probably didn't think twice about it. Still, I felt uncomfortable, but I went along with it because that was what I was supposed to do.

After a while, I got involved with a fraternity guy. I liked him because he was obnoxious the way a fraternity guy is supposed to be, which also allowed me to keep him at a distance. No one really understood why I liked him. But I thought I liked him and that we were good for each other. Throughout our relationship, however, it just didn't feel right, and I couldn't figure out why. I was usually such a good judge of character. Had I really chosen to date someone so wrong for me? The relationship felt so forced. When we broke up, I wasn't very upset and couldn't understand why. He made me laugh, my mother liked him, we had great conversations, yet something was missing. I could not or maybe would not acknowledge the truth about myself. After all, I was supposed to grow up, find a good job, get married, have 2.5 children, and live in a house in the suburbs with a white picket fence. At this point, that dream didn't look likely. Almost everyone had believed I was in love with him, and they truly thought we'd end up together. That was certainly the *last* thing I wanted. But what did I want?

I had no idea what was going on inside. I was graduating with my bachelor's degree, but I felt that even with the well-rounded education I received, I didn't know myself. I didn't know what I wanted to do, who I wanted to be, what I wanted to accomplish in life. I was confused and scared. I was supposed to be the one who had it all together, the one who knew what she was doing and where she was going. Everyone told me I was just going through a rough period and that it would all work out. I often smiled and said "I know," knowing there was something else, something I couldn't reach, something I couldn't talk about. I felt apart from everyone else, even when I was in a room full of people, so I overcompensated. I felt so different, yet I knew on the outside I was just like everyone else. It was killing me, but I couldn't risk losing who I appeared to be when I didn't even know who I was.

The only thing that seemed to be a constant was the sorority. I got a job as a sorority consultant to travel to chapters throughout the country to provide guidance and support. I met many wonderful people, including national officers whom I had always admired from a distance. I knew I'd made a good decision. I looked at women who were initiated 40, 50,

60 years ago who still came back. I wanted that to be me someday. I wanted to make sure that all sisters had as wonderful an experience in the sorority as I did, so I worked hard at my job and made a lot of friends.

That year also led to a lot of soul-searching—about who I wanted to be and who I was. Along the way, I met a true angel, Christine, who became my best friend. We talked for hours and hours about the most obscure things, about spiritual things, about deep issues of self. She helped me stand up for myself and sort out my life, staying with me every step of the way. I'd never felt so close to someone in my life. She was special, such a great friend, a truly terrific person. I couldn't explain how we had gotten so close, how we had suddenly become lifelong friends. How could one not love her? She was an amazing person who touched the lives of everyone with whom she came in contact. There was a special intimacy to our friendship too, unlike any other friendship I'd ever had. I knew I wanted to spend as much time with her as possible, that I wanted to live my life with Christine by my side. How lucky I was to have such a special person in my life.

Then it happened. One night we went out to dinner. Afterward, on our way to visit one of her friends, we were talking about some issues that had come up recently. For the past few days, I had felt tense around Christine—that unmistakable feeling you just can't put your finger on but feel nervous about. As we were driving, I suddenly felt sharp tension in the air. Was something wrong? Then Christine told me what she had wanted to say for so long: She was gay. She hoped I still loved her and knew she was the same person I'd eaten dinner with. I didn't say much, and we arrived at her friend's house. I was stunned. How could you know someone so well and yet not know such a huge part of her life? The entire time we were there, I thought only about what Christine had told me, reviewing the past few years of our friendship to see if there'd been any clues. When certain things jumped out at me, I felt uneasy. I had the exact same characteristics and qualities. I did the same things that gave me clues that Christine was gay without ever verbalizing it. So much of my life now made sense. She said exactly what I'd always tried to suppress. Was I gay too? This wasn't supposed to happen to me. Yet when she said those words, it was as if she were showing me a mirror and daring me to look in it. It clicked. I didn't want it to, but it made more sense than anything else I'd ever heard or felt.

It took a while for me to internalize my feelings and deal with who I was. It's frightening when your mind floods with memories about something you knew all along was your truth. I realized why I was so unsettled with my life after college and why I was so confused. But I couldn't admit or deal with what I felt. I felt as if God had truly sent Christine as my angel. Her brave declaration allowed me to come to terms with who I was and gave me the strength and courage to explore my inner being even more deeply. Together, we could support one another and deal with the "whys" of our orientation. We could grow together, develop our friendship, our love, our spirituality.

With Christine's guidance, I became a volunteer national officer, maintaining friendships with sisters across the country while working for the betterment of the sorority. The sorority was right there with me throughout all my troubled times and all my happy moments. I truly love being a member and love giving back in a unique way. Each time I'm with my "national" sisters, I feel such an incredible sense of friendship and sisterhood. We all love the sorority, and we're all part of an incredible organization that fosters unity and love. But what would happen if one of their own was a lesbian? I'm fearful of what they might say. As in most national sororities, our nondiscrimination clause doesn't say anything about sexual orientation. It's a private organization, and I could be dismissed from my duties. I don't honestly think that will happen. Still, I'm afraid of exposing myself and allowing me to be me, wholly and completely.

I'm living a dichotomy. I want to be honest and truthful and pave the way for future lesbian sisters who want to become involved with the national organization. I want to reduce some of the stigma of being a lesbian. I want to help those lesbian and bisexual sisters in our chapters deal with their sexuality and accept it, unlike what I did for so long. On the other hand, I'm scared. The sorority has been the constant in my life, and it's difficult for me to reveal so much of myself, to put so much at stake without knowing what will happen. What if I'm a square peg trying to fit into a round hole? Should I take that risk and reveal myself with the possibility of losing it all, or remain quiet and subtly hope to effect change in the organization? I don't know the answer. As much as heterosexuals don't want to feel uncomfortable when people tell them they are gay, gay people want to feel comfortable with their heterosexual friends. Is it my responsibility to go forth and reveal myself, in order for the sorority to create a place of tolerance, acceptance, and education? Do I now become "the lesbian" in the sorority? Will my sisters feel comfortable around me? Will I feel comfortable around them? I've told everyone in my close circle of friends, including a few fellow national officers, and so far everyone has been very accepting. I often think how much easier it would be to be heterosexual; I would just go about my business and everyone would assume I was heterosexual. But I'm not. Each day I discover a little more about my sexuality. Each day I find I do have a responsibility to educate those around me to make the world safer for gays, lesbians, and bisexuals. Gay people are no different from heterosexual people; we all work, sleep, eat, shop, watch TV, dance, play, bicycle, go to the movies, laugh, cry, get angry, and join sororities and fraternities. I hope that sororities and fraternities become groundbreaking organizations that promote tolerance, acceptance, and inclusion of all people. And it is my sincere hope that leaders of every national organization read our stories and begin to educate their membership so that gays, lesbians, and bisexuals can be free to be open about who they are.

The Back Steps
by Tiffany Hendrix

"We're not like other houses," a senior once told me when I was a pledge. "We don't tear our pledges down just to rebuild them into carbon copies of ourselves. We want you to stand up for what you believe in." One of her younger sisters had done just that, and she was being ostracized. What did that say about our sisterhood, our values?

There's nothing like getting your hair done at the end of the last decade of the 20th century. At 16, my friend, now a professional stylist, was a blond hurricane. OK, not entirely blond—sometimes black and sometimes cinnamon and sometimes plum. Back in high school, she tried tirelessly to get me to let her cut my hair, which I never did until I was well into college. I sat myself in her kitchen during academic breaks; there were designer scissors, bowls of color, and tint brushes scattered across her dinner table. She'd either straddle me or kneel on my thighs. I wanted this, the pressure of her, the smell of her skin drowning out bleach fumes, more than I wanted a new hairdo. She'd give me a different style for every semester, nothing too drastic. One style for my first term at the university in Ohio. A new color for pledging. Cut and color for my last semester in Ohio before I transferred. Highlighted chunks for my first five months at Indiana University. Then one day I said it, and she replied, "What? No, Tiffany. You're not. I know you better than you know yourself. You're so straight. Give yourself two years and you'll figure out you're straight. I know you. You like boys." With those words, everything broke into tiny shards and landed in the pile of hair at my feet. Everything, including the memory of her sugary kiss and passionate touch. She had reacted in a similar way when I told her I was planning on going Greek. "What?" she had said. "No, you're not." At one time I would have agreed with her.

It's hard to say why I chose to pledge, but on bid night, January 26, 1996, any doubts I had about my decision vanished. The small Ohio sorority house stripped itself of the evening gown and chocolate mousse pretension and became a madhouse of sensory overload, the most prominent aspect of which was the professional photographer's flash. No sooner had my pledge sisters and I crossed the threshold than we were shoved into big baggy sweatshirts with sorority letters splashed across them. We experienced a sort of collective mind meld. We weren't sure exactly what was happening or whether we liked it, but it moved so quickly that I think we were all somewhat taken with it. At the very least, I know I was intrigued. We were ushered to a carpeted stairway festooned with white holiday lights, and a photo was taken of us with our new "sisters." One by one each pledge class arranged itself for one fully clothed photo and one not so fully clothed. Then came the pictures on the columned front porch, same motif. We pledges were herded from room to tapestried room amid the smells of beer, whiskey, tobacco, and weed, occasionally summoned from our celebration by the beckoning of boy pledges who had come to serenade and kiss us. That's how it started. As time passed, "sister" lost its quotation marks. The small Ohio campus lost me. A volume called *Vice Versa* found its way into my personal library.

It wasn't until the first semester of my sophomore year, the semester of nightly after-dinner cigarette breaks with my sisters on the front porch of the Ohio house, that I suspected the deviant term *bisexual* applied to my life. My relationship with my sisters took on a whole new dimension, one that I was convinced they could never have guessed. Never one to take much action, I would lust after one of three or four boys in my history class during the afternoon. Then, after dinner, I would lust after one of three or four sisters with whom I was sharing intimate conversation. Maybe it was predatory. It doesn't matter. They did not have to know.

A rough year later I stood on the front porch of my apartment in Bloomington, Ind., where I currently live and study, a beer in one hand and a cigarette in the other, with tears streaming down my face. "I know," I said to my Big (sister). "You and Beth drove a long way to come to this party tonight and to see me. But I...I need to be given some time to hang out with this girl from my class. You just don't understand."

"Sure I do," she said, employing her best tone of sisterly camaraderie.

But I suspected she didn't. In this strange place I was no longer Greek (my sorority does not have a chapter at IU). I felt like we lived on two different planets. I should've had two separate parties, I thought. One for me to try to learn what it's like to be gay, and one where I could be with my sisters without having to tell them. But since my sorority life and bisexual life were headed for a head-on collision, something had to be said. How would she take it?

"I just...I..." I was half drunk and having trouble expressing myself. In choosing to become my Big, this woman had taken on the special responsibility of being available for me under any and all circumstances. One year earlier I had sacrificed the intimacy of the school where we had both pledged, Everyone-on-campus-says-God-bless-you-when-you-sneeze University, for anonymity. I had felt suffocated in Ohio, and anonymity was the one thing I'd needed more than anything else. So I had turned my relationship with my Big into something long-distance. She knew me, so she knew I had a flair for melodrama. In a huge tearful blurt I released the confession: "I'm bisexual, I'm attracted to her, and I'd rather explore that right now than (sob) go off on adventures with you and Beth."

"O-o-oh," she crooned. I was lulled into a false sense of security by the comforting tone of her voice, the tone so familiar to me. "Just because you have feelings for girls, and even though you may have had feelings for Beth, you still have to realize that Beth and I drove four hours to see you. You can hang out with this other girl any time." I had already figured that out, but... "*What?* Feelings for Beth? No, you don't understand. Not at all." Beth was my sister and friend and no more than that. How could I explain that to my Big?

I had met Beth during my freshman year when we lived on the same floor. We enjoyed the same social circle, and although the small town where we studied didn't offer much in the way of places to explore, we did what we could, cruising through a tunnel of laughter into a spattering of Ohio starlight. Beth loved the Indigo Girls' music. As for the singers' sexuality? "Yuck," she'd say. She was obviously not the only one who felt that way.

Gay college women can be heard mocking "sorority bitches," but I'd never heard one of my sisters make a homophobic comment. They didn't have to, since the gay, lesbian, and bisexual community at that university barely exists, but a lot of my sisters agreed with Beth's "yuck." I found this out on mock pledge night in October 1996. when I was still a present and active member of my Ohio sorority. The fall pledge class was going to a little brother's house to drink and share sorority secrets. This particular night freshman girls were milling around. We had to hold back, lessen the impact of our activities, due to rush rules. We tried to amuse ourselves, but we still felt disappointed. All 20-plus sisters were seated in a circle in the living room when a little brother took it upon himself to liven things up. "They say," he said, "that 10% of the population of the Western world identifies as homosexual. By that estimation, at least three of the women in this room have engaged in sexual activity with other women. I would like to know by a show of hands who those women are."

My stomach sank. At that point, I had just admitted my feelings to myself. What if one of my sisters who smoked spoke up and said, "Well, I've seen the way Tiffany looks at us out on the porch!" I was mortified, and there was no way in hell I was going to raise my hand. My justification was semantic; I had never consciously acknowledged being sexually involved with a woman. Therefore, the question did not apply to me. As a student of history, I was aware that any manipulation of the facts could be labeled revisionism. I chose to interpret my situation as I saw it. That I longed to be with a woman was beside the point. As I was pondering all of this, I thought, *Relax your facial muscles, Tiffany. Anything less than sto-icism in this moment will betray you,* when suddenly the only senior sister we had in the sorority that year raised her hand. "*What?*" her room-mate shouted. "I'd like to know by a show of hands who's never sleeping in a room with you again," she fumed as she threw her hands into the air. "You can take your iguana and you can take your tendencies and you can sleep somewhere else." Eventually, that was exactly what happened. Our one and only senior and her iguana moved down the hall from the room they had originally shared with our closed-minded sister. That conversa-tion became a turning point for relations within our house. Dinner ban-ter and all sorts of other talk revolved around who was right and who was wrong and who would sleep or share a room or have sex with which other woman in the house.

For the rest of that painful and strange semester, we often sat around lighted candles and talked about respect. Women chose to pledge our chapter because we all had different perspectives. We could learn from and strengthen one another through our diversity. These dark sessions often reminded me of my intense pledge period. "We're not like other houses," a senior once told me when I was a pledge. "We don't tear our pledges down just to rebuild them into carbon copies of ourselves. We want you to stand up for what you believe in." One of her younger sisters had done just that, and she was being ostracized. What did that say about our sisterhood, our values? Within my pledge class, strong doubts were expressed as to whether our sorority could survive this conflict.

When I finally admitted that it very well could have been me who had raised my hand that night, I was removed from my chapter and my sisters by 200 miles and a semester-long infatuation with a butch bull dyke. I had come out to my Big on the porch of my Bloomington home. Now I had to go inside the apartment, walk past my crush, find Beth, and tell her before my Big had the chance to "out" me. Beth, however, was enjoying herself immensely, and I wasn't even sure she had heard me tell her until I got her E-mail message a week later. "It doesn't matter to me. Sure, it is something I'm not into, but that doesn't mean friends of mine can't be…. Is that the whole reason you were so upset that night? I don't agree with it when it comes to myself because I know I don't feel that, but for anyone else, you can't help how you feel. The one thing you must know and ALWAYS REMEMBER is that you are my friend and I am yours no matter what."

Some parts of coming out must be remembered even though they beg to be forgotten. I'm thinking of the phone call to my mother on that very first day when I realized my feelings would not disappear. I remember the moment I realized that talking to my straight female friends about this was not gaining me understanding. Those common filler words "you know?" were answered with blank stares. I recall talking with straight male friends and finding out how many different ways the word *woman* could be interpreted. These are the things my mind chooses to emphasize as much as that first blue-eyed, me-too smile. The best response of all was my Bloomington roommate's: "Who cares?" Slowly, over time, I've learned to trust my instincts. I also have learned to tone down the drama just a little bit.

Visiting my pledge sisters in Ohio is always a rich and valuable experience for me. They have exploded outward from the sorority house and landed scattered around the outskirts of the little campus, which is still just as picturesque as its recruitment brochure. The rented houses where my sisters live now are no less photo-collaged, no less painted, no less textured than the crowded rooms they shared at the sorority address. They survived. They have accomplished the goal they have striven toward since pledging: the status of senior. As the one who chose to leave, I see these women as alive as their houseplants and as delicious as their spaghetti dinners, as selves who have reached definition independent of, aided by, in the context of, and in spite of one another.

Sometime between the time that I left Ohio and now, decisions were made within the sorority that have allowed two other sisters to "come out" without being kicked out of their rooms, verbally abused, or scandalized. Now, two years after I left Ohio, my sisters provide a safe and empowering emotional environment, where the label that describes my orientation does not matter. By virtue of having such a figurative but powerful space, I have the strength and the will to defend myself when I encounter those who think that a label is all I am. The creation of this space was not why I went Greek. It was simply the result.

This past January, Beth recited the following line at sorority preference desserts: "In the end, our house can only be a better way to stumble up the back steps and walk out the front door." I'm not saying every queer should go Greek. I'm certainly not suggesting that all Greek women should sleep with other women. I am, however, suggesting that Greek women confront this issue for themselves, so that they and their sisters might be comfortable raising their hands, in the living room and out on the street, if ever the question is asked. We should all have the same back steps up which to stumble—God draws us all different maps for finding that front door.

On Trial
by Ali Cannon

Ruthie celebrated my uniqueness and my nonconformist spirit; such witnessing, however, took place under the guise of Theta belonging—a place where nonconformity was acceptable only if it fell within the guidelines of compulsory heterosexuality.

In 1982 at the University of California, Berkeley, I was put on trial at Kappa Alpha Theta for being a lesbian. I was 18 years old.

Before I was put on trial I was a well-loved member of the sorority, even though I always had mixed feelings about being a member. I went through rush in kind of an ambivalent state, not knowing much about the Greek system. My father had been in a fraternity at the University of California, Los Angeles, but that was for Jews only. And my mother had been in a sorority for a brief time (also at UCLA) in the '50s, but she quit after her independent spirit got the best of her. What sticks out most in my mind is that she spent her final sorority days in a state of bratty rebellion, and even put a fish in the housemother's bed.

So my mother did not have some overarching need to see her daughter join anything; well, maybe just a bit. I mostly wanted to look into joining a sorority because I knew I liked being around big groups of women. The most fun I had in high school was being in a Mariner scout troop. Women a couple of years older than me in that organization had provided motherly (sisterly) love and encouraged something grounded and confident in me—things I now know were pieces in my coming-out journey.

Still, I didn't like the rush experience, finding it incredibly fake and way beyond any class level to which I'd been exposed. I didn't have the outfits or debutante mind-set. They all had monogrammed sweaters; I was living in a co-op. My lower-middle-class upbringing in homogeneously Jewish Los Angeles hadn't prepared me for these interactions. By the end of rush I was kind of mocking the whole experience, wearing a cowboy hat and an ERA T-shirt. That week, though, I met a couple of women whom I really liked. Both were members of Kappa Alpha Theta.

Ruthie was the woman who came to call me "little sister." She was warm, loving, intelligent, nurturing, and probably somewhat familiar to me. She had grown up in the same neighborhood as I. My dad, coincidentally, had sold her parents their first home. After four months of sisterhood, she wrote me this letter:

From the first day we met, I saw in you an independent woman through and through. Spunky and cute and with good things to say, you're my type of Theta lady all the way.

Fun times, warm talks, our friendship has grown, and from early on a seed was sown. A seed that will flourish as the years roll on past, a friendship, a bond, guaranteed to last.

You're different, Ali—bright and unique—you'll never conform so you'll never be beat. Let no one convince you that "being together" is wrong, and never fear to sing your own song....

Ruthie celebrated my uniqueness and my nonconformist spirit; such witnessing, however, took place under the guise of Theta belonging—a place where nonconformity was acceptable only if it fell within the guidelines of compulsory heterosexuality.

While the Theta house stood on pillars of conformity, I went busting out down the coming-out road. I met Sharon, my first girlfriend, the spring of my freshman year. She had another girlfriend at the time. I knew I wanted her from the moment I met her and heard her cute voice at a meeting I was facilitating at the campus Women's Center. I was not out to myself at the time, although I had questioned my sexuality in high school, having fallen in love with a woman the summer before my senior year.

Sharon and I had one sexual encounter at the end of my freshman year—an exciting, yet odd, encounter. We fooled around in her bed at the end of a big party. A couple of her drunken friends were passed out in the room, but I didn't care. I stayed late at the party hoping something would happen, and when she grabbed my hand and led me upstairs, I knew I was ready. After this initial tryst, I wrote her the most romantic and sweet letter—young puppy love all turned on, coming-out fever gushing forth. She had called me "fireball" because of all the sexual energy I had that first night, and that's how I referred to myself in the letter. But she blew me off. I was too young to be bothered with, according to the advice she got from one of her friends, and that actually seemed to be more of a reason than the fact that she had a girlfriend. I was crushed.

But then, when I returned for my sophomore year, she called me. I had just moved into the sorority house at the time. Actually, I didn't want to live there, but the rule was that you had to live there if you were an underclassman. It seemed they needed us younger ones to pay their damn rent. Anyway, I liked the sorority enough to move in, and that was that.

It didn't bother me that Sharon had blown me off the previous semester; I was just happy she had called. And she was very sweet and tender and wanted to see me. We got together right away. Those first few weeks of school were totally blissful. I was rarely at the sorority, staying most of the time at a house in Berkeley where Sharon was house-sitting. One of my fondest memories is our making love on the floor while listening to Fleetwood Mac. It was all like a dream, my longing for a woman unfolding. It was all too blissful to even stop and think, *Hey, I'm a lesbian.* Love was in the air, in addition to passionate sex, and that was all that mattered…until the ugly hand of my "sisters" came crashing down on my head.

The misogynist rule at Kappa Alpha Theta was that boys were not allowed upstairs. I always tell this story by saying that basically, as long as you were on Theta property you were a protected vestal virgin. You could get gang-raped at a fraternity, though, and it was none of their business; you, the whore, surely had brought it on yourself.

The "accepted" place to mess around with guys at the sorority was in the chapter rec room. One night, Sharon and I decided to check it out. We were alone in the rec room and barricaded the doors at one end to protect ourselves. Sharon had given me balloons that night, and we were feeling good, not knowing there was a side entrance to the "rec room." Sharon and I were making out when Trish and her boyfriend walked in. Evidently, they were seeking out the rec room for the same purpose.

I don't really remember what happened then. They probably

entered and left, but I didn't notice too much. But then it happened. I walked into the house one day to discover that I had been reported. Sitting in a small entry room (probably a sitting room for the genteel ladies) was the Standards Committee. Trish had reported me, and they were ready for me. I was thrown totally off-guard. Sitting there in judgment were elected officers in the house and a few random alumnae. The trial had begun.

They told me about "the incident," and I had to defend my sexuality. I had no language for this. I think I said something like, "I'm not a hairy-armpitted dyke," meaning I was trying to say I wasn't the stereotype, which of course was a problematic thing to say and rife with internalized homophobia. Then I cried, saying my parents didn't even know. The Standards Committee was not compassionate. They all sat there glaring at the lesbian on display. I was a member who had gone awry, and that was all that mattered.

Under duress, I flew home that weekend to tell my parents. It was OK but not great. I think I barely mentioned the sorority trial. I basically just told them I had fallen in love with a woman. My parents freaked out after I left, but that's another story.

I returned to my place of residence, the Theta house, and had to report to the Monday night meeting. I was told that everyone in the sorority would be voting on me at a meeting without me. Later that week, I received a memo from the representative alumna whom I shall call Melissa. Melissa was a perfectly coiffed upper-class Protestant white woman. Order and formality were important to her, and she probably had a fair amount of leisure time on her hands.

On her cute little stationery, I was told that I was charged with "behavior unbecoming a member of the fraternity that causes embarrassment to the house or chapter members." Note that they used *fraternity* instead of *sorority*—language that supports the patriarchal underpinnings of the Greek system, in that the female counterparts of fraternities cannot even refer to themselves officially as such. So I was being told that this broad bylaw covered me. One can only imagine the "criminal" behavior it was used to denounce in previous decades when people of color and Jews were not allowed to belong. The letter went on to cite my offenses. I had been seen at the following locations:

(1) The chapter rec room

(2) The Sigma Alpha Epsilon Fraternity parking lot (adjacent to the Theta house)

(3) On campus

Actually, number 3 always cracked me and Sharon up and does to this day. What it reveals, however, is the pervasive, all-encompassing eye of the sorority. My sorority sisters had the right to control my behavior anywhere I went. I was a member of their institution, and anything I did in the public sphere reflected on them. I could not be an out lesbian. Any public display of affection or even the slightest suggestion that I might be in the presence of my lover violated the rules of the sorority. *Embarrassment* was a code word for their need to regulate my behavior.

More than 100 of my peers voted and placed me on probation. The alumnae admitted to me that they didn't kick me out because they were afraid of a lawsuit. I should have gotten a lawyer right away. But I naïvely thought my homophobic sisters would come around and eventually grow to accept me. That never happened.

Much of my probation was focused on Sharon. She was the intruder, the dyke who invaded their pristine, protected, ensconced sorority world. Never mind that I pursued her. Sharon was treated like a man; in line with the Theta policy on male visitors, she was not allowed upstairs. Additionally, she wasn't allowed in the house for more than five minutes at a time.

Sharon was scapegoated in the wider campus environment, as word spread like wildfire through the Greek system about "the lesbians." Sharon frequently encountered anonymous individuals on campus who pointed at her from afar shouting, "There she is! There she is!" While I was waiting for my sisters to get a grip, Sharon and I retreated into the sanctity and comfort of our relationship. We were isolated, yet we clung to our romance.

A month went by. I didn't hang out at the sorority very much. Some members had written me encouraging notes, and I tried to believe that their promise of sisterhood stood for something. I had a leadership role in my pledge class, and a lot of my peers respected me. One letter demonstrates one woman's attempt to combat institutionalized homophobia:

Howdy, kiddo,
Of course some people are uptight. You force them to reexamine their

own sexuality; therefore you are a threat! I suppose your openness about your relationship has a dual purpose: to make you happy and also to expose and educate your sisters on the options in life.

If you leave, the prejudice and bigotry will breed in ignorant bliss. But be careful; educate through wisdom and consideration. To realize that some people may feel uncomfortable seeing you hug another woman is very important.

Don't let your fighter instinct hold you back from being tolerant of people's prejudices. OK? Who I am is unimportant. What is important is that my feeling of love and respect for you is not exclusive. You have the support of your sisters. Remember that.

This anonymous letter was written on a Boynton animal card with the inscription, "Don't let the turkeys get you down." Underneath, my sister added, "They're just a bunch of dumb chicks."

I innocently expected the whole probation thing to blow over. Then one day Sharon, who worked as an undercover security guard at the student store, busted Donna, a woman in my sorority, for stealing a candy bar. It was quite the sweet revenge; Sharon really read her the riot act.

Rumor got around later that night that Donna had gotten busted. A couple of pot-smoking, rowdy girls in the house were dying to hear the dirt on Donna. They invited Sharon and me to hang out with them on some weird internal staircase of Theta. While they passed a joint around, Sharon regaled us with the glory of the bust. They lapped it up. We took it as a sign that maybe it wasn't such a big deal for us to be together around Theta. The storytelling definitely lasted longer than Sharon's sanctioned five minutes. After they'd gotten their fill, Sharon and I still wanted to be together. We went upstairs and kept talking in the bathroom. We hid out in a large shower stall, not feeling totally safe to just be hanging out. We were not having sex, just talking.

Some girl in her Lanz nightgown heard us talking when she walked into the bathroom and let out a blood-curdling scream. It was awful. I guess she thought we were going to rape her or something. That was the beginning of the end. The mass hysteria and fear became more targeted, more oppressive, and more violent.

In less than a week, I was in the midst of another trial, this time without rules. It was on a weekday evening. I'd eaten dinner at the sorority, and I was supposed to meet Sharon at a café around the corner at 9 P.M.

I never showed up. Instead I was told to report to that god-awful sitting room. There was no advance warning; the Standards Committee was waiting for me.

Their faces were hideous, twisted, and glaring at me. I'd been reported again, this time by the Lanz-nightgown girl. The committee wanted me to answer for my crime; I had "violated my probation." I was distraught. I was angry. I felt completely oppressed. What I had to say didn't matter.

It was 10 P.M. by then. The interrogation had gone on for some time. The whole house would be voting on this again, they informed me. Then we heard a knock at the front door. Sharon. The girl who answered the door refused to let her in. Policy was being set in a state of homophobic anarchy. The girl shut the door in Sharon's face; Sharon later told me she felt she was being treated like an animal. She was. She pounded on the door. "Let me in, I want to see Ali," she demanded. She always had been allowed in the house for five minutes; she had every right to be let in. But the girl at the door wouldn't let her in, and Sharon paced outside. The sisters enjoyed the knowledge of the trapped "big bad wolf" outside their precious door.

Someone told me Sharon was out there. I immediately went outside to be with her. It was awful. We huddled at the side of the building, weeping, distraught, anxious, enraged. This went on for quite some time. One or two women tried to console us. We clung to each other. We moved cautiously onto the path leading to the front door. Suddenly the door swung open. Barbara, a supposed friend, walked over to us. She put her hand on Sharon's shoulder in a condescending manner and said, "Sharon, I'm sorry, but you'll have to leave the property." Sharon flung her arms in the air. "Get your hands off me," she said. And just at that moment the president of Theta, a senior and close friend of Barbara, appeared in the doorway. "Don't you hit Barbara," she screamed.

It was shocking. We were shocked. Theta headlines were already reading "Violent Lesbian Attacks Sorority Girl!" Sharon and I gathered ourselves. We put our arms around each other and walked off the property.

The following Monday was the chapter meeting. This time they were going to let me speak to my sisters. I would have a voice in my own trial. I got up before all 100 sisters, after listening to the Christian call to order: "…now we see through a glass darkly, but then face to face…." My face was dark, my glass was broken. I spoke my piece. I said I'd been through enough and that they should let me move out. I was strong, grounded, out, and proud. They were silent, vicious, hounding. I left the room. They voted to keep me on probation, and as a punishment, Sharon was no longer allowed in the house.

I resigned my membership, and Sharon and I went to the Student Advocate Office on campus. The advocate wrote a letter to Kappa Alpha Theta offering to do sensitivity training. Theta refused. It was still years before lesbian-gay-bisexual student alliances began appearing on campuses. The student advocates encouraged us to go to *The Daily Cal,* the campus newspaper. We were too afraid, felt too isolated, and needed time to recover.

On the day I moved my stuff out of the sorority, I saw Ruthie, my "big sister," in the parking lot. She somehow had heard we were thinking of approaching the newspaper. She said, "Ali, I just want you to know, if you and Sharon approach *The Daily Cal,* I personally will feel compelled to write a letter on behalf of Kappa Alpha Theta."

So much for sisterhood.

In the following months, Sharon and I tried to restore some semblance of normality to our lives. I basically moved in with her. Our love was still passionate, magical, and tender, but we had been severely damaged by the sorority experience. We lost many of our friends and bore the brunt of the scapegoating on ourselves and on our relationship. By the end of the summer, Sharon had found someone else. We had an ugly breakup.

Greeks have an unspoken rule that you're never to reveal the secret rituals that bind you together as sisters. Here are some Theta mysteries revealed: They speak to the obvious white Christian culture that sororities and fraternities celebrate. When I was initiated into Theta, all of us pledges were gathered in the chapter rec room. We drank out of some medieval chalice. Our big sisters spun us around, disoriented. When we opened our eyes, a secret door was opened in one of the walls. Standing on a wooden platform was an old woman—a Theta alumna—probably a member from the '20s or '30s. Standing on one side of her was a young Theta with blond hair. On the other side crouched a young Theta with dark hair. The blond woman held a glass of water. The dark-haired woman held a bottle of ink. The old woman motioned for the blond woman to raise the glass of water. The dark woman stood with the ink dropper. The old woman said, "One spot can spoil the whole thing." The dark haired woman squeezed the ink dropper, letting one spot fall into the glass, dispersing through its oppressive clarity.

Sharon joked that I was the ink spot. I was.

PanHELLenic Experience
by Helen Harrell

Helen Harrell in a sorority
formal composite
photograph

When I signed on as a pledge, I'd expected some form of initial haz-
ing, even though it was against school policy. But I could never have pre-
pared myself for the constant barrage of harassment that became my
daily existence.

The stark black-and-white days of the '50s were gratefully behind us,
and the early '60s had begun. Although there were signs of the pending
cultural revolution and African-Americans were becoming increasingly
vocal in their demand for much-deserved recognition and equality from
both fellow citizens and government, some things remained constant
enough for most individuals to feel secure in their ennui. It was a time
of forewarning, and personally it was a time of major change as I ven-
tured off to college and began the early stages of establishing my own
independence.

Since I had always lived in major metropolitan areas, it was nothing
less than culture shock for me to arrive in a small, conservative
Midwestern town to attend my father's alma mater. Although I did
receive an excellent liberal arts education, the small private college with
its scattering of liberal faculty could not offer much relief from such a
stifling environment. Further, as I have a solid background in theater
and the arts, I found little offered in the way of entertainment or

extracurricular activities, and I ended up joining a sorority to alleviate my pervasive boredom. At the time sorority life looked like it might provide me the opportunity to establish a network of friends and perhaps offer a venue for social activity. Eventually, the actual experience verified that one should carefully evaluate wishes and desires, because sometimes the fulfillment can be disappointing and painful. The need for belonging is strong in youth, and the value of a life lived both introspectively and independently comes as a result of both age and experience. Such a life cannot be fully appreciated until one at least learns that bylaws are not necessarily a foundation for creation of a family and that people who come together as a result of oppression are not necessarily enlightened.

In retrospect, I'm not sure if my displeasure with sorority life could be so easily dismissed as a reaction to inherent homophobia, because at that time no one talked about sex, or sexual issues, as politic. Certainly the expectation was one of heterosexuality, although no one discussed that either. Prior to this experience, I was unaccustomed to having my friends and associates monitored by anyone, much less by a self-designated group well entrenched with the attitude that it was their responsibility to shape my college experience within the context of the Greek experience. Perhaps my actual Greek heritage didn't recognize itself in this framework of panHELLenic experience; or perhaps my as-yet-undeclared lesbianism was obvious in my inherent personality, and that was enough to somehow set me apart from the mainstream. Regardless, I quickly became the "problem sister" who needed extra attention—the odd sheep who continued to stray from the flock.

When I signed on as a pledge, I'd expected some form of initial hazing, even though that was against school policy. But I could never have prepared myself for the constant barrage of harassment that became my daily existence. I found a puddle of water on the floor outside my door each morning (very slippery if overlooked), Vaseline on the doorknobs to my room and closets, shaving cream in my slippers and shoes, hand lotion spilled in my lingerie drawer and on my bedsheets, my hair being cut while I was sleeping (which I still consider physical assault), false fire alarms, fake emergency telephone calls from family in the middle of the night, and on and on. I had little recourse in addressing these hostilities, because school officials as well as sorority officials considered such actions mere teasing and fun, antics all pledges must endure. But I didn't find such sophomoric stunts amusing, and my anger increased daily. I struggled to prevent my anger from affecting my studies and determined to avoid the house as much as possible. I studied in the library, took on two part-time jobs to pay for meals at the college cafeteria, thus avoiding house meals, and spent as much time with friends who lived off campus as I possibly could.

Three women—I always referred to them as the fearless triad—in particular nominated themselves as the committee to make life difficult for me. Ever alert to any minor infraction, they constantly reminded me if I was late for study time or not in bed at a decent hour. Most significantly, they seemed obsessively concerned with whom I dated. I either dated the wrong people or, at the very worst and completely polar opposite, I most certainly had too many boys chasing me. At that time, I was so busy living life and accumulating experiences that I was fairly oblivious to anyone's amorous inclinations toward me, regardless of her or his gender. And since I had grown up in a theatrical climate both as a semi-professional dancer and ice skater, it was no coincidence that I called many lesbian and gay couples and drag queens my friends while I was still in elementary school. It hadn't occurred to me that there was anything different about such people, because I hadn't fully realized that these friends lived rather clandestine existences. They had always seemed perfectly normal to me, and although I knew I was a lesbian, I didn't talk to anyone about my sexual interests. I had yet to examine the implications of gay life as applied to me personally.

Because of their seeming obsession with me, the triad became a focus of my attention. I observed them more closely as individuals while trying to understand their lifestyle as it played out in the house environment. They were always together, seemingly inseparable; they never had dates with boys, spent weekends in their rooms, and, most notably, drank themselves into oblivion nearly every evening after 10 o'clock. Since alcohol consumption by students was an infraction of both the sorority and the college rules, I took great delight in learning such a bit of information, given the tireless energy they expended to ensure that I obeyed the rules. It was not until a friend of mine from home mentioned that the triad were perhaps lesbians and had a crush on me that I began to consider their actions and behavior more seriously. Many of us did not date boys, but because romance, marriage, and children were remote among my personal goals, I assumed that it might be the same for others as well.

I was slow to grasp the idea that there were many lesbians and gays on campus who lived only a shadow of their/our lives. Naïve and idealistic, I was, indeed, to assume that just because no one discussed homosexuality, sexual orientation didn't matter. In fact, the opposite was true. To talk about homosexuality and to admit that one was attracted to those of the same sex was a social death sentence and could put one in harm's way. So much for thinking there might be a direct correlation between academic freedom and an enlightened philosophy as applied to living life with a sense of acceptance and generosity.

As I tested the theory that the triad were lesbians, I conjectured that maybe they were simultaneously interested in me while hating me as the object of their affection. Perhaps they believed they were socially prevented from acting on their natural desires; or maybe they resented me for my own casual approach to friendships and relationships and how I was seemingly unconcerned by social ramifications; or they hated themselves and me because of what we now call internalized homophobia (homosexuality is considered to be a sin, and because it consists of aberrant behavior disapproved by greater society, then we were all defective and a disgrace). Then again, maybe they weren't lesbians and didn't like me because they suspected that I was.

I will never know exactly what motivated their hostility toward me. As can be imagined, I didn't have much interest in discussing their behavior with them or in their welfare at the time. After two years of misery, I left the sorority and moved into my own apartment. I didn't have contact with any of my "sisters" once I left and do not know what became of two of the "triad" members. I did learn that one of them committed suicide shortly after graduation. I took this action to be a confirmation of my suspicions because there were, and still are, many suicides among lesbian, gay, bisexual, and transgendered students, but to this day I have no proof.

As dreadful as my experience with sorority life was, I did learn much about discrimination and how it feels to be harassed and targeted for being different from group expectation. This was my first experience at being the victim. I had spent a good deal of my youth, along with other family members, involved with groups and activities that tried to deter discrimination and hateful behavior directed toward Hispanics, African-Americans, Jews, and my drag queen and transgendered friends, and it wasn't until I came to Indiana that I found myself a target of similar behavior. I guess I can thank the Greek system for providing me with a learning experience that only reinforced my determination to strive for an end to such group behavior. I certainly came to a better understanding of why so many chose to live silent and closeted lives. It has never been my nature to accept injustice passively, and to live as someone other than who I am would be unthinkable, but not everyone feels as confident or safe as I.

As I relate my experience with Greek life that took place around the midpoint of the 20th century, I'm all too aware that although there has been some improvement in the acceptance of homosexuals by and within the Greek system, the incidents of violence, abusive language, and menacing attitudes that come to my attention daily tell me we still have a major struggle ahead of us. The system is an inclusive one that, by definition, must then also be exclusive. What is acceptable in terms of exclusiveness? Do such groups have the right to determine whom they want as members? If exclusion is acceptable, how are criteria that determine nondiscriminatory requirements for membership monitored? It seems sensible to assume that homosexual and heterosexual individuals can most certainly share the same organizations, living quarters, and social activities, and that this will be achieved through educational programming, personal contact and growth, and open communication. I raise the above questions, however, because I have to ask, "Why would anyone who has been so discriminated against at all levels of our culture, as have homosexuals, want to participate in such exclusionary organizations? Where does discrimination stop? Which group or individual is excluded and why?"

As an early advocate of the elimination of the Greek system, I have accepted that there is enough support for such organizations as to make their demise unlikely. Still, Greek proponents and participants should seriously evaluate the purpose and function of their system. We live in a society that is struggling to become more tolerant and accepting of all individuals, and a group that qualifies its standards for membership, acceptance, or belonging in a way that counters such positive societal direction and growth is an anachronism that thwarts the progressive educational experience.

A Chance to Reject
by Chris Hampton

Not long after, I was watching TV with another member when a news piece about some sort of gay pride event came on. "I just hate fags," she muttered. "I can't stand them. I don't know why they have to shove their lives in our faces." This time I couldn't bring myself to say anything. I just got up and silently walked out of the room.

I had just turned 18 when I arrived at the University of Arkansas in fall 1985. I roomed with a girl I'd gone to high school with, and we could not have been more opposite. I had been on the newspaper staff and was something of a loner; she was on the drill team and extremely popular. We decided to live with each other for no other reason than that we didn't know anyone else at UA. That summer she called me one day and asked if I wanted to go through rush with her. I didn't know what she was talking about. She explained that it was the process you go through to get into a sorority. Clueless about what I was getting myself into, I agreed. How much time could it take?

We both ended up pledging Kappa Alpha Theta. I was a bit surprised at how much time I had to spend doing things with the sorority, but I was swept up in the parties and other activities, how friendly the other girls were to me, and how the older members were almost motherly in their concern and caring for the pledges. When I look through my old Theta scrapbooks, I remember how much love and acceptance I felt from my sisters. It took a while for me to realize how conditional that love was.

At my first walkout party (a bonding activity planned by and for pledges), I drank way too much. I hadn't been a big partygoer in high school and had no idea what my limitations with alcohol were. I didn't know how to drink in moderation, and I certainly didn't think anything bad would happen to me at a walkout. After all, there were several older members present as "sober sisters"—chaperones who acted as designated drivers to keep an eye on the pledges and make sure we got home safely at the end of the party. It was held at the home of an alumnus of the fraternity that cohosted the walkout. I joined a game of quarters with kamikaze shots.

I don't remember how I ended up alone with the boy or how much I had to drink. I just remember him pulling me behind some tall bushes next to the side of the house. I kissed him, and then the kissing turned into something I was too drunk to stop. He was unbuttoning my blouse, and I was trying to push his hands away. He kept saying it was OK because nobody could see us; the fact that I might not want to have sex with him never occurred to him. I told him to stop. Instead he shoved me against the house, kissing me roughly, and unzipped his jeans and pulled my hands to his crotch. Lucky for me, the kamikazes intervened. "I'm going to be sick," I gasped, and stumbled out of the bushes and into the house. I avoided him, staying in the bathroom until everyone went home.

The next afternoon, when I recovered from my hangover enough to go to the house for study hours, our pledge trainer told me she and the chapter president needed to meet with me. She was clearly angry, but she wouldn't tell me why. She told me to go into the study room and work on my homework until the president was ready to see me.

I tried to work on my assignments, but of course I couldn't concentrate. I had never seen a member act disappointed or upset with me, and I had no idea what I might have done. I knew I'd gotten really drunk the night before, but so had most of my pledge sisters, and I certainly wasn't the only one who ended up sick or hungover. Finally, after almost two hours, the pledge trainer opened the door and asked me to come with her. I felt everyone's eyes on my back as I quietly gathered up my books and followed.

The president, the chaplain, and one of the members who had been a "sober sister" the night before were waiting for us in the president's room. The chaplain served as something of a moral leader to the house, and she was the officer to whom people went whenever they were worried that someone might be behaving in a way that would call us all into question on campus. That year a born-again Baptist senior, studying pre-veterinary medicine, held the office.

"We realize a lot of this is new to you and that you had a lot to drink last night," she told me as the others looked on. "But the fact remains that when you're out at a party or a bar or anywhere, you represent this house. And we can't have people doing things in public that will reflect badly on the reputation of everyone else in the house," she told me, smiling kindly and patting my hand.

As it turned out, the "sober sister" had seen me going away with the boy, and she had crept up to the bushes and watched my "loose behavior." I didn't question them or explain that I hadn't wanted things with the boy to go so far. It was made very clear to me that what happened was my fault because I was drunk. I was put on notice that any further incidents would result in my being asked to leave. This was my first lesson in how much the members of the house worried about what others thought of us.

Other lessons came later, like the next year when Tina, one of the girls who had been in my pledge class, dated a black football player. While he was a big man on campus and was cheered wildly at Razorback games, Tina's boyfriend was persona non grata at the Theta house. One night he came over to study with Tina in the living room, where many girls entertained their boyfriends. Shortly afterward a nasty rumor circulated around the house that he had given Tina herpes. People started refusing to do their laundry in the machines she had used. "Can't we do anything about this?" people would demand when Tina was not around.

It was agreed that while we could not tell anyone whom to date, Tina would be asked privately by the president if she could be "discreet" about her boyfriend. Tina, who had to sit through a meeting similar to mine after my nearly being date-raped, reluctantly agreed. When girls sat around in the TV room talking about their boyfriends, she was silent. Her boyfriend stopped coming to the door to pick her up; he just sat quietly in his car waiting. While no one ever said anything to her face, the whispering and gossip did not die off until after Tina left school to marry him a year later.

College was increasing my awareness of issues, helping me notice the type of thing that happened to Tina. In addition to being involved with my sorority, I was also volunteering at the campus radio station, which exposed me to a broader spectrum of people. I was hanging out in the underground music scene, going to little punk rock clubs, and meeting people of different races and, more significant for me, people who were openly gay. While my sisters thought my involvement in campus radio was cool, they often expressed their distaste with the music I liked and the places I went. "Aren't you afraid you're going to get hurt?" they asked as I headed out for another all-ages show. I'd think about the party where I was nearly raped and about all of the nondrinking, peaceful, straight-edge skateboard punks at the shows, and then I'd laugh at the suggestion.

During my junior year, a pair of roommates attracted their fair amount of behind-the-back gossip. Amy and Megan were incredibly close and always together, often holding hands or falling into riotous tickle fights in the TV room. One of the members claimed she had gone into their room one night to ask them to turn down their music and walked in on a similar tickle fight, only this time Amy and Megan were naked. "Are they lezzies or aren't they?" people asked in disgust. "Ugh, that's just so gross, the way they act," a member shuddered one night after Amy and Megan ran through the TV room giggling. Still, no one said anything to their faces. I often wondered if they had any idea how badly their sisters talked about them behind their backs. That year, however, there would be no meeting, because Megan held the office of chaplain.

Throughout all of this, I was starting to feel an attraction to women, but I didn't understand what it meant. Looking back, I know I was completely and utterly in love with my new roommate, Janine, but at the time I didn't realize why I was so jealous whenever she had a boyfriend. She'd come to me crying after yet another relationship had soured, and I'd put my arms around her. I'd bury my face in her long red hair, smell her perfume, and wonder what it would be like to kiss her. I didn't dare question it, and I never told Janine about it. It was too confusing for me to handle. I knew I liked men, and while I had feelings for women that I couldn't really fathom, those feelings were too scary for me to contemplate. I thought about the comments people made about Amy and Megan, and kept my mouth shut.

One day I finally lost my temper in the TV room after several members had been making remarks about the boyfriend of one of our pledges; he was Malaysian, and they were horrified that someone in the house was dating an international student. After one member referred to him as a "chink" and another called him a "big-lipped gook," I blurted that I couldn't believe how racist they all were and stormed out of the room.

Not long after, I was watching TV with another member when a news piece about some sort of gay pride event came on. "I just hate fags," she muttered. "I can't stand them. I don't know why they have to shove their lives in our faces." This time I couldn't bring myself to say anything. I just got up and silently walked out of the room.

I never thought for a moment that the people who had bigoted ideas and used such hateful words might be right, but I felt terribly alone. Surely I wasn't the only one who felt this way, but why didn't anyone else speak up? I wondered whether anyone would ever speak up for me if people discovered I might not be everything my sisters had expected. I liked to think someone would, but then I'd remember Amy, Megan, Tina, and that meeting when I was a freshman, and I knew that all I could expect was whispering behind my back and cold glares.

While I can look back on these experiences now and see how they led up to my leaving the sorority, no single event made me decide to get out. I never experienced discrimination myself, because I wasn't dealing with my own sexuality. I never said a word to anyone about my feelings. Indeed, I think my fears about how the others in the house would react just made me bury deeper any thoughts about loving women. So I went about my business, holding small offices like corresponding secretary, halfheartedly volunteering for committees, being a little sister for one of the smaller fraternities on campus, and trying to hide my envy whenever Janine started dating a new boy. My feelings about women were too complicated and dangerous for me to handle on my own. And I knew of no one I could trust to talk to about them, so I just ignored them and hoped they would go away.

I left the house at the end of my junior year by going inactive. I didn't make a big show of quitting, and, I'm ashamed to say, I didn't explain all my reasons for leaving. I applied for inactive status on the basis of financial difficulty, which was certainly true enough, but I never told anyone that I really wanted to leave because I was fed up with the prejudices and hate I'd witnessed.

I don't mean to make it sound like the entire experience was bad. It was great to have a place on campus where I felt I knew everyone, where I could hang out and feel relaxed and welcome. Some of my sisters were remarkably kind and accepting. There were lots of fun parties and late-night talks and beer runs. Unfortunately, the attitudes and intolerance of some members, coupled with the silence of so many others, became too uncomfortable for me. Even when things were going well in the sorority,

I was having a hard time forgetting about the growing list of incidents of bigotry.

A few years after leaving college, I started dealing with my bisexuality, and by then I was in contact with only a couple of people from my Theta days. While those people were understanding when I came out, I know it wouldn't have been that way if I'd ever come out as an active member. It saddens me to think about what it would have been like if I'd come out while I was involved in Theta. Maybe what I was really doing when I left was rejecting them before they'd have the chance to reject me.

Belonging to Myself
by Jennifer "Smitty" Smith

I grappled with the thought of the local adviser and national executive board silencing me. Being represented by these women made my stomach turn. I couldn't see myself being part of an organization that didn't live up to its founding statements while expecting me to keep quiet about being a lesbian in order to keep from tarnishing its image.

Sleek, stylish, normal—words to some, but dreams to me. The desire to belong, to be loved, to fit in consumed me in 1997–98 during my freshman year in college. I wanted to be somebody. I wanted to wash away the invisible ink that had saturated my skin in high school. I wanted to dissolve the sarcasm I had created in order for people to see me...the real me. I yearned to belong.

I searched for resolution. My answer: a sorority. I ached to become a part of a Greek organization. The women were beautiful, respected, energetic, involved, but, most of all, uniform. Sorority sisters, with their own personalities. I could be sarcastic; I could be outgoing; I could be unique, once I had the security that I belonged. I'd no longer be simply Jennifer Smith, but rather Jennifer Smith, sorority sister.

Through high school I played the clarinet and bass clarinet, softball and field hockey, was a member of Peer Outreach, served on the newspaper staff and on the yearbook committee. Still, I felt...alone. My closest friends were six girls: Rosie, Dia, Ashley, Amanda, Lindsay, and Tory, and we were all very involved in the school. We were the "leaders." Though I hung out with these girls on weekends, I still felt alone. I didn't hang out with the "popular" crowd because I didn't smoke pot or drink. I was an outsider.

College, "the beginning of the end," would provide a new start, a new person, a new Jennifer Smith. Determined, I rushed five sororities at the University of New Hampshire, instantly drawn to the picture-perfect image they displayed. I yearned to become one of them. Two weeks into the school year I did. The Mu Alpha chapter of Chi Omega welcomed me into its family. For 18 weeks I pledged. I learned the oaths, the history, and everything about the sisters. I learned the ideals of Chi Omega: "To be in the best sense, democratic rather than 'exclusive,' to be womanly always, to be discouraged never…to be loyal under any and all circumstances to my fraternity and her highest teachings…." I committed it all to memory. I became "super pledge." I knew everything there was to know about Chi Omega, which helped me form the bond I so badly desired.

I spent my days at the blue house on Strafford Avenue with the giant white Greek letters on the front. I went out Thursday, Friday, and Saturday nights every week, my social schedule revolving around parties. My phone rang constantly, and I never had to eat in the dining halls alone. By the end of spring, as an active sister, images of living in the house the next fall and becoming president were in the forefront of my mind.

Returning to school sophomore year, I wasn't the same. I'd fallen in love that summer, with a woman. Working at a summer camp in Vermont, I met Christine. By the end of the first two weeks, this red-headed woman, whose brown eyes could reach into my soul, and I were inseparable. I'd help out as much as I could at the barn, as she was head of the riding program. We also spent time together every evening after our campers had gone to bed, often in her bedroom, its walls almost completely taken up by windows overlooking the lake that lapped up underneath the floor. We were falling in love.

By the end of the summer, we knew we wanted to continue our relationship outside of camp. She was going to be teaching at a boarding school in Vermont two hours away, but we were willing to deal with the distance. Unlike my sorority sisters, I was unable to talk of my relationship, because it was not like theirs. I said nothing. I feared losing the security I had created for myself the previous year. I had worked too hard and had grown too dependent on Chi Omega to throw it all away. Chi Omega had become my home; my sisters had become my friends and support system. So I chose to keep silent and allow the facade to grow. I still wanted to belong.

As the first month of school progressed, I changed with every second that passed. The bubbly, happy-go-lucky "Smitty" everyone knew had disappeared. Parties transformed into watching TV, beer into water, and laughter into silence. My sisters began to notice. I no longer hung out with anyone but myself. I yearned to tell them there was nothing wrong with me; I had simply found my true self. But I didn't have the strength.

I became increasingly uncomfortable with leading a double life. At the beginning of October, I moved out. Giving no other reason than needing a place that condoned better study habits and had more privacy, I moved my belongings to a single in one of the dorms, Christenson Hall.

A few nights before I moved into Christenson, I had to talk to someone in the sorority. I could confide in my "kid," or so I'd hoped. I could no longer hold this information hostage within myself. She had been one of my best friends during the previous year and was the only person I felt I could tell. The air felt dense, and my palms were clammy as I walked into the room we shared.

"I need to talk to you about something. Can you come on deck with me?" I said nervously.

The 50-foot hallway felt like a mile. We entered "deck," which held 15 beds, and shut the door. I sat down on my denim comforter so I wouldn't faint onto the floor. My heart was beating as if I had just run the Boston Marathon, and I couldn't sit still. I was scared.

"I told you I was going to move out, and I am. But I have to tell you the real reason I'm leaving. I'm leaving because I can't live here and be myself. I'm gay."

Tears ran down my face like raindrops on a windshield. I was shaking.

With tears in her eyes she said, "Don't worry. I'll still love you no matter what. You're my best friend. I knew something was wrong. But what are you going to do about the others? They're asking questions. People are starting to ask me what's wrong with you. Some people here might not be accepting of a gay sorority sister. I don't know. Are you going to tell them? Are you going to stay active?"

I thought I could continue my role in Chi Omega and secretly have a girlfriend. Friendship, laughter, security, sisterly bonds, smiles, parties, sister functions—I wanted it all as well as the ability to be openly gay. Content with the idea for the most part, I occasionally grappled with the issue of being dishonest. To uphold everything the house stood for, I needed to tell them.

Shortly, somehow, word got around that I was leaving not just because I needed a quiet place to study. Some sisters were even beginning to question my sexuality. Their questions were filled with worry and concern, as well as a desire for answers. Word got back to me.

"Smitty, Diane asked me at the bar Friday night if you're gay," my big sister told me.

With each thought of a sister finding out that I was a lesbian, my stomach ached, but my conscience got the best of me. I could not lead two lives. To pretend to be a sister to these women meant ultimately hiding from them a huge part of who I was.

It was Friday. The leaves were the color of pumpkins, cooling lava, and the setting sun. The air was warm enough for khaki shorts yet brisk enough for my long-sleeve, navy-blue Chi Omega shirt that read THE BEST IS YET TO COME! Soon the Thomson Hall clock, standing proudly in its spot overlooking the rest of the campus, struck noon. I was free. With the Chi Omega house song "I Think I Love You" by the Partridge Family playing in my head, I grabbed my things and made my way to Vermont to see my girlfriend.

Anxiety lurked deep inside me when it came to facing Chi Omega. I never went to the house. I saw sisters, but little was said. I was certain their minds were filled with questions. Did I have a giant pink triangle on my forehead? I no longer had the desire to be involved, even after a year and a half of devotion. Could I still be accepted as a sister, even though I wasn't who they thought I was? If only I could hear them say that the oaths and symphonies created by the founding members mattered. They simply had to say they would be "loyal under any and all circumstances" and "lovable rather than popular." I needed them to say I still belonged.

Surrounded by the faces of the past Chi Omega sisters, the damp chapter room where the secret rituals are held was saturated with my fear. The chapter adviser had been informed I was a lesbian and wanted to tell the chapter. About to learn my fate, I felt the color drain from my face and beads of sweat collect at my hairline. I was scared and angered by the response I felt sure was coming. Watching the Mu Alpha chapter adviser peer at me over her blue reading glasses like a nun looks at a student who has not learned her Hail Mary, I waited patiently for the verdict. All I heard was:

"Why are you doing this?"

"What do you plan to gain from telling the house this information?"

"This is a Chi Omega issue and needs to stay a Chi Omega issue!"

"Your private life should *not* be brought into the house!"

"If any waves are caused by this, further action will be taken!"

I refused to cry in front of this woman, to let her see my pain. I shook, not in fear but in disgust. What happened to being "democratic rather than exclusive?" Her words played over and over in my mind. No! I made the decision right then, right there. This woman who didn't know me wasn't going to tell me I couldn't tell my sisters and my friends who I was. The decision had to be mine.

On October 12, 1998 (ironically, during National Coming Out Week), I walked into the Chi Omega house for the last time. Standing behind the mauve love seat, my knuckles were white from clenching the cushion. One by one, the sisters made their way into the room. I saw the unanimous question in their eyes: "What's Smitty going to tell us?"

My mouth felt like cotton candy—soft and sticky—but without the sweetness. I felt as though I were in confession and had to tell the priest I had sworn at my mother. My goal was to confess my "sin" without crying, without showing my weakness and vulnerability.

When the room was overflowing with women, all of whom were staring at me with curiosity, I said, "I'm here tonight to put to rest rumors that have been making their way through the house. I moved out a few weeks ago, and with my moving out came a lot of questions. One question is about my sexuality."

My voice cracked. Fighting back the tears, I continued. "I'm telling you this because I feel all of you are my friends and I respect you. For me to be true to myself and to Chi Omega, I have to tell you the truth."

I couldn't fight it any longer, and neither could the other members of the house. Tears were streaming down the faces of nearly every woman in the room.

"I'm gay. I'm a lesbian. But I'm still the Smitty I was when I rushed. I'm still the same Smitty I was when I pledged, and I'm still the same Smitty I was when I sistered up."

I couldn't believe they were crying. Were they crying because I was and they felt bad? Or were they crying because they couldn't believe what they were hearing? Nearly every sister in the room came up to me, gave me a hug, and told me how proud they were of me. They said I was strong. Though my tears blurred my vision, I still saw how sincere they were.

Two months later I had still not set foot into the three-story blue Chi

Omega house. Though the sisters voiced their desire for me to remain active, my desire was no longer there. I knew the minute the chapter adviser opened her mouth and said all of those things that I would not remain active. My black pants, black platform shoes, and pastel top had turned to jeans, sneakers, and a sweatshirt. I tried to envision taking my girlfriend to a party or cocktail hour. I laughed. I wanted to believe this could happen, but I knew it couldn't. The Greek community focused on the heterosexual community, not the homosexual one. I didn't want to be the "Greek gay poster child." I just wanted to be me.

Though I considered remaining active, I grappled with the thought of the local adviser and national executive board silencing me. Being represented by these women made my stomach turn. I couldn't see myself being part of an organization that didn't live up to its founding statements while expecting me to keep quiet about being a lesbian in order to keep from tarnishing its image.

Going inactive meant starting over. I'd be giving up everything I knew. Though I was sacrificing my right to wear my Greek letters, I knew in my heart there were sisters who would be there when I needed them. They would still be my friends. By going inactive, I'd finally belong—to myself.

Sisterly Love and Friendship

Friendship with oneself is all-important, because without it one cannot be friends with anyone else.
—Eleanor Roosevelt, Alpha Kappa Alpha

And Then I Kissed a Woman
by E. Guzik

At a rush retreat, I casually mentioned, "My 'boyfriend' is named Amanda." I wasn't surprised, but I was relieved when no one was shocked. No one slipped unobtrusively from the room. No one gasped or awkwardly cleared her throat. No one pulled me aside quietly and suggested I not say this publicly.

And then I kissed a woman. Again. My coming out was that simple. In college I kissed a woman.

Well, not quite that simple. In my college 20th-century American poetry class, I first heard Adrienne Rich's theory from "Compulsory Heterosexuality and Lesbian Existence." I remember the horror I felt as my professor summarized Rich's argument: "Straight women can never really be sure they are straight—doubt is always inevitable, because the culture has so strongly socialized us all to heterosexuality that any such choice is always suspect." His explanation was probably more nuanced than that, but all I heard was that I couldn't be certain I was straight. I thought I was. I thought that fooling around in middle school was ado- lescent experimentation, but now I realized I could never be sure. The room all but spun.

Then I kissed a woman and was sure. Sure that I wasn't straight.

Kissing Amanda couldn't have happened at a more charged moment in the intersection of queer politics and Greek life at Tufts University. After all, it was Tufts University in the early 1990s, a school developing a reputation for being politically progressive. Just before I came out to myself, a man had been forced out of the most prestigious fraternity on campus after his brothers learned he was gay. Upon leaving his fraternity, he made public a notebook kept in the bathroom of the house in which graphic depictions of extreme violence against women and racist remarks were commonplace. This incident, making explicit the basis for accusations of racism, sexism, and homophobia within the Greek system, prompted campuswide debate about whether that system should remain at Tufts in its present form.

And in the midst of all that, I was faced with multiple possibilities. Should I stay in my sorority? Should I come out to the house? To the queer community? To the Greek system? To the campus as a whole?

One cold, clear morning as I walked across campus, I stopped abruptly at a corner of campus near a dining hall, and it came to me. If Amanda had been a man, the whole sorority would have known about her. I might have left a rose at the president's door to prompt a ceremony in which I'd have told the sisterhood about my new infatuation. Or some sister who had learned an especially juicy bit of gossip about one of our recent dates would have teased me about it during "Good and Welfare" at the end of an informal meeting. If Amanda had been a man, everyone would know. It seemed awfully silly that, based on that one difference, my latest relationship had become a secret. So I decided to come out to the chapter.

I considered what the consequences of such an announcement might be, but I was fairly certain the women in my house would react well. My sorority sisters had always pleasantly surprised me. I rushed only because a good friend from freshman year had recently told me she was part of a new sorority. Though I was shocked, I agreed to go to her rush party as a favor. Since I was still interested in men then, the lure of a sorority was certainly linked to the possibility of formals and mixers. I never, however, would have joined if the women had not been so different from what I expected. As we stood around veggies and dip and punch, we talked about campus politics, career goals, and community service. Every woman seemed like a leader in the making. When I received a bid, I accepted, and members continued to defy my expectations.

So at a rush retreat, I casually mentioned, "My 'boyfriend' is named Amanda." I wasn't surprised, but I was relieved when no one was shocked. No one slipped unobtrusively from the room. No one gasped or awkwardly cleared her throat. No one pulled me aside quietly and suggested I not say this publicly.

Even though my chapter was overwhelmingly supportive, there were some awkward moments. That spring, my chapter's semiformal was a joint production with another chapter from a different school. When I took Amanda, I was worried about introducing her to a room full of people we didn't know. The photographer would ask all the sisters to get into one big picture, and the room in front of us would be a sea of men in black tuxedos and suits—and Amanda. In terms of the small group or couple pictures, the photographer seemed to miss that we were a couple ourselves, splitting us up by arranging her on one side and me on the other of other people's dates. Only after we had spent a few slow dances on the floor together did he seem to get it. I was equally nervous about taking my next girlfriend, Ruth, to the Inter-Greek Council formal held the following fall. I knew the sorority women at Tufts were at least tolerant, but I wasn't sure, especially given the previous incident with the gay fraternity brother, how a ballroom full of drunk fraternity men would react. Though that evening passed uneventfully, I remember being circumspect about any displays of affection between Ruth and me.

I was perhaps more nervous about how the gay community on campus would feel about a sorority sister in their midst. Members of Tufts's Lesbian, Gay, Bisexual Community had been some of the most vocal advocates of radical change to the Greek system. Through my network of friends and extracurricular activities, I already knew a number of students involved in the group. In fact, Marcus, a hall mate from my freshman year, and I had startled each other at a TLGBC meeting the year before I came out. He was afraid I'd tell everyone that I had seen him there, and I was afraid of the same thing. Despite personal connections, however, I was not at all sure I would be entirely welcome in TLGBC meetings. In retrospect, I realize I had more cause to fear homophobic reactions from the Greek system. When encountering resistance from the Greek system, I always felt as if I had the more ethical position. I could be justifiably outraged by their ignorance. Rejection by the gay community, though, was more problematic. If TLGBC objected to my Greek affiliation, I'd have to question whether my decision to stay was traitorous.

Because of my initial success in coming out and my chapter's support, I began doing educational work with the queer community at Tufts. Small groups of the TLGBC members went to freshman classes and gave presentations to dispel some of the stereotypes and myths about gays, lesbians, and bisexuals. Usually each speaker briefly told his or her coming-out story and then took questions. I spoke at these panels, usually wearing my sorority letters to show my Greek pride. The only workshop where I was seen as some kind of oddity occurred the year TLGBC spoke at the Greek Life 101 workshop on homophobia. There I was, in my letters, in front of every pledge from every house on campus, talking about being a dyke, the label I still prefer to define my queer identity. Most of the questions were polite, but one fraternity pledge said what I suspect many less candid people in the room were thinking: "Aren't you afraid of representing your house this way?" I don't remember exactly what I said, but I know I didn't get angry about it until afterward—partly because he assumed there was something wrong with me and partly because I was afraid he was right. Walking from the workshop to our sorority executive board meeting, I realized how angry I was. I arrived at the meeting, and we began working through business. About halfway through the meeting, I recounted what had happened. One of my sisters without missing a beat said, "Elizabeth, I'm proud to have you represent our house 'that way.'"

As I came out to an increasingly wide circle of people on campus, though, I discovered not everyone was as supportive as Elizabeth. Though I was admitted to Order of Omega, a few months after my initiation one of the sisters from my sorority told me quietly at a house dinner that my nomination had caused some debate among the members of the Order of Omega. Some people questioned whether someone who was "that way" was suitable for membership. Though women from other houses seemed cordial, I wondered about their sincerity, especially since I'd heard rumors about women in other houses who were also queer but hadn't come out. Looking back, I wonder if the sororities could afford to be so accepting, since having one dyke in the system gave the Panhellenic Council a token liberal credential without endangering recruitment efforts, consciously or not.

Perhaps most significant, our national organization heard about the "lesbian" in our chapter, though they never seemed to know who it was. Occasionally, national personnel made heterosexist or homophobic remarks about the "problem" to me or other house members. When members of my chapter proposed an addition of sexual orientation to the national nondiscrimination policy at our convention, members of the national argued that it was "unnecessary." At a planning meeting for one of our rush events, the division undergraduate president suggested we put pictures of our pretty sisters with their boyfriends up on the walls. Though no explicit mention of the reason for this new recruitment technique was fully articulated, the message was clear enough.

A few years later I attended the installation of a new chapter at another school in the Boston area, a school known for its focus on communication and broadcasting. As a result of the strength of those majors, that school had a higher than average percentage of undergrads who were artsy in how they dressed and expressed themselves, a style that apparently could be read as "queer" by some people. Another national representative mentioned to me and two of my sisters, one of whom identifies as bisexual, that the school was having some trouble with recruitment. The national sorority suspected it was because the school had a higher than usual population of students who were "that way," and we certainly didn't want sisters like that. I didn't make some witty response, because I was too hurt and shocked by their overt prejudice. In addition to having hurt feelings, though, I was amused by the fact that they apparently didn't know a sister who was "that way" when one walked up to them and said hello. The sorority national representative seemed to think our chapter's recruitment problems were more related to a reputation on campus as the "lesbian sorority" than other issues, such as our status as the only sorority without a house and our newness to the system. So while other sororities held their rush events in the living rooms of their houses and we had only classrooms to use, our national sorority, rather than pressing our Panhellenic to conform to National Panhellenic Conference rules, focused on ways to make us look more like the other (straight) houses on campus. Even now, years after college, I still have conflicted feelings about whether the national was right. True to form, the sisters I keep in touch with assure me that our problems at rush were the result of those other factors far more than any reputation we gained on campus on my account.

I continue to believe that sororities, more than coeducational environments, can provide the kind of women-only space in which women can develop leadership and confidence skills. In some ways, sororities can introduce these resources to women who are alienated from or uncomfortable with the resources provided by women's studies departments or women's centers. I have not, however, ever believed that sororities are the only route to such skills nor that they are necessarily the best way. Unfortunately, more often than not, most sororities do not prioritize such strengths, but, in fact, perpetuate the problems women face with alcohol abuse, eating disorders, and sexism.

Today, as a graduate student at a campus with a far more traditional

Greek system than Tufts', I'm not convinced of the possibility of substantive change. Too often the stories I hear from students demonstrate only the worst aspects of Greek life. The campus at which I study is not one where many women would feel safe coming out in their sororities. My colleagues, many of whom did their undergraduate studies at large, public California schools, look at me with a mixture of horror and wonder when I tell them I was a sorority dyke in college. The very process of formal rush, with its highly specific rules set by the NPC, perpetuates a system in which sororities differ from one another more cosmetically than substantially.

Despite my objections to structural weaknesses in Greek organizations, I continue to be grateful for the experiences I gained through my sorority membership. My college experience would have been entirely different and markedly impoverished without my struggles to figure out the paradox. The friends from college with whom I speak regularly are almost entirely women from my sorority. When I went through a nasty breakup with my first girlfriend and our mutual friends did not support me, my sisters assured me that I wasn't crazy and that they were there for me. I can't imagine how I would have gotten through some of the roughest times I had in college without the support of my sisters who stuck by me when even my closest non-Greek friends did not. Nor can I imagine how dull my life would be today without their long-term friendships to enrich my life.

This summer I had an opportunity to see a number of my sisters in the way that I suspect many sorority alumnae do: One of my sorority sisters got married. It was a seaside wedding in a suburb just north of Boston. Before the wedding, we had sent a flurry of E-mail messages among the sisters expected to attend. The bride had been our recruitment chair and was a sucker for sentimental tributes. So one sister, particularly adept at transforming normal songs into occasion-specific ones, was working up alternative lyrics for "Love Me Tender," since the groom was an Elvis fan. I protested the use of the sweetheart song, which I found heterosexist and sexist, not to mention just plain corny. At the reception, we quietly sneaked out to a lawn behind the reception hall to rehearse both the Elvis song and a traditional sorority song. As we serenaded the bride and groom, despite my lingering embarrassment that if my grad school friends saw this they would double over in laughter, I realized that still, years past my college days, I felt at home with these women in a way I felt with few others. Choices that might seem to require justification elsewhere, appearances that might require pretense on the other coast, simply did not matter. It was enough to sit and reminisce about our college days.

On the drive home after the reception, I realized our sisterhood has only grown over the years, despite the distances among us all, and has come to mean what it always should: an unconditional acceptance of people with whom you have a bond that cannot be dissolved. The bond may have been formed through activities that non-Greeks find to be useless or silly, but the bond still remains. Just as with biological sisters, we have had plenty of disagreements and periods in our lives where there were sisters we could not bear to be around. All too like family, we often know entirely too many embarrassing stories about each other's younger years.

While I look forward to sorority weddings as an excuse to see old friends, I cannot see even such happy occasions as purely celebratory because two of my roles—member of a sorority and dyke—do not fit easily together. Part of the struggle for equal rights is the struggle to allow individuals to be themselves no matter how closely or distantly those selves match up to assumed standards. My struggle to negotiate the relationship between roles that seem contradictory to so many may be why my closest friends from college were women from the sorority. The women who knew me in both of my roles knew me more thoroughly and completely than those who knew me in only one of the two contexts.

As I look back on this today, I think back to when I first kissed a woman. I have come full circle.

Who I Am
by "Christina Galabres"

My relationships with the other women in the chapter continued to grow stronger than ever, because I finally felt confident enough to show them the real me. I trusted them all enough to let them get to know me for who I really am, and that sense of honesty between us brought us closer than ever before.

Until I was a senior in high school I was always anti-Greek. I assumed all fraternity members were chauvinistic, racist, homophobic guys who just wanted to party. I assumed all sorority members were rich, anorexic, stuck-up snobs willing to sleep with any man. I never wanted to put myself in a position where I could not be myself and where I could not feel confident in all I have to offer. I wanted to surround myself with people who would love me for who I am, not for who they'd want me to be. Yet the more I thought about it, the more I realized I had no basis for my judgments. My brother had been in a fraternity, and he and his friends were respectful, well-rounded, open-minded men. The only sorority women I knew were my mother and her friends, whose experiences were 25 years old. I realized I was judging sorority women because I assumed they would judge me. I decided that to gain a clearer understanding of Greek life and the sorority community, I would go through formal fall recruitment, thus gaining concrete experiences on which to base my opinions.

I pledged Chi Delta the fall of my freshman year in 1997. At that point, I dated only men, yet I'd had crushes on girls since my junior year of high school. I'd never acted on any of my attractions toward women, partly because some of them were directed toward famous singers and actresses, and partly because I assumed the repercussions would be more severe than the satisfaction of acting out my curiosity. The Chi Delta chapter I joined, along with all of the other sorority chapters on campus, seemed greatly focused on men and alcohol. We had several date parties my first semester to which I would invite, and kiss, my male date. My tendency to end up kissing my male dates became a joke between me and my sisters.

I was also on the university's track team. As any athlete can vouch, members of sports teams often become extremely close. I immediately became a bosom buddy with another runner, Melissa. We did everything together, studying, going to the beach, taking weekend getaways. I even invited her to some date parties in addition to the male date I would bring, and we occasionally slept in each other's dorm rooms when our roommates were gone.

In December of my first year, I had a sexual dream about Melissa and I freaked out. I didn't know how to handle sexual attraction toward one of my best friends, especially since the best friend was a girl. Any sexual feelings I'd had toward women before had been crushes from afar, never someone to whom I was actually close. What did it mean? Did it mean I was a lesbian? I talked to my older sister about it, and she said it was normal to have dreams like that and it didn't necessarily mean anything. I tried to suppress the thoughts for several months, convincing myself that the dream meant nothing. But it became more and more difficult to deny these thoughts, and I started to think consciously about my attraction to Melissa.

I had been diagnosed with depression my junior year in high school, and it got really bad during the winter of my freshman year in college. The cold weather, combined with 10 long track practices a week and my constant state of fatigue, added to my mood's fast deterioration. Melissa was there for me through all of it. I even found out later that she had called my mom to find out how to help me. Melissa would drop everything to jump in the car and drive to the city so we could sit and look at the lights. We'd escape for the weekend to go to the beach, to walk at sunset, and to talk about everything on my confused mind. She helped me sort through one of the hardest times in my life.

By late February I could no longer pretend my feelings toward Melissa were purely platonic. We confided our mutual attraction and began seeing each other secretly, not telling anyone of our love for each other. I continued to go to sorority date parties with men, but I stopped kissing them. My heart belonged to Melissa, and I couldn't deny that to myself. Yet somehow I found myself completely unable to confide in anyone else about my feelings. Once my mom confronted me, and I denied it all. I've always been very close to my parents, and to lie about something like this was difficult. I felt I was betraying them while at the same time protecting them from the reality that their daughter might be a lesbian instead of just an experimenting college student. I continued to talk to my Chi Delta sisters about crushes I had on random men, all of which were falsified to cover up my love for another woman.

At the spring formal my freshman year, I was set up with a random guy and had a horrible time. The entire evening I couldn't stop thinking about Melissa and how much I wanted her there with me. That same night, a senior Chi Delta showed up with three other women, and I asked my big sister in the chapter who they were. She responded, "Oh, just some of her lesbian friends or something." I was overwhelmed with mixed emotions. My big sister didn't seem thrilled that there was a lesbian in the chapter, which was really hard for me, because she was one of the people to whom I felt the closest. On the other hand, this senior who had brought a few of her female friends to the date party was acting in a way that showed her sisters that it was OK for women to date women. She was a person who had added a lot to the growth of our chapter, and she wasn't going to be ostracized as a result of her attraction to other women. Seeing her dance with her friends that night gave me a sense of liberation, and I felt I could do the same. I felt I could bring Melissa to a date party and hold her in my arms, just as so many of my sisters did with their boyfriends, and everything would be OK.

But there was still that cold response from my big sister. Did she really feel that way, or was it just an off-the-cuff comment? My fear of being dismissed by the ones I loved prevented me from telling anyone about my relationship. I was truly scared—scared of how people would perceive me, that they would look at me as weird, as different, as a lesbian, instead of as a Chi Delta sister who was the same unique, loving individual as before. I was scared my sisters would feel uncomfortable sharing a room or a bathroom with me. I grew up in a conservative, upper-class town, and I feared the judgments of others. I was scared of being ostracized from the track team for fulfilling the stereotypical image of the lesbian athlete.

I spent the rest of freshman year living a lie. I returned home for the summer and confided in my closest friends as well as my family. My parents cried and told me how much they loved me. My friends hugged me, and I just kept getting closer to Melissa. Many relationships were reaffirmed for me that summer. When I returned to school that fall, no one in Chi Delta knew Melissa and I were dating, not even my three roommates, one of whom was my big sister.

Upon my return, I met a girl in the chapter, Naomi, who had been abroad my entire freshman year. During fall recruitment, Naomi and I were decorating our house for theme night, standing in the hall amid other sisters. She randomly turned to me as I was hanging a poster on the wall and asked, "Have you ever kissed another chick before?"

I stopped what I was doing and just stood there, my heart pounding in my neck, my hands shaking as I gripped the poster. I stared at the blank wall where I was about to hang the poster, my mind moving a mile a minute.

Oh, my God! I thought. *She knows! Naomi knows I have a girlfriend! What do I do?*

I had spent so much time concealing the truth that I was dumbstruck when faced with the opportunity to tell the truth. As I continued to stare at the blank wall, I mumbled, "Yes."

"Really?" she said, "Who? Melissa?"

"Um…yeah." I can still feel the lump in my throat that prevented me from swallowing. I felt the room closing in on me, the lights dimming, a spotlight on my conversation with Naomi. I felt my world shutting down, my hands trembling, my body temperature rising.

"Cool," she said. "I've kissed girls before too."

The whole time we had been having this conversation, as I experienced hot flashes and felt faint with the truth hitting me in the face, Naomi just continued to hang stuff on the walls without pausing. She talked so smoothly, so calmly, as if we were discussing our summer vacations. She continued to ask me questions in a steady voice, at a normal volume level. I answered truthfully in a trembling, soft voice. All I could think about was how this conversation was going to change my position in the sorority. How would my sisters react to having a bisexual woman sharing their home?

Naomi and I became instant friends. She was the one person in the chapter I truly opened up to. I told her everything about my journey, which began with my first crush on a famous singer and carried me to the present, having had a girlfriend for six months. She kept my secret tight, respecting my desire not to let the other sisters know yet. For the time being, I continued to pretend I was someone else. At night, I made up excuses to tell my three roommates why I would sleep over at Melissa's apartment. I said I needed to get away from the sorority, or that I was studying late with Melissa and didn't want to walk home alone. They never questioned me.

The time came for our first date party of the fall, and I decided I didn't want to put myself through the pain of being set up with another random guy just to put up the facade of being straight. I brought Melissa but also a couple of guy friends, telling everyone it was just a group of us all going together as friends. But as the night wore on and more alcohol was running through my body, my inhibitions were lowered. Melissa and I moved closer and closer together, and by the end of the night we had kissed on the dance floor among all of my sisters and their dates.

I never came right out and told anyone in the chapter about me and Melissa. I didn't have to. They all saw it. They saw me spend every available moment with her. They saw me leave the house late at night to sleep over at her house. They saw us kiss on the dance floor. After that first date party with Melissa, I felt a huge sense of relief. I no longer had to pretend to be someone else. I opened myself up to my sisters and let them know I was the same person they had known and loved for over a year; I just had a girlfriend.

I never encountered any problems once my sisters found out about this new aspect of who I am. After that first kiss on the dance floor, Melissa was my girlfriend, and everyone knew it and accepted it. I was never faced with homophobia or a lack of interest or support in my life. My relationships with the other women in the chapter continued to grow stronger than ever, because I finally felt confident enough to show them the real me. I trusted them all enough to get to know me for who I really am, and that sense of honesty between us brought us closer than ever.

Melissa and I have been together now for almost two years. She comes to all of the Chi Delta date parties and is loved by my sisters as a best friend. It has meant the world to me to be able to love her as much as I do without worrying about being judged by my sisters. They've all gone above and beyond the support I ever hoped for. After Melissa and I opened our relationship up to the chapter, my big sister told me how happy she was for me to have found such an amazing person. My fears of her lack of support vanished. She was as supportive of me as anyone else. A few months ago one of my good friends told me she was so happy that Melissa and I are together and that she has honestly never heard a negative thing said about our relationship from the other sisters in our chapter.

The support I've received from my Chi Delta sisters has given me the confidence to open myself up to others and allow them to get to know me for who I really am. I no longer deny to others whom I really love. Melissa and I are soul mates. She has filled my life with happiness, and we have built a relationship of trust, honesty, and true love. I feel lucky to be able to share the happiness of our relationship with my closest friends, my Chi Delta sisters. If it were not for their support, I would not be able to live my life in as honest and self-confident a manner as possible.

More Than a Token Lesbian
by Dianne Catalano

I watched as my fellow feminist sisters, openly feminist, unknowingly changed themselves for a man. I was always saddened by their frequent passivity around men or how they silently suffered from another drunken hook up, as they wondered what possessed them.

"If there's something you want to tell me, you know you can," my mother said.

I wasn't hungry, and I'd been staring at my dinner. The thought of eating made me nauseated, as I tried to swallow the words I'd kept inside for as long as I could remember. I shifted my gaze from my plate to her eyes. I couldn't trust her; she couldn't handle it yet.

"I'm fine," I said. I moved the food around my plate, trying to make it seem as though I had eaten.

"You've been really quiet for the past few days…" she said, her voice trailing off. I sucked in what little air I could, knowing what she would ask next.

"Is it about that poem?" she asked. And there it was, hanging out there, the question that would start and end all conversations until I cheered up or confessed. I silently cursed at myself for even mentioning the poem, but keeping her at bay about my silence took too much energy; I had to give up some information if I was going to get through the rest of my high school days.

"Nah. Just tired," I said. I felt the heat pulsing in my ears from embarrassment. That stupid poem.

The drama began toward the middle of my freshman year of high school. I'd been taking private basketball lessons since the summer, hoping I would make the team my sophomore year. In my quest to become part of the team, I had fixated on one player and had written a poem for her, which at the time I'd earnestly thought was about sheer admiration. In what I saw as a chance to impress her, I had told her about the poem and given her a copy. She then showed the poem to the girls' basketball team, all of her friends, and anyone else she could find. Thus I was branded a "dyke" for the rest of my high school days. It took me months to climb out of the depression, which ensued shortly afterward, as I considered that I might be a lesbian and that I had no friends. In my attempt to fight and suppress my sexuality, I dated a few guys, who were wonderful boyfriends. In the midst of each relationship, though, the hollow feeling inside my chest never dissipated.

On my 17th birthday I came out to myself and began to battle my personal demons. I told no one until three months after my birthday in a painful long-distance conversation with my soon to be ex-boyfriend. I couldn't even say the words out loud; he had to say them for me.

By the middle of second semester of my senior year I had a girlfriend, and although we were covert, rumors flew again. While my family often commented on how mannish my new "friend" looked, they didn't want to see the truth, and I helped the illusion. I placated them by dating boys occasionally. I decided that Mom and Dad would not pay for college tuition if they knew who their daughter really was.

Needless to say, I was excited about going away to college. Carlisle, Pa., is a long drive from Long Island. Dickinson College was a new place, with no one from my high school, and no one to brand me "the dyke." I was conflicted about how I would deal with my sexuality. I made sure that Dickinson had a group for lesbian, gay, bisexual, and transgendered folks, just in case, and fraternities and sororities, again, just in case.

When I stepped onto campus I thought I had stumbled into a bad '80s sitcom. My soon-to-be resident advisers were dancing and singing to "Ice Ice Baby." Somehow, the 1990s had never reached south central Pennsylvania. Not that Long Island had escaped the '80s, with the decade's ever-prevalent acid-washed jeans and big hair, but I was a Gap kid, dressed in my khaki shorts and polo shirt. Fortunately, my floor mates dressed similarly to me, and I would later realize, most of the campus did too. All of the doors had door tags with *The Lion King* as the theme: crayoned-in coloring book pictures with borders of decorated construction paper with our names on them. My door tag was a zebra in rainbow colors, and my border was triangles. Dear God, someone from my high school had called ahead to my RA and told her I was a lesbian. It only took until the first floor meeting for me to realize that my RA had no clue what the rainbow stood for, and my fears subsided.

I wanted to fit in desperately. I went to fraternity parties, got drunk, and tried hooking up with guys, but I felt like a traitor. In two months I knew I had better tell someone about my sexuality before I continued to silence myself with alcohol. I started preseason training for tennis, decided to drop out of ROTC, and told both RAs in my building. The two of them, not knowing that the other knew, decided to play "Guess what I know about one of our residents that you don't know" at their staff meeting. They wound up outing me to their staff, who outed me to everyone they knew. With fewer than 1,800 students on campus, it didn't take long before everyone knew. Welcome to the nightmare that was my reality.

I started dating a woman, and we soon became known as the campus lesbians. I rarely, if ever, saw my floor mates, choosing to separate myself from them because I couldn't deal with their possible rejection. I became active on campus, playing a varsity sport, being a member of the new student orientation committee, becoming an RA, working as social chair for Allies (a group for LGBT folks and their allies), etc. I stayed away from Greeks, however, because I was scared of fraternity men and their homophobic reputation.

My world shifted during sophomore year. I was on staff with three sorority women with whom I talked of the possibility of there being a place for someone "like me" in a sorority. I served on the orientation committee with almost all sorority women (in the same sorority), including the chair of the committee. My girlfriend and I broke up, and I was in search of a new identity. I was sick of being the token lesbian; I wanted to be a part of the status quo. The women on the orientation committee showed me so much friendship and kindness that I wanted to be part of their organization. They opened their doors to me. Kara, Sarah, and Naomi showed me what sisterhood meant. The women who lived in the chapter house my sophomore year proved to be the most amazing and open-minded women. When I visited them, they asked me about my love life and never became skittish when I answered. Yep, I wanted in.

I couldn't go through rush, though, since I didn't want to be subjected to the whole process. I had friends in almost all of the chapters on campus, and I didn't want to be isolated from them during the two weeks of rush. They saw *me* when they looked at me, not just a lesbian, and I saw them as friends, not as members of a sorority. So I did the mature thing and moped. I sat around while they all had rush parties, listened to my female residents as they returned from round robins, etc. I told my sorority friends good luck before their parties and focused on something else, trying to block out my feelings of sadness and jealousy. I waited impatiently for bid day weekend to pass so I could be part of them again, as an unofficial sister. On Saturday morning, bid day, that all changed.

"Hello?" I answered the phone, sleepy at 10 A.M.

"Dianne, this is Mags, the rush chair from Panhel. You've been offered a snap bid from Tri Delta," she said in an unusually perky voice for her.

"Mags, it's early…and not funny," I said.

"I'm not kidding…hold on, someone wants to talk to you."

That's when I heard Sarah's voice, and I had to laugh at her formality. I thought for sure this was a joke, but hoped it wasn't.

"Hello, this is Sarah, the president of Delta Delta Delta," she said. "On behalf of my chapter, we'd like to offer you a snap bid."

"Oh" was all that I could mutter. I was a whiz at early morning articulation. "Seriously? You're serious, Sarah?"

"Yes, so take some time and think it over. Come by to Greek Affairs to let us know either way by 12…OK?"

I was beaming. I didn't think of myself as the token lesbian. I thought I had finally overcome the stigma. I was going to be a part of the Greek community. I could make a difference; just being a part of a sorority as an out lesbian could make a difference. I was going to be a Tri Delta.

I impatiently waited for the bids to be handed out. Bid cards were delivered to your door; then chapter members came to your building and took you to the rest of the chapter's members, who waited by a designated spot in the academic quad.

"Reider, shouldn't you be over at the house by now? You don't want to miss announcement of the bid list, do you?" I asked my roommate. I didn't tell her I had accepted the snap bid; in fact, she didn't even know I'd been offered one. I knew that I'd see her in a short while, since she was a Tri Delta.

"Yeah, I'm going. What are your plans for the night?" She was worried about me being lonely on bid night.

"I gotta write a paper. Give me a call later."

"OK...you know you're boring, right?"

"Yup. Get out of here before you miss it. I'll be fine...really."

I was elated when I got to the academic quad wearing Sarah's letters.

"You little shit. I can't believe you let me leave without telling me," Reider said as she hugged me. We both had smiles on from ear to ear.

"I felt all bad leaving you...you little shit!"

That night was one of my best. My friends from other chapters came over and gave me hugs. I couldn't have been happier. I knew all of the sisters at Tri Delta from the previous semester and felt like I was home. My pledge class seemed pretty cool. Some of the other pledges were my former residents with whom I was good friends. I slept in my letters that night, afraid that if I didn't, I'd wake up to realize that it had been a dream. Waking up in those letters was an amazing feeling.

Life was incredible. I was elected pledge class president, probably because I knew all of the sisters, including our new member educator. I loved every minute of pledging. I wasn't sure how many other members of my pledge class knew I was a lesbian, and I didn't bring up the topic. Those who knew were awesome. I knew the sisterhood supported me, so I thought I'd take everyone else in stride. About two weeks into our pledge program a speaker came to campus to talk about bridging the gap between the Dickinson Christian Fellowship and the LGBT community. About half of my pledge class went with me to this program, along with sisters. During the program, there was a segment when people were asked to stand up if they fit into an identity such as single-parent background, person of color, etc. Then the presenter uttered the phrase that always made me nervous: "Stand if you're lesbian, gay, or bisexual."

I took a deep breath and stood. My pledge class stared at me; I think I shocked a few of them. As I sat down, I said to Naomi, who sat next to me, "I'm sorry. I think you can expect some people to depledge tomorrow because of me...I'm sorry."

Naomi put her arm around me. "If they do, we don't want them in our sorority. We wanted you as part of the chapter...we don't want them if they can't handle this."

I was comforted by her words, but I still felt horrible. No matter how many times, in an attempt to beat internalized homophobia, that I've told myself it didn't bother me if other people had a problem with my identity, it was always hard. It's difficult to lose friends, or potential friends, by uttering a simple phrase. But no one depledged because of my coming out. Some of my favorite coming-out stories are from when I came out to my pledge class.

It was late one night. We were sitting on the second-floor porch, smoking cigarettes. A couple of sisters and other pledges were there, along with Suzie.

"My parents still don't know I swear or drink," someone said.

"Mine don't know I smoke," someone else said, as she exhaled.

"Yep, mine still think I'm a virgin," another chimed in, as we all laughed.

"That's OK. Mine still think I date boys," I said. Everyone laughed at that one. I looked around, and Suzie appeared stunned.

"Oops! Suzie didn't know," I said. "Suz, I'm gay."

Her brow lifted as she made the connection and smiled. "Oh, that makes so much sense now." We all started cracking up. Her response was pretty indicative of everyone else's. Surely there were some who were awkward at first, and I had to battle a lot of my internalized homophobia. I always tried to be careful of my personal space, not wanting to stand or sit too close to anyone, for fear they might think I was hitting on them. The semester of pledging was difficult for me as far as making connections with straight women, but it helped me deal with myself. It was Sarah, however, who was always there for me. She became my big sister and a wonderful friend, helping me through the semester of pledging, my long distance relationship, classes, and anything else, supporting me as a friend and a sister.

I don't want to paint a picture of perfection surrounding my sorority experience. There were horrible days along with great ones. There were times when I felt as if my sisters were nothing more than "intimate strangers," as the Indigo Girls have said. Once, at a fraternity social function, I saw the word *fag* on their wall next to a brother's name. It enraged me that they would leave something like this up, as if it were something they were proud of. I don't know how many of the brothers knew I was a lesbian, but I didn't feel safe, so I left the party. Not many of my sisters understood why it bothered me. I couldn't find the words to explain to them why I felt so angry and upset. I felt so isolated from those men and isolated from all of my heterosexual sisters who had no idea what I felt. If I tried to explain to them how the Greek system is embedded with heterosexism, I knew only a few would understand. It was frustrating, and sometimes I couldn't remember why I was part of such a system.

Fraternity men's use of the word "fag" constantly grated on my nerves. "That's so gay," uttered from the mouth of a sister did not help either. The disclaimer "I don't mean you" or "You know I don't mean it like that," never made me feel better. Greeks were and continue to be the embodiment of heterosexuality and normality. I could never be that, and I didn't want to be that. I didn't want to be asked what gay people thought about the movie *Chasing Amy*. I didn't have a rainbow-colored phone that tapped me into the "official gay opinion." I was no longer the token lesbian on campus; instead, I was the token lesbian sorority woman. Sure, faculty members were surprised, and I think a few reconsidered their opinion of Greeks when they found out that one chapter had an openly lesbian member. I felt as if few minds were changed, mostly in my sorority, and I give them credit, since many had never before met an openly gay or lesbian person.

I learned a lot about heterosexuality from my sisters. I watched as my fellow feminist sisters, openly feminist, unknowingly changed themselves for a man. I was always saddened by their frequent passivity around men or how they silently suffered from another drunken hook-up as they wondered what possessed them. I felt lucky that I didn't have to deal with the heterosexual drama that comes with being a single woman in college. I wanted them to see themselves as the amazing and strong women they were—not what the fraternity men thought they should be. My sisters were filled with passion during chapter meetings and somehow neglected themselves when they were in relationships. I wanted them to be the same feminists they were in class when they were out on Friday or Saturday nights, but college culture is not set up that way, nor is the culture at large. I don't blame my sisters, nor do I think poorly of them. Rather, I am thankful for hearing their stories and being able to take a look at what their lives were like.

Sister-only functions often proved difficult for me. Women teased or flirted with me for fun. Sometimes I think they flirted because it was a thrill or they were curious or knew I was safe, since I was in a relationship, or because I was the closest thing to a man around. Usually, I took it all in fun, but on a few occasions it went too far and I felt used. But I was using them too—to be a part of the status quo. I was using my membership to gain the prestige and elitism that came along with it. I appreciate all that I learned from being a part of my sorority, the women whom I call my sisters, and other members of the

Greek community. There were days, however, when I was sick of being the poster child for lesbians. Lesbians didn't exist in other sororities. Sometimes I felt completely alone.

The loneliness I felt crashed into the pride I felt surrounding my sexuality during senior year. My best friend, Ifer, who had been abroad junior year, was back. We were reunited, two out lesbians ready to take on our senior year. At first it was awkward to communicate to her that I was still me even though I had joined a sorority. I often teased her that if she hadn't gone abroad, I wouldn't have gone Greek. Ifer helped me negotiate the dichotomous identities I juggled, always there to help me sort out what it meant to be a feminist, lesbian, and sorority member. I began to feel connected to all of the communities that constructed my identity and manage to deal with my contradictions. Could I be an advocate for women's liberation in the Greek system? The topic of my proudly being an out lesbian and out Greek often came up in many late night chats. But any reconciliation between my identities was turned upside down when I heard about the tragic beating and death of Matthew Shepard.

Ifer and I were on the committee to plan a rally against homophobia and hate crimes. She was chosen as a speaker for the rally, and she worked hard on what would turn out to be an emotional and extremely poignant speech. I brought the event to the attention of my chapter and told them how much I'd appreciate their support. I often separated my LGBT functions and my sister functions, but I was scared and needed the two worlds to come together.

Only a few of my sisters attended the rally. Another sorority to which I was moderately close also attended and gave me hugs and smiles of support. Still, I felt defeated. Cooney, a sister in my chapter, encouraged me to address the chapter that evening.

"I was hurt today that the sorority who supported me the most was not my own. I don't often preach to any of you about LGBT activism, and I don't expect all of you to attend Allies functions, but today was different," I said through my tears.

"What will it take for you to care? Why do I have to stand in front of you, crying, for you to understand how important it was for me to have your support today? Will it take me not making it home from the bars one night? Will it take my death for it to sink in that something terrible has happened and it scares the shit out of me because of who I am?" I was angry, and I wasn't going to hold back how I felt. It wasn't completely fair that I let out all my frustrations with the world on my chapter, but the words kept coming out. I knew they all supported me, but they hadn't shown it when I'd needed them the most. I know I reached them, and many could not look me in the eyes. I love my chapter, and I love my sisters, but that day I needed them to be supportive of their *lesbian* sister.

Later that night I was in the student union working on a paper. On my way out I spoke with a few guy friends from one of the fraternities. It was well past midnight, and I was nervous walking home alone, even though it was a short distance. For the first time in my four years at Dickinson, I didn't feel safe on my campus.

"I can't believe how much all of this has gotten to me," I said to the guys.

"You're really shaken up, aren't you?" one of them said.

"Do you mind walking me home tonight?" I asked.

Although Hibbs made me promise to give him a cigarette as compensation, he walked me to my building. Along the way, he asked me about how I was feeling; he was genuinely concerned. Who I was affected him. This is the same fraternity man who wore a rainbow sticker on National Coming Out Day in support of me and had gotten some of his brothers to wear one too. He helped me feel safe that night, and he showed he cared. I couldn't have asked for much more than that.

I still keep in contact with many of my sisters and visit them when I can. They'll always be my sisters, and many of them will be my friends for the rest of my life. I changed them, and they changed me. Who they are is a part of my world, and who I am is a part of theirs. I couldn't have asked for much more than that.

A Quiet Acceptance
by Katie Stuckemeyer

*Katie Stuckemeyer and her
Kappa Delta sorority sisters enjoy
margarita night at Pepe's.*

I felt like a 10-ton weight had been lifted from my chest. If this woman, who had been one of my most vocal enemies the previous semester, could not only become a close friend but also give me her full support and acceptance, anything could happen. I continued confiding in my sisters, receiving their unconditional love and acceptance.

"Sometimes the best way to figure out who you are is to get to that place where you don't have to be anything else." When I decided to pledge Kappa Delta sorority, these words were placed before me as the motto of the previous pledge class. Far from embracing them as truth, I cringed inwardly. As a lesbian, I believed it was my fate to remain closeted within the Greek system. I couldn't conceive of a welcoming environment, one where I would be loved and accepted for who I am. I envisioned myself leading a double life for the remainder of my college career, unable to integrate my identity as a lesbian and a sorority woman.

I made the decision to join a sorority in January 1998. I was a sophomore in search of an alternate social group as well as a new experience. I had watched friends rush my freshman year, and I vowed I would never, and I mean *never*, join a Greek organization. Although I was not yet out, even to myself, I felt I had little in common with these women. I pictured a sorority as a group of women so similar they could have been cut out with a cookie cutter, leaving little room for diversity or individuality. My freshman year came and went with my best friend coming out as a lesbian, leaving me with a barrage of internal struggles regarding my own sexuality.

I returned to Valparaiso University for my sophomore year, and within a month I became involved with a woman. I finally came out to myself and my closest friends. I couldn't believe no one was surprised; I guess they all knew what I had worked so hard to deny. Far from ready to be out to the entire campus, though, I kept my relationship a secret, which served only to hurt both me and my partner. Our relationship ended within two months.

I think I decided to rush not only to "try something new" or "make new friends" but also to create an environment where I'd be forced to closet myself, where I could deny my sexuality indefinitely. I thought joining a sorority would force me to be straight, at least outwardly. And maybe, just maybe, if I were outwardly straight for long enough, I would become heterosexual.

I began rush when I returned for the 1998 spring semester. At that point only one sorority at Valparaiso, Chi Omega, had affiliated with a national sorority. The remaining seven chapters were local sororities, though all affiliated with national chapters during the spring semester. Although we were supposed to rush all eight sororities, I had narrowed my choices to two chapters by the end of the second day of rush. Two weeks later I sat in the final party of the sorority I was to choose. I decided, albeit halfheartedly, to pledge Kappa Psi Omega.

Some of my sisters claim their pledging period was the best time of their life. Unfortunately, mine was not. Consumed with internal struggle, I alienated myself from the gay community I had previously associated with while isolating myself from my new sisters. I made my pledging period as difficult as possible, attempting to ease the rejection I saw as inevitable by causing it myself. In my mind it was easier to have my sisters reject me because of the unpleasant, sarcastic facade I projected than to have them reject me because I showed them my true identity. The more my sisters tried to embrace me, the more forcefully I pushed them away. To my dismay, I was activated in February 1998 and became a member of Kappa Delta sorority once we affiliated with the national organization in April 1998. My attitude didn't change once I was activated, and I pushed my limits in every way possible. My plan was working.

I had made a couple of good friends in my pledge class, but for the most part, the actives disliked me. I came out to two or three of my pledge sisters at the end of the year, and they received the news nonchalantly. I couldn't believe, though, that the entire chapter would react so calmly.

I moved into a room on my sorority corridor fall semester of my junior year, living with one of my pledge sisters. I dreaded the year to come, feeling the situation would be nearly unbearable. I hated everyone. They hated me. Why was I even part of this organization? I had built a wall between myself and my sisters that seemed impenetrable, simply because *I was afraid.*

I soon realized that living among these women, I'd have to remove my mask sooner or later. I reintegrated myself with the gay community and was elected support chair of Alliance, Valparaiso's group for gay, lesbian, bisexual, and transgendered students and their straight supporters. When my sisters asked where I was going on Wednesday nights, I answered them honestly. "I'm going to Alliance," I said, and they simply nodded and continued what they were doing. I found myself slowly growing closer to my sisters. Strangely enough, as I revealed more of my true identity to my sorority sisters, the women who had once disliked me were now becoming my closest friends.

As I grew closer to these women, I experienced an internal tug-of-war. As some of my best friends, my sisters deserved to know about my sexuality, if only to understand me more fully. At the same time, though, I feared that the friendships I treasured would instantly disintegrate when I told them the truth. One of my best friends within the sorority was of particular concern to me. Rachel had grown up in a conservative small town in southern Indiana and had been raised in the Lutheran Church-Missouri Synod. She had probably never known anyone gay or lesbian before, and I feared her response to my revelation. Since she was my best friend, though, I knew she'd find out eventually, and I wanted her to hear it from me first.

So I slowly dropped hints. When talking about relationships, I'd play the "pronoun game," referring to my significant other as "they" rather than "he" or "she." I tried to pick the best time to tell my sisters, and had several one-on-one conversations. All were well received, with my friends asking me questions and listening intently to my answers. One of my best experiences coming out to a sister occurred in October, when I told my former pledge educator. We had a long conversation outside her apartment building that culminated in her telling me how much she admired me and how much I had to offer to Kappa Delta. I felt like a 10-ton weight had been lifted from my chest. If this woman, who had been one of my most vocal enemies the previous semester, could not only become a close friend but also give me her full support and acceptance, anything could happen. I continued confiding in my sisters, receiving their unconditional love and acceptance.

I wish the responses of all of my sisters were positive, but this wasn't the case. My worries about coming out to Rachel were well founded; after I told her, we didn't speak for about six months. When we finally spoke again, she told me what I had expected. She had never dealt with these issues before; she was afraid, and she would rather run away than face an uncomfortable reality. I told her how much her rejection had hurt me and that I would not compromise my own identity for anything or anyone. Thankfully, we have since been able to rebuild our friendship into one that is stronger and more honest than ever, one based on the unconditional love between best friends and *sisters*.

My senior year has seen a world of changes both within myself and within my chapter. For the first time, my sexuality is an accepted reality instead of a "dirty secret." With the support and love of my sisters, I've been able to stop masking my sexuality to the Greek community. In January 2000, I was invited to participate in a panel discussion on diversity in the Greek community. I hesitated, then accepted the invitation. For the first time, I would be coming out to my sisters and the Greek community at large. I was nervous before the discussion began, but as I surveyed the standing-room-only crowd, I realized the first two rows were filled by my Kappa Delta sisters. A wave of pride rushed through me as I realized, once again, what a source of encouragement these women are in my life. When the discussion ended, I walked up to my sisters, still trembling with excess nerves, and was greeted with hugs and congratulations. I don't know who was more proud, my sisters or myself.

My sisters' acceptance and encouragement culminated recently when I decided to bring a woman to a Kappa Delta date party. I'd wanted to do this for some time, but I'd had neither the courage nor the faith in my sisters' promises of support to act on it. Usually, when we had a sorority function that involved a date, I drafted one of my male friends into action. I enjoyed myself on all of these occasions, but I always felt I wasn't being true to myself or honest with my sisters.

This winter, though, I became involved in a casual relationship with a woman who was extremely interested in my life as a member of a Greek organization. She mentioned several times that she wanted to accompany me to a sorority function, and I truly felt my sorority sisters would enjoy spending time with her. Once I had asked her to my date party and she accepted, I began to prepare my sorority sisters. I told them I was bringing a woman to the date party, and it went without saying that she was not "just a friend." My sorority sisters were very excited for me, saying they just wanted me to be happy. To prevent any shocked glances when we entered the room, they all told their dates beforehand that a lesbian couple was attending. I had complete faith in my sisters, but this did little to alleviate the nervousness I felt as we drove to the party. When we entered the room, however, we were immediately greeted by several of my sisters, welcoming me and introducing themselves to my date. Their ease with the situation enabled me to relax and enjoy the evening, and when my date and I walked onto the floor and began to dance, no one gave us a second look. This quiet acceptance and lack of attention meant the most to me. To my sisters, we were no different from any other couple.

As I reflect on my three years as a member of Kappa Delta, I'm proud to say that I, with the help of my sisters, have reached a point I never thought possible. My sisters have quietly accepted my sexuality. They don't discuss it constantly, as they understand it is only one part of my identity. They have learned, however, to accept and understand that it is an integral part of my identity, and they encourage me to express it as such. My sisters treat me with the same respect and love that I show them, urging me to be true to myself in all that I do. I've learned that "sometimes the best way to figure out who you are is to get to that place where you don't have to be anything else." I am truly thankful to have found that place, and it is among my Kappa Delta sisters.

Sharing My Secret
by Michelle Fouts

My fears slowly fade as I realize the issue is not my being a lesbian, but my not being myself.

I never once thought it would be easy to come out to my sorority sisters or anyone at the small private college I attend. Ashland University has approximately 2,500 undergraduates, and the majority of students come from small farming communities. The school is located in the middle of nowhere in Ohio, completely surrounded by the Amish community. The closest metropolitan area is an hour and a half away. There's not much to do around here, and of course, it's very hard to meet people who live alternative lifestyles.

It was not that I was scared to come out because I did not consider my sisters my friends, because I did. My fear stemmed from the idea that if a person was not from a large city, which many of my sisters were not, they would not be able to accept others' individuality. Preconceived notions I had about "country girls" convinced me that none of the women in my sorority would accept my difference in sexuality. For a while I was convinced that if any of them ever found out I was gay, I'd be kicked out of the sorority and shunned. I had recurring nightmares of standing in front of the Formal Standards Committee and being told I was unfit to wear the sacred pin of Alpha Delta Pi. I pictured myself standing in front of the executive members trying to convince them I should not be turned away for being different. I thought for sure none of the women would want to associate with a lesbian.

I came across as very uptight and never talked about whom I was dating or my plans for the weekend. I avoided mixers, date parties, semiformals, and formals as if they were the plague. This was hard for me, because I wanted to be actively involved and had always been outgoing. I used school and work as excuses, telling my sisters I was falling behind in my classes or unable to change my work schedule. I figured that the more I avoided these situations, the less anyone would notice my absence. But my plan backfired, and people often questioned my whereabouts.

While I was determined to run away from the truth, my diamond sister, Natalie, considered my big sister in the sorority, was trying to find it. Natalie was there when I had questions about what was taking place during meetings, initiation, and other sorority events. Over the months we built a strong friendship. But even though I trusted her and looked up to her, I didn't feel comfortable talking to her about such a controversial subject, which didn't stop her from trying to find out what was going on with me. She never pressed for answers, but she knew I was struggling both mentally and emotionally. One night during a sisterhood, I left the room, unable to control my emotions. When my diamond found me sitting on the bathroom floor, she rushed to hold me and listen to my cries. I told her how I was struggling with my life and was unhappy. Before I could think of anything else to say, I bluntly came out and said, "I am a lesbian. I will understand if you don't want to associate with me anymore. I just don't want to lie to you or anyone else anymore. My life is a joke and I can't possibly be happy when I'm living a lie. Hopefully you don't hate me for keeping this from you." As I told my story she held my hand, listening with open ears and an open heart. Never did she judge me or become offended. During this, I realized we shared a special bond that nothing could destroy. She listened to all that was on my mind before speaking. "I realize that this isn't easy for you," Natalie said. "I don't understand exactly what you're going through, because I've never felt that way. What I do know is that I love you no matter what. That's what I'm here for. I'm your sister and always will be, no matter what you're afraid to talk about. You just have to remember that you're not alone, and all of the sisters love you and will stand behind you no matter what. They all might not agree with it, but if they can't love you for who you are, they're not worth it. You have to be yourself. That's why you're in Alpha Delta Pi. We asked you to be one of us because of your great personality and individuality. Please don't feel like you have to hide from us. We love you."

My spirit felt free after I talked to my diamond that night, as if a huge boulder had been lifted from my heart. She made me realize the true meaning of sisterhood. While I didn't run out of the bathroom, interrupt the meeting, and tell all my sisters I was gay, I did begin to open my eyes and see that the women who made up our chapter did not judge one another, as I had imagined.

A year has passed since the night I shared my secret with my diamond. Since then I have come out to many of my sisters, including our advisers, whom I felt would be supportive. Everyone who has learned this from me personally has been wonderful about it. I don't feel at all like they look at me any differently, which was my biggest hurdle to overcome. As of today, about 20 of the 65 women who make up our chapter have heard me directly proclaim that I am gay. Probably more know, which doesn't bother me. As long as they don't treat me as an outsider, I don't care who knows. Don't get me wrong, though. Just because I've told only a few people, that does not mean I'm ashamed of being a lesbian, because that's who I am. I just want to make sure that I'm discussing the topic with those who will support me and not feel different around me. In a way, since all of the reactions have been positive, I'm still waiting for the one negative response that will send me back into hiding. I hope that doesn't happen, and I know that as long as I take my life one step at a time, I won't have any major problems.

Even though I have a great support system, it's still not easy to talk with all of my sisters about whom I'm dating or my plans for the weekend. I still don't feel 100% comfortable about bringing my girlfriend to a sorority social function or sharing pictures of the two of us. That's all beginning to change, though, and my goal is to take my current girlfriend to the upcoming date party that just happens to have the theme "Find a Mister for Your Sister." I find this theme quite ironic, but I'm taking it lightly and still plan to have a blast. The date party is a dance, and I'm slightly worried how everyone will feel or react when they watch us slow-dance for the first time. I hope this will be the icebreaker I need to make me feel more comfortable being the person I am. I realize that I'll be taking a huge risk, but I'm ready to take it on and change tradition.

None of this has happened overnight. It's taken a lot of believing in myself and my sisters to open up and share secrets about my life. I've been lucky that everyone has been so wonderful and accepting of the "new me." Proclaiming myself as a lesbian has not prevented me from prospering in the sorority either, which had been one of my worries. For example, I recently finished my one-year term as the Panhellenic delegate who oversaw all of the Greek philanthropy and public relations issues. Also, this past January I was appointed as the Alpha Delta Pi chaplain. My fears slowly fade as I realize the issue is not my being a lesbian, but my not being myself.

Over the past couple of months I have come to see the true meaning of sisterhood and why I joined the sorority. We have a bond that no one or nothing can come between or alter. I have gained valuable life lessons while dealing with the emotional issue. I have to remember that I'm not an outcast or living in sin. Most of all, I must keep in mind that my sisters always stand by my side. Just as our motto says, "We Live For Each Other."

My Sister, My Love
by "Jessi Opynth"

*"Jessi Opynth" (right) posing with
her sorority sister Meg*

With our first mention of a commitment ceremony to be held sometime in the next year, our sisters reacted with more enthusiasm than we did. Although they probably don't realize it, each has been crucial in the acceptance of ourselves individually and as a couple.

"Do you really think he is? I mean, I've never seen him with a girlfriend or anything, but he's so cool."

"Yeah...but just *look* at him. Have you ever watched him? He's such a homo."

This conversation about one of our beloved, longtime advisers was the first I'd heard my soon-to-be sorority sisters have on the topic of homosexuality.

As I grew up in a liberal town, but with conservative parents and a close-knit, religious extended family, I hadn't had much exposure to homosexuality. In fall 1994 I enrolled in college, following a typical, happy adolescence. Despite the uncomfortable feeling of being different from my friends because of my attraction to other women, I left home identifying myself as a normal, heterosexual 18 year-old. My alma mater, although located in a conservative area of the country, was like any other college: teeming with youthful ideas, diversity, self-exploration, and individuality.

I never saw myself as someone who would join a sorority, but Greek life was different than I'd expected. A considerable portion of the campus is Greek, and they seemed to offer a lot. I found myself at a sorority rush and was impressed; the members were down-to-earth, thoughtful women, not the mindless young coeds portrayed in movies and books. I quickly made friends and enjoyed being a part of Greek life. I pledged Lambda Chi Zeta the winter of freshman year, just as I was beginning to understand and accept the feelings I had toward women.

The atmosphere around the sorority house was friendly. Sometimes they threw a loud party or the television blared from the living room. At other times everyone disappeared to campus or into their rooms. Although I felt at home, as a pledge I had that uncomfortable feeling of not always being included. Several weeks into pledging, I overheard that conversation about the sexuality of our adviser. It was obvious this conversation had taken place before. It was also obvious that my sisters were homophobic and ignorant of gay people and gay issues. As I came out to myself, that conversation loomed over me from time to time.

Toward the end of pledge period, a similar incident took place, but this time I spoke out. My pledge sisters and I were in a separate room while members took turns demanding that we sing songs. I'll never forget the moment I heard Kris, one of the oldest active members, scream through the door, "Sing 'I love you, you love me, homosexuality!' "

I froze for several seconds, and she repeated herself. "Hello!? I said sing 'I love you, you love me, homosexuality!' Hurry up!"

Without thinking, I shouted back, "No!"

There was complete silence throughout the house; pledges never refuse. But there were no more requests for that song.

I still wasn't completely in touch with my sexuality, and both of these incidents disturbed and discouraged me. What kind of organization was I joining? But I enjoyed the sorority, and for the most part I pushed the incidents out of my head. I finished pledging and became a member the spring of freshman year.

The following fall was full of excitement. I was finding my place in the sorority, taking on more responsibilities as a member, getting involved in new activities, and making friends throughout the Greek community. I took on the task of public relations for the sorority and avidly participated in philanthropic activities in the community. I quickly got to know my new sisters better. Some of the members I hadn't particularly liked during pledging became close friends. I discovered immediately that my friendships and support grew stronger, and I could count on my sisters to stand up for me. Late in the fall of sophomore year, I was eligible to have my own little sister.

I met my little sister, Meg, at a party. Rachel, another sister, knew her from their hometown and wanted to introduce her to the sorority. Meg and I hit it off immediately, quickly becoming close friends. Like me, it didn't take long for her to realize how well she fit in at Lambda Chi Zeta, and she pledged that winter. I was thrilled when Meg became my little sister.

Our friendship continued to grow as she pledged. One night at a small party at the Lambda Chi Zeta house, I was sitting on the couch with my friends Morgan, Mike, and Paul. We had been drinking and playing a game of our own invention: pass the piece of candy with your mouth. Meg saw me pass the candy to Morgan and asked if she could talk with me in private. She bluntly asked, "Are you gay? I saw you kissing Morgan." She stared hard at me, waiting for my answer. Without thinking, I half surprised myself and said, "Yeah, something like that." She told me about her relationship with Laura in high school, and we were both surprised at our mutual lesbian feelings. Our conversation didn't go into much detail, but it gave us a stronger bond. We knew the subject of this conversation was off-limits within the sorority. Only one other time did the subject come up while Meg was pledging. One night I was walking her home after a rough night. She said to me, "Jonas is so lucky. I'm really jealous of him." Jonas was one of my best friends at the time. He had been coming out to himself for the past year, and I'd been going through the ups and downs with him. We had a strange relationship; most people—and sometimes myself included—thought we were more than friends. "What do you mean?" I asked. "That doesn't make any sense." She refused to answer at first, but finally said, "Because I'm interested in you."

To say I was bewildered would be an understatement. Despite our common feelings, I'd never considered a romantic relationship with Meg. I'd never had a relationship with another woman, which probably contributed to my apprehension. I realized that even though I was anxious about the situation, I was excited about the idea of exploring my growing attraction to her, and I could see our relationship develop. I spent a lot of time talking with Jonas, frantically saying things like, "Jonas, what do I do? She's my little sister—we're in the same sorority!" Despite his dislike of fraternities and sororities, he was supportive. I decided that if anything were to develop between Meg and me, there was no question that it would have to wait until she finished pledging. Members and pledges play distinct roles, and the line between the two is clear. Even though there's no explicit sorority rule that a sister cannot date a pledge, there's no room in a member-pledge relationship for an intimate relationship. Again I thought of the conversation about our adviser. The idea of being an out lesbian in the sorority and in a relationship with another member seemed risky. I had no intention of affecting the friendships and sisterhood that had become integral parts of my life. Added to this were terrifying images of being out to the Greek community. None of this could be whispered to anyone, let alone advertised to our peers.

The evening after Meg was initiated, we were in my room talking. We hadn't mentioned our growing feelings for one another, but that night Meg did something that would be a huge turning point for both of us, as well as for the sorority. She climbed up to my loft, leaving me standing in the middle of my room, bewildered. We spent the night talking. We discussed our feelings for each another, our fears of homophobia, and most of all, how our relationship would affect the sorority. We agreed emphatically that our relationship would remain secret.

Being a part of a meaningful sisterhood makes it even harder to conceal such a big part of your life. My sorority roommate, Karen, figured out what had developed between Meg and me. Karen and I were close friends, and we spent some of our best moments in heated debate. I would say she was homophobic at first, but after a while she accepted Meg and me. She was the first sister who was close who knew about my sexuality, and her acceptance gave me hope. But I also had my first experience being outed and worrying about how my relationship with Meg would affect my other friendships.

One night Karen and another of our sisters, Stephanie, were at Iota Mu Kappa, a sorority that had always been one of my favorites. That night, after spending the evening drinking beers with the Iota Mu Kappas, Karen said to everyone, "Well, how would *you* feel if you just found out your roommate was a lesbian?" To my horror, she shared this with me the next day. They were the last people I would have told. I appreciated her honesty but was disappointed by her betrayal.

Meg and I discussed how each of our sisters might react. "Myra wouldn't care, but Stacy would definitely not handle it well. And can you imagine what Lucy would say?" One night at a party, we had an urge to tell one of our sisters, Rachel, so we asked if we could talk to her alone. "Rachel, we really want to tell you something," I said. "We don't think you'll care, but we'd like you to know." She didn't blink an eye; we were so relieved. She actually laughed at us for thinking it would be such a big deal. Feeling inspired and full of confidence, we decided to tell another sister, Carmen. We realized we were picking "safe" people, knowing that both Rachel and Carmen were not homophobic. But it was still a big step for us. Carmen was ecstatic. At first she didn't believe us, because she thought it was so wonderful. Throughout the next year, one by one, more of our sisters found out about us. Often they figured it out on their own. Sometimes they asked another sister. Eventually the entire sorority knew, but Meg and I were still never openly affectionate around the house. We didn't want to upset the applecart that seemed to be settling so nicely for us.

Meg and I were enjoying the time we spent together, but we each had our own niche in the sorority and were respected as individuals. I was elected treasurer and also designed the sorority Web site. Meg held several offices, including membership chairperson. She was busy planning sisterhood events and making friends with many people both in and outside of the sorority. Looking back, I see that although we were seen as a couple, our individual talents were appreciated as well.

Erin, who had joined the sorority through Meg, was one of the last to find out—or so we thought. Meg cherished their friendship and was fearful of what Erin might think about our relationship, so I left it up to Meg to decide the right time to tell her. One day on campus, we ran into Erin. "I'd like to talk to you guys later, OK?" Erin said. Meg and I panicked. We could only guess that she found out about us and wanted to confront us about it. After we worried and second guessed Erin's intentions for the rest of the afternoon, she finally approached us that night at a party. "Look, you two, if you think I don't know what's going on, you shouldn't be so stupid. It's obvious." We were dumbfounded. We discussed it with her for a while and she admitted that she had figured us out a long time ago but found it entertaining that we thought she was oblivious. Once again we were encouraged that our sisters accepted our big sister-little sister romantic relationship.

Other times we heard negative comments from other sisters. Near the end of my college years, eight of us went to Las Vegas for spring break. Carmen told us in private that two of our sisters on the trip had complained to her. "I wanted to tell you something that Georgia and Josie said on the flight out here. They said you two better not hold hands and dyke out when we're walking down the strip in Vegas. Just wanted you to know." I was sad to hear my friends were saying this behind my back. I realized we would always have to deal with this and that there would always be friends who were worried about how our relationship would reflect on them.

Over the next couple of years we became more comfortable as a couple and as members in the same sorority. It was great to be sorority sisters and in a relationship; we had the best of two worlds. With each new pledge class, we felt uncomfortable about our new sisters finding out, but we always found an opportune moment to tell them about our relationship. We didn't attend sorority date functions together for a long time, though. After 2½ years, we finally stopped bringing friends or brothers as dates and went as a couple.

Two springs ago one of our sisters gave us a wonderful gift. Stephanie had recently seen Beth, a friend she had grown up with. In high school they had grown apart, and Stephanie never understood why. "I wanted to thank you both," she told us. "You've made it possible for Beth and me to become friends again. In high school, she came out to herself as a lesbian. She knew I was homophobic and eventually pulled away from me and our friendship. Now, almost five years later, she finally came out to me and explained why she had deserted our friendship. But after knowing you, and knowing you as friends, sisters, and as a couple, I've realized you are wonderful people and have a wonderful relationship together." Meg and I cried. At Stephanie's wedding several months later, we met Beth and her girlfriend, and Stephanie told us that nothing would make her happier than to see us acting as couples at her reception…dancing and, well, being couples.

That all began over four years ago. The first spring formal Meg and I attended as dates was a huge step both for us and the sorority. We're now comfortable showing affection in front of our sisters. For a long time the subject of Meg and me was an issue once in a while, but now our relationship is seen as ordinary, just another couple in many respects.

Today, Meg and I are still together. I graduated in May 1998 and started a job in a new city. Meg finished school the following spring, and we're finally living our life together in the world. With our first mention of a commitment ceremony to be held sometime in the next year, our sisters reacted with more enthusiasm than we did. Although they probably don't realize it, each has been crucial in the acceptance of ourselves individually and as a couple. Our sisters stand by us, and within the Greek community at large our relationship is commonly known and accepted.

I've heard that some of the sorority alumnae are concerned that Lambda Chi Zeta will be known as a gay sorority, while others are happy to see a diverse sisterhood. Barbara, one of the sorority's most involved alumnae, recently told me that many of the alumnae were interested in hearing about our relationship and how the sorority reacted. I realize how lucky Meg and I are to be a part of such a supportive group, and I hope that more women will experience what we have.

Jonas told me long ago about *passive activism*. It was a new phrase to me at the time, but eventually I learned that I was a passive activist. I know Meg and I have touched a number of lives, and I never predicted such acceptance. Although we had some rough times, I would never change a moment. When I think back to that conversation about our adviser, I'm amazed at the changes I have seen. I'm reassured about moving through the rest of my life holding on to the experiences Meg and I had with this diverse group of women.

Unconditional Love
by "Marie Baker"

The feeling of community in my chapter deepens for me week by week. During one meeting, as we talked about upcoming boy/girl sorority events, my big sister reached over and squeezed my hand to let me know she was mentally adding "or girl/girl." As I went through the painful coming-out process with my family, I knew I had many sisters who knew and loved me the way I am.

I have known several things about myself for almost as long as I can remember. I had always known I was different from the other little girls. I couldn't pin down exactly why I felt that way, except that I didn't enjoy playing dress-up or playing with dolls. I always preferred skinned knees to makeup. And I knew I did not want to be in a sorority or any other "girly" club. Sororities were elitist, and they would make me wear dresses. Besides, what sorority would want me?

Twelve years later, in 1997, as a freshman at Princeton University, I reflected on some of these feelings as I waited in line outside a sorority rush party. OK, so some of my opinions had changed in the intervening time. I had learned to appreciate dresses and makeup, although I had continued to skin my knees. I had also long since figured out why I felt different from other girls my age: I was attracted to women. Even more bizarre in my eyes, I was also attracted to men, and realized I was bisexual. This was a realization that years before had caused me great anxiety, because I thought I was simply indecisive. By the time I entered college, however, I had fully accepted that I was never going to decide one way or the other, and I was fine with that. I also had resolved that I had to hide it from everyone at all costs. I had seen the discrimination and fear that people in my conservative high school suffered when they came out. In fact, I'm ashamed to say that even as I struggled with my own sexuality issues, I gossiped about those "gay people" myself.

Now, 600 miles away from my past, I was haunted by the fear of that happening to me. I determined never to act upon any of my same-sex attractions and instead concentrated only on being attracted to men, as are "normal" women. With those thoughts, I filed in to a room full of girls who I felt were waiting to judge me against those standards of normalcy.

You might wonder where my childhood resolution against sororities had gone. Actually, at this point the resolution was still firmly lodged in my mind. I didn't go through rush to join a sorority; I rushed to meet other girls and to enjoy being fawned over for four days before dropping out and leaving sororities way behind. The problem was, despite my intentions, I actually liked one of the sororities very much, a new sorority on campus that had not yet assumed a specific stereotype. The chapter attracted a lot of people who, like me, had never seen themselves in a sorority. Some of them were strong leaders who envisioned the direction in which the young sorority should go and wanted to be a part of creating chapter traditions. When I was offered a bid I accepted. Many of the members were not a lot like me, but that was one of the reasons I wanted to join. The bottom line was that I had fun during rush, and I had fun as a pledge. Later, I enjoyed being a full member even more, and soon I was entrenched in the Greek life I had sworn never to pursue. Meanwhile, I remained an interested but remote observer of lesbian, gay, bisexual, and transgender life on campus.

In my sophomore year, however, around November 1998, my life began to change. I was growing dissatisfied with the helpless feeling of being closeted. I felt a vague, nagging sensation that something was missing from my life. I realize now that it was not my lack of same-sex dates that bothered me; it was my deceit. I hated the feeling that each time I met someone new, no matter how close we got, I would never be able to reveal my identity out of my personal fear. My bisexuality was an aspect of my life that I was ashamed of, even though I knew I hadn't done anything wrong. I didn't want to live like that. I decided that it was time for me to come out.

One night while talking to a good friend who was openly bisexual, I took a deep breath and told her, "I understand what you're talking about.

I'm bisexual too." I don't think she realized there was anything special in my having said that. She didn't know she was the first person I had ever told. Although I was terrified, I was also thrilled. This was one of the bravest things I had ever done, but I knew even then that more difficult tasks were to come.

For several months I struggled through a series of little steps. More of my close friends found out, and with each person I told I got stronger. Lured by pumpkin pie (the one food I cannot resist) I went to my first LGBT meeting. Soon after, I kissed a girl for the first time, and we began to date. Bit by bit, I was coming out, and it was one of the most exciting periods of my life. The distinction must be made, however, between being out to other queer people and being out to the general population. The risks involved are decidedly different. I'd been living two connected but distinct lives. On one hand I had my girlfriend, the Pride Alliance, and the "a cappella" group I had joined which is, by self-proclamation, open to "all sexual orientations and gender identities." On the other hand, I had my family, my classes, and my sorority. In January 1999 the two halves collided. I had been dating my girlfriend a couple of months when our sorority announced our annual formal. I wanted to take my girlfriend to it. I remember thinking that my situation was unfair. For most members of the sorority, dating someone made the choice of whom to bring to the formal easy; for me, dating someone made it more complicated. It would've been easy for me to invite a male friend, but I didn't want to take the easy way out.

My feelings weren't the only thing fueling my fear; I also knew I had a strong responsibility to my chapter. Of course, I didn't want anyone to think less of me personally because I dated girls, but I was braced for it. And I didn't want to hurt the sorority in some way by coming out. It was unacceptable to me that some members might no longer want to be in the sorority or that new members might think twice about joining because of me. In the end I decided to trust that the women of my chapter, whom I had grown to love, would still love me after I told them. After a long discussion with my girlfriend to make sure she was game for it, we decided to go together. Along with my decision not to bring a boy, I decided not to pretend that my girlfriend was just a friend. I wanted people to know the truth. I didn't want them to think I was afraid, even though I was terrified of what they might say.

Periodically, a subset of sorority officers meet to discuss problems the sorority might have and to talk with members of the chapter if they have concerns or questions. I decided to express my fears to them and to make sure they knew the whole story and could answer questions if anyone approached them. I was nervous telling the entire group of officers, since most of my experiences had been one on one. I was also afraid that they'd tell me I couldn't bring my girlfriend. I forced myself to enter the room where they were meeting. Shaking all the while, I said, "I'm bringing a girl to the formal." I paused. "She's my girlfriend." I stiffened for a blow that never came. Most of them were surprised as my meaning sank in, but none appeared shocked. They had a few questions for me but reassured me that they weren't overly concerned about it and that I shouldn't be either. I left feeling wobbly but relieved.

The remaining days until the formal flew by in a mixture of school-work and preparations. There were, I admit, a few glitches. I had not anticipated, for example, having to argue with the florist to get her to give me a corsage instead of a boutonniere. Throughout it all, my roommates (who are also in my sorority and supported me throughout the process) and a handful of other people who knew helped whenever they could. Finally, having taken care of all the details, I was on the bus sitting next to my girlfriend on the long-awaited night.

I have to hand it to the people who design charter buses—they're an excellent way to encourage coming out on the way to a sorority formal. For one thing, the seats are in sets of two, so it was immediately clear that I was with a girl who was not in the sorority. Also, the seats are high enough to muffle conversation across rows, so that anyone who was interested could discuss it and get it out of their system on the way there. I got a couple of interested looks, but mostly people didn't stare. I'd advised those people who knew about my girlfriend to answer any questions freely and honestly, so I think they might have defused some of the curiosity during the hourlong ride to the formal. The formal itself was in some odd way almost anticlimactic, poised as I was for an affront. We ate and talked and danced like everyone else. Perhaps some people thought we were just friends, but that we could also be accepted as a couple was evidenced by the number of my sisters who approached me to talk during the evening. Many were curious, and some were taken aback, but they still asked questions, which meant much more to me than if they had ignored us for propriety's sake. A few thanked me for my bravery.

Of course, despite the overwhelmingly positive response of the chapter as a whole, there were isolated incidents of sorority members who were less able to accept me as a bisexual than as a straight woman. I will never be looked at the same by some of my sisters, whether or not they condone homosexuality. Every controversial issue is different when it hits close to home. One of my sisters actually refuses to accept it whenever I date a woman, and although she refrains from saying anything derogatory to me, she continually asks if I have a boyfriend, sometimes even in response to a statement on my part about a current girlfriend. In some ways I have become an example of what it means to be out in a sorority at a small, conservative, Ivy League school. It's sometimes lonely. I feel strongly, however, that there comes a time when you must grab on to what you believe in and hold on tight. If by making my life a little more complicated, I have also made it easier for others to come out in sororities here, then it's worth being that example.

Even when I feel the most isolated, however, I know I am loved by my friends, which has been an immense relief to me. Most of my sorority sisters and other friends have never let me wonder if they still care about me. When I have a bad day or a good day, my sisters are there to commiserate or to party with me. The main difference between now and before is that I don't have to suffer through sexuality issues by myself. The more people I come out to, the more people I have to cheer me up when I have a "bad sexuality day." In fact, although there are a few people to whom I will probably never be close because I'm bisexual, there are a good number to whom I feel even closer. Some of them might be able to relate to my situation. Others merely understand that by coming out I made myself vulnerable. The feeling of community in my chapter deepens for me week by week. During one meeting, as we talked about upcoming boy/girl sorority events, my big sister reached over and squeezed my hand to let me know she was mentally adding "or girl/girl." As I went through the painful coming-out process with my family, I knew I had many sisters who knew and loved me the way I am.

Coming out is an ongoing trial, and as more people find out, I'm thankful to my sorority for continuing to accept me; the process has been almost seamless. I'm thankful that the atmosphere of my chapter is one in which I feel safe to be myself and in which I know instinctively that the love of my sisters is unconditional.

Out and Proud

The one thing that doesn't abide majority rule is a person's conscience.
—Harper Lee, Chi Omega

In Pursuit of Ani DiFranco
by Lindsay Hey

*Lindsay Hey (left) and her
sorority sisters hanging out at
a fraternity party*

The alumnae in charge of Gamma Iota chapter could not understand why I needed to stand up and tell everyone about my girlfriend when "other girls don't stand up and read letters about their boyfriends." Because my sisters reacted so positively, however, I don't have to worry about alumnae or the national sorority breathing down my neck.

With a D, an E, an L, T, A, a G, A, M, M, A
That's Delta Gamma, that's what I am, ah!
With a D, an E, an L, T, A, a G, A, M, M, A
That's Delta Gamma, that's what I am, ah!
I'm Delta Gamm born and Delta Gamm bred
And when I die I'll be Delta Gamm dead!
So rah! rah! for DG! Rah! rah! for DG!
Rah! rah! for DG! Delta Gamm....
HOT DAMN DELTA GAMM!

I stood openmouthed, staring at the bouncing, screaming girls as a rushee my freshman year, 1997. My freshman experience kept getting stranger and stranger. Not only was I plucked from my home in sunny Los Angeles and plopped down in the middle of the Indiana countryside, but a huge group of girls was screaming at me from their front porch 50

feet away. I was adjusting slowly. But as soon as the 65 girls at the Delta
Gamma house finished chanting for me and the other 30 freshmen in my
rush group, our Rho Chi led us up the steps for an hour of smiling, nibbling, and answering—smiling just because you're positive that your face
is stuck that way; nibbling even though you're famished; answering questions about yourself, though you've forgotten who you are because you've
answered "How do you like school?" and "What's your major?" too many
times to count.

My problem was, however, that I could not have answered the questions truthfully. Even this early in my freshman year, I knew that being a
lesbian at my school was absolutely unacceptable. Gay students were not
safe there. All throughout my freshman year, I saw flyers posted saying
that two girls were raped in their dorm room because they were suspected of being lesbians. In the police blotter in the paper, I read a story about
a gay student who was beaten in the middle of the night while walking
through a dorm parking lot. Such incidents terrified me and kept me in
the farthest reaches of the closet, but there was not a secret deep enough
to keep me from joining a sorority. The thought of an "out" lesbian going
through rush, though, was absolutely ridiculous, so I remained closeted.
My university is 75% Greek with fewer than 1% out-of-the-closet queers,
which led to some mathematically intimidating numbers. This system
centered around heterosexism and undeniably left no room for queers.

On the other hand, I wasn't going through rush because I was pretending to be straight but because I wanted to live in a huge white house
with pillars. I wanted the T-shirts with the appliquéd letters. Most importantly, I wanted the friendships that I saw blossom out of the Greek houses. At this point in college, I already had discovered that sorority membership was synonymous with a shoulder to cry on, an ear to listen, and
a family to help me grow individually. During rush, I heard story after
story about what sisterhood meant to the Gamma Iota chapter of Delta
Gamma. The women in the house were not typical sorority girls.
Sisterhood meant staying home and ordering a pizza with someone who
was sick while everyone else went to party. The sorority encouraged me
to be as different as I needed in order to be myself. Sisterhood meant
appreciating the differences among the girls in the house, even if it meant
cheering on your sisters at a field hockey game when you know nothing
about field hockey. The sorority didn't want to change who I was; it
wanted to help me grow internally. That was the meaning of sisterhood

for the women of Delta Gamma. All of these ideas of sisterhood that I heard during rush coincided perfectly with my ideas of friendship, so I accepted a bid to join the chapter. That Sunday night, as I ran to the house to greet my new sisters, I was overcome by emotion…and still kept my secret.

As the weeks went by after I pledged, each day grew harder and harder. I wanted badly to tell my newfound sisters about my long-distance girlfriend, Elizabeth, whom I'd been dating for a year. Instead, when they asked why my phone bills were so high or who sent me packages once a month, I'd grin and bear it as I mumbled "my best friend" under my breath. She *was* my best friend, true, but she was also my lover and my life partner. I pretended to be interested during talks of fraternity boys and traditional marriages, until one day I'd finally had enough.

Two of my closest friends, one of whom was my sorority sister Eileen and I were traveling to Indianapolis for an Ani DiFranco concert when the subject of homosexuality came up. It seemed to appear in conversation more and more, and I felt as if I had to take advantage of this opportunity. Determined to uncloset myself right then and there, I turned off the music filling the car with comfort noise and announced my sexuality.

"I'm a lesbian!" I exclaimed in what seemed slow motion. To my amazement, the world did not stop turning because I had uttered these words. My friends asked me a few questions about my girlfriend, if I was planning on coming out, and what my parents thought. I survived the not-so-traumatic "inquisition," and the three of us continued on I-70 in pursuit of Ani DiFranco.

With this positive experience, I slowly came out to more of my close friends, including several of my sorority sisters. All were extremely accepting, which further boosted my confidence. Their biggest concern, however, was for my safety. My university has a history of antiqueer hate crimes, and my friends certainly didn't want me to become a victim.

My freshman year continued like this. I came out of the closet to many of my peers, answered their questions concerning my sexuality, and all was well. Although this situation of select openness was much healthier for me than being completely closeted, I knew I couldn't spend four years of life, the "best years of my life," worrying about who knew which truths concerning myself and my girlfriend.

After my freshman year, I returned to Los Angeles for the summer, extremely excited about moving into the sorority house in August. I had become close friends with several of the girls in my pledge class and grew more and more excited to become a true member of DG. My excitement, however, was tainted by a large dose of horror. I was out to only three girls in my house of 122. I planned to keep my fear, my girlfriend, and, most important, my sexuality, out of the Greek system. I wanted to keep up the facade that I was, in fact, just a typical sorority girl, wearing her lettered shirts from her informals, interested in fraternity boys, and living in a house with huge white columns.

But that was before I experienced living in a sorority house firsthand and realized that every waking and sleeping moment was spent with my sorority sisters. My opinion completely changed. As scary as it was, I made a vow to myself. No more lying. If people asked me if I had a boyfriend, I'd correct them and say I had a girlfriend. If people used the word "gay" in a derogatory way, I'd ask them to use a word that wasn't personally offensive.

One instance that sticks out in my mind occurred at a band party in the cellar of a fraternity house. A group of my sisters and I were dancing as the band played, and one of my close friends in the house, Sara, who didn't know about my sexuality, stood next to me. I had been nervous about coming out to Sara for a few reasons. First of all, Sara is an amazing person, and I was extremely afraid to lose her friendship and her sisterhood because of my sexuality. Also, I had always viewed her as a conservative person. She comes from a small town in Ohio that's not known for liberal politics. Similarly, Sara is a religious person; and earlier in my coming-out process, I had a terrible experience with one of my religious friends. And, I had always told Sara that she looked like my "best friend," Elizabeth, who is actually my girlfriend. I had no idea whether Sara would be uncomfortable with me when she discovered that I had been telling her for two years that she looked like my girlfriend's twin sister! All of these things made it difficult to come out finally to Sara, but I felt I had to or it might never happen.

The perfect opportunity arose. Between songs she leaned over and whispered, "Lindsay, you should go talk to the drummer. He is totally 'your type.' "

Tell her the truth, I told myself. I took a deep breath and held it until I uttered, "Sara, he would be if I weren't a lesbian."

She smiled, laughed introspectively, embarrassed at the heterosexual assumption, and continued dancing. I took a well-deserved sigh of relief.

As the first semester of my sophomore year passed, I continued to grow more and more courageous. I talked to anyone who would listen about my emotions, my worries, my sexuality, and my girlfriend. During this gradual self-acceptance, I came out to the president-elect of the sorority, Stephanie. When I told her I was a lesbian, she grew silent, muttered "OK," and seemed shocked. I wasn't sure what she was thinking until she approached me later that night. "Lindsay, I'm sorry if you thought that I was uncomfortable with what you told me earlier. I want you to know that if you decide to come out to the entire house, I'll completely support you."

When these words flowed from her mouth, it felt as if someone had pulled the plug and let the nervousness and fear drain out of me. Stephanie's words sparked a new concept in me. I'd never considered coming out to Delta Gamma until then. But with this, Stephanie encouraged me to undertake a "mission" of sorts with her help. Together we chose a date for my announcement to the chapter, a task that seemed almost impossible at the time. I later discovered that choosing *when* would be the easiest step. I had absolutely no idea *how* I was going to bring 122 girls, most of whom were from the "Bible Belt," into my most private affairs and, consequently, my bedroom. So I decided to write a letter and read it aloud to the chapter. Stephanie agreed that this would be the best way to handle the situation, and she helped me with all of the formalities. We decided that if our sorority truly believed in the ideas of sisterhood that we spoke so proudly of each year during rush, I'd have no problem coming out.

As the day grew closer, I latched on to several of the girls in the house for their support and comfort. One of these girls was Sara, the sister who'd found out about my sexuality in the fraternity basement. During the weeks between the night I came out to her and the night I read my letter to the entire chapter, Sara talked me through many nervous breakdowns and fits of hysteria. She had never been close friends with a gay or lesbian person before and admitted that she did not know exactly how to react when I told her at the party. She wished it had been an atmosphere in which I could have answered her questions and she could have answered mine. I told her that I had been so incredibly nervous about telling her and if I hadn't told her at the party, she still might not know.

My coming out brought me closer to all of my sisters, but this was especially true with Sara. During the weeks preceding the night when I read my letter to the sorority, Sara dragged me on walks, knocked on my door in the middle of the night to make sure I was holding up all right, and smiled at me across the dining room so that I'd know she was thinking of me. She truly exemplified the closeness and individuality that describes sisterhood in Delta Gamma.

All of this support and practice led up to the day when I had planned to read my letter, February 8, 1999. As the girls filed in to the chapter room, I could have cut the tension that surrounded me with a knife. With sweaty palms and chattering teeth, I stood as Stephanie announced, "Lindsay has something she'd like to share with the chapter." Deep breath. My voice shook as I read the first sentence of my letter.

I must have heard the word "diversity" 300 times during rush last year. Each house claimed that they had athletes, music students, studiers, and partiers. Yet, when I looked around at some of the houses, such diversity appeared to be hidden. For me, however, Delta Gamma was different. I could tell that the diversity existed here by simply talking to girls. I suppose that you could say that I have gradually been testing this diversity for the past year and a half. Today, I am going to challenge all of you to decide for yourselves how much you believe in the diversity of Delta Gamma. I am standing up in chapter tonight to tell you that I am a lesbian. I have been out to myself since my sophomore year in high school. I have had a girlfriend for over two years, and she is everything and more to me. But I am not standing up here to tell you who my girlfriend is but instead who I am. The truth is, with or without her, I would still be a lesbian.

So many people have asked me why I need to do this—to tell my most intimate thoughts and concerns to 122 girls with different backgrounds, different beliefs, and different concerns. I had never thought of this as a why or why not issue. For me, this is completely who I am. I have never asked myself why I should tell my sisters who I am. Instead, it has always been why shouldn't I share myself completely with them? But that is not the only reason for this. Every single person that I have shared this with so far has become much closer to me. By telling this to my sisters, I hope for so many things—open conversations, honesty, and, most important, closer friendships. I am completely in the closet at home…I can't talk about this with even my parents. I don't want to have that same walking-on-thin-ice feeling here in the [sorority] house and on campus. Also, I am trying to prevent the rumor mill from taking its vicious toll. The control is so important to me. I want to be the one to share each and every piece of information truthfully and at the same time prevent gossip.

I wish I could promise that I know what each and every one of you is thinking, but I can't. I can promise, however, that at least once in my life, I have felt the same confusion, denial, nervousness, and uncertainty about my life as you are feeling right now. I have had people that shun me and tell me that it is a phase. I have had people grow silent and completely unsure of what to say. Kim told me that I was brave. Sara has said that I am her encyclopedia into a world that she is working to understand. Krissy just smiled and let me know that I was all right. Emily held my hand as I sobbed because it just got so hard. But none of these people would have been able to understand unless they asked me questions. So please do not be afraid to talk to me about how I am feeling, how you are feeling, what I want, or what you want. There are so many girls in this house who have spent hours upon hours listening—talk to them. Ask me if there is someone close to you that you feel comfortable talking to who understands and has been able to swallow this. But please, if you can do one thing for me and for this house, remember the Lindsay that you know. I am not fighting, I am not a poster child for lesbians in sororities, and I don't want an army. Whatever you think of the life that I am leading, please remember that I am still Lindsay.

They clapped. I sat down, and they looked at me and clapped. I hadn't cried, I hadn't fainted, and I hadn't needed physical support. The girls knew how hard it had been, this road I had been tripping slowly down for a year and a half, and they clapped. After this outward show of support died down to a dull roar, I seemed to enter another world.

Sara and Roberta, two of the girls who had helped me since the beginning, stood with their guitars in hand. "Lindsay has shared an important part of herself with us tonight, and we want to play this to thank her for that." They played "The Wood Song" by the Indigo Girls, which starts with the lyrics "The thin horizon of the plan is almost clear. My friends and I have had a tough time." It had been a tough time; my life was almost clear, and I let it all out. I completely lost control and bawled through Sara and Roberta's song.

February 9, the day after, was almost as scary as the letter-reading session had been the night before. I had no idea whether the 2,200 people on campus had heard about my sexuality yet, but no one in my classes knew. Or if they had heard, they didn't care enough to give me a second glance. My appearance hadn't changed outwardly, but I felt my face had taken on a new glow and I had a new confidence in my step. My coming out gave me a brand-new sense of freedom, shedding a new light on the opportunities to make the queer community on campus more visible. I finally was able to get involved in the gay, lesbian, bisexual, and transgender group on campus. Amazingly enough, next semester I'll have a leadership position in the group. I have three antihomophobia buttons on my backpack; before I came out I was too afraid to put one on. My openly gay friends on campus visit the sorority house, and I don't have to worry about people second-guessing my sexuality. Everyone already knows.

The reaction to the letter was not all positive, however. The alumnae in charge of Gamma Iota chapter couldn't understand why I needed to stand up and tell everyone about my girlfriend when "other girls don't stand up and read letters about their boyfriends." Because my sisters reacted so positively, however, I don't have to worry about alumnae or the national sorority breathing down my neck. Thank goodness.

I'm presently the only openly gay member in the Greek system, which is shocking considering that 75% of my university is Greek. Perhaps some people are still in the closet because they had no example to follow. I was worried about how to come out, when to come out, and what to do if my house deserted me—maybe they are too. By allowing myself to be labeled as a lesbian in the Greek system, I open myself up to other closeted Greek members. If I can help one person avoid the heartache I went through, the positive aspects of coming out of the closet far outweigh the negative.

People constantly ask if being Greek was worth it, even though I knew I was a lesbian long before I came to college. This question is confusing to me. Are the lifelong friendships worth the year of secrets that I kept? Are the memories and photographs I have posted on my walls worth answering the questions my sisters ask about my sexuality? For me, these questions don't take more than a moment's thought. I know my four years spent as a Delta Gamma are nonrefundable and irreplaceable. Being a lesbian anywhere in this world is not easy, but the support and affection that I received from my sisters helped me from the second I accepted my bid card. My coming out has not come close to reforming the Greek system across the nation. In a 150-year-old international system, one girl is not going to put an end to the terrible traditions of homophobia and heterosexism. The Greek system at my university is no different.

My sorority is not my only activity or concentration on campus. But it is where I live, where the majority of my friends are, and where I'm able to completely be myself. A few people on campus still call me names, though. A group of guys on a fraternity porch yelled "go home, dyke." The difference, however, is that I now have 122 Delta Gammas right behind me, ready to run up to that porch and give the homophobic people of the world a piece of their mind. Delta Gamma has stood by me for the past two years. They have stood by the gay me, not the in-the-closet me, but the girl they all now know *is* me. They had no idea what they were going to experience that night as they screamed "Hot Damn Delta Gamm" out of the window. But maybe they have experienced just a small spoonful of diversity, which is exactly what Delta Gamma is all about.

It's Nice to Have a Dyke Around the House
by Erin A. Lawson

Erin A. Lawson's sorority sisters show their love and support for Erin at her coming-out party.

To this day I don't know how my sorority truly felt about having a lesbian in the house. But I think most of them genuinely appreciated the diversity and made an effort to be more inclusive.

"When you see a Kappa, wanna be a Kappa, wanna get to know KKG!" I like to joke that this catchy song phrase expresses the truth of why I joined my sorority—I saw a member and wanted to get to know her. I only wish it could have been that easy.

It was fall 1994, and I was 18 years old. And I faced one of the toughest decisions of my college career: to rush or not to rush. Imagine being at such a small school that anyone could rattle off at least three labels for anyone else in attendance, even without knowing the person's name. "You know her, I know you know her. She's a Kappa...jock...English major...hangs out with so-and-so?" You see, if the world has six degrees of separation, Whitman College has two degrees at most. And the first identity qualifier is inevitably "Greek" or "independent." As a freshman, I was rushed just as hard by the independents (persons who did not join a fraternity or sorority) as by the Greeks. The tactic of the independents seemed one of fear, implying that if I went Greek I'd be looked down upon by those strong enough to remain independent. Well, that struck me as ludicrous, because I couldn't imagine what I'd become dependent on if I did join the Greek system.

The self-righteous semantics of the independents offended me and caused me to look harder at their enemy. I attended the first Greek rush party with my friend Liddi, who identified herself as God on her name tag. We thought it would be a funny way to test the social etiquette of the high society femmes. Surprisingly, though, I met some women who didn't fit that stereotype. I met women like myself: women wearing scrubby clothes, irreverent women, women who could make me laugh until it hurt. So I began to perceive a sorority as a means to be involved with a community of women without the physical pain or athletic skill required of my previous experiences with groups of women. So, I talked myself into pledging a sorority.

That year I was a Kappa loner. I idolized the senior class and some of the juniors, but I was annoyed by those in my own pledge class. I sometimes wandered from frat party to frat party, completely invisible, watching women in my group become vain, pathetic, and annoying around boys. It infuriated me to see someone ditch her friend for a guy, and I cringed with each sip of my cheap frat beer. It was obvious that I didn't fit in.

During sophomore year my pledge class moved into Section, a corner of an H-shaped dorm on campus. Sororities at Whitman lived on campus in sections of dorms. By the end of that year, most of my closest friends were Kappas, and no one was more shocked by that realization than I. Living with them—Saka, Symons, Morton, Emo, Magill—forced the undercurrent of my pledge class I could love and respect—beautiful and talented women who constantly revealed new depths of personality. It was also at the end of my sophomore year that I discovered a new element of my own personality.

The night before my last final, I had not slept for more than two-hour bouts for a week due to shameless procrastination. It made sense to think a good night's rest would enable a productive cram session the next morning. Unfortunately, I was meant to realize more than REM sleep that night. After hours of agonizing, sleepless thrashing, I finally settled onto my back and opened my eyes in resignation and disgust. There near the ceiling hovered the words YOU ARE GAY. They appeared in green neon, so it was probably too expensive to use the phrase, YOU ARE LESBIAN. But this realization didn't come as a complete shock. I had finally admitted to myself that I thought my friend Jenny was more than just "a cool girl." But why could the "eureka" not have waited one more day? My thoughts fell out like a waterfall, and I was still in a panic when the sun rose: "Is it nature or nurture? How would I tell everyone? How would I find a girl-friend? Would I have kids?" Needless to say, I failed my exam the next day. And worse, the girl I had a crush on was in that class—not only looking nice, but acing the test.

I returned to my room that evening and sat on the floor in numbness until dinnertime. At food service I saw my love, her smile as big as the cup of Coke from which she was discreetly sipping rum. I couldn't even taste my food. When I returned to my room I was surprised to find Genie, my soccer buddy, waiting in my reading chair. I had hardly seen her all semester. Her timing was impeccable, because she was the only person in the world who could have pulled me out of my funk.

Whiskey-spiked Slurpees in hand, we walked around country roads for hours catching up on the semester. She quickly noticed Jenny's unfa-miliar name among my roster of friends. When prompted, I exploded with the confession: "I just met her this semester and I have such a crush on her." Genie was ecstatic to learn that I was finally dealing with what she had known about me for so long. As we chatted, I felt my isolation dissolve. I felt happy. We passed out that night in my room to the Indigo Girls playing so loudly they drowned out the sound of my concerned friends pounding on the door to make sure I was breathing. The night before, I had heard only chaos amidst the silence. This raucous night I heard not a sound. And when I awoke the next morning, Genie was still there beside me.

When I returned for my junior year, in fall 1996, I decided to come out to my sorority sisters. I took any opportunity I could to reveal my news. One night when one of my sisters was trying to teach me how to insert my contacts, I slipped into the closet when she wasn't looking.

She said, "Hey! Where'd you go? Are you in the closet?"

I popped out dramatically and said, "Not anymore!"

And there was the time I made Emo guess whom I was kissing. She would have named every boy at our school had I not interrupted her. Hell, if you can't have fun while you come out, what's the point? And in this vein I chose to out myself to Kappa Kappa Gamma my senior year.

The first chapter meeting of the 1997–98 school year coincided with the first day of classes. On that day every Kappa member received a surprise in her mailbox—a handful of rice wrapped in veil-like material and tied with a matching ribbon. The gossip was out of control. Every good Kappa knew someone would be getting pinned at chapter that night. Which lucky woman would receive her boyfriend's fraternity pin as a symbol of his undying commitment? And did the rice, as opposed to oatmeal, suggest the next level of commitment—engagement? Everyone had her theory of who the mystery couple would be.

After the normal course of business at the chapter meeting, the mass of bodies spread into a circle around the room. The candle was lit, the lights dimmed. I watched as the candle passed from woman to woman, anticipation lighting every face differently. The flame stopped to illuminate "accomplice number 1," who fought laughter as she read an ambiguous poem about the importance of creative expression. The candle passed to "accomplice number 2," who read a love poem lacking gender-specific pronouns. The candle was passed this way in an effort to tease suspects into blowing out the flame. One more accomplice read a poem, and suddenly the candle was in my hand. I was a textbook example of fight or flight, but there was no escape. I was the guest of honor. My grin was overly dramatic as I unfolded and read aloud a poem by Pat Parker titled "My Woman Ain't No Woman" which concludes, "My woman ain't no woman, but that's OK, 'cause I ain't no man." Then, "Poo!" I blew out the candle. Gasps. Minds reeled. "She just returned from Spain; she must have met a hot Spaniard and fallen in love!" So I laughed and rushed to quiet their straight thoughts. "No, no, it is not what you think! Actually, I wanted you all to know I'm a lesbian."

Silence.

Complete silence while thoughts were grinding to a halt and shifting direction.

Then, suddenly. Cheers. Claps. Hoots and hollers!

Once everyone had settled down, I attempted to launch into the spiel I'd prepared in my head for more than three months. Not only did I fail to recognize my own voice, but I also failed to remember any of the words I had prepared. Magill had been prepped with a series of questions to remind me of the highlights of my speech, but others beat her to the punch.

"We're so happy you felt comfortable enough to tell us!"

"Congratulations! Do you have a girlfriend?"

"Do your parents know? How did they react?"

Although I no longer recall my responses, I'm sure they were almost completely unintelligible, like "Uh huh. Thanks. No. Yes. Fine." And I probably answered Magill's more politically pointed questions with even less grace. I hope I at least threw in a few of the key *H* words, such as *homophobia* and *heterosexism*. Either way, by the time it was over, with a little help from my friends, I had at least made a point. I was a lesbian.

This story probably seems magical and unreal to many queer Greeks. Could a sorority be so accepting? Well, at Whitman it has to be. The first thing any Whitman Greek will tell you when confessing to being Greek is that "it's different at my school," and to an extent this is true. First of all, Greeks at Whitman seem to take Greek life in stride, with amused detachment in many cases. Whatever the extracurricular commitment, whether athletics or a sorority meeting, school comes first for everyone. Also, Whitman is such a homogenous culture that each Greek group is basically just a cross-section of the campus at large: athletes, musicians, thespians, academics, peer counselors, potheads, even queers. While the sororities would seem biased toward money and vanity, that's only because most groups are characterized by their most high-profile members, which often happen to be the beautiful and prissy rich girls. There are plenty of beautiful, prissy, and rich independents as well. What unites everyone at Whitman, regardless of social affiliation, is the influence of the greater "political correctness" of the campus. The peer pressure is almost the reverse of that of larger schools. Some Kappas did have a problem with my announcement and my identity as a lesbian. But for them to have expressed it would have meant being labeled closed-minded, ignorant, and homophobic. Given this atmosphere, consciousness-raising at Whitman is tough. How does a minority group fight for change and growth when it encounters no resistance? What can you do when you feel you're always preaching to the choir, because you can't determine who is lip-synching?

Another question I struggled with was whether I was hypocritical to remain a part of a heterosexist institution such as the Greek system. The thought had, in fact, occurred to me to deactivate. I simply could have declared that I had "gained a broader perspective" while abroad, as had many of my predecessors who could no longer find reason to be Greek. I saw my choices as either resigning from the group, only to complain about the Greek system to no functional end, or remaining in the group to use my insider position to create dialogue and raise issues. I chose the latter.

To this day, I don't know how my sorority truly felt about having a lesbian in the house. But I think most of them genuinely appreciated the diversity and made an effort to be more inclusive. After the mock pinning ceremony, my sorority sisters and I hosted a coming-out party. I sported my T-shirt that says IT'S NICE TO HAVE A DYKE AROUND THE HOUSE. The nicest gesture of the evening came from Bridget, who suggested we make my shirt into a Kappa shirt. She loved the pun on the word "house." In being so serious about her idea, she made it clear that she was proud to have a lesbian in her sorority.

Since graduating, I have been informed by many that Whitman is now teeming with baby lesbians. It was just my luck that Whitman went from having a queer dating puddle in my time to just one year later having a queer dating pool. I can only laugh. I have such a different perspective now, finally being surrounded by a lesbian community. Yet I try not to judge. As most "card-carrying dykes" will tell you, "it's all about process." So when it comes right down to it, there's not a lot I regret, not even being a Kappa.

Truth or Dare
by Kelly Steelman

Kelly Steelman (left) and her sorority sisters at a sisterhood flower-planting activity

Coming out to my sorority was definitely a positive experience. I spent nearly two years worrying what they would think, only to find that most of them already knew and didn't care.

In fall 1997, when I arrived at the Illinois Institute of Technology, I was determined to be straight. For the past year I had been questioning my sexuality, but I hadn't experimented, and I didn't want to be gay. I didn't want to disappoint my family or all of the other people who were proud of everything I had accomplished. I'd spent my high school years doing the "right" thing. I excelled in school, participated in several extracurriculars, and was the best daughter and sister I could be. After all, I had to set a good example for my five younger siblings. I felt trapped by the expectations of my family and conservative environment, but even more so by my personal expectations. While I was excited to finally leave home and be myself, I still couldn't bear the thought of being a lesbian. I thought that if I were more social and dressed a bit more femininely, I could feel straight and find a guy, any guy that I could be attracted to. After all, IIT was the perfect school for me to achieve this. There were three men for every woman; certainly there had to be one for me.

The first week of school coincided with rush. At that point in time

IIT had only one prominent sorority. That week I attended several activities with the sisters of Kappa Phi Delta. I had never considered joining a sorority, but the prospect of meeting people while attending parties, going on Mardi Gras boat cruises, and swimming at the beach appealed to me. During events, I spent a lot of time meeting the sisters but even more time observing them interact with one another. It wasn't until the last day of rush that I felt fully included. Before leaving for an event at the beach, I stood on a fraternity's deck watching the Kappas. Those with swimsuits were sitting in a hot tub, and two girls in shorts and T-shirts sat on the edge. One of them, Meg, noticed me watching them and dared me to go in. I was wearing jeans and a tank top and wasn't thrilled about hopping in fully clothed. All of the Kappas beckoned me to join them, and Meg promised to go in with her clothes on if I would. I couldn't resist, so I jumped right in. I then spent the rest of the day at the beach goofing off with the Kappas. The next day I was offered the opportunity to pledge, and I accepted. I liked the girls in the group; all were smart, and some of them were Girl Scouts, as I had been throughout high school. I felt as if I'd found a great organization of which to be a part.

I became very involved in Kappa as well as other student organizations. I made a ton of new friends and even met some guys who seemed interested in me. Out of all of them, Steve was the most persistent. I had danced with him at a party, and he invited me back to his frat house to watch movies with some of his friends. I innocently agreed, and we headed back to his place where we briefly joined a game of poker. After a few hands, we went into his room with his roommate and two others. Shortly into the movie the others left, leaving Steve and me sitting alone on his bed. The next thing I knew, he was on top of me shoving his tongue down my throat. I tried not to mind. He was a nice guy, and I thought maybe I could get used to this if I stayed long enough. Long enough ended about 10 minutes later when he undid the buckles on my overalls. In two seconds flat I was off the bed, rebuckled, and screaming "look at the time" as I ran out the door.

While having an eventful social life exhilarated me, I now knew something was wrong. I spent many nights chatting online with Hailey, a good friend of mine in Boston. She was a lesbian and the first and only person to whom I had confessed my internal struggle. She told me that no matter what I decided, in the end I'd be a stronger person for it. She always knew the right thing to say to make me feel that questioning my sexuality was not wrong.

By the middle of my first semester I still hadn't admitted I was gay, although I thought about it constantly. Deep down I knew I wasn't straight, but I couldn't admit anything to myself, let alone to any of the Kappas. I trusted them all, but I wasn't picking up many clues about how they would react if I shared my inner turmoil with them. I especially wanted to share my feelings with my big sister, Meg, but I was unsure of how she might react due to mixed messages in past conversations.

The first time Meg and I really talked, our conversation scared me to death. We were sitting in the BOG, our campus bar, and she was telling me about the guys she was usually attracted to. She told me she had a problem with always falling for gay men. She revealed her latest crush and asked me if I thought he was gay. I blurted that I could never really tell about those things and that my friends had always unjustly accused me of being gay. I was afraid she had figured out my secret, and I suddenly became defensive. She went on to confide in me about how several years back she was at a sleepover when she was awakened by her friend stroking between her legs. She moved her friend's hand and spent the rest of the night in the guest bedroom. The next morn-ing she confronted the girl, who apologized profusely and was adamant that she thought it was the cat. Only a couple of years later Meg discovered that "the cat woman" had come out and was facing issues as the pastor of a church. It was a rather funny story, but still I couldn't discern her opinion on homosexuality. Why did she tell me these stories the first time we seriously talked? Did she suspect I was gay? Was I that obvious?

Only one week after that conversation with Meg, I went to the room of one of my sisters to obtain her signature for a pledge project. As soon as I walked in I was immediately distracted by her roommate, Jess. She had half-naked pictures of Madonna on the wall and a ton of Indigo Girls CDs. I spent the entire time talking to Jess and totally ignoring the person I had come to see. Inadvertently, one of my sisters had just introduced me to my first girlfriend. Soon after, I began to spend every night sleeping on the beanbag in her room. Although it was obvious that we were a couple, Jess and I vowed to not tell anyone. She was in the Army ROTC program and worried about the repercussions. I, on the other hand, agonized over how everyone would react, especially my sisters. I was afraid I would never be initiated into Kappa if they had the slightest notion I was gay. Luckily for both of us, her roommate rarely stayed there and didn't seem aware that Jess and I were more than friends.

As my pledge semester wore on, I became more and more uneasy about how Kappa members would react if they found out about me. Close to Thanksgiving, one of my pledge sisters overheard another pledge, Gina, saying, "Kelly was really cool before she started hanging out with that obviously homosexual girl." About a week later I found out she had been telling some of the ROTC people that Jess was gay. I freaked out. At my next pledge meeting I almost cried, and I told them I couldn't believe they were spreading rumors about me and Jess. I pleaded with them to talk to me and not everyone else if they had problems or questions about my friendships. I was overcome with relief when my pledge sister Rebecca, who was also in ROTC, stood behind me and told everyone she was disappointed with their behavior. The rumors stopped soon after, or at least stopped getting back to me. I silently rejoiced when Gina depledged after being reprimanded by the active chapter for the way she treated me.

I frequently asked my big sister if I could be kicked out of Kappa for anything. One day in particular, while Meg was helping me study, I confided in her that I was worried about not being initiated into the sisterhood. When she asked why, I explained, "If the Kappas knew about certain aspects of my life, they might not accept me." I tried so hard to tell her I was gay without saying the words. Meg grew very serious, telling me I had nothing, absolutely nothing, to worry about. She assured me that the sisters liked me, and nothing I could say would change their opinion of me. All that mattered was my dedication to Kappa. I tried to convince myself that she had no clue what I was talking about, while she tried to convince me that she did. I attempted once again to explain myself. I told her I had a big issue that she didn't really understand. Meg looked me in the eyes and told me she did. I still wasn't convinced. I decided to test her, and I asked her to guess. She hesitated, and I saw she didn't want to guess specifics. Instead, she told me there was nothing I could not be accepted for. Meg reiterated, "We know you love Kappa and think you'd be a good sister. Nothing will ever change that."

After that conversation, I needed to tell Meg. I didn't want to hold back anything from my big sister, who had been so open with me from the beginning.

One evening I called her and asked her to come to Jess's room. She came, and after some prodding from Jess, I blurted that Jess and I were dating. Meg smiled and said she knew and was waiting for me to tell her. She immediately apologized for telling me about her lesbian, cat-stroking friend and hoped her story hadn't offended me. She had wanted to apologize since that conversation but had felt the time wasn't right. Meg assured me that Kappa would accept me for who I was and promised to support me, whether or not I came out to the entire sorority. I was impressed by Meg's unconditional friendship, but it wasn't enough to assure me I could tell the whole chapter. She said none of the sisters would mind if I was gay, but she swore not to tell a soul.

After talking to Meg I felt as if I should tell my pledge class, but I couldn't muster the courage to tell them as a group. Jess and I decided to tell Rebecca together. I had the feeling that Rebecca didn't approve of homosexuality, but I also believed we were close enough that it wouldn't matter. I knew she had some gay friends back home, so I figured she'd be receptive. Luckily, I was right. Rebecca didn't approve of being gay, but she didn't feel it was her place to judge. She guaranteed that it would not affect our friendship or our sisterhood, and she promised not to tell any of our other pledge sisters.

The next semester, despite my fears, I was initiated into Kappa Phi Delta sorority. While this was an exciting time, I had just returned from an emotionally draining Christmas break. I had come out to my parents, and even though they tried their best to be supportive, tension was definitely in the air. I had planned to move in with Jess that semester, but as I expected, my parents were less than thrilled. Nevertheless, I came back to IIT and moved in with her, which turned out to be a life-changing experience for me. Within weeks of moving in with me, Jess became extremely possessive. She envied the time I spent with Kappa and tried to prevent me from being with them. She constantly picked fights, and I became torn between my girlfriend and my sisters. I feared choosing Kappa, because I thought Jess would break up with me and I'd be left in a horrible roommate situation. I couldn't stand to let my parents be right. So I chose Jess and let my other relationships suffer.

I felt extremely guilty, missing Kappa events and abandoning my friendships. The separation from my life outside Jess overwhelmed me. Combined with the tension between my parents and me, I just stopped functioning. I spent much of that winter sick, and my grades suffered.

Worst of all, I didn't talk to anyone about it, because I didn't want them to be disappointed in me. As a result, I felt completely isolated.

One of the only Kappa activities I participated in that spring was our annual Jac Rose Formal. I planned to go alone since I didn't think I could bring Jess as my date, but the day before the formal several of my sisters encouraged me to bring Jess so I wouldn't have to sit alone. So we attended the formal together. I was feeling very sick that night. My back was in pain and wearing a dress didn't help. Aside from my physically discomfort, the night was fun. Jess and I even danced to a couple of songs. My sisters did everything in their power to make us feel comfortable that evening—even including Jess in the photos of sisters and their dates. A week later the Greek adviser, who was also at the formal, approached me and said that even though I wasn't out to the sorority, he thought it was wonderful that I brought a girl as my date. I was surprised that he knew I was a lesbian, but I found out later that after my big sister and I had talked, she went to him for advice on dealing with diversity within the sorority. He had evidently seen me and Jess on a date downtown and put two and two together. I felt relieved, knowing I wasn't being supported only by my big sister, but also by an administrator.

The semester finally ended, I went home to work at a summer camp, and Jess went home to Missouri. We kept in touch until halfway through the summer when I broke up with her. Although it seemed a spur-of-the-moment decision, her possessiveness had increased amazingly, and I could no longer handle the intensity of our relationship. Jess called several times a week and wrote every day all summer. For a while, it was nice knowing that she missed me, but she was constantly guilt-tripping me for my lack of communication. I wrote as often as I could, but I had other obligations that consumed my time. I had spent the summer trying to rebuild friendships that were destroyed when I started dating Jess. Then one day, during another guilt-ridden phone call, I snapped and broke off our relationship, and I didn't talk to her again until a few days before I went back to school. I received a phone message from Jess and, with a sinking feeling, realized that I was still assigned to be her roommate. I called her, and though it was a tense conversation, it seemed like our reunion might not be nearly as bad as I expected.

In fall 1998 I went back to IIT ready to jump into my academics and rush week with Kappa. Unfortunately, this didn't happen. I was unable to move out of my room with Jess due to housing complications, so I was thrown into an emotional hell. I spent the first night back at school completely in tears. There was no way I could attempt to rush girls feeling this way, so I wrote a letter to Kappa asking to be excused from the beginning of rush so that I could take care of some personal problems. I still wasn't ready to reveal the truth to Kappa. Two days later I wrote a letter asking to go inactive for the semester. I wanted to be able to live sanely with Jess, and I knew I'd have to put a lot of effort into mending our friendship. Kappa demanded a lot of my time, and I, once again, felt pressured from Jess to choose either her or the sorority. At that point, I felt taking time off from Kappa was my only option. My sisters were obviously concerned. Angela, one of the executive board members, called and asked if I could offer a more specific explanation as to why I was leaving Kappa for the semester. I went up to her room and broke down and told her everything. This was difficult for me, because Angela and I were not close at this point, and I was still worried about being out to my sisters. But Angela seemed genuinely concerned about me, so I answered her questions and tried to convince her that going inactive was the only way I could deal with the Jess situation. I gave her permission to tell the rest of the executive board, but only if she felt it was necessary. I secretly hoped she would keep it between just the two of us. To my knowledge, she did.

As the semester progressed, life with Jess took quite a toll on me. Every day after class I knew I was coming home to a potential fight or emotional breakdown. Jess was supposed to be on antidepressants, but she rarely took her medication. As a result, I woke up often in the middle of the night to her crying and asking me to stay awake with her. I gradually grew less and less sympathetic and more and more distant. As she saw me slipping away, her dramatic episodes grew more frequent and explosive. She lied constantly and even threatened suicide. As Jess grew more psychotic, I grew more depressed. My grades continued to drop, and I missed being a part of Kappa. I vowed to to get more involved as soon as spring semester began.

When I returned after Christmas break, I jumped back into Kappa. I was elected assistant pledge educator and sisterhood committee chair. I was excited to spend time away from my prison and more time with my sisters. One night in our room Jess yelled at me for coming back later than I had planned. This was a normal occurrence, but that night I'd had enough. I grabbed my bag, went down to the chapter room, and informed several of the Kappas that I was moving out of my dorm room. I had planned to sleep on one of the couches in the chapter room that night, but I was persuaded to go to Libby's apartment to talk with a few of the sisters.

I wasn't sure how much information I wanted to reveal, because of my recurring fear of outing myself. I ended up saying little, but I did tell them what was going on with Jess without actually telling them why. I told them about Jess screaming at me that evening and divulged stories of her lies and deranged behavior and how emotionally draining living with her had become. I never mentioned that we had at any point been anything but friends. Then one of them said, "Well, what do you expect? You're living with your ex." I was shocked by the statement, but even more shocked because the conversation went on like nothing out of the ordinary had been said. They continued to talk about how they could never live with their ex-boyfriends and wondered how I'd dealt with it for so long. They asked questions about my summer and why we broke up. Everything was extremely casual. We joked, we laughed, I got everything off my chest, and it all seemed normal. None of them cared that I was a lesbian.

Although six of my sisters now knew I was gay, more than half of the chapter was still in the dark. I was uncertain about the reactions of the others and wondered how to tell them all at once. In March, as part of the sisterhood committee, I planned a retreat at a camp in Wisconsin. One of our spring retreat traditions centered on each sister bringing a song describing her life, playing it, and telling everyone what it means to her. The previous year everyone except me had opened up and talked about personal things. I knew this would be the perfect time for me to come out to Kappa as a whole. I brought a song by Melissa Ferrick called "Everything I Need." After I played my song I explained to them that my life now seemed perfect. I had moved out of my room with Jess, and I was in love with my best friend, Hellen. A wave of relief washed over me. I finally had done it: I'd told all of my sisters I was gay. Libby, who was lying next to me on a sleeping bag, smiled and put her arm around me. I was shaking. As happy as I was that everything was now out in the open, I was worried that some of the younger Kappas would not accept my orientation. But Libby's smile assured me that everything would be fine, and I felt a thousand times better.

Later that night we all sat around a campfire and decided to play Truth or Dare. It turned into more of a question-and-answer period. The topic turned to crushes, and someone asked me who mine was. I was perplexed. I thought I had just told them who I was totally in love with. I repeated myself and told them about Hellen. Most of my sisters had met her before and knew we had been best friends since high school. One of the Kappas looked confused and asked if Hellen knew how I felt. I couldn't help laughing. I hoped Hellen knew, because we'd been dating for five months. My deepest secret was now in the open, and to my delight no one seemed to mind.

After the retreat I found a note in my mailbox from Libby that read, "I understand how hard it was to share everything with the chapter, and I'm really happy you did." Every bit of reassurance I received made me feel I had made the right decision about coming out to Kappa. When the 1999 Jac Rose formal rolled around, they even gave me an invitation for Hellen. As it turned out, she couldn't go, but I know without a doubt she would have been more than welcome there. I brought her to Kappa's Family/Friend Luncheon, and she often came to the Kappa room to watch movies with some of the chapter. I never felt any hesitation about holding her hand in their company. My sisters asked me about past girlfriends, and some of them joked about being lesbians. Two of them even tried to convince me that they were an interracial lesbian couple, which soon became a running joke. Kappa was becoming more than comfortable with my sexuality, and the executive board even added sexual orientation into the antidiscrimination clause of our bylaws. My big sister, Meg, continued to support me, even attending a Gay, Lesbian, Bisexual Student Association meeting with me.

Coming out to my sorority was definitely a positive experience. I spent nearly two years worrying what they would think, only to find that most of them already knew and didn't care. Not only did they not change the way they treated me socially, but they also treated me fairly in leadership roles. One thing I had feared was that I would never win an election in Kappa if I came out, but that spring I was elected president. I was excited to have the respect of enough Kappas to be voted onto the executive board, because this was the first time that they knew exactly whom they were voting for.

Diversity within Kappa is what has made the group so accepting. Although we're a small group, we have people of different races, cultures, religions, and sexual orientations. Their actions toward me and one another reflect what sisterhood is supposed to be all about. The Kappas are a magnificent group of women, and I'm proud to call them my sisters and my friends.

Out Greek Leader
by *"Sheryl Solomon"*

And so it came out, the flowers were from Anna, and we were dating. I didn't feel like lying to Sara. I'd thought I could trust her, and I expected her to act maturely. Clearly, I was wrong.

Before I entered college, I knew I wanted to be in a sorority. I don't consider myself a typical sorority girl, but the sisterhood and community included in the image of sorority life appealed to me. I'm from an upper-middle-class family and grew up in a New York City suburb. I attended a small high school and am now a student at a large northeastern university. I'm a sister of one of the several national sororities at my school and was recently elected president of our chapter for the 2000 calendar year. And I am bisexual.

During my first college semester, I attended a weekly discussion group for lesbian, bisexual, and questioning women. It wasn't until I came to school and began to go to these meetings that I met other women like myself. One woman with whom I became acquainted over the course of the term was Jessica; like me, she was a white, upper-middle-class Jew raised outside New York City. She had graduated from the university the previous May and was a few years older than I. During one conversation the group had about how to meet people at our large and sometimes impersonal school, Jessica said she had joined a sorority to make more friends. I'd been having a hard time finding people with whom I really clicked and was considering joining a sorority; Jessica's comment increased my interest.

I returned to school a week before second semester to participate in formal sorority rush. The temperature hovered around freezing, and the ground was covered in slush as I trekked around the campus with hundreds of other freshman girls. But by the end of the week I found a sorority in which I felt truly comfortable. Bid night arrived, and the house I wanted to join offered me a bid. The first person I saw when I walked in that night was Jessica, an alumna of the sorority. We smiled and hugged, and I knew I had made the right decision.

The following Friday night I went to a party at a fraternity with our pledge educator (the sister responsible for teaching new members about the history and sisterhood of our sorority), some sisters, and a few other pledges. I stood talking to someone when a woman who looked slightly familiar walked into view.

"Did you go last Thursday?" she asked.

"Did I go where?" I was a bit confused, and then I realized that the sexuality discussion group met on Thursday nights. She looked familiar because I had seen her at one of the meetings.

"Oh, OK. No, I didn't," I responded.

"I'm Danielle," the girl said. "I'm one of the sisters."

Within minutes, Danielle told me all I could have ever wanted to know about the sorority I had just joined. There were a few other bisexual sisters (besides her and Jessica) in the house and a few straight sisters who knew about their sexual orientation. She had even dated one of the sisters. But in general, everyone was discreet.

Danielle and I clicked from the moment we met. We have much in common and even look similar. I remember one time when we walked into a friend's apartment and my friend's roommate, whom I had never met, said, "Oh, look. It's Danielle…and a little Danielle."

There's one traditionally queer bar/club in the town where I go to school, and I went for the first time with Danielle and the two other bisexual sisters in the sorority, Liz and Anna. We were dancing when Danielle took me aside to talk.

"Dude, I'm not supposed to tell you this, but I really want you to be my little sister."

How could I say no to that? So I chose Danielle as my big sister, and she asked for me as her little. She's been a great big sister, and with me being an only child, she's the closest I have to a real sister.

I met many wonderful women and made some incredible friends when I joined the sorority. One such person is Anna, another bisexual sister in the house. When I first started spending time with Anna,

Danielle, and their friends, Anna didn't really like me (she later said she found me "tolerable"). But over the course of my pledging semester, we built a solid friendship, and as the academic year drew to a close, we became more than friends. From the beginning Anna and I had a hard time defining what we were to each other, in addition to being friends and sorority sisters. She wanted to keep our relationship a secret from our friends, but they quickly found out we were involved. Over the summer we saw each other a few times, including one weekend when we visited Marie, a friend of ours who was at school working in a lab. She's also Anna's little sister in the sorority. Danielle and Marie were probably the only friends who supported my relationship with Anna at that point, and their support helped me realize that Anna and I were a "good thing."

While most of my sorority sisters who know I am bisexual accept me and love me, I have encountered problems with one sister. Sara is a year older than I am, but we were in the same pledge class. She was the first person in the house I came out to, besides Danielle and our bisexual friends. Even though Sara comes from a conservative background, she seemed quite liberal and was supportive of my sexuality, at first. When Anna and I originally got together, Sara was the first person I told. I expected her to be supportive, as she had been in the past, because she knew how happy this made me. Unfortunately, this was not the case. Sara vehemently opposed the idea of Anna and me being involved, whether we were friends seeing each other or dating. She was worried about how such a relationship would look to other sisters and concerned about the possibility of it tainting our sorority's image on the campus. So before I went home for the summer, I told Sara that Anna and I were no longer involved (a lie), and had decided to just be friends. When we got back to school in the fall, I didn't mention my relationship with Anna to Sara at all.

A few weeks into the semester I hurt my foot, and Anna sent me a huge bouquet of flowers. They were delivered to our sorority house right before a sisterhood barbecue. A handful of sisters stood at the door when the delivery man walked from his truck holding a great display of flowers with my name on the card. I told everyone the flowers were from my parents (at first I thought they were), but a few days later Sara confronted me.

"So who sent you those flowers?" she asked.

"Oh, a secret admirer," I joked.

"Really?"

"No, I'm kidding."

"Were they from a certain person?"

"Who do you mean?" I said innocently.

"Did Anna send them to you?" Sara asked.

And so it came out, the flowers were from Anna, and we were dating. I didn't feel like lying to Sara. I'd thought I could trust her, and I expected her to act maturely. Clearly, I was wrong.

We held elections for our chapter's 2000 executive board the first weekend in October. I knew that a sizable portion of the sisterhood thought I'd make a good president, and I wanted to hold a position on the executive board. By this time in the semester, about 15 sisters—my closest friends in the house—knew I was bisexual, and most of them were aware that Anna and I were a couple. Sometime between January, when I pledged the house, and October, I stopped feeling paranoid about people finding out about my sexuality. Much of this was due to my relationship with Anna; I loved her too much to constantly worry what people thought of me. At the same time, I wasn't ready for the whole sisterhood to know I was bisexual. I was especially discreet about my relationship in the weeks prior to elections, and hoped my sexuality would not become public and be used against me in the electoral process. Despite my anxieties, elections went well. I was elected president for the 2000 calendar year, and nothing was mentioned about my sexual orientation during the process.

About an hour after elections had ended, I was talking to one of my close friends about the day. "Sara spread a rumor in the sorority saying that you're a lesbian," she told me.

Later that night another friend said that everyone had heard the rumors but that no one had told me because they didn't want to upset me. I could not stand up; I could barely breathe. I felt confused and alone and extremely angry. I ran up the stairs and knocked on the current president's door. We talked for more than an hour about the entire situation. She too had heard the rumor, but said it obviously didn't matter since more than 90% of the sisterhood had voted for me. I maintained that the principle of the situation bothered me; Sara's actions went against the concept of sisterhood and blatantly violated sorority policies. I sought justice, and wanted Sara to be disciplined for her unsisterly conduct. I walked out of that meeting confident she would get what she deserved.

A month later I got the chance to confront Sara with the truth: that in the weeks before elections she started a rumor that I was a lesbian, presumably to sabotage my chances to be elected president so she would get the position. I had a meeting with Sara, the current president, the current personnel chair responsible for enforcing sorority policies, and the personnel adviser, an alumna who advises the sisterhood on all matters, especially those concerning policy and rules. All of them had apparently heard the rumor, but my claims still fell on deaf ears. Sara cried and told them she hadn't said anything like that; she insisted she was concerned for me during elections, not about me potentially being president.

After much internal deliberation, I recently decided not to go after Sara and other sisters who, I felt, didn't act in my best interest or in the best interest of our sorority. I sent out an E-mail message to my close friends in the house alerting them to this decision:

It's been a long week; all of you have seen me with a pensive look on my face and have heard me talk about whether I am going to act on my convictions and go after justice or sit this round out and focus my energies on my upcoming presidency. Well, I choose the latter. As much as I think something needs to be done to address the behavior of certain sisters in our house, and as much as I feel discriminated against, I feel that I am not in a position to cause trouble in our chapter and with our national organization to see that justice is served. I believe that it will be more beneficial in the long run for me to concentrate on the future of this chapter—on our next executive board and on spring rush and on all of you, whom I love very much—as opposed to burning bridges behind me. So, thank you all for listening to me vent and giving me a hug when I needed it and for supporting me. I hope that I will not let you down as I work to build up this sorority, and I hope that somehow those girls will receive back what they have given to me and to our sisterhood.

This was quite possibly the hardest decision I have had to make in my 19 years. It upsets me that someone to whom I used to be especially close, one of my own sorority sisters, would use information about my private life—that I am bisexual—in a blatantly hurtful and selfish way. Sara is still out there campaigning for "biggest gossip," and she was never reprimanded for her behavior, but I feel I am being the better person in this situation by not fighting back and by moving on.

To the best of my knowledge, the rumors have died down. Although it's not discussed in my midst, most of the house knows that I'm bisexual and that Anna and I have been involved. While I believe in keeping my personal life private, the fact that much of the sisterhood knows about my sexuality has been a blessing in disguise. I feel much more open in the sorority house than I did at the beginning of the semester; it's easier to take a deep breath and relax, because I no longer have anything to hide. No one has said anything negative about my sexual orientation to my friends. If people are cowardly enough to talk about me behind my back, I'm not going to waste my time worrying about them.

Anna and I began to date officially when the fall semester started. I spent many hours at the apartment she shared with Danielle, Liz, and two other sisters, and our friends quickly grew to accept the relationship. Anna and I were involved for almost seven months and dated for three. We still care for each other and are still in each other's lives as friends, but our romantic relationship placed too much stress on our friendship for us to continue to be together.

My story is as yet unfinished. This semester has been one of tremendous growth. A sister whom I thought was a close friend betrayed my trust, my first relationship ended, and I found a great friend in the process. I was elected president of my sorority and will have the chapter's support when I'm installed next month. From this process I have learned I have amazing women as my sisters and friends. With their love and support, I will lead my sorority into the new millennium as someone proud of being both Greek and queer.

The True Test
by Sara Sperling

*Sara Sperling (left) with her soror-
ity sister Celia at bid initiation
night, 1991*

*I held his hand and we stepped out of the closet together. Every face
in the room turned and stared in curiosity, wanting to know what had
just happened. Could they tell from my face that I had just admitted I
was gay?*

My Farewell—Spring Quarter

For the first time in my life I'm nervous about speaking in front
of others. In about five minutes I'm going to stand in front of 140 of
my sorority sisters to give my senior farewell. We're all sitting in the
meeting room of our new sorority house. The walls and furniture are
silver and bordeaux, our sorority colors. Many women are giggling,
expecting me to get up and tell jokes about the Greek system or sing
songs and play my guitar, as I've done many times. Most of them are
expecting another stand-up comedy show, but this time I'm not
going to deliver jokes or announcements of mixers with fraternities.
I'm about to tell my Alpha Phi sisters I am a lesbian. With my palms
sweaty and my breathing short and rapid, I sit in the front row waiting for our chapter president to call me up. How did I get to this
point? Wasn't it just a couple of years ago that I was dating a nice
Beta guy?

Celia—Summer Break, 1989

As a freshman at the University of California, Irvine, I attended the summer orientation program and met some incredible people. One woman in particular, Celia, made a lifelong impact on me. Celia, a junior, was involved with many groups. She had a magnetic personality that radiated throughout every room she walked into. Everyone knew her and wanted to know her better. For some reason Celia took me into her circle of friends. We studied together for economics and hung out at fraternity parties and around campus. I admired her and wanted to get as involved in college life as she was.

Celia founded the Alpha Phi sorority at UC Irvine, and her pride and admiration for her sisters made me more interested in sorority life, but I didn't think any sorority would want me as a member. I was a tomboy, more interested in playing softball and "thumper," a popular drinking game, than decorating cute cups and photo albums with "puffy paints."

Rush—Summer Break, 1990

Despite my concerns about the Greek system, I decided to go through sorority rush. I spent each day at the Red Lion Inn in Costa Mesa wearing Ann Taylor clothing I had bought a week earlier with my mom at the mall, talking about my interests and what I wanted out of college. Since this was my second year of college, I knew there was some sort of process for the sororities to choose members. Were these women going to really know me after a week? I went through rush with the goal of meeting new women friends. I had spent most of high school hanging out with my boyfriend and our seven best friends, all boys. I was "just one of the guys" and had few female friends.

At the end of the week I met with my rush counselor in the hotel lobby to pick up my bid card. To my surprise, the card had the Alpha Phi emblem on it. After screaming "No way!" for about a minute, I rushed to the buses that would take me and my new sisters to meet the rest of the Alpha Phi house. I couldn't believe I was going to have a group of female friends. I was so excited that I got the whole bus to sing "We are Family" by Sister Sledge.

Pledge Class—Fall Quarter, 1990

At the beginning of sophomore year, I immediately got involved with sorority life. I was elected pledge class president and was already planning my speech for when I'd become sorority president in a couple of years. My pledge class consisted of 40 women of various ethnic, religious, and social backgrounds. The Gamma pledge class was unstoppable, and each woman had a special place in the pledge class. We won most of our intramural sporting events, took trips to Las Vegas together, made up funny songs for the sorority, and were always the life of the party. I rarely went to sorority events without my best friends in the pledge class, Emily and Colleen. Emily was dubbed my "evil twin." Whenever we were together we caused trouble, and we were usually the ones who started drinking games or were loud and cracking jokes all night. We even lived together in a house with three other women. Not a weekend went by that Emily and I were not out partying or sneaking into the casinos in Las Vegas. Colleen was the spirit of the group, always involved with sorority sports and the center of every fraternity party. Colleen knew everyone and made a point to say hi to them at every weekend social event. The three of us were quite a crazy team. Now that I had a group of close female friends, life could not have been any better.

Sorority Dance—Winter Quarter, 1991

My first formal Alpha Phi function was a dance at the Santa Ana train station in Orange County, Calif. I took Paul, a boy I'd met the previous summer. A comedian, he was always trying to make people laugh. We were the perfect pair. We danced most of the night away. Halfway through the evening, Celia showed up with her date, Megan. Was I the only one staring? Everyone knew Celia and Megan both had boyfriends, but this was the first time a sister had brought a woman to a formal function. They both looked absolutely beautiful, each of them in a dress and wearing very little makeup. They both seemed so happy to be there together. Throughout the evening it was clear they were having the best time out of all the girls there. They danced all night long. Not one person questioned Celia. She was straight. It was not an issue. Even though I was having a great time with Paul, I felt something that night I would always remember. Someday I wanted to bring a woman to a sorority formal and dance with her.

Life as an Alpha Phi—Fall Quarter, 1991

The next year I moved into a house with three of my sorority sisters on Balboa Island. "The Island," as we called it, was located 10 miles from campus and a ferry ride away from Newport Beach. Every house had a beach decor with large windows to let in the sun. There were only two ways of getting onto "The Island," by ferry or over the two-lane bridge. It was paradise, and we were all having a blast living there—parties on the weekends, Alpha Phi events during the week, and tons of boys coming to visit. Even though I was having a great time with my sorority sisters, the desire to date women stayed with me.

Ivan—Late Fall Quarter, 1991

UC Irvine hosted a student leadership conference for 100 student leaders in the desert. There I met my college soul mate, Ivan, the male equivalent of Celia. Ivan was an attractive guy, 5 foot 6 with sandy brown hair and a smile that could win anyone over. His lean body was strong from years of high school swimming. He was UC Irvine's "big man on campus" and a member of my brother's fraternity, Sigma Nu. We immediately hit it off, joking on the bus ride to the conference. For those around us on the bus, it seemed like we were flirting and on our way to "hooking up."

That evening several students threw a party in their room for those who wanted to drink the night away. At the party Ivan and I talked about the day's activities and workshops. Looking for a quieter place, we ended up alone in a smaller room discussing our passions and dreams. As the liquor warmed me up, my questions to Ivan became more risky. At one point I asked him if he would consider having a threesome, with one woman and one male. He said, "Sure." Without missing a beat I shot back, "What if the woman wasn't there?"

"What are you trying to ask me, Sara?" Ivan said defensively. Oh, boy, I was truly letting the alcohol take over. Then Ivan surprised us both by saying, "Yeah, sure, what about you? Would you ever be with just a woman?"

"Yes," I replied instantly.

For a couple of seconds we sat there and stared, realizing what we had just done. We had admitted our attraction to people of the same sex. I had never said it out loud to anyone, much less a stranger or someone in the Greek system.

"Hey what are you two doing in there?" someone outside our small room shouted. Out of nervousness and relief, we started laughing hysterically.

"Do you realize where we are right now?" Ivan asked. I looked around and saw some clothes hanging on a rack.

"The closet!" I shouted.

"Are you ready?" Ivan asked me.

To me it meant more than just going back to the party. He was asking if I was ready for my new life, for letting others know and love me for who I really was.

I said, "Absolutely. Let's go."

I held his hand and we stepped out of the closet together. Every face in the room turned and stared in curiosity, wanting to know what had just happened. Could they tell from my face that I had just admitted I was gay?

That night left me with one big question: How was I going to live a gay lifestyle and still be in a sorority?

Berkeley Bound—Spring Quarter, 1992

After several months of thinking about what I'd told Ivan, I decided it was time to leave Irvine for a while to explore my sexuality in the perfect place: the San Francisco Bay area. I applied to summer school at UC Berkeley. At the end of June, I packed my bags into my yellow Volvo and headed off in search of some answers to my constant questioning. As I got closer to Berkeley, my mind raced with the possible scenarios that could take place over the summer. I imagined all of the people I could meet and the places I could go without fear that someone might know me as Sara, the Alpha Phi.

My First Kiss—Summer Quarter in Berkeley, 1992

As soon as I arrived in Berkeley I found a lesbian, gay, and bisexual group that met on campus once a week to talk candidly about sexuality. Through this group, I became empowered to be honest and to explore my feelings. Away from Irvine I was able to be true to myself and admit my attraction to women. I felt as if I were given a new lease on life. Now it was time to try out this new lifestyle. I wanted to date and kiss as many women as I could.

Halfway through the summer my friend Shari, a Gamma Gamma Gamma from Irvine, called to see if she could visit. I knew that if Shari came to visit I'd want to tell her about my attraction to women and that I'd had a crush on her for about a year. This could change everything back home if she wasn't cool with it. But I took a chance and told her to come up north.

A week later Shari arrived. When she got out of her car she took my breath away; she was wearing a bandanna in her hair and a sleeveless shirt that showed off a daisy tattoo. I knew I was in trouble, because she'd probably be able to see how much I was attracted to her by the look on my face.

That night we went out for dinner with a bunch of my friends to a dingy restaurant on Telegraph Avenue. After dinner we went back to our dorm rooms and hung out, listening to the Steve Miller Band on the stereo. Shari wanted to sit outside on the low wall separating the dorms from the cafeteria and have a smoke. She caught me up on what was happening back home and what everyone was doing for the summer. Irvine and Alpha Phi seemed so far away, emotionally and physically. Then Shari asked me about Berkeley and whether I was dating anyone. My whole body got tense and my voice cracked. "I wanted to take some women's studies courses," I said. *Oh, man, this isn't what I wanted to say. OK, here I go…* "Shari, I'm gay, and I wanted to come up here and figure everything out."

Oh, shit, did I just say that? "I'm sorry. Are you uncomfortable?" I asked.

"No, not at all," she replied. Then Shari did something I'll always remember. She kissed me. Not the way I kiss my sorority sisters when I see them, but like I did with Paul. Everything I'd dreamed of. Her lips met mine, and we kissed softly at first and then the passion kicked in. Even though I'd kissed boys a million times, this felt like my first kiss. We started kissing faster, as if someone would tell us to stop what we were doing. Neither of us pulled away until we heard a voice in the distance wanting to know where we were.

"Sara, where are you?" my friend Noah yelled.

"I'll be right there," I shouted back.

"Was that OK to do?" I asked.

"Definitely," Shari assured me.

The rest of her visit was like a dream. We walked around Telegraph Avenue gazing at each other, oblivious to the hectic scene of students and foreign visitors around us. The time went fast, and her visit was soon over. She had to go back to Irvine, and I was left in Berkeley with my thoughts of her and questions about what I was going to do in September. At the airport we held hands under my coat, still insecure about what we were doing. "Final boarding call," the announcer said. I looked at Shari and told her I would miss her and wanted to be with her when I returned.

The rest of the summer raced by as I went to many gay and lesbian events in San Francisco and Berkeley, including book readings and concerts performed by gays and lesbians. Why could Irvine not be like Northern California and have more open-minded people? What the hell was my sorority going to say when I returned and they found out I'm a "dyke," a word I heard often in the sorority?

Two months later my brother, Mark, flew up to help me drive my car and belongings to Irvine. We talked about his summer and how much fun he had in Newport Beach surfing and hanging out with friends. He wanted to know about my summer, but I wasn't ready to let him know much. I felt newly comfortable with who I was, but I didn't want to lose my family. I dropped Mark off in Newport Beach, a cute town 10 minutes away from Irvine, then met up with some of my friends.

When I arrived in Irvine, I met Ivan, Shari, and a couple of my sorority sisters in one of their campus rooms. I felt like I couldn't breathe. I hadn't expected to see my whole world in one room so soon after my arrival. Shari was excited to see me and asked me to stay with her at her brother's house that night.

At the house with Shari, we discussed the upcoming year and what we were going to do about us. My senior year was about to start, which meant lots of sorority events and date functions. We admitted our intense attraction for each other and our desire to be together as girlfriends. I knew I had to take a chance on this one. My first girlfriend, Shari, was going to be a sorority girl. Could I have chosen a more complicated situation?

Rumors—Fall Quarter, 1992

Shari and I thought we were doing a good job of hiding our relationship, but it didn't take long for people to start talking. Many of my sorority sisters questioned our friendship and why I was spending so much time with a Gamma Gamma Gamma. My relationship with Shari didn't last much longer, but the gossip surrounding our friendship did. Throughout the rest of the academic year I learned that some of my sisters were trying to find out if I was gay by asking my close friends. They took it upon themselves to tell people I was gay before I was even comfortable with the word. The rumors were so frequent and sometimes hurtful that I decided after a year that I'd had enough.

Coming Out—Late Fall Quarter, 1993

After a year of dodging rumors, I recruited the help of my friend Neil, an active member of the lesbian, gay, bisexual, and transgender student group at UC Irvine, to come up with a plan to get people to stop talking about my relationships. After many late-night talks, Neil and I decided I should come out to the whole sorority at once, instead of one member at a time. This way the rumors wouldn't continue. I found myself slowly becoming disillusioned with my community of "sisters" and wanted to make sure the facts were told correctly.

Two months later I called my president to tell her I wanted to let the chapter know I was a lesbian. Our president was a dynamic woman named Michelle, who had been in the pledge class after me. It was interesting having a younger member as my chapter president and having to ask her permission to "come out" to the chapter. Michelle was nervous because no one in Alpha Phi had ever done something like this. "Why now?" she asked. I explained that I was upset by the labels and ridicule directed toward me, and I was stressed that many of my sisters thought they didn't know someone gay. I thought they would benefit from hearing my story and knowing some facts about homosexuality. Michelle asked if she could let me know in a couple of days after she talked it over with our adviser and district governor. After a week, Michelle gave me the go-ahead to tell my sisters, even though our district governor, who happened to be our previous adviser, didn't understand why I wanted to do this. The district governor told Michelle that if I was allowed to tell my story, then the sorority must make time for everyone who is different to tell her story. I wasn't sure if this was really what the district governor thought or if it was just an excuse to try to discourage me from telling my chapter. It was clear to me that the district governor did not support my decision, but luckily Michelle backed me up 100%. Michelle and I both decided it should be done in the spring when all the seniors were doing their farewells.

A Test of Sisterhood—Spring Quarter, 1994

"OK, everyone, Sperls is here to talk to you all," Michelle announced.

I said to myself, *Don't pass out. Just get out of your seat and get to the front of the room.* I looked at Neil, who sat in the front row giving me the thumbs-up sign.

"I asked Michelle if I could speak tonight so I could tell you all at once that Neil and I have something in common besides our good looks." The sisters started laughing. "We're both gay."

Boy, was it silent! I guessed I had better talk some more.

"As you all know, I've dated Betas and Thetas." Giggles erupted in the room. Oh, my gosh! I had just said "Theta," as in Kappa Alpha Theta, the sorority. "I didn't mean Thetas...oh, do any of you have any questions?" Well, that was smooth, Sperling. I hung my head not really knowing what to say. As I lifted my head to face my humiliation, I saw women raise their hands as they began their incredible journey of being one of the few national chapters to accept their gay sister. Questions began to flow:

"How did you know?"

"Was it hard for you to come to date functions with a guy and not bring a woman?"

And my favorite, "Do I still have your phone number so we can go out?"

This was amazing. I felt empowered. For the next hour I told more of my story and answered their questions. I felt overwhelmed with the same feelings I recalled when I first received my bid card saying I was an Alpha Phi. It had been so long since I'd felt the same closeness as on bid day when I rode the bus to meet my Alpha Phi family. At last, I felt a part of the sorority again.

The Food Chain
by E. Plemons

The sorority system was a frighteningly sobering pit of horrors in itself, but wasn't my involvement in the situation even more problematic? Since I wasn't just "another female" but also a dyke, I fell completely out of the Greek life food chain. I was on my own.

Looking back on the whole experience now, it seems surreal. None of my friends believe me, and I certainly can't blame them. "You were in a what? You?" "Are you kidding? You're kidding, right?" Of course, these responses come only from the few people to whom I've confessed my past Greek affiliation. Most of the time, it's a detail that I conveniently leave out of conversation. We all make mistakes in our youth, right? I've made it to the ripe old age of 22 without any signs of permanent damage from my sorority days. I'm sure I will be able to look back at the whole affair in a few years and laugh. Right?

I didn't go to DePauw University intending to rush. The images of Greek life that had come to mind before I'd ever set foot on DePauw's campus in Greencastle, Ind., were ones of blond-headed girls who cared more about dates and diets than their grades and cap-headed boys who knew more pickup lines and keg prices than you could count on both hands. I spent my first two years there trying to convince myself that my first impressions had been wrong and my last two years kicking myself after learning that I'd been right all along.

Upon arriving on campus I felt sure I wouldn't become a part of the Greek system. It was the '90s, after all. A time of individuality and personal space. The thought of "sorority" brought to mind images of languid Georgian women daintily sweating through southern belle gowns, fanning themselves while skillfully fending off advances from Billy and Hank, the dashing fraternity men. How could I be in a sorority? I didn't own a single pair of high heels or a dress, except for the cheap floral print skirt I was forced to buy and wear for my high school graduation. But the recruitment pamphlets were right; Greek life at DePauw was "different." It was different because everyone I'd met before rush was in a sorority. I mean everyone. Though it seems like a cliché, Greek life seemed the only option. And, because of the time-honored tradition of rushing early in the year, the sorority system snatched me up before I'd had a chance to formulate an opinion of what modern Greek life was really about.

So I rushed. But I didn't like it. The only women I talked to who were at all like me were my friends from the soccer team, who all happened to be in the same house. Of course, I later learned I had been targeted as a potential pledge, and it was well planned whom I would talk to at that house. (Did I feel misled? You bet.) They assured me that their house was different from the others, that they truly valued individuality, and that I would fit in there. I bought it again. I pledged Alpha Phi. All in all, I liked being in the sorority at first. One, two, three—instant social group. As pledges, we were always going to the house, meeting what appeared to be endless ranks of women whose names were nearly impossible to learn, since most of them looked, dressed, and spoke exactly alike. "Oh, my God! It's so great to finally meet you! We've heard so many awesome things about you!" I thought, *How strange. I've only been here for three weeks. I didn't realize anyone here knew anything awesome about me. And I know I haven't seen you before.* It seemed strange to me, this idea that because the women in my pledge class had all happened to choose the same house, we would become best friends overnight. My roommate from the dorms and several members of the soccer team were in my pledge class, so I was able to avoid the awkward, forced interaction that seemed to define the majority of our house events. As a freshman, I was relieved that the house provided things to do when there had been so little entertainment before, but I soon realized that those "things to do" were the problem.

Sorority life was by far the straightest thing I've ever done, seen, or been a part of. Straighter than your first junior high dance. Straighter than prom night—so I've been told. Every activity centered around fraternity boys. There could be no picnic, no party, no good time unless droves of them were present. As a closeted baby dyke who had just left a two-year high school relationship with an older woman, this change was jarring, to say the least. I really liked some of the women in the house, and I wanted to spend time around them and try to cultivate some friendships. Many of the women seemed bright and independent—that is, until the boys came around. I sat back and watched how completely the dynamic changed when a group of men entered the room. I did what any baby butch would do; I stuck my chin out, stopped smiling, and shook their hands, while the other women fell all over one another trying to be cute and funny, and obviously trying not to appear intellectually threatening. There was no more talk of sisterhood and friendship; instead there was talk of hooking up and formal dates. It wasn't long before their priorities were made crystal clear.

I suppose it's only fair to put Greek life at DePauw in its proper context. From the perspective of a student, the Greek system seems to be the singular force that controls your universe. It has a hand in every decision that is made, from social to political to personal. It defines your group of friends, affords you instant social status, and, depending on which house you're in, ranks you on the totem pole somewhere between "loser" and "cool kid." You see, at DePauw, Greek life is the only life. With roughly 80% of the student body affiliated with a Greek organization in some form or another, one can imagine that the overwhelming majority of campus resources and considerations go toward Greek affairs and are dominated by Greek interests. We even have (believe it or not) a university-sponsored "Go Greek Week," an entire week of events set aside to showcase the benefits of the Greek system and encourage new students to rush. The motivation of the university seems like a simple law of proportions—at least that's what Greek students and the university, which is dominated by Greek alumni money, like to tell themselves. If most of the student body is Greek, most of the time and money should go toward Greek-centered events. Most of the policies should create ways for the Greek system to thrive. It all seems to make sense, until you're part of the invisible and voiceless independent 20%.

As a result, a person entering the university as a promising young student, after being run through the wringer of social pressures and slender molds that define the Greek system, emerges as a well-manicured, fanatically overachieving, insecure sheep. DePauw is about desperate belonging. Maybe *clinging* is a better word. DePauw is about desperately clinging to some established group for fear that without group identification, there will be no way to define one's self at all. I admit that I buckled under that pressure, at first. And these women, my new "sisters," were living under that pressure every day and had lost the self-respect and the initiative to get themselves away from it. Seeds of doubt planted themselves in my brain.

During the summer after my freshman year, things turned around for me. With a little help and reassurance from some wonderful friends at home, I decided it was time I came out of the closet. It started, like most coming-out processes do, with coming out to a few close friends at home. I also wanted to come out to my close friends at school. DePauw is a lonely place to be queer; you don't have to ask a queer person to figure that out. There was also something appealing about coming out to a group of people so far removed from my life at home. I thought I could establish my life at school and think through some things before coming out to my parents.

So I came out to my Alpha Phi roommates the second day back on campus. Looking back on the whole thing now it seems so ridiculous. I think I showed them a picture of a woman I'd been dating back home and said, "This is my girlfriend." I wasn't quite ready to say, "I'm gay," out loud yet. Though I'd been in a long-term relationship with a woman with whom I'd been very much in love, I was still trying to escape from the whole "we were just really, really good friends" syndrome. The friends I told were wonderful, and I don't know how I would have made it in the sorority without them.

A few days later I came out to a senior whom I admired and who was also captain of the soccer team. I was concerned about how the team would react, and I needed her opinion on how to best handle this matter within the sorority. She consulted another friend in the house, and so on and so on, and soon all of Alpha Phi knew Plemons was a dyke.

Though it was sort of nice to sit back and let the rumor mill do all of my outing for me, I worried about the reaction within the house. Alpha Phi was a mixed bag of women. There were some totally progressive, cool people there, but there were also some hard-core, ultraconservative religious people. Let's face it: The sorority system isn't known for social liberalism. I was confident that I was well liked, but I wasn't prepared to deal with adverse reactions. I was afraid people would feel weird showering while I was in the bathroom or changing in front of me. Luckily, the hostility I knew existed was kept fairly well hidden and didn't impair my daily living. I learned that there is indeed some value in the learned facade most of the sorority members wore.

Slowly but surely, I found myself involved in several late-night question-and-answer sessions. I might be sitting on the front porch swings with a few girls and all of a sudden one of them would turn and ask, "Hey, Plemons, how do lesbians have sex?" or some other such question. People slowly came to me for information. Though many of their questions were intrusive and inappropriate, I answered them and was grateful for the asking.

While I know many of the women in Alpha Phi had had no prior personal contact with an openly queer person and my willingness to talk was enlightening to them, the process of self-declaration was valuable for me too. Through endless conversations and a newfound desire to read and learn everything I could about queer history and politics, I learned a lot about myself. I considered the response from the house to be positive, because I had nothing against which to compare it. Since my greatest fear was that I would be asked to deactivate and be shunned by all of my friends, anything short of that reaction seemed like bliss to me. I was setting myself up to be treated badly, because I didn't expect to be treated well.

Things changed a lot the spring semester of my sophomore year. At the beginning of the term I submitted a one-act monologue to the University Playwrights Festival. My piece was selected and performed with the help of two amazing women, and that performance constituted my outing to the entire campus. The piece, titled *Gunfight,* was my best attempt at what I would have said to the world if given the chance and a sturdy soapbox to stand on. It was full of politics and personal accounts, but what caught most people's attention were the detailed accounts of lesbian sex and intimacy. Most reactions were what I later learned to expect from people at DePauw. Those who approached me had nothing but praises, but there were many who lacked the courage to approach me with objections. At a school that small, I heard a lot of the trash talk secondhand. But despite the offhand criticism, I had thrown myself into the fire, and I felt invincible.

After *Gunfight* was produced, I gained the confidence to become involved with queer causes on campus. I had come out to my family during winter break, so I didn't feel there was anything keeping me from investing myself in queer activism. Shortly into spring term I joined United DePauw, our university's gay, lesbian, bisexual, transgender, straight, student, staff, and faculty alliance. Even though it has a really big name, it was a small group at that time. I was terrified to walk in the first time. I knew there were professors in the organization whom I admired, but the handful of students were people whom I had never before seen on campus. No one else—surprise, surprise—was Greek.

My initial reservations about being a part of the Greek system reemerged during that meeting. It became quite clear that many of the problems that queer students faced on campus could be traced either directly or indirectly to the Greek system and its peculiar manifestations at DePauw. It's impossible to have such an overwhelmingly heterosexist governing system and not alienate those who aren't heterosexual. In addition to the "you don't belong here" messages constantly being sent to queer students and any independent, there was a great deal of antiqueer violence perpetrated both within and outside of the fraternity and sorority system. This violence included everything from name-calling to rape—both men against women and men against men.

I remember sitting in that room and learning for the first time about the scared and marginalized queer community at DePauw. I was ashamed that I hadn't heard of these atrocious events before that day. I really never had any idea, as impossible as that sounds. I spent my evenings leisurely swinging on the porch of my sorority house feeling lucky that all of my new "sisters" still allowed me to use the common showers, and meanwhile, other queer students around campus were being assaulted or locking themselves in their dorm rooms out of fear of what their hall mates would do if they finally broke the door open. I felt like an asshole. I didn't tell the queer group I was an Alpha Phi. I didn't want to be identified as part of the problem when I desperately wanted to be part of the solution. Several weeks passed before I went to another United DePauw meeting.

Day-to-day life at Alpha Phi was getting harder for me—and anyone with a social conscience. As I was finding a larger picture in life, about the ways we treat one another and what is right and wrong, it was continuously demonstrated to me that the women I was living with saw little of what was happening around them. No one questioned the rules governing their lives. Instead, they slipped further and further into a system that was denying them choices and compromising them as individuals.

So I determined that the sorority system is, in essence, all about men. I liked to think of it as a high-priced, historically legitimized, intensely destructive dating service. Charming, heh? The sorority system was a frighteningly sobering pit of horrors in itself, but wasn't my involvement in the situation even more problematic? Since I wasn't just "another female" but also a dyke, I fell completely out of the Greek life food chain. I was on my own.

My feminist principles, coupled with the awkwardness and sheer physical disgust I felt upon setting foot in a fraternity house, changed my life at DePauw. I stopped going to fraternity parties, which for all intents and purposes meant that I stopped going out altogether. Suddenly, all of the women at Alpha Phi who had vowed to be my lifelong friends and love me for my differences began to disappear. They were my "sisters" until something better came along. Usually the "better" was in a baseball cap and a pair of overpriced khakis.

I didn't attend spring formal my sophomore year. Instead I stayed home with one other Phi who had also decided not to go. We sat together in the dining room. All the lights had been turned out, and there wasn't a soul left in the house. Needless to say, we felt very important. I'd decided that going to straight events with guy friends in order to play along and not upset anyone wasn't OK with me anymore. The decision was made: "I'm a dyke. I date women. If I don't have a female date, then I don't have a date, period, and I don't go to formal events." I was getting tired of putting my feelings on hold to ensure that the rest of the house would be comfortable with my queerness.

Many of the girls seemed to take great pride in there having been no confrontation surrounding my living in the house. As if just because no one screamed at me and called me sick it was the same as openhearted acceptance. They didn't notice the subtle, and sometimes not-so-subtle, messages that defined the boundaries of where my "lifestyle" should stop and my obligation to the "sisterhood" should begin. For example, I was allowed to comment on girls I found attractive, but wasn't allowed to add the tales of my sexual escapades to the collection of stories told around the breakfast table on Sunday mornings.

Near the end of sophomore year, life in the house took an unexpected turn. The entire house was off campus for our annual second-term informal. My three roommates and I had decided to go to the informal together, so none of us had dates to worry about. Everyone had been drinking pretty heavily, and we were all out on the dance floor. Out of nowhere a freshman pledge, whom I'll call Jane to protect her privacy, started dancing with me. Now when I say dancing, I mean really dancing. I was more than a bit surprised, but she was really sexy, and in that state of mind I saw no reason not to dance with her. Later my friends told me that several people stopped dancing and watched us, but at the time I wasn't considering the possible reactions of our "sisters."

Jane and I started spending a lot of time together. My roommates made fun of me because Jane, who was still living in the dorms at the time, spent so much time in our room. Everyone knew what was going on, despite what Jane would have liked to believe. I was Plemons, the big dyke as far as everyone in the house was concerned, so Jane didn't have to say much before everyone considered us together. A senior in the house even let us use her single room to sleep in one night, but Jane was nervous. She hadn't decided definitively whether she was queer, so she didn't want anyone to know what was going on between us. Luckily for her, school was out for the summer.

In my junior year, I returned to Greencastle with a flat-top and much less patience. I had spent the summer at home working with and hanging out with so many empowered young dykes who offered me the energy and intelligence I had been longing for at DePauw. I wasn't willing to be as quiet as I had been for the past two years. Overcrowding due to extremely successful rushes in the previous years caused me to live in the dorms, which was such a good thing for me. Thinking back, I really don't know how I would have survived that time if I had been living in Alpha Phi.

My politics were becoming more radical than they had been in the past, and I was frustrated with the way the sorority, an organization that was supposed to be about helping women succeed, was so obviously hypocritical and, in fact, acted to hinder women. The very rules that we were told were enforced to protect us were the ones that put us in the greatest danger. Women who wanted to be with their boyfriends for the evening were forced to leave the safety of the sorority house full of friends and walk to a fraternity full of men who saw them as trophies. Because no alcohol is allowed in sororities, women who wanted to drink had to do so in a male-dominated environment away from the safety of their female friends. I knew something was wrong. It was so clear to me, and I was furious that I was the only person out of more than 60 women to feel this way.

I went to the officeholders in the house to discuss some of my concerns. Remembering the awkwardness I'd felt as a freshman being pressured into extremely heterosexual situations (including kiss-ins and being forced to watch straight porn movies at a fraternity during a sorority event), I wanted to change some of our chapter practices to save other young women from similar situations. These women, who had championed the benefits of the leadership experience gained in the sorority, stared at me helplessly. The overwhelming response I received was that they could not change any of these things. "Oh Plemons, lighten up! It's tradition."

One woman, whom I considered a friend and who was a senior at that time, actually said to me, "Plemons, you're right. We know you're right. And if everyone was a gentleman like you we could change these things, but people just don't care as much as you do. The house would never agree. We can't do anything." I was furious. I began to doubt my association with such an irresponsible body.

Despite my growing frustrations with Alpha Phi, I remained involved with the sorority into the beginning of my junior year. Jane and I continued to date into the fall, and we went to our fall formal together, she in a gorgeous black dress and I in a tuxedo. Despite the opinions of the prevailing literature, I'm proudly all about butch/femme. While this affected my appearance at the formal and in daily life, it also affected my relationships with the women in the sorority. I was respected and seen as a caretaker by many of the sorority members. Big surprise for a butch dyke among girly-girls, heh? No one said a word to me about our attendance at the formal, but Jane felt the pressure of her friends' watchful eyes. I was so angry. This group of women whom I was supposed to call my "sisters" made my date feel guilty and self-conscious about being with me.

I was teetering near the edge. Jane had decided that the pressures of having a relationship at DePauw and in the sorority were too great, and we stopped seeing each other. The final straw came when in one weekend three different women in my house made sexual advances toward me. It was all casual. They just wanted to see what it would be like to make out with a girl. These women had claimed to be my friends, but were treating me like a science experiment. Again, I was furious.

In one weekend I lost the girl I had been dating and nearly all of my close friends. I wrote a letter announcing my deactivation and delivered it to the house at our chapter meeting the following Monday night. Of all of the people I honestly believed cared about me, only three people said anything to me about it. After my deactivation, not a single person from the house came by my dorm room to see me.

All of the hypocrisy of the system was opened like a split melon and laid out in front of me. I was angry that I had wasted so much time and effort on these people. I tried to better the system and ended up getting burned by it. It pained me to think of the hours I spent sitting in the dark during asinine chapter meetings, listening to petty and selfish rants, and giving my "honest" opinion of an endless array of outfits. All I had to show for my two years of involvement with Alpha Phi was a couple of ridiculous sweatshirts I had never worn and a lot of reasons to apologize to independent students for being a part of this hypocrisy.

After I left the Greek system, I became one of its most vocal critics on campus. I became the copresident of United DePauw and worked to improve the lives of queer students, staff, and faculty on campus. Our group challenged the status quo by implementing policies, bringing big-name queer speakers to campus, and opening a resource center for queer people and allies. I watched the Alpha Phis doing their ridiculous philanthropic activities and realized I was helping others while they were just fulfilling their obligation to appear to be helping others. I also made more amazing and wonderful friends as an independent than I ever would have made in the Greek system.

In some ways I'm glad I experienced the madness that is the Greek system. I learned some important lessons about people and interactions. Most of all, I learned what I don't want in my life. I don't need that structure and group validation. I don't want to surround myself with people who don't feel qualified to think for themselves or direct their own lives. I gain energy from action and initiative. My involvement in the sorority has better equipped me to dismantle racist, classist, homophobic, asshole ideas—like those that define the Greek system—in the future. And I am making it my business to do just that.

Sisterhood
by Krista Dunbar

As I looked at the women preparing to be initiated with me, I realized this was the first group I had ever belonged to in which sisterhood was unconditional. If someone didn't agree with how I dressed or what I thought, she was still my sister, not an adversary. It was almost too good to believe.

"This is so strange," I remarked to Devon and her girlfriend, Jessica. We stood in the piano lounge of Hershey Hall, the graduate student dormitory at the University of California, Los Angeles, early in October 1992. Through the long casement windows facing Hilgard Avenue, we had an excellent view of sorority row's weekly courting rituals. "Why do people join sororities?"

Devon replied, "We both belong to a sorority."

I looked at them skeptically. "You do?" I had known Devon and Jessica for a little more than a month. They worked in the hall's cafeteria and had "adopted" me as soon as they had confirmed I was a lesbian. I knew Devon played rugby with the university club team and Jessica liked to paint, but they had never mentioned the sorority to me.

"I'm president of Lambda Delta Lambda, the lesbian and bisexual sorority. Jessica's going to be pledge mom for the next class. Would you consider rushing?"

"I'm a grad student," I hedged. "I thought only undergrads did that sort of thing."

"Come to our meeting next week and see for yourself."

So I went. I told myself it was because I was still new to UCLA and wanted to make more friends, although when I arrived at the meeting, the six LDL actives were all people I had met before at Devon and Jessica's apartment. I was also curious. What I knew about sororities ran between stereotypes and nothing at all. In Canada, my homeland and where I took my undergraduate studies, Greek societies didn't play a large role in the social and academic lives of most university students. I had never once considered rushing—until now. I tried to go into that first meeting with an open mind, but underlying everything was the assumption that this was going to be like every other lesbian association I had joined over the years and the desperate hope that it would indeed be different.

Devon started by introducing the LDL council to the prospective rushees, all seven of us. There was Jessica, of course, then Sandy, the vice president, and her girlfriend, the treasurer. The secretary was Farrah, Devon and Jessica's roommate. Devon explained that they were attempting to revive the sorority; in the past year rush had been suspended, and no new pledges had been initiated.

In turn, the rushees introduced themselves. As I had feared, I was the only graduate student. I had expected, however, to be surrounded by freshmen. Most of the rushees were juniors and seniors with diverse majors, including Asian-American studies and film and TV production.

Devon told us, "We don't have our own house, but that means you don't have to pay dues you can't afford. Our brother frat is Delta Lambda Phi, and they're gay, so there's no pressure to date guys from there. We want progressive women who would like to experience sorority life without the negative aspects we all hear about."

Intrigued, but not necessarily convinced that this was going to be a unique moment in the pantheon of lesbian experience, I agreed to become a member of Kappa class. Our first pledge meeting was to be held at Devon and Jessica's apartment the next week.

Over the next month, that apartment became the sorority house we supposedly did not have. We would often assemble for take-out before the scheduled meeting times and stay late to watch movies. Several times I camped out on the couch along with other members of the pledge class. The history of Lambda Delta Lambda and its traditions were taught to us subtly, almost effortlessly. We learned that UCLA was the Alpha chapter of LDL, begun five years earlier as a coffee klatch of seven women that had then been incorporated as a sorority. We learned the founders' names, the chapter histories, the colors, and the handshake. Jessica, who was three years younger than I and younger even than most of the other pledges, acted like a mother in the truest sense of the word. When we remembered the teachings easily, we were rewarded with a smile. When something slipped our minds, we were encouraged to try again and usually were prompted along.

Devon and Jessica's apartment became a home to me, and I was desperately in need of one. I had just moved from Halifax, Nova Scotia, to Los Angeles to study Slavic linguistics and at the age of 22 was living far away from my family and close friends for the first time. I had gone to graduate school with the naïve assumption that it would be no harder than my undergraduate course of study had been, then had felt sandbagged by the weight of all of the expectations by the end of just my first week of classes.

If the apartment was home, then the fellow members of my pledge class were like family. We bickered as we wrote our class song, then felt satisfied when we finally reached a consensus. When Shari, the film and TV studies student, got an internship with Madonna's production company, we were all proud of her. Everyone groaned at my bad jokes and admired Vicki's freshly pierced nose.

Midway through the pledge process I realized Lambda Delta Lambda was more than just another lesbian organization. For one thing, one of the most active members was straight. Farrah had rushed with Devon and Jessica. I was curious about her reasons for choosing Lambda Delta Lambda over a more traditional house. Her response was straightforward. "Devon and Jess are my friends, so of course I wanted to go where they went," Farrah said. "But also, a more traditional sorority just isn't for me."

Over the pledge period the women in my class revealed themselves to be a diverse group. Vicki and her girlfriend, Helen, were rushing together. Shari and another woman considered themselves bisexual, with varying degrees of experience in relationships with other women. Another pledge was in the process of establishing her identity as a lesbian, and I had been out to my parents and friends since age 18 and felt I had a sound idea of who I was and where my life was headed.

What I noticed from the very first meeting was that there was no pressure to be a certain type of lesbian. Devon was a classic blond-haired, blue-eyed Southern Californian beauty who had been planning on rushing Delta Delta Delta, her mother's sorority, until she arrived at UCLA and found LDL. Jessica had come to Los Angeles from Oklahoma. Vicki was Latina, and Helen, Sandy, and her girlfriend were Asian-Americans.

Farrah's background was Middle Eastern. We were together as a purely social group with no more of a political agenda than to foster sisterhood.

That being said, LDL was not quite nirvana. The occasional thoughtless word did pass between us. My summer job had involved reenactments of 19th-century British military drills, since I was working at Halifax Citadel National Historic Site as a military animator. After four months of marching two miles every working day and standing sentry at the front gate for the equivalent of four full days, in October I still had what we could charitably call a military bearing (although my partner Kathleen refers to it in an entirely different way). Before one of our classes, a fellow pledge asked me what my job had entailed. I gave her an abbreviated demonstration of bayonet drill with an imaginary rifle. At its conclusion she said, "My God, you really are butch."

I never let her see how much her definition of me rankled. Until that moment I had thought I was just another color in the spectrum that was supposed to make up Lambda Delta Lambda's membership. I worried how I could feel sisterhood for someone who formed such a quick opinion of who I was. I worried that this was going to turn into yet another organization pulled apart by abstracts of the "ideal lesbian."

I had no reason to worry. When I told Jessica about the comment, she was appalled. "Look around. None of us conforms to an ideal. We have fat chicks, skinny chicks, Asians, and Latinas. Hell, we even have Farrah, who's not gay. Don't worry about so-and-so. I'll talk to her." That fellow pledge never again passed comment on my appearance in front of me.

Preparations for initiation intensified toward the end of October and into November. The actives wanted us to become full members before Christmas so that we could assume a wider role in the sorority. "There will be no hazing," Devon assured us the weekend before the initiation ceremony.

Instead, there were presents left behind by our big sisters during what other houses might have called Hell Week. We would not know who our big sisters were until the ceremony itself, so it became something of a game to see if we could catch them in the act of leaving their gifts at our apartments and dorm rooms. One day I came home from a particularly trying lecture and found a book tied to my doorknob, along with a small snack of chocolate. The timing was perfect; I ate the chocolate and lost myself in the story. By suppertime I felt refreshed and ready to resume studying.

As pledges, we had to observe certain traditions whenever we encountered an active on campus, but they were fun more than anything else. One tradition demanded that whenever a pledge met an active, she immediately had to give that active a piece of Dubble Bubble. Pledge training became crazy, as we tripped over one another in our haste to distribute gum. Finally Devon had to say, "No more Dubble Bubble! My cavities are getting cavities!"

Initiation night was remarkably clear and warm for November, the start of Los Angeles's rainy season. We were to meet at Devon and Jessica's, then were to be taken on our round of duties that made up the "test" part of the ceremony. The stereotype I knew of sororities had pledges running through heavily populated areas wearing only a bed sheet or a diaper or a similarly degrading article of "clothing." I was relieved to arrive at the apartment to find the other pledges dressed in white from head to foot. Jessica found a pair of white jogging pants for me and said, "These ought to fit." That was the end of my worries about parading through Westwood in a toga.

The test was intended to be fun and slightly embarrassing but certainly not humiliating. We performed three or four activities in West Hollywood, the gay area of greater Los Angeles, then went on a scavenger hunt through the actives' apartments. A few hours after initiation began, we returned to Devon and Jessica's place for the ceremony itself.

As we waited for the actives to change, we pledges sat on the couch and the floor in one huge huddle. Everything seemed hysterically funny because we were so nervous. One woman kept repeating, "That wasn't so bad," until it seemed like a mantra. I found it hilarious and had to cover my mouth with my hand to keep from disturbing the solemnity of the moment.

The actives emerged from the bedrooms dressed in black and carrying candles. I was surprised to see two alumnae in the crowd, not knowing that in most houses it's a tradition for them to attend initiation ceremonies. Jessica's demeanor killed the hysteria; as pledge mom she had to guide us through the ceremony, and she was determined to get us through without a glitch. Belatedly I realized that none of the actives had been paying lip service to the concept of sisterhood during the pledge period. They had meant it.

Without betraying the secrecy of the ceremony, I can tell you that it moved me in a way I hadn't expected. I had participated in gay and lesbian groups of all stripes as an undergraduate and had tried not to take sides during the polemics that always seemed to break out in the first meetings. For four years I had listened to the members of campus gay and lesbian group at Dalhousie argue about their agenda: Was this supposed to be a political group or a social group? One faction argued there could never be enough voices in the political arena. Another said there had to be a social outlet somewhere, and that this should be it. It was always agreed in the end that a compromise would be made and a balance struck between activism and socializing, but not before people quit the group over bruised feelings or disagreement with the direction we were taking.

This dynamic had carried over into every group I had belonged to. If you didn't believe in a certain set of principles and dress in a certain kind of way, then you weren't considered a true member of the group. As I looked at the women preparing to be initiated with me, I realized this was the first group I had ever belonged to in which sisterhood was unconditional. If someone didn't agree with how I dressed or what I thought, she was still my sister, not an adversary. It was almost too good to believe.

As I pledged my oath to Lambda Delta Lambda in a hesitant voice, prompted along by Jessica, I believed every word of it. Once we had passed through initiation, I expected the degree of closeness to diminish. We weren't spending the same amount of time together as we had during the pledge period, when we'd had classes and an activity at least once a week. While the bonds did ease slightly, we still had plenty to keep us occupied. Our charity for the winter quarter was the AIDS Rock-a-Thon. In the spring the pledges had to plan and execute the pledge-active party.

In late June I left to go home for the summer. Devon, Jessica, and Farrah came to my dorm room to see me off. They had chipped in and bought me a going-away present: a Pittsburgh Penguins T-shirt and hat and a copy of *Newsweek* to read on the plane. I expected to return in mid September to help them rush new candidates.

When I returned to L.A., everything had changed. Devon and Jessica had broken up, and Jessica had moved back to Oklahoma. Farrah and Devon had given up their place to take separate apartments in other areas of West L.A. Sandy and her girlfriend had also split up, with her ex moving to another university well away from the city. Shari had graduated, Rachel had transferred to the University of Southern California, and Alex, my big sister, had transferred as well, to California State University, Long Beach. Suddenly the core of actives we had counted on had diminished considerably. Much of the cohesiveness had also fled with the breakup of the two executive couples.

That year Devon made several stabs at getting Lambda Delta Lambda back together. She had a party in October with her new girlfriend and tried to spur interest in the sorority. But she needed help from the remaining actives. We lost touch with Farrah; my workload increased steadily that year as I prepared for my MA exams; and Vicki and Helen also split up that winter, both leaving UCLA. Reviving LDL was too much for Devon to do alone. I saw her less and less often as the year progressed. By the time I sat for my master's exams, any thoughts of Lambda Delta Lambda were buried under a pile of Old Church Slavonic verb conjugations and Serbo-Croatian adjectival endings.

I understand that Lambda Delta Lambda is currently active on only two campuses, UCLA and the University of California, Berkeley. While Delta Lambda Phi, the fraternity for gay and bisexual men, has grown every year, LDL has shrunk from an all-time high of 12 active chapters to its Alpha and Beta, the original two. Even trying to contact actives is an ordeal; Berkeley's listed E-mail address no longer works, and UCLA doesn't have a contact person for the chapter on its listing of active sororities. Why is there such a contrast between LDL and DLP?

All I can offer is speculation based on my experience both in LDL and the lesbian community at large. The first is that when I joined LDL, its feeling of sisterhood stemmed mainly from the fact that six of the 12 actives were in relationships with each other. When the couples split up, the emotional glue that bonded us dissolved. We all made new ties and pursued separate courses. Tied into this is that all of the pledges knew at least one of the actives before rushing. I knew Devon, Jessica, Farrah, and Alex. Helen and Vicki were friends with Sandy and Livia. Devon met Rachel in English class. Getting us to rush LDL was like preaching to the converted. There wasn't enough outreach to the UCLA community at large to prime any lasting source of prospective rushees.

Lambda Delta Lambda also had an uphill struggle against the sorority image. When I mentioned earlier that what I knew about sororities ran between stereotype and nothing at all, I can tell you exactly what I had in mind: beautiful blond girls without a single physical flaw, standing around the ballroom of a posh hotel in black cocktail dresses, sipping champagne while their equally gorgeous and flawless dates dote on every word. Many women who come out in college have a picture of sororities that may match mine in some or all of these points. Why would a lesbian want to join a society that even slightly suggests it perpetuates these stereotypes?

I firmly believe there is a place for sororities in the lesbian community. It now becomes a job for active lesbian members of any Greek society to help the community believe that. Sorority is not all about formals and Homecoming. Sorority is sisterhood, something that sometimes is missing during the battles over what makes the ideal lesbian. Sorority is about learning to live with people who differ from you, yet with whom you can laugh after you have had an all-day debate.

In fall 1993 LDL's sisterhood was drawn and quartered. The remaining actives lost heart and drifted away. Hopefully, another generation of UCLA students will pick up where we left off and rebuild the chapter. A sorority is the best way to learn sisterhood.

Rushing Out
by Leanna L. Heritage

Leanna L. Heritage and her
sorority sister Erin flash big
smiles at an Alpha Sigma party.

*"You do know that the Bible says it's a sin, don't you?" she asked me with
a concerned face. I looked at her in complete amazement. I was about to ask
her what Bible she had been reading, but I bit my tongue and smiled.*

The desire to belong has always motivated me to be involved in everything around me. I hated high school, but not because I was open about
my sexuality. No one disliked me or harassed me for being a lesbian. I
hated school because no matter how many things I was a part of, I still
didn't feel I belonged. I was a member of the National Honor Society,
captain of the soccer team, and an editor for the yearbook, and I still
wasn't happy. I was a part of the social elite, and I had friends everywhere.
People liked me and always have, but I've never felt a sense of belonging.
I was on top of the world by my senior year. I graduated with honors and
was ready to start my life over in college. I chose to head south for my
education and get away from everyone I knew. Missouri seemed like the
perfect place.

Let me start this adventure by describing the town in which Truman
State University is located. The first thing one will notice is its size. There
are only 17,000 people, yet there are more than 80 churches. Yes, I counted. "Huntin' season" is a really big deal. The stoplights are turned off at 6
P.M., and the biggest crime ever dealt with is theft. Right in the middle of

this sits the prestigious and beautiful campus of Truman State University. I loved the campus from the first day I visited and knew this was where I was destined to belong.

I had a great time my freshman year at school. I did everything I could, except rush a sorority. Becoming a member of the Greek community my first year at Truman, I felt, was not an option. Every invitation I received in the mail from the various sororities got a one-way ticket into the trash. Besides, I was involved in PRISM, Truman's gay, lesbian, bisexual, and straight alliance, and there had always been an unspoken hatred and tension between PRISM and the Greek community. I wanted to stay loyal to my fellow queers, but by the start of my sophomore year I was aching to experience Greek life.

"Tri Sigma because everyone else has!" my friends yelled when I told them I was interested in joining a sorority. Everyone was such a joker, but in a way, they were right. It had been a year since I'd come to Truman, and a lot of people knew I was involved in PRISM and was fairly open about my sexuality. I got the impression right away that if I was interested in joining a sorority, I had to keep it quiet around my PRISM friends. They frustrated me by telling me I wouldn't be welcomed in any sorority and that if I was accepted, I'd only be their sideshow attraction. Their resistance only made me more determined to go Greek.

Some of my friends on the rugby team were heavily involved in their sorority. I pleaded for them to let me come when they went to their various functions so I could meet more of their sisters.

"Leanna, we love you to death, but these girls won't be…uh…very accepting." This is all that they would tell me, but what they said wasn't quite the truth. I knew about half of the members of their sorority, and no one had a problem with me. At least, I couldn't tell if they did. I know they were just trying to be my friends, and they didn't want me to get hurt in the event I did not get a bid. I finally gave up the sorority pursuit, angry and frustrated.

Later that year, the same friend who discouraged me from joining her sorority handed me a flier for another. "Here," she bubbled. "I've heard nothing but good things about this service sorority, and I think you should check it out. The informational meeting is tonight, and we're all going. Come with us."

It was more of a demand than a request. I think she invited me only because she wanted to perk me up after my disappointment with her sorority. Joining a service sorority was not exactly what I had in mind, but it was only an informational meeting and it would give me an opportunity to hang out with my friends.

It was a damn cold January evening, and I was dressed more warmly than that little boy in *A Christmas Story*. My friends and I headed across campus for the meeting, and I didn't even remember the name of the organization we were going to. Since it was standing room only when my friends and I arrived, we opted for floor seats in the front.

The meeting started and dragged on for an hour, but I wasn't paying attention. I just kept looking around the room. Seeing all of these girls made me concerned for the first time since I began my quest for Greek status that maybe my PRISM friends were right. Maybe I didn't belong here and I would only be laughed at and criticized for my decision to rush. I struggled to hold the fear and doubt inside, but I was doing a fine job…and then came "The Game."

I had no idea this "Get to Know You Better" game was on the agenda. Maybe it was mentioned and I just didn't hear. Anyway, it was a simple game. Within the little pocket of people you were with, one was to take a small piece of paper and write on it something unusual about herself. The paper would then be placed in a pile, and everyone had to guess what characteristic belonged to what person. I was at a loss as to what to write, and I was holding up the game for my group.

"Just put down you're gay!" one friend hissed. So I did. It wasn't as if any one in that group didn't already know, so I just figured it would be an easy guess. No sooner had I finished writing "I'm gay" on my paper than someone walked by and collected all of the slips from our group. I panicked.

"What's going on?" I yelled.

"Oh," the girl who picked up the papers yelled back. "We thought it would be more fun and productive to do it as a whole group." I was ash white. "Don't worry, it'll be fun. Just stand when they read yours out loud."

"What?" I squeaked. My life in Alpha Sigma Gamma was officially over, and it hadn't even started. I was planning on approaching the executive board after the meeting and telling them privately about myself, but now everyone in the room would know in just a few minutes. I was so frightened I wanted to vomit.

"Just don't stand up." One of my friends whispered. Good idea. It was so painful to watch the pile of papers shrink as the president of the organization read them off.

"'I have a tattoo on my bum,'" she would read, and the room would erupt with laughter as a girl (or two) would stand up and introduce herself.

It was just like a sitcom. Before they had even read my note, I knew they'd chosen it. First the president gave the note a double take, and then she looked around the room. She turned to the vice president, standing next to her, to show her what was written. Her eyes lit up, and she looked around the room. Everyone waited patiently for her to read it off, curious with laughter about who was going to stand up next.

"'I'm gay.'" She read it off slowly and precisely to make sure she was saying it correctly. The room had fallen silent. I wasn't going to stand up, and I thought this was a horrible game. She was just about to toss the slip of paper to the side when she looked over in my group's direction on the floor. My "friends" were snorting and chuckling with amusement at the predicament I was in. I had been the only girl in the group not laughing, which tipped off the president to whom it might be.

"Is it you?" she asked. "Please stand up and introduce yourself." She was still smiling as I stood up. I turned around slowly to all of the girls, and everyone was staring at me. I felt like I was at an AA meeting.

"Hi, my name is Leanna, and I'm gay." No one made a sound. I was too frightened to move, standing like a deer in the headlights. But then something wonderful happened. Someone clapped, and then someone else joined in and then another and another until the entire room was clapping and smiling. I sat down, grinning from ear to ear, and I felt things weren't as bad as I had thought they were going to be.

Life began to zoom by at a million miles an hour after that meeting. I don't remember all of the details of my rush season, but I do know that I've never been as busy as I was that semester.

There were about 30 girls in my pledge class to start with. A few girls had quit a couple of weeks into rush season when the responsibilities of maintaining classes, interviews, and social lives collided. There were still a lot of girls participating when the elections for our pledge class officers came around. A friend of mine was kind enough to nominate me for treasurer, and I won the position. It was a great feeling to win, because it made me feel as though I no longer had to worry about my sexuality being a problem with anyone in my pledge class. Everything was great until I started to fall behind the quota we had to meet every week for active member interviews.

The interviews were to be very casual. We, as pledges, were to contact active members of Alpha Sigma Gamma and schedule a time to interview them for the purpose of getting to know them better. It seemed easy enough, but on top of everything else I had to do, those simple interviews became a huge hindrance. Sometimes the interviews would last hours and sometimes 10 minutes. Sometimes I forgot to meet someone for an interview, and sometimes the active didn't show up. Either way, I knew I had to start cutting back on my other activities if I was serious about continuing on with ASG.

My attendance at PRISM meetings and rugby practices began to decline until I stopped going to both of them altogether. It was hard to do, because as much as I wanted to participate in everything, I knew in my heart I could not. The rugby team didn't seem to mind, but a lot of my PRISM friends took real offense to my quitting PRISM to join a sorority. Some called me names like "lemming" and "conformist" and it hurt terribly, because it came from the group of people who had first accepted me on this campus for who I was. I forced myself to ignore them. I knew I was breaking free of the chains that had kept me from my dreams of belonging to a sorority.

Though rushing ASG was hard, I was starting to feel I belonged with them. Everyone was so happy that our pledge season was almost over, and I had worked hard to catch up on all of the interviews. All of the girls I had interviewed were friendly and genuinely excited to see me becoming a part of ASG. Only one person I interviewed made me so angry that I wanted to quit.

I met this active member after her class, and we sat down in the hallway to begin the interview. We went through the generic questions first, such as "Where's your hometown?" "What's your major?" and "What year are you in school?" Every question I asked had been answered in a friendly, relaxed manner. We finished with the interview, and I was just about to leave when she stopped me with a question.

"Are you really gay?" She was sincere as she smiled with curiosity.

"Yes, I am." I smiled back.

"You do know that the Bible says it's a sin, don't you?" she asked me with a concerned face. I looked at her in complete amazement. I was about to ask her what Bible she had been reading, but I bit my tongue and smiled.

"Really?" I asked. We were both standing, and though I towered over her by at least seven inches, she made me feel as though I were three feet tall.

"Yes, it does. Are you a Christian?"

"Well, yes, I am actually."

"And you didn't know this?" She was starting to make me mad, and I was fighting back tears. Yes, I am a Christian. I do believe in God, and here was my own sister doubting my beliefs and condemning my lifestyle.

"Well, truthfully, I don't believe I'm any more a sinner than anyone else," I replied. By the look on her face, one would have thought that I had just killed her dog. She edged closer to me, and her voice was stern with anger.

"Homosexuality is a sin in God's eyes. You may be a member of Alpha Sigma Gamma, but you're no sister of mine." With that final comment she turned and left me standing there, crying with frustration. I went back to my room and made the painful decision to discontinue rushing ASG. I cried the whole time as I wrote my speech about my depledging for the executive board. I went to bed early and was just about to fall asleep when my phone rang. It was one of the active members of ASG calling to ask if she could interview me. After much pleading, I reluctantly agreed to meet her at the library that night.

We met, exchanged pleasantries, and found a lost corner of the library where we could talk. We sat down, and she started her tape recorder. We must have talked for hours about our lives and the hardships that we dealt with daily. Somewhere during our conversation, I told her that I was quitting ASG.

"What!" she screamed. "You can't quit now—you're so close to finishing." I just smiled and told her about the horrible interview experience I had had earlier.

"You're going to quit because of that?"

"It really hurt my feelings, and if there's one person who feels this way about me, who's to say there aren't others?" She just looked at me shaking her head with disapproval.

"Leanna, the women of ASG need you. You bring us a new kind of diversity, and that's something that's been missing from this sorority. I broke the color barrier a few years ago when I rushed. Do you think everyone in ASG was overwhelmed with excitement about a black woman rushing?" I shook my head no. "There was resistance, but I still joined, and it was the smartest choice I could have made." She paused to let what she had said sink in. "You see, ASG needs you to save it from conforming like every other group on campus. ASG prides itself on diversity." She paused and smiled at me. "So finish your pledge season and make us a proud organization."

Those words of inspiration moved me to plow full force into finishing my pledge season, and I became an active member of Alpha Sigma Gamma on April 26, 1998. Becoming a member of ASG was one of the greatest moments in my life, but it would have meant more if all of my friends from PRISM supported me. The tension between the Greek community and the gay community had cost me my friends. I was so angry that I vowed that this nonsense would end before the start of the next semester.

PRISM had been petitioning the student senate for years to create a gay, lesbian, bisexual, and transgender resource center. But their efforts had been in vain because PRISM wasn't a strong enough organization to sway opinions and beliefs. I approached the executive board of ASG and asked if they would write a letter of support for the PRISM resource center. They thought it would be a great idea, but they had to present it to the active body to vote on. The letter of support was presented to the active body, voted on, and passed by a nearly unanimous vote. It was one of the happiest days of my life when I saw all of the hands rise in response to our president's question "All in favor?"

Alpha Sigma Gamma was one of the largest organizations on campus, and once it sent a letter of recommendation to the student senate, other organizations began to follow. It was like a domino effect. Alpha Phi Omega, our brother fraternity, sent its support, followed by other social sororities and fraternities. After years of fighting, PRISM won their campus resource center.

Things have settled down around campus, and I have slowly eased my way back into PRISM while maintaining my active status in ASG. I still miss a few PRISM meetings for ASG events, but everyone in PRISM seems to understand, and they still welcome me back when I'm able to come. I never paid much attention to what happened to the one active ASG member who was negative about my being openly gay. We avoided each other, and she eventually graduated.

Rushing a sorority is not for everyone, regardless of their sexuality. The idea of being in a sorority, as I have learned over my years of being active in ASG, is not to rock the boat but rather to become a fellow rowing mate for the benefit of reaching a common goal. It's about having a shoulder to cry on when relationships go bad or having an ear to listen to me when I need to vent about school. Above all else, though, I have learned that being in a sorority is about having friends whom I love unconditionally and whom I am proud to call my sisters.

Straight Sisters' Perspectives

A friend gathers all the pieces and gives them back in the right order.
—Toni Morrison, Alpha Kappa Alpha

Friend for Life
by Jessie Strauss

Jessie Strauss and sorority sister Cris Rivera at an Alpha Epsilon Phi pledge formal at Duke University, 1995

The lessons my friendship with Cris taught me proved invaluable this past autumn when one of the sisters in the chapter brought her girlfriend to the fall semiformal. When some of the sisters in the chapter started asking questions—"How would people act?" "What would people think?"—I was able to show them from my own experience just how easy tolerance and acceptance could be, especially for your sisters.

I came to college in fall 1994 with no thoughts of joining a sorority. I even chose the college I did—Duke University—over the other one I was considering, because the Greek system was too dominant at my other option, Washington and Lee University. I had visited Washington and Lee the spring of my senior year and had to keep myself from laughing out loud at the exploits and antics of my two hosts, freshmen who were both pledging sororities. When they left me with another visiting high school senior to attend a pledge party that was going to be held in a big open field, I knew without a doubt that Greek life was not for me. I would later be proved wrong.

I was born and raised in a picture-perfect suburb of Washington, D.C. In me, it produced a good student and a fairly good citizen who knew absolutely nothing about the way the world worked. I always knew I was sheltered, but I had no idea what I had never been exposed to until I left my hometown of 17 years and headed off to college. Granted, Duke University was not then, nor is it now, the great melting pot of universities, but my horizons needed a lot of broadening, and so any start was a good one.

Looking back from the outside, I realize that my four years at Duke were interesting for the gay and lesbian community on campus. Beginning as a low-profile, quasi-underground organization known as DGBLA (Duke Gay, Bisexual, and Lesbian Association) and a political nonentity my freshman year, the community put itself at the forefront of the campus scene during my sophomore year. It evolved by my senior year into a very vocal group called Gothic Queers. A friend from my freshman dorm, who came out to me at the end of our senior year, told me he wished that Duke had been as open-minded and accepting toward gays for all four of our years there as it had come to be by the time we left.

None of this, of course, had anything to do with me—nothing beyond what I'd read on the front page of the campus newspaper about the group, then known as DGBLA, fighting for recognition and acceptance in a campaign to allow same-sex marriages in the Duke Chapel. I saw the events in purely political terms and was interested in them as such, but my interest was mostly objective. As a straight person, these were issues that interested me but did not particularly involve me.

At first I wasn't involved in much of anything, to tell the truth. When I arrived at college my freshman year, I put off making any big commitments for a while—no boyfriend, no extracurriculars of any type. I was determined to take a small detour from the hectic life that I'd known in high school.

Without knowing it, though, I made one of the biggest decisions of my life that lazy fall semester, one that would forever change how I viewed myself, my friends, and the world around me. In November of my freshman year, my next-door neighbor and best friend convinced me to sign up for sorority rush. Well, she didn't really have to do much convincing. In spite of my earlier prejudices, the idea of sorority life had started to grow on me. At the end of rush, I considered myself lucky to have found a group of people I genuinely liked and wanted to get to know—and, imagine, they seemed to like me too.

I joined Alpha Epsilon Phi, knowing I was making a fairly big life decision but completely ignorant of the impact that my experience in the sorority would have on my life. It was a heady time for me, meeting new people left and right and changing my opinions and personality almost every second, whether or not I realized it at the time. For someone who had been as sheltered in their upbringing as I was, it was almost like information overload. I loved every second of it.

I cannot remember being in the sorority and not knowing Cris. I met her on my first day in the sorority, and we became fast and immediate friends. Cris was a fifth-year senior, and although we seemed a mismatched pair at first, we formed a bond that held like Super Glue throughout my first semester in the sorority. I looked up to Cris and saw her as everything I wished I could be—a little sister in a fraternity with friends of all kinds in every place we went and the type of personality that demanded everyone's attention when she entered a room. What's more, she could attract men like a magnet, a talent that had thus far eluded me.

Looking back on memories of freshman year and the semester I spent pledging the sorority, I cannot help seeing Cris everywhere. She was a mentor and a best friend, guiding me through the days when I started to experiment with men, with alcohol, and with my sense of self. No matter what stupid thing I did, Cris was always behind me to catch me when I fell. We were inseparable.

My freshman year passed too fast, and before I knew it, it was time for me to head back to my home in Maryland for what I knew would be an interminable summer. I stayed in the dorm almost until they kicked me out, spending my last few days almost exclusively with Cris. Unspoken between the two of us was the knowledge that things might never be the same as they had been that semester. Cris would be staying in Durham and would be there when I came back to school in the fall, but neither of us knew if our friendship would change with Cris out of school and me still a student. I didn't want to lose the wonderful friend I had found and bonded with in such a short time.

When I first arrived back at school in the fall, I was ready to pick up where I had left off. Cris was as much a part of my life as she had always been, and I started to spend almost all of my time with her and a few other sorority sisters. We were easy to entertain—put us in a room together and we would talk for hours. Throw in a few beers, and we would have conversations beyond my wildest dreams, intellectual and hypothetical and spiritual all wrapped up into one.

Cris always liked to get us started on "what if" conversations. I remember one evening at the beginning of my sophomore year when a group of four or five of us had one of our infamous late-night talks. "What would you do if someone in the chapter posed for *Playboy*?" Cris asked, spurred by a recent audition held on campus for the magazine's "Girls of the ACC" issue.

The response was varied. "What? Do you mean would we kick her out?" my friend Meredith asked.

"I don't know," said Susan, another sister. "I'd have an awfully hard time calling someone who did that my sister."

Robyn added, "I don't think it would give the sorority a very good image."

"Or maybe it would give us a great image," Meredith chimed in, and we all laughed.

I turned in with my two cents. "Plus, it's not considerate to do something like that to put your sisters in a situation to have to deal with. And besides, it is not like anyone forced her to do it."

We continued the discussion until we finally settled at an even stalemate on whether we would let the sister in question stay in our chapter. Cris's next question seems significant only in hindsight. "Well, what if you found out that one of your sisters was a lesbian? Would you let her stay in the chapter?"

The response was unanimous and fairly quick. "Well, sure," Robyn said.

"Why not?" I asked, the naïveté of my suburban upbringing showing its face once again.

"You don't think it would give the sorority a bad image?" Cris asked.

"Of course not," Meredith said.

We all agreed, and I added, "It's not like posing for *Playboy*, where you have a choice of whether to do it. You are who you are, right?"

I remember those two questions so distinctly because, posed together, they provided the moment where I got my first grasp on dealing with the issue of homosexuality and the mind-set that has remained with me to this day. Comparing the action of posing for a nudie magazine with the inherent sexual orientation of being a lesbian called to mind similar comparisons of apples and oranges—the two were on opposite ends of a very wide spectrum.

As my sophomore year went on, Cris and I slowly drifted apart as I had feared. A lot of the fault was mine. I had met a guy and fallen head over heels in love with him, or so I thought, losing a lot of my perspective on how important my friends were. By the end of sophomore year, Cris's role in my life had diminished more than I had ever wanted it to, yet I felt too ashamed of how I had neglected our friendship to try and make amends.

I had largely lost track of Cris when I got an E-mail message from her via our sorority mailing list in November of my junior year. The message, sent to active sisters as well as alumnae, started out by encouraging us to vote in the upcoming election. By the end of the message, Cris had come out.

Chris's E-mail message caught me so off-guard that I had to read it twice to believe what I was seeing. Of all my friends, Cris was the last I would have expected such a declaration from, but there it was. Meredith, who was my roommate at the time, wasn't surprised a bit. She had been close friends with Cris before I had met both of them, and she had known for quite some time that Cris was gay. I was surprised but tried not to show it. I didn't want to mention the E-mail message to other sisters, because I was afraid that they would think I was making a big deal of it, which I certainly didn't want to do, or be thought of as doing.

In retrospect, I reacted pretty badly to Cris's E-mail, although not as badly as I could have. I did nothing. I didn't congratulate Cris on the courage it must have taken for her to make such a declaration to the sorority, a group that was important to her and people whose opinions she valued, myself included. I didn't use the message as an impetus to reestablish the bond that had been so strong between us just a few months ago. I rationalized it all by saying I was busy dealing with problems of my own and that I just didn't have time to have dinner or coffee with her. What I wouldn't admit was that I just didn't want to deal with the issue. Or was it even an issue at all?

I found myself caught in a cycle of confusion and self-doubt. I wanted to call Cris, but I was afraid she would think I was calling only because she had come out, and then my old guilt about letting our friendship deteriorate surfaced again. Then again, I wasn't sure how I should act if we did get together. Should I mention the fact that she had come out or not mention it? And if I was to mention it, how? I had never really been exposed to people talking about gays and lesbians in a normal, nonoffensive way; even using the terms "gay" and "lesbian" used in normal conversation seemed a little unusual to me. Sinking in a quicksand of political correctness, I was unsure which terms I could and could not use, and I was almost afraid to talk to Cris out of fear that I would use the wrong ones.

I struggled with all of this for about a year, silly as that may seem. Maybe I just needed to do some growing up. I finally made a concerted effort to reestablish my friendship with Cris toward the end of my senior year. Once we finally got together, I realized how silly I had been to put this off. It finally dawned on me that Cris was still Cris, that picking up where we had left off was not going to be difficult just because she had come out in the time since we had been close. When we finally got together, I wasn't worried about what I would say or how I would say it. It was just like old times. Cris came to the initiation group in the spring of my senior year, and I couldn't help looking over at her during the ceremony and thinking how far we had both come since our initiation three years before.

Cris and I are both advisers for our chapter now. I'm glad the chapter has the benefit of her perspective, not just as a lesbian but also as someone who has been through the sorority and found out more than most people do about what sisterhood is really about. The lessons that my friendship with Cris taught me proved invaluable this past autumn when one of the sisters in the chapter brought her girlfriend to the fall semiformal. When some of the sisters in the chapter asked questions—"How would people act?" "What would people think?"—I was able to show them from my own experience just how easy tolerance and acceptance could be, especially for your sisters. I made a point to talk to nearly all of the sisters in the chapter to make sure they weren't apprehensive for one reason or another, and I'm happy to say that the semiformal's biggest obstacles were a few sore feet and a bad DJ.

I'm also glad I get a chance to see Cris more often than I did in years past. Since we both have different lives, different responsibilities, and different friends, we're not as tight as we once were, but every once in a while we run into each other in a bookstore or a bar, and it's just like old times. When Cris came into my life, somehow I knew ours was a friendship that would have a lasting effect on my personality and my life. Looking back, I can't tell you how glad I am that I was right.

Unnaturally Close
by Selene Jones

Selene Jones (left) and two sorority sisters pose for a group shot at a sorority event.

Even though Amber didn't live the life that I had envisioned, it didn't make her bad or evil. She has to run her own course and live her own way. By telling me she was a lesbian, she wasn't asking my permission or opinion. She was asking for what we all crave: unconditional love and understanding.

When I was growing up, I remember thinking, *Gee, I must be one of the most open-minded people in the world.* I now know that that naïve statement wasn't quite true although the fact that I grew up in a working-class, very ethnically diverse part of New York City's borough of Queens made it easy for me to think it was. Before I go any further, let me tell you how I came to be here.

I'm the youngest of three and the child of a divorced Southern couple. Though many of our ancestors have a variety of beginnings, we simply consider ourselves "Black" or African-American. As I was growing up, it was apparent that I wasn't anything like my older brother and sister. I was often one of a handful of African-American students in my classes and had friends from ethnic backgrounds that were different from mine. I committed the "sins" associated with being myself—all of the things that would not be traditionally associated with African-American women in the minds of my family. I challenged that. I played tennis, I liked rock music, and in my junior year in college, on November 26, 1996, at the ripe age of 20, I became a sister of Theta Phi Alpha, Alpha Epsilon chapter.

When it came to college choices, for many reasons, I stayed close to home. In fall 1994, I enrolled at St. John's University, also in Queens. It was still the home of "The Redmen," and the school enjoyed NCAA basketball notoriety. Of course, being a naïve freshman, I promptly went to rush as my orientation adviser suggested. At the time, there were eight sororities on campus, with only two being nationals. After receiving a bid from my first choice, a local sorority called Gamma Chi, I was promptly introduced to the world of hazing. I decided sisterhood wasn't worth that much pain, so I "dropped." After that, I threw myself into my schoolwork and held several jobs. It took me a while to recover from the severe hazing I had endured.

In my junior year, with the urging of a friend who worked with me on campus, I gained the courage to go through rush again. She reminded me that I was never one to let someone get the last word or "beat me." I couldn't let Gamma Chi win. I needed to go through rush again to make sure they weren't keeping me from a group of women worthy of being my sisters. This time I hit pay dirt; I found Theta Phi Alpha.

After initiation, I became a friend to many of the sisters, though not all. During pledging, I met Amber, who was already a sister, and soon realized we had a lot in common. She lived in another borough of New York, but we didn't live far from one another. We had hobbies in common, were emotional, and had a passion for ice cream. She was an older sister who had risen through the ranks of the chapter and would be graduating soon, with a degree in pharmacy. Everyone held her in high esteem. After she graduated, we kept in touch. I was floored that she even remembered to send me an invitation to her graduation party.

After graduation, Amber moved to Pennsylvania and decided to do some work for our organization on the national level. We madly sent E-mail messages to each other during her first year as a national officer, and I enjoyed her correspondence. I guess she enjoyed mine too, as she wrote back. During this time I realized she was one of my best friends. We talked about her trials in her new position and what was going on back in the chapter. I even tried to fix her up with one of my cute male coworkers through the Internet. During my remaining time in college, I became involved with many activities and also rose through the ranks of the chapter. Somehow, by default, I found myself vice president of the chapter. Though I was happy to graduate in May 1998, I was even more thrilled that Amber and I now shared two passions: Theta Phi Alpha and *still*...ice cream. With the same ease I had in becoming vice president, I stumbled into becoming a national officer.

In many ways, Amber was an important role model for me. With her, I had a closeness I had not had with my older sister. Amber filled that void.

In Pennsylvania she enrolled in a graduate program, and I enrolled in a graduate program at New York University in Manhattan. We spoke often both by phone and E-mail. We talked about the rigors of grad school and how we couldn't wait for it to be over. We also bounced ideas off of each other about Theta Phi Alpha and how we could improve it.

While in grad school, I became a sexual health advocate. I learned many mind-expanding facts, among them what it feels like to be in the sexual minority. I was one of a handful of straight people in the program, and learned to validate the feelings of others and put the issues associated with coming out into perspective: It is not about me, what I want or think; it is about the person and who he or she is. There I learned what could be going through a person's mind before and during the conversation in which they came out. That only made me ready to lend my support. I had no idea that the coping skills I learned would be put to use so quickly.

At our sorority's biannual convention in 1998 I noticed Amber's "unusual" friendship with another sister, Claudia, who was not from our chapter. I didn't know how they met, but I knew they seemed attached at the hip. As time wore on, I consciously acknowledged the nagging suspicions I had about her sexuality. Amber's "unnaturally close" relationship with Claudia was something I tried to ignore. It occurred to me that their closeness would not be "unnatural" if they, or at least Amber, were lesbian.

I debated and wrestled with myself for more than a year until one evening in October 1999. Amber was visiting from Pennsylvania and said she had something to tell me. I thought it was an odd announcement and immediately suspected the worst. We went to the living room of my mother's house to talk. As we sat across from each other, I felt the tension emanate from her, and I grew more anxious. I turned to humor in an attempt to break the spell. I would say things that I "knew" were not true. So I screamed, "You better not be prego! There's not enough space in your room for a baby and you and me when I visit!" It worked. She laughed, as did I. Then I exclaimed, "I'd be really angry if you got married. I can't afford this place on my own!" We continued to chuckle. My next instinct was to say, "You're gay? Yeah, no shit!" But I held back. Finally, I gave her the silence she needed to speak her truth. I heard the clock ticking as I waited patiently. She began slowly and shakily, "Well…Selene…I don't like men in that way…." That was it. As the words poured out slowly, time seemed to slow down. In mid sentence, I knew things between us would always be slightly different. At that moment, I felt many things, but above all, I wanted to scream, "I knew it!" Even though I was in shock, I was ecstatic that Amber came out to me. We continued to talk about her worries, her family, and finally her "unnaturally" close relationship with Claudia.

She confided in me her worries, her hopes, and that, in fact, she and Claudia were in a relationship. More shock! She was from a Catholic family, and her road ahead would not be smooth. Something within me reached out to her as she rejoiced in her relationship yet fretted about her parents' reaction. She also worried that her siblings would not take the news well, that she would lose those important bonds. She knew what she was and accepted it. She didn't seem upset by it, only worried about the reactions of others.

While Amber expressed her confusion and her fears about her siblings, I was still reeling from her coming out. She explained that there were a lot more aspects of her family that contributed to her fears, including an aunt whom some of her relatives did not speak to or mention. Her fears became real to me. At that moment, it didn't matter what I felt, only that I knew she needed me. She needed me to know her, to accept her, to be her friend, to love her, to be her sister.

She and I hugged after she finished talking about the ways she should prepare to deal with her family's reaction. As we hugged, I felt tears burn my eyes. I couldn't understand why, so I hid them as best I could. After our hug, I went back into my room and cried. Again, I couldn't understand why and, in fact, was frightened by it. Suddenly, I realized I was mourning the loss of plain, straight Amber, much like the process parents go through when they find out their child is gay. I, like parents, would have to let go of what I thought she was. Like parents, I had to let her life be about her—much easier said than done. I didn't know if I could do it. Could the closeness we had developed over the past three years withstand this "confession"? As I lay in my bed that night, I felt relieved to finally have my suspicions confirmed. It also explained Amber's last boyfriend, whom I found repulsive. Yet, I wrestled with some of the most rudimentary notions, which I thought I was above. I thought, *She doesn't look like a lesbian...Amber, a dyke?...my Amber?...How?*

The bigoted notions I thought I'd conquered returned. She and I were not as similar as I thought. I finally had a gay friend. Was I ready for it? Could I actually be a good friend *and* sister? Was I actually as "cool" as I thought? Who exactly was Amber? When other people find out, will they think I am a lesbian too? All of these questions and more swirled in my mind. They were all about me! How could I be her sister yet be so selfish? How could I be an ally while I was concerned about being identified as a lesbian too?

For the next few weeks I was almost afraid of Amber. She wasn't what I thought, and I felt betrayed. What alarmed me the most was my ambivalence. Amber was a lesbian, and that both scared and saddened me. But if I was a true friend and sister, how could I not be happy for her? Not only did she know who she was, but also she had someone she loved to share her life with. How could I begrudge her that? I didn't want to hurt Amber, and I wanted to accept her, so I was careful to hide my ambivalent feelings. I needed for this mourning of my "straight sister Amber" to be about my feelings and me, not a concern for her.

Soon after she told me, I learned I wasn't the first person she had told. In fact, she had told some of our friends from the chapter. She next told her parents, who were surprised, but actually took it well. Still, they're cautious about her revealing her sexual orientation to other relatives. The mourning I went through must be a small fraction of the anguish they are going through.

I found I had to be a lot like a parent of a teenager to get through this with my friendship with Amber intact. I had to realize that what I thought, believed, and wanted was not what Amber's life is about. Her life is about her and what she wants. A few short years earlier, she was my friend; later that developed into a sense of sisterhood. Even though Amber didn't live the life I had envisioned, it didn't make her bad or evil. She had to run her own course and live her own way. By telling me she was a lesbian, she wasn't asking my permission or opinion. She was asking for what we all crave: unconditional love and understanding. That's all you can offer a sister who chooses to come out to you—your love, your understanding, *yourself.* It is a time for truth, and that may come with a multitude of questions. Don't be afraid to ask questions that come to your mind or to even challenge assumptions. Her path to self-actualization will only be made easier if she knows she has your support. I truly believe sisterhood is based in the best parts of the human soul, the parts that are selfless and come from love.

It wasn't until Claudia came to visit, about two weeks after Amber came out to me, that I began to reconcile my inner demons with my outer demeanor. I'm now in touch with all of the feelings that rage within me. They still conflict every now and then, but now they don't interfere with the way I see Amber or Claudia.

I know there are more Ambers and Claudias who are Greek. If you have all of the building blocks of sisterhood, you can overcome the destructiveness of homophobia. It saddens me that some of those women have to hide. I wonder if my organization would support Amber if she were completely out. I'd like to think they would, but I know some sisters would have problems with it and feel uneasy. Some would unfairly judge her. This brings sadness and anger to my heart: sad that they are so closed-minded; angry that I cannot do much to control it. I hope that one day Amber will get all that she wants—love, happiness, and acceptance. I'd love to see her come to an event, completely out, and not feel as though she was on display or being whispered about. I want for her and Claudia what I would want for any couple. As an ally and sister, I must foster an environment that makes all the things I wish for Amber and Claudia a reality. My role also demands that I conquer my own fears. I still do that every day.

Now I watch Amber struggle. She's trying to be a new professional in her field; she's making a name for herself away from all that she grew up with; she's trying to remain "just a sister"; she's trying to be true to herself and to Claudia. The struggles she and I both face never cease. They certainly become easier and sometimes less important. She's struggling to live the life that her appearance dictates she should, and she's trying to be true to herself. I watch her deal with the reactions of her parents. And the fact that they will not allow her to tell her close relatives saddens her, and she often wonders if her parents are ashamed of her. It's easy to see the strain on her of keeping all of the "balls in the air." Sometimes when I think of her, I feel guilt and relief. I think to myself, *Thank goodness it isn't me!* Then I wonder what kind of friend could think such a thought.

I spend a lot of time deliberating the many ways I can become a better ally and sister. To me, the best way I can do that is to accept all that she is and is not; to realize I do not have to like the fact that Amber is gay, but I can support her pursuit of happiness.

Amber is still involved in the sorority and is now living with Claudia. We still talk and laugh about things old and new. I can say, with great pride and jubilance, that it will take a lot to destroy true sisterhood. Amber is still Amber. She is and always will be my sister. It has taken me a couple of months to fully realize that.

Conclusion
Listening to the Voices of Secret Sisters
by Shane L. Windmeyer and Pamela W. Freeman

"I hear you."

"I'm listening."

Sometimes listening to a different voice can be the most powerful way to learn about and experience another person's life. Hearing a different voice changes the perception, what story is being told, and how we believe.

Indeed, there are secret sisters in every Greek letter organization. For the first time, we hear from each story the individual echoes and the resonance of their collective voice: the questions, the struggles, the fear of rejection, the anger, the love, the sisterhood, and the need to listen.

Nancy Evans, in the introduction to this book, raises the question, "If lesbian and bisexual members are good for sororities, is sorority membership good for lesbian and bisexual women?" The voices of "secret sisters" allow us to recognize a different perspective on sisterhood.

All sororities extend the promise of sisterhood, as characterized by friendship, truthfulness, camaraderie, respect, shared values, and mutual support. Listening to the voices of lesbian and bisexual women, though, we discover that this meaning of sisterhood is not always a fulfilled promise. Emerging from what these voices are telling us are eight factors that can influence the development of sisterhood, either negatively or positively. We have attempted to identify these factors and to provide direction for the Greek system to reinvent itself. These factors, if not acknowledged and managed, can jeopardize the founding principles of sorority life.

1. High Value Placed on Relationships. Evans identifies "fear of disclosure resulting in rejection" as a significant influence on a lesbian or bisexual woman's decision to reveal her identity to her sisters. Most of the stories support the conclusion that this factor can discourage lesbian or bisexual women from building truthful relationships with sisters.

Of all of the factors to be discussed, this one is probably the least surprising. Studies suggest women typically place a high value on relationships.[1,2] With women often joining a sorority primarily to form close bonds with other women, a sorority sister can experience trauma when faced with either of the following prospects: (1) jeopardizing the bonds of sisterhood by revealing her sexual orientation; or (2) protecting the bonds by keeping her sexual orientation a secret, thereby being dishonest with her sisters. Both decisions can lead to rejection, either because of homophobia in the first case or dishonesty in the second.

Another conflict faced by lesbian and bisexual women in sororities occurs if they decide to participate in lesbian, gay, bisexual, transgender groups outside the sorority. Several women write about their feelings of hypocrisy when trying to maintain their sorority affiliation while developing friendships with members of the LGBT community. A strong perception among LGBT people is that Greek letter organizations practice exclusion and intolerance. Not all of the writers were able to resolve the dilemma inherent in being a sorority woman and a lesbian, and some of them felt rejected by one or both groups after their secrets were out. Rejection from either group was difficult to accept for women who valued highly their relationships and their need to belong, as do most women.

This factor also underscores the importance of what sisters may consider to be casual conversation. For a closeted sister struggling to protect relationships while trying to decide whether to be honest with her sisters about her sexual orientation, a seemingly innocuous comment about gays or lesbians can intensify her internal struggle and push her further into the closet. When faced with the prospect of destroying her relationships with parents, sisters, and the LGBT community, a lesbian sister may not know where to turn for help.

The high value placed by women on relationships leads to the conclusion that the fear of rejection so commonly felt by persons who have kept their sexual orientations unknown may be even more intense for lesbian or bisexual sorority women. Allies are especially necessary in sororities for this reason, and understanding among sisters about the intensity of a sister's fear of rejection because of her sexual orientation must be developed through educational efforts and leadership within the organization and from campus resources, such as advisers and LGBT resource centers.

2. *Governing System Based on Control.* Colleges and universities are founded on the value of the pursuit of knowledge. Sororities, to the contrary, appear to control the discovery of any information that their leaders fear may damage their desired image. For example, through the National Panhellenic Conference's "Unanimous Agreements," which all member organizations are required to follow, members are forbidden to respond to questionnaires without prior approval of the NPC Research Committee.[3] In our effort to understand what women were telling us about their national organizations, NPC members were invited to answer questions about their antidiscrimination policies. Only two organizations responded. One responded that no information could be given without prior approval from the NPC Research Committee. The second response conveyed an unwillingness to cooperate. At least one sorority issued an edict that forbade all members from contributing stories to this anthology without approval from national or international officers. We speculate that such an edict would never have been issued if members had been invited to submit stories outlining their academic accomplishments or their philanthropic endeavors.

Is it not homophobic to fear what might be learned about sororities if members talk about their sexual orientations? Clearly, sororities on the national or international level tend to control their image rather than challenge it when it comes to sexual orientation. When we began work on this book, a colleague shared that a member of the NPC Research Committee had warned him to remove a question dealing with sexual orientation on a survey if he wanted to facilitate the approval process.

The pressures against learning about sexual orientation issues in sororities is also evident in member organizations of the National Pan-Hellenic Council and among other multicultural organizations. An example of this reluctance to speak about sexual orientation was articulated on the Lambda 10 Web site bulletin board, where a member posted:

"It has occurred to me that within the African-American community many of us tend to be closeted; therefore, it is not surprising that those of us in Black fraternities and sororities (and non-Black Greek organizations too) are not out about our sexual orientation. Many times it is because of fear or

*not enough support. So I wanted to voice myself to let you know that I'm
here if you need support. DST til [sic] the day I die!"*

We tried persistently and in vain to attract contributors from these
organizations, leading to at least a suggestion that the sisters in these
organizations are not comfortable openly discussing sexual orientation
as related to their chapters.

In the absence of a free flow of information, how are local chapters
expected to learn about issues facing their organizations? Control of
research and responding to questionnaires, judgmental responses to
unpopular ideas, and a near absence of educational efforts to increase
understanding about sexual orientation hinder learning about the issue
of homophobia in sororities. As a consequence, members often are ill
prepared to respond appropriately when they learn a member is lesbian
or bisexual.

Numerous stories in this anthology refer to the constraints placed on
their sisters by alumnae, national or international officers, and advisers.
To their credit, sisters in some of the chapters offered their support to
"secret sisters" even though this placed them at odds with their national
or international leaders. Currently, more than in past decades, some
women are emerging as leaders in denouncing homophobia in the Greek
system and are challenging the exclusionary tactics that have been prac-
ticed when it is learned that a sister is a lesbian or bisexual. In spite of the
tight control that works against a sister's coming-out process, acceptance,
and celebration of diversity, stories show that there are chapters with
strong women with the courage to stand by their sisters in the true spirit of their vows. More sisters are needed to challenge the tight bonds of
control and to replace them with strong bonds of sisterhood.

3. Religion as a Basis for Sorority Ritual. Members of sororities must
somehow resolve differences between what they have been taught about
homosexuality, ostensibly on the basis of religion, and their vows of life-
time support for their sisters. Such religious foundations for ritual can
perpetuate homophobia in organizations. Sometimes these foundations
may be used by those members wishing to exclude lesbians and bisexuals as license to discriminate against them. Accordingly, women who may
be questioning their sexual orientation, or who know they are lesbian or
bisexual, may suffer in an atmosphere of intolerance, causing them to
remain closeted.

Religion, then, affects lesbians and bisexual women in sororities in more than one way. The importance of religious doctrine in sorority ritual condones secrecy and promotes traditional Christian beliefs. The second way has to do with the individual beliefs of sisters, including those who have been raised to believe that anything other than a heterosexual orientation is sinful. For a woman who values highly her affiliation with the sorority and the relationships she has built with sisters, the effect of religious teachings that condemn same-sex relationships can be devastating.

4. *Social Expectations Leading to Unsafe Domains for Women.* A theme found in stories from each section of this book is that women both voluntarily and involuntarily participated in social activities in which unsafe conditions existed for them. Excessive use of alcohol, arranged dates based on an assumption of heterosexuality, and attempts to hide attempted sexual assault are cited as unsafe and unhealthy realities of the social scene in Greek letter organizations. The assumption that all sisters date men is extremely strong, and there is an expectation that physical attractiveness, as determined by narrowly defined criteria, is necessary for acceptability. Going against the grain of social acceptability in sororities can be extremely taxing, especially when a sister adds concerns about her sexual identity to the mix. A setting in which social expectations create unsafe conditions for all women does nothing to support lesbian or bisexual women who are struggling with uncertainty about how well they will be accepted if their sexual orientation becomes known among their sisters. In fact, such settings can hinder a woman's understanding of self and hinder the coming-out process for lesbians and bisexual women. These unsafe domains are directly linked to issues of sexism, homophobia, and pressures on women to conform. It is important to recognize that these issues are interrelated and to question the avoidance of addressing them.

5. *Authenticity of Relationships.* A sisterhood relationship that is genuine is more likely to withstand the challenges involved in learning that a sister is lesbian or bisexual than one that is superficial. Several contributors to this book described hurt feelings and disappointment when women who had been believed to be true sisters made homophobic comments or failed to show support for sisters who did not comply with certain standards of acceptance. For a lesbian or bisexual sister to feel comfortable coming out to her heterosexual sister, there must first be some

sign that the sisterhood relationship is strong enough to endure the unexpected. Experiences presented in this book, especially from the perspectives of straight sisters, support this conclusion. Stories also suggest that sorority women come out to their sisters before coming out to their families, underscoring the value of a strong sisterhood in supporting a sister who is struggling with the coming out process.

It is difficult to build a climate of acceptance for lesbian and bisexual women if the foundation of sisterhood is weak, lacking in trusting relationships, and guarded in the extent to which persons are tolerated when they deviate from a mold. Sometimes women who have felt success in their sororities have discovered success and acceptance are not the same once they come out as lesbians or bisexual women. Success, as measured by achievement of chapter goals, may be attainable, even in a superficial sisterhood. Acceptance, though, can be achieved only in an authentic sisterhood that can withstand deep understanding of the women in it. There should be no "secret sisters" in a true sisterhood, because relationships are based on honesty and openness when the sisterhood is authentic.

6. *Ability of Bisexual Women to "Fit In" Socially in a Heterosexual Environment.* A quarter of the writers for this anthology identify themselves as bisexual. The information provided in their stories leads to several observations about what sorority life is like if you are a bisexual woman. First, confusion about one's sexual orientation often is prolonged because of the comfort level of bisexual women in relationships with men as well as with women. In a setting in which heterosexual dating is the norm, a sister's bisexuality can easily remain hidden, even to herself. Likewise, once the bisexual sister has discovered her sexual orientation, it can be even harder to convince those around her of her difference than if she were lesbian or straight. In sum, bisexuality can involve more confusion involving more people than homosexuality. It can be harder for a man to disassociate from a bisexual woman than for him to disassociate from a lesbian. His involvement with a bisexual woman can add pressure for her to conform to a heterosexual lifestyle, even though she instinctively may wish to engage in relationships with either men or women. Consequently, a bisexual woman's coming out can be prolonged and unsettled.

7. *Conflict Between Traditional Sorority Image and Feminist Theory.* Feminism is defined as "the doctrine advocating social, political, and all other rights of women equal to those of men."[4] Lesbians have been a

visible part of the women's movement, and sexuality has been a focal point of discussion within the movement.[5] Sororities, by contrast, have not been known for their activism in the women's movement or for promoting feminist ideology. Research findings presented in the introduction to this book portray sorority women as typically being wealthier, more physically attractive, more highly involved in social and extracurricular activities, and less accepting of diversity and nontraditional roles for women than are non-Greeks. Lesbians do not conform to all of the norms for gender roles that sororities often espouse. It is understandable, therefore, that as the lesbians and bisexual women who wrote for this book became more open about their sexual orientation and more involved in campus activities with lesbian, gay, bisexual, and transgender student groups, the conflict between the value systems of these women and their straight sorority sisters seemed to intensify. The chasm between value systems of a woman's LGBT group and her sorority sometimes led to her decision to disaffiliate with the sorority rather than try to lead a dual life as a lesbian and a sorority sister. Several of the women in this book describe themselves as being "too butch," "too intellectual," "too inclusive," or "too nonconformist" to fit into the sorority system, irrespective of their sexual orientations.

In 1988 the Lambda Delta Lambda sorority was formed with the purpose of the inclusion of lesbians and bisexuals. While this sorority fulfilled a need to bridge this gap, the president of LDL attributed recent dwindling numbers in membership to a lack of interest in joining sororities among lesbians because of their belief in the validity of stereotypes portraying sororities as being "superficial and exclusive."[6] Clearly, as long as sororities maintain their traditional image, they will have difficulty attracting and sustaining a diverse membership, and lesbian and bisexual sisters will be likely to face tension between their value systems and those of their sisters.

If anything, sororities today, at least those that are members of NPC, could be perceived as becoming even less akin to feminists in how they describe themselves, adopting the masculine language of "women's fraternities" rather than calling themselves "sororities," supposedly out of concern that "sorority" is a diminutive term. None of the writers in this book describe themselves as belonging to "fraternities," even though most of the organizations represented are members of NPC.

8. *Individual's Sense of Self.* Just as sororities support leadership

development, involvement in philanthropies, and social skills, they need to nurture individual self-respect and understanding of self-identity. Many of the sisters recognized internalized homophobia as a result of low self-esteem and failure to devote attention to one's personal self-development. Once the sister gained confidence in discussing her sexual identity with someone, it enhanced the sisterhood and allowed other sisters to be more comfortable with different sexual orientations among the membership.

The importance of this factor is supported by research that suggests that students with high self-esteem have less heterosexist attitudes and better experiences accepting someone who is gay or lesbian.[7] Coming out in a sorority can be problematic if there is a concentration of members with low self-esteem and a solid sisterhood structure does not exist to help these members build confidence in themselves. Women who are generally more comfortable with who they are, including their sexuality, view homosexuality as less of a threat to themselves. Such an understanding of sexuality leads to a more positive self-identity for all members.

These eight factors mandate that sororities take proactive measures to educate and foster sisterhood to be inclusive of lesbian and bisexual sisters and, in the process, to overcome homophobia. Several key interventions and resources specifically relating to these factors are provided in the closing section of this book to assist in such efforts.

Having compiled anthologies about being lesbian, gay, or bisexual in the Greek system, we believe homophobia exists in both fraternities and sororities and that change in the Greek system is a slowly evolving process. The resistance to change in sororities, however, seems more visible, at least in part because of the strong hold of national and international organizations on local chapters. Local sorority chapters are controlled by policies at the national or international level that suppress individual expression and difference. If we look back at the directive from one national or international headquarters to prohibit contributions to this book by its members, we can see the ease with which this organization asserts itself. We did not observe this tight control by national or international fraternity officers when we solicited stories for *Out on Fraternity Row: Personal Accounts of Being Gay in a College Fraternity*. In fraternities, perhaps due to looser national or international control, individual members may be more likely to influence changes in nondiscrimination policy. One example since pub lication of our first book is Sigma Phi Epsilon fraternity's adoption of sexual orientation as part of its international bylaws in direct response to concerns at the local chapter level. Based on the stories in *Secret Sisters* and on the expectation issued by NPC policy for local chapters to follow "Unanimous Agreements," we can surmise that change leading to empowerment of individual members seems less likely in sororities than in fraternities at the present time.

A positive comparison between sororities and fraternities is that in both, those organizations with strong and authentic foundations of sisterhood or brotherhood can provide environments in which true inclusiveness can be achieved. Likewise, if the sisterhood or brotherhood is weak or superficial, it will be difficult, if not impossible, for a lesbian, gay, or bisexual member to feel comfortable being herself or himself. In these situations, problems are exacerbated by excessive alcohol consumption and coerced heterosexual relationships, leading to a generally unhealthy, unsafe, and dysfunctional organization.

A final comparison of fraternities and sororities concerns fear. Whereas there is some fear of violence associated with coming out in both fraternities and sororities, the fear of sorority women is more often a fear of rejection than a fear of violence. While men fear rejection, they also fear violence and physical harm that could be inflicted by their fellow members to a greater extent than did women.

Beyond these observations, the Greek system as a whole must seriously seek ways to reinvent itself and return to its founding principles of "an appreciation of learning, a commitment to lead, an ethic of service, a love for one's brothers and sisters, and a belief in democratic ideals."[8] Policies and procedures that exclude entire populations of students serve to deprive lesbian, gay, and bisexual students of the opportunity to attain these ideals. The Greek system cannot continue to hide behind a myth of diversity. In a survey conducted in 1986 about perceived issues and problems facing the Greek system and society at large, national and international fraternity officers and advisers most strongly denied homosexuality and racism as being problems or issues in Greek organizations, out of a list of 41 predetermined categories.[9] National and international leaders erred in concluding that these issues were not pressing. One result seen today is the rapid growth of multicultural and ethnic fraternities and sororities on college campuses—a growth rate exceeding that of NPC and National Interfraternity Council member groups.[10] If this growth pattern continues, Greek letter organizations could risk becoming even more homogenous and exclusive along racial and sexual identity lines. In a survey published in the year 2000, 42% of incoming freshmen indicated that they either already had or would like to have lesbian and gay friends.[11] Accordingly, Greek letter organizations should expect to attract new members who assume that their college experience will continue to involve close relationships with diverse friends. Fraternities and sororities should prepare themselves to either accommodate this expectation in the future or risk losing membership.

Fraternities and sororities were formed with a purpose that included free exchange of ideas, healthy debate, challenging the status quo at the time, addressing difficult issues, and preparing their members to think broadly in order to provide much needed vision and leadership for society.[12] Today, sexual orientation issues, including homophobia and learning about sexuality, are examples of difficult issues facing the Greek system. The question remains whether or not Greeks will rise to the occasion of addressing these issues and, in so doing, reinvent themselves. This process of rediscovery and returning to its founding principles could help the system survive in the midst of changing student populations and broadening values of inclusion.

Perhaps as part of reinventing the college Greek system, we need to listen once again to the voices of those women whose stories have been the focus of this book. Stories in this anthology communicate clearly that it is possible for women who are lesbian or bisexual to enjoy the benefits of sisterhood in sororities, but to do so requires a genuine sisterhood based on truth. A strong sisterhood can overcome the ills of homophobia. Further, the individual must be able to resolve conflicts in image and conscience that may occur when trying to preserve her relationships with both sorority sisters and friends in the LGBT community.

Within the Greek system, there are women today who are willing to take a stand in support of lesbian and bisexual sisters, even though the pressures against doing so from alumnae and national or international officers are oppressive. As more and more women enter college with already established friendships with LGBT persons, it will be increasingly difficult for them to turn their backs on sisters who may be lesbian or bisexual. If sororities continue to thrive, they may well have to loosen the constraints they currently place on their member chapters, in order to be more understanding and accommodating of sisters who do not conform to traditional norms. If they are to respond to the needs of their membership, sororities may be forced to revise policies that impede the learning of information they currently view as unpopular.

Finally, accommodation of greater diversity by national and international leaders could serve to promote healthier and safer social environments, in which sisterhood can develop among women who are both independent and interdependent. Independence in thinking, combined with interdependence in friendship and support for one another, can result in strong, thriving organizations that are, in fact, reflective of the wishes of college students of the 21st century.

Voices of lesbians and bisexual women in sororities are easily hushed in the face of adversity. More allies and out role models are needed to show support for individuals and to bring about change in the Greek system. We all have a responsibility to challenge the status quo and to recognize that all of our organizations need to be open and accepting of lesbian and bisexual sisters.

We have brought attention to the factors that influence sisterhood and have provided direction for the Greek system to move forward on sexual orientation issues. Now is the time. The presence of "secret sisters" in every sorority cannot be denied. Nor can complacency prevail over responding to their voices and creating a Greek system free of homophobia.

The voices are deafening. The secrets are revealed. We must not let them be lost.

NOTES

1. V. C. Cass, "Homosexual Identity Formation: A Theoretical Model," Journal of Homosexuality 4, Spring 1979: 219–235.

2. J. B. Miller, Toward a New Psychology of Women (Boston: Beacon, 1976).

3 "Unanimous Agreements, 1999," in Manual of Information, 13th edition (Indianapolis: National Panhellenic Conference).

4. Webster's New Universal Unabridged Dictionary, s.v. "feminism."

5. Carla Golden, "The Feminist Movement and Sexual Orientation," chapter 3, "Our

Politics and Choices" in Lesbian and Gay Psychology, edited by Beverly Greene and Gregory M. Herek (Thousand Oaks, CA: Sage, 1994).

6. Maureen Bogues, "Keeping the Lambda in the Greek Alphabet," The Advocate, October 14, 1997: 31.

7. Jane M. Simoni, "Pathways to Prejudice: Predicting Students' Heterosexist Attitudes With Demographics, Self-Esteem, and Contact with Lesbians and Gay Men," Journal of College Student Development 37, January-February 1996: 68–78.

8. Smith Jackson and Amanda Harless, "Returning Greek Organizations to their Founding Principles," About Campus 2, September-October 1997: 23.

9. Roger B. Winton Jr. and Michael J Hughes, "Resources and Emerging Issues," in Fraternities and Sororities on the Contemporary College Campus (New Directions for Student Services, no. 40) (San Francisco: Jossey-Bass, 1987), 105–117.

10. Leo Reisberg, "Ethnic and Multicultural Fraternities Are Booming on Many Campuses," Chronicle of Higher Education 7, January 2000: A60.

11. Jonathan J. Mohr and William E. Sedlack, "Perceived Barriers to Friendship with Lesbians and Gay Men Among University Students," Journal of College Student Development 41, January-February 2000: 70–80.

12. W.A. Bryan and R.A. Schwartz, "The '80s: Expectations, Challenges, Predictions, and Recommendations," in The Eighties: Challenges for Fraternities and Sororities, edited by Bryan and Schwartz (Carbondale: Southern Illinois University Press, 1983), quoted in Bryan, "Contemporary Fraternity and Sorority Issues," in Fraternities and Sororities on the Contemporary College Campus (New Directions for Student Services, no. 40) (San Francisco: Jossey-Bass, 1987), 37–56.

Interventions and Resources

How to Use Stories as Educational Tools

Half the battle in getting people to understand homophobia and become more accepting involves getting them to acknowledge that it is a real issue for them. Use of true stories can be an effective way to demonstrate that homophobia in sororities is real and affects the lives of *all* sorority women.

Several examples of how stories in this anthology can be adapted for use in educational programs are given in this chapter. Two of the stories have been condensed into case studies with discussion questions. Brief quotes have been pulled from others for use as "Read-Arounds." A description of how the stories can be used in role playing concludes this chapter.

Regardless of the approach taken, one important guideline should be followed by program planners and presenters. The intent of the program and the nature of the audience must be the foundation for selection of stories and methods. For example, if the program focuses on recruitment and education of new members with a goal of helping incoming members learn about the value of diversity and the intended audience is to be pledge trainers and other chapter officers, then stories that cover more details of rush and pledging will be more relevant than would a story focusing on the role of a national officer or chapter adviser. If the intended audience is to be student affairs professionals who advise Greek organizations on their campuses, then stories that cover a sister's entire college experience and beyond may be more helpful than one that focuses only on the pledge period. If the program is to be directed toward all members of a particular chapter and the members already have a good understanding of homophobia but are having the program to build on what they already know, then stories that are more unusual than others may provide more stimulating, in-depth discussion.

These are just a few of the ways that the stories can be useful in educational efforts. Other uses are limited only by the extent to which the educators use their imaginations, as the scope and substance of experiences that are portrayed through the voices of the sisters who shared their stories in this book contain relevant material that can be directly applied to most, if not all, sororities in a variety of settings.

Case Studies

The two stories that have been selected as case studies are "My Sister, My Love" by "Jessi Opynth" and "Unconditional Love" by "Marie Baker." Details about pledging and the "big sister/little sister" relationship are highlighted in the first case study. In the second, the special circumstances involved in being bisexual and active in both a sorority and campus LGBT group provide excellent discussion material, especially for audiences in which basic information about sexual orientation and homophobia has been covered in previous sessions.

Case Study #1: "My Sister, My Love" by "Jessi Opynth"

Even before she came to college, Jessi knew she was attracted to women. Still, she left home identifying herself as a heterosexual, "normal" 18-year-old. A considerable portion of her college was Greek, and she quickly discovered through the rush process that the women she met were down-to-earth and thoughtful and that they were not like the stereotypical mindless coeds she had seen portrayed in movies and books.

Jessi pledged her sorority during the winter of her freshman year, just as she was beginning to understand and accept her feelings for women. She enjoyed being in the friendly atmosphere of the house, and most of the time she felt at home. Several weeks into pledging, though, she overheard a conversation among her soon-to-be sisters about the sexual orientation of one of their advisers. "I've never seen him with a girlfriend or anything" and "He's such a homo" were among the sisters' comments that first revealed their homophobia and ignorance about gay people and gay issues. What otherwise would have been a perfect second home for Jessi became a place where she could not always feel included. She could not help asking herself what kind of organization she was joining, although she enjoyed other aspects of sorority life. She finished pledging and became a member during the spring of her freshman year.

The next year, as an active, Jessi became a "big sister" for one of the pledges, Meg. After observing Jessi and some of her male and female friends playing a game they invented, which involved passing a piece of candy from one person's mouth to another, Meg bluntly asked Jessi, "Are you gay?" Surprising herself, Jessi responded, "Yeah, something like that," after which Meg told her about a relationship she had had with a girl in high school. Both were surprised at their mutual lesbian feelings, and the bond between them was strengthened as a result of this brief conversation. Both knew, though, that the conversation was strictly off-limits within the sorority, and the subject came up only once more during Meg's pledge period.

As Meg's freshman year progressed, Jessi was aware of a mutual attraction developing between her and Meg. She confided in her good friend Jonas, who was going through the ups and downs of his own com-ing-out process. Both agreed that if the attraction between Meg and Jessi were to lead to a romantic relationship, the first for Jessi, it would have to wait until after Meg had finished pledging because of the distinctive roles of members and pledges. Despite there being no explicit sorority rule that a sister could not date a pledge, there was no room in a member-pledge relationship for an intimate relationship. Jessi's thinking returned to the conversation during her freshman year about their adviser, and she realized being an out lesbian in the sorority and in a relationship with another member could jeopardize the friendships and sisterhood that had become integral parts of her life. She and Meg committed themselves to secrecy.

Being a part of a meaningful sisterhood, though, made it hard to have such a big part of their lives concealed. Over time, some of their sisters figured out what had developed between Meg and Jessi. To their delight, even those sisters who were the most homophobic were eventually able to accept the relationship. This acceptance gave them hope that it could become possible to be truthful with the rest of the sisters.

Both Meg and Jessi were respected members of their sorority and became elected officers. Even though most sisters knew Meg and Jessi were a couple, they still were valued for their individual talents. At times they heard about a comment that had been made by someone in the house, usually someone who was concerned about how Meg and Jessi's relationship would reflect on the image of the sorority. While such reports saddened them, they were able to accept that they would always have to deal with such concerns. Eventually, they became sufficiently comfortable and accepted to attend a date party as a couple, and finally they were seen by their sisters and friends as just another couple. When some alumnae raised questions about how their presence would affect the sorority's image, their sisters were supportive of Meg and Jessi. They considered themselves fortunate to be part of an organization that had been successful in changing from the days when they sat around and made homophobic comments about their adviser to one in which the sisters supported one another honestly and openly.

Underlying Issues and Questions for Discussion

Underlying issues include homophobia and how it can affect a person's ability to come out, ethical considerations related to dating a sister, how to deal with homophobic alumnae and national officers, and image as a factor in the success of sororities. Discussion questions may include:

1. How typical do you believe Jessi's pledgeship to be? Is the conversation about the sisters' adviser believable? Could such a discussion occur in your sorority?

2. How do you think your sorority would react if two sisters became romantically involved with each other? What action, if any, would your sorority take? Would you agree with your sorority's response? Why or why not?

3. Do you think the special care exercised by Jessi and Meg to be discreet about their feelings for each other during the time preceding Meg's initiation was appropriate? Was it necessary? Why or why not? Is your opinion influenced by their "big sister/little sister" roles?

4. Who should take responsibility for intervening when homophobic remarks are made among friends in a setting such as a sorority house? Why?

5. How would your sorority respond if alumnae raised questions about the sexual orientation of members? What if the questions were raised by national officers?

6. When it is known that a lesbian or bisexual sister or sisters live in a sorority, is the sorority likely to be labeled as a "gay" sorority? If so, how should/could the sorority respond?

7. Have you known about sororities on your campus in which lesbian or bisexual women were members? If so, what was the response on campus? Did you agree with the response?

8. What other issues might be involved with sisters being out as lesbians or bisexuals? Are the issues different when two sisters are involved romantically?

9. Would it be homophobic for a sorority chapter to have a policy against romantic relationships between sisters who live in the house? Why or why not?

Case Study #2: "Unconditional Love" by "Marie Baker"

Marie had fully accepted that she was attracted to both men and women, even before she enrolled in college. She had resolved that she had to hide her bisexuality from everyone, because she had observed the discrimination and fear experienced by persons in her high school who came out. She even recalled engaging in gossip herself when the topic of "those gay people" came up. As she participated in rush during her freshman year, Marie was prepared to concentrate on being attracted only to men and being "normal." She found rush to be fun, she liked the women she met, and she became a pledge. Meanwhile, she observed LGBT life on campus, but from a distance.

During her sophomore year, though, Marie's life began to change. Being closeted led her to feel dissatisfied and helpless because of her deceit. No matter how close she got to a new friend, her fear prevented her from revealing the truth about her sexual orientation. She felt ashamed, even though she knew she had not done anything wrong.

One night Marie decided to break her silence by coming out to a friend who was known to be bisexual. Her friend did not realize this was Marie's first coming-out experience and treated it as nothing special. Marie was thrilled and felt empowered to tell more of her close friends, all members of the LGBT community. She continued to lead two connected but distinct lives—one among her LGBT friends, who knew she was bisexual, and the other among her sorority sisters, her classmates, and her family, who had no idea she was bisexual. Marie was feeling increasingly uncomfortable about hiding her true identity in one part of her life, and she decided to take another bold step when plans for her sorority's annual formal were announced. She wanted to take her girlfriend.

Marie agonized over how to go about going to the dance as part of a same sex couple. She feared rejection by some people who would be at the dance, but even more she feared harming the sorority. Knowing that a group of her chapter's officers met periodically to discuss problems and talk with house members about concerns, she decided to talk with them prior to the dance. Shaking all the while, she said to the group, "I'm bringing a girl to the formal. She's my girlfriend." Most of the officers were surprised, but they assured Marie they were not overly concerned about it. She was relieved.

The night of the formal arrived, and Marie and her date boarded the charter bus. Being the only woman sitting on the bus with someone other than a man or another sorority sister, Marie knew the bus ride would provide the first opportunity that evening for her and her date to come out. The response was a mixture of curiosity, surprise, and acceptance. Throughout the evening, numerous friends greeted Marie and her date and talked. Some asked questions, but again the atmosphere was one of acceptance.

Despite the overwhelmingly positive response of the chapter as a whole to Marie's bisexuality, there were some isolated incidents of sorority sisters who were not completely accepting. Even so, Marie felt a strong sense of caring from her sisters and felt comforted knowing she no longer had to suffer through her sexuality issues alone.

Coming out was an ongoing trial for Marie, making her thankful to her sorority for their acceptance. Her sisters made her feel safe to be herself and provided for Marie an unconditional love.

Underlying Issues and Questions for Discussion

Underlying issues include bisexuality as distinctive from other sexual orientations, safety, stages of coming out, effects of remaining closeted on the development of sisterhood, effects on individuals of living a dual life, same-sex dating in a heterosexist environment, and the importance of allies. Questions for discussion could include:

1. What might be the greatest fear for a bisexual sister when deciding whether to come out to her sorority? What might be the basis for this fear? Do you think the fear would be justifiable?

2. Would the issues to be dealt with by a bisexual sister in a sorority setting be the same or different from those of a lesbian sister? How might they differ from those of a heterosexual sister?

3. When taken by surprise by the coming out of a bisexual or lesbian sister, what might be some supportive ways to respond? What

responses might a supportive sister want to avoid? Why?

4. What reasons might be given by some sisters for *not* being supportive of a bisexual or lesbian sister? Are these reasons valid? Why or why not?

5. In an authentic or sincere sisterhood, is it to be expected that responses to a sister's coming out will be varied? If so, would this imply that the sorority is homophobic? Can a sisterhood be authentic and *not* have a range of responses from members? How can a sorority deal with varied responses to a sister's coming out?

6. Do you think safety is more of an issue for bisexual women than for other women? Why or why not?

7. Are there traditional practices in your sorority that could impede a sister's ability to show support for a bisexual sister? If so, what are they? If so, how could these practices be altered to neutralize their effect as obstacles to showing support?

8. How common is it to have someone in a sorority who is bisexual? Do you believe most members of your sorority understand what bisexuality is? If not, what resources are available on your campus for learning about bisexuality? How could you facilitate learning in your sorority about this topic?

Read-Arounds

One technique proven effective in setting a tone and sustaining interest in a program about homophobia is the use of "Read-Arounds."[1] This training tool involves placing quotes on small slips of paper, numbering them, and handing them out to people in the audience prior to the beginning of the program. At selected points during the program, participants are asked to read aloud the quotes on their slips as their numbers are called. Quotes can be placed in the program according to topic, or they can be read at the beginning or end of the program to set or end with a particular atmosphere. Another benefit of this technique is that it gets participants involved in the program in an impersonal, nonthreatening way.

Every story in this anthology includes quotable material that could be used as "Read-Arounds." The following are some examples.

• Once when she drank too much at a frat party, she asked me to hold her hand to stop the bed from spinning. I held her hand the entire night as I lay on the edge of her bed with her, which caused some gossip in our hall. One of my sorority sisters told me that if I didn't have a boyfriend, they would "wonder" about Angie and me. The fact that I had posters of Olivia Newton-John, whom I worshiped, on every wall in my dorm was a further indictment. (From "Anchor of Denial" by K.P. Brown)

• During freshman year, I dated a guy named Paul who lived on my dorm floor. When he came back the following fall, he came out to me as being gay. My first response was, "What will my sorority sisters think about my dating a gay guy?" This probably was not the reaction Paul was hoping for. (From "In Your Eyes" by Kristin H. Griffith)

• During my sophomore year I spent a lot of time sitting in the window seat of my 10th-floor dorm room reading any gay material Paul got his hands on, including *Out* and *Deneuve*, gay and lesbian magazines. Unfortunately, everything seemed to be about gay people who were really "out" and comfortable with their sexuality. They had lives that seemed far removed from what I was going through. Reading about them just made me feel more alone. (From "In Your Eyes" by Kristin H. Griffith)

• I was excited, not only for the chance to take a leadership position, but also to be fully immersed in Greek life. Then again, that summer, I realized more and more that I wasn't into guys. My best friends from home had boyfriends, and I found myself constantly jealous or not understanding why they'd want to spend their time with these "boys." I wanted to spend all my time with women. "Why didn't they?" I'd ask myself. (From "Never, Never Land" by Elana Mendelson)

• Certainly I lacked the strength and integrity to come out to my sorority sisters. Coming out at that time is still unimaginable to me. The revulsion I saw among my sisters in regard to homosexuality made certain I could never reveal myself as a lesbian and stay in that living arrangement. Since I had no real model of a relationship and thought I never would have one, I wondered if I was even entitled to that identity. Those college years are part of a past life I know was mine yet find difficult to claim. (from "Mistaken Identity" by Nancy Haver)

• No one ever seems to believe my sexual orientation. As if it wasn't difficult enough for me to just come out of the closet, I have to constantly justify my sexual orientation to the straight world *and* the gay world. The gay world thinks I'm in some sort of transitional stage and that one day I'll realize that I'm really gay. Well, it's been one hell of a long stage. A 27-year-long stage, to be exact. And the straight world thinks I'm in some sort of experimental phase and that one day I'll wake up and realize I'm really straight. I have news for all of you. I am bisexual. That's the way it is, and it's never going to change. You all need to start believing me. (From "One Heart, One Way" by Mollie M. Monahan)

• Is it my responsibility to go forth and reveal myself, in order for the sorority to create a place of tolerance, acceptance, and education? Do I now become "the lesbian" in the sorority? Will my sisters feel comfortable around me? Will I feel comfortable around them? I've told everyone in my close circle of friends, including a few fellow national officers, and so far everyone has been very accepting. I often think how much easier it would be to be heterosexual; I would just go about my business and everyone would assume I was heterosexual. But I am not. (From "Nightmare of a National Officer" by "Carolyn")

• Some of my sisters claim their pledging period was the best time of their life. Unfortunately, mine was not. Consumed with internal struggle, I alienated myself from the gay community I had previously associated with, while isolating myself from my new sisters. I made my pledging period as difficult as possible, attempting to ease the rejection I saw as inevitable by causing it myself. In my mind, it was easier to have my sisters reject me because of the unpleasant, sarcastic facade I projected than to have them reject me because I showed them my true identity. (From "A Quiet Acceptance" by Katie Stuckemeyer)

• Two of my closest friends, one of whom was my sorority sister Eileen, and I were traveling to Indianapolis for an Ani DiFranco concert when the subject of homosexuality came up. It seemed to appear in conversation more and more, and I felt as if I had to take advantage of this opportunity. Determined to uncloset myself right then and there, I turned off the music filling the car with comfort noise and announced my sexuality. "I'm a lesbian!" I exclaimed in what seemed slow motion. To my amazement, the world did not stop turning because I had uttered these words. My friends asked me a few questions about my girlfriend, if I was planning on coming out, and what my parents thought. I survived the not-so-traumatic "inquisition," and the three of us continued on I-70 in pursuit of Ani DiFranco. (From "In Pursuit of Ani DiFranco" by Lindsay Hey)

• I found I had to be a lot like a parent of a teenager to get through this with my friendship with Amber intact. I had to realize that what I thought, believed, and wanted was not what Amber's life is about. Her life is about her and what she wants. A few short years earlier, she was my friend; later that developed into a sense of sisterhood. Even though Amber didn't live the life I had envisioned, it didn't make her bad or evil. She had to run her own course and live her own way. By telling me she was a lesbian, she wasn't asking my permission or opinion. She was asking for what we all crave: unconditional love and understanding. That's all you can offer a sister who chooses to come out to you…. (From "Unnaturally Close" by Selene Jones)

Role Playing

Educational programs that do not involve the audience can quickly lose the attention of those in attendance. Particularly for small groups, one effective technique for involving participants is role playing. Each of the stories in this anthology includes material that can be used in role playing to demonstrate personal decision making and problem solving. By having two or three members of the audience act out a scenario in which the characters are forced to make choices about an issue, then discussing the scenario and the choices made by the characters, the audience learns through observation and discussion. With strong facilitation, role playing can work with large groups, but extra care must be given to logistical needs such as easy-to-use and functional sound equipment, a stage area that is clearly visible from all parts of the room, and participants who are willing to act in front of a large audience.

Role playing usually works best if the scenario being enacted is short. It can be written in script form and given to volunteers from the audience to read. Or, perhaps a more effective approach is to write a short paragraph which the volunteers read, then act without a script. How familiar and comfortable attendees are with one another may determine which approach is best; more familiarity can facilitate a more relaxed, free acting approach without use of a script. In a sorority setting, where attendees know one another well, the unscripted approach can be relaxed and engaging. If the facilitator wants to ensure that certain messages are stated in an unscripted role play, she or he may be an actor in the role play, along with volunteers from the audience.

Following the role playing of each incident, it is important to process what has just been observed, paying special attention to feelings evoked in actors and observers. One technique is to have actors stay in position and describe their feelings in their character roles immediately follow-ing the role play and before group discussion.[2] If the facilitator believes that altering a certain part of the role play will emphasize a point, the scenario can be performed again, but with modified instructions to the volunteers.

An excerpt from one of the stories in this book, "Rushing Out" by Leanna Heritage, is presented here to show how all three methods could be employed for role playing. In the first example, the scenario is fully scripted. In the second example, the same scenario is written in para-graph form to be given to volunteers for improvisational acting. In the last example, the scenario is again scripted, but with an alternate ending.

Example #1: Scripted

Ask for five volunteers to play the roles of Sue, the sorority president; Donna, the vice president; Leanna; and Leanna's friends Jane and Paula. Place three chairs together at the front of the room. Place a fourth chair several feet away from and facing the other three chairs. Have persons playing the roles of Leanna and her friends sit in the three chairs and have the vice president sit in the fourth chair. The president will not use a chair.

Sue: "Greetings, everyone. We're going to get the meeting started today by dividing into small groups and playing a little game to get to know one another better. Each of you has been given a small piece of paper. Write something unusual about yourself on it. After you are fin-ished, all pieces of paper will be placed together within your group, and as one member of the group reads each aloud, the member whose unusu-al feature has been read will stand and introduce herself to the group. Please begin now by writing "I am unusual because…""

Leanna to her friends: "I don't know what to write about myself!"

Paula: "Oh, just write down that you're a lesbian." [*Giggles*]

Leanna: "I can't do that!"

Jane: "Yes, you can. We're the only ones who'll know. Now, hurry; she's asking us to turn them in." [*All three appear to be writing quickly, laughing as they do.*]

Sue: "OK, everyone should be finished now. Your vice president and I just chatted and think this would be even more fun if we did it as a whole group instead of by small groups. Everyone, please turn in your papers to Donna." [*All act as if turning in papers to vice president.*]

Leanna: [*Saying in horror to Donna*] "What are we doing? Why are we doing it like this? I can't do this!"

Donna: "Don't worry; it'll be fun. Just stand up when yours is read out loud."

Leanna: "What? I can't!" [*Looking terrified*]

Paula: [*Speaking softly to Leanna*] "Just don't stand up. No one will know."

Sue: [*Appears to draw paper from basket, then reads it aloud*) "OK, here's the first one. A tattoo on my bum." [*Everyone laughs*]

Paula: [*Stands up, laughing*] "Hi. My name's Paula."

Sue: [Acting as if looking at next small paper; hesitating, then looking seriously at Donna, the vice president] "I'm...gay." [*Looks slowly around room; no one stands right away; looks as if she is getting ready to toss paper away and draw another one, then sees Jane and Paula laughing while Leanna looks horrified*]

Sue: [*Looking at Leanna*] "Is that you?"

Leanna: [*Slowly standing up*] "Hi, my name is Leanna, and I'm gay." [*Room is silent.*]

Jane: [*Slowly at first, without speaking, begins to clap*]

Paula, Sue, Donna: [*All join Jane in clapping; all smile. Leanna smiles broadly, and scenario ends.*]

Discussion Questions

1. Paula thought it was a joke to have Leanna write that she was gay. Is it ever OK to assume that someone you know is heterosexual? Is there any harm in joking about being gay if you know everyone in the group very well and believe that they all are heterosexual?

2. Once it was learned that Leanna was gay, was the group's response acceptable? How do you think the clapping and smiles made Leanna feel? What message was communicated to Leanna by the clapping and smiles?

3. Was Paula's joke homophobic? Why or why not? What is homophobia?

4. Is there anything that members should do the next day, or the next week, in regard to this game and Leanna's coming out?

Example #2: Unscripted

It is the first chapter meeting after pledges have been given their bids, and the president of the chapter, Sue, is about to convene the meeting. She and the vice president, Donna, are seated at the front of the room. Leanna and her pledge sisters Paula and Jane are seated together. The mood is festive, as Sue welcomes everyone and says they are going to play a game to become more familiar with one another. She has everyone write something unusual about themselves on pieces of paper and turn them in. The instructions at first say that the papers will be kept within the small groups, and people in the group will draw one paper at a time, read it, and the others in the group will guess who it describes. Leanna cannot think of anything unusual about herself to write, so Paula jokingly says for her to just put down that she is gay. When the writing is completed, Sue announces that she and Donna have decided to make it a whole-group activity instead. Leanna is horrified. Paula tells her just not to identify herself when her paper is read. Sue reads several other papers first, then pauses before slowly reading Leanna's. After a moment of silence, just as Sue is ready to throw aside the paper, Leanna slowly stands and says she is, in fact, gay. After a pause, everyone claps and smiles. Leanna's facial expression, after seeing their acceptance of her, is joyful.

Discussion Questions

1. Is this an incident of homophobia? Why or why not? What is homophobia?

2. If Leanna had not been gay, would the joke have been acceptable in this setting?

3. Was the response (clapping and smiling) of the sisters acceptable? What message do you think this response conveyed to Leanna? To other sisters?

4. Is there anything that the president could have done differently?

5. Is there anything more that should be done as a follow-up the next day or the next week?

6. Should Leanna feel comfortable in this sorority as a gay woman?

Example #3: Second Outcome

In this scenario, the outcome has been changed, and the scene is role-played a second time by the same or different volunteers. The example given here is scripted, but the paragraph used in a free acting approach could also be modified and used with an alternate ending. Again, four chairs are needed, with three of them grouped together and facing the fourth. The president is standing. Volunteers are needed to play Sue, the chapter president; Donna, the vice president; Leanna; and Leanna's friends Paula and Jane.

Sue: "Greetings, everyone. We're going to get the meeting started today by dividing into small groups and playing a little game to get to know one another better. Each of you has been given a small piece of paper. Write something unusual about yourself on it. After you are finished, all pieces of paper will be placed together within your group, and as one member of the group reads each aloud, the member whose unusual feature has been read will stand and introduce herself to the group. Please begin now by writing "I am unusual because…""

Leanna to her friends: "I don't know what to write about myself!"

Paula: "Oh, just write down that you're a lesbian." [*Giggles*]

Leanna: "I can't do that!"

Jane: "Yes, you can. We're the only ones who'll know. Now hurry, she's asking us to turn them in." [*All three appear to be writing quickly, laughing as they do.*]

Sue: "OK, everyone should be finished now. Your vice president and I just chatted and think this would be even more fun if we did it as a whole group instead of by small groups. Everyone, please turn in your papers to Donna." [*All act as if turning in papers to vice president.*]

Leanna: [*Saying in horror to Donna*] "What are we doing? Why are we doing it like this? I can't do this!"

Donna: "Don't worry; it'll be fun. Just stand up when yours is read out loud."

Leanna: "What? I can't!" [*Looking terrified*]

Paula: [*Speaking softly to Leanna*] "Just don't stand up. No one will know."

Sue: [*Appears to draw paper from basket, then reads it aloud*] "OK, here's the first one. A tattoo on my bum." [*Everyone laughs*]

Paula: [*Stands up, laughing*] "Hi. My name's Paula."

Sue: [*Acting as if looking at next small paper; hesitating, then looking seriously at Donna, the vice president*] "I'm…gay." [*Looks slowly around room; no one stands right away; looks as if she is getting ready to toss paper away and draw another one, then sees Jane and Paula laughing while Leanna looks horrified*]

Sue: [*Looking at Leanna*] "Is that you?"

Leanna: [*Looking nervous, shakes her head "no"*]

Sue: [*Tosses paper aside and goes on to another one*]

Paula and Jane: [*Chuckle nervously as they notice that Leanna is not laughing*]

Discussion Questions

1. Paula thought it was a joke to have Leanna write that she was gay. Is it ever OK to assume that someone you know is heterosexual? Is there any harm in joking about being gay if you know everyone in the group very well and believe that they all are heterosexual?

2. Once it was suspected that Leanna may be gay, was the group's response acceptable? How do you think the chuckling made Leanna feel? What message was communicated to Leanna by the chuckling? What could Paula and Jane have done or said?

3. Was Paula's joke homophobic? Why or why not? What is homophobia?

4. Is there anything that members should do the next day, or the next week, in regard to this game and Leanna's obvious embarrassment?

We hope the examples that have been given to show how the stories of "secret sisters" can be used in case studies, "Read-Arounds," and role plays will stimulate additional ideas for educating about heterosexism, homophobia, and sisterhood. Using real-life examples to raise awareness can be extremely effective, especially when the methods used are interesting and actively involve those in attendance.

NOTES

1. Daniel Watts and Tammy Lou Maltzan, "Some of My Best Friends…Lesbian, Gay, and Bisexual Awareness for Greek Letter Organizations" (training materials presented at the joint conference of the National Association of Student Personnel Administrators and the American College Personnel Association, Chicago, March 1997).

2. Nancy Schniedewind and Ellen Davidson, Open Minds to Equality: A Sourcebook of Learning Activities to Affirm Diversity and Promote Equity, second edition (Boston: Allyn & Bacon, 1998), 72.

Shane L. Windmeyer and Pamela W. Freeman, Lambda 10 Project.

Meaning of Sisterhood
Concentric Circle Exercise

The premise of sorority involvement is the ability to foster sisterhood. Many of us share different individual experiences when we speak of sisterhood and what it means to us. Some of these ideas of sisterhood may include words such as friendship, truthfulness, camaraderie, respect, shared values, and mutual support. Often the meaning and practice of sisterhood are just as varied as our individual thoughts on what sisterhood means to the sorority chapter. Such meanings of sisterhood are communicated through our rituals, what we say we value, the actions we do or do not take in given circumstances, older members' comments and interactions, and so forth. Even though we may say the word "sisterhood" and use it as a key way to identify who and what we do, seldom are we given the opportunity to discuss and agree on what sisterhood means for us as individuals and as a sorority. Having a continual dialogue about the meaning of sisterhood enables all sisters to have a shared experience defining their sorority sisterhood.

This activity is designed to give all participants the chance to interact on a one-to-one level to define the nature of sisterhood for their chapter. Through our work on this book and our companion book *Out on Fraternity Row: Personal Accounts of Being Gay in a College Fraternity,* we believe wholeheartedly that a strong sisterhood enables sorority members to overcome homophobia. We also believe that those chapters who share an understanding of sisterhood are more likely to respond in a supportive manner to the lesbian or bisexual sister who comes out to the chapter. The phrases and questions listed below create a dialogue on the meaning of sisterhood and assist in building a foundation to accept diversity more readily. Such an exercise may be used as a warm-up activity prior to a leadership retreat or in combination with other chapter functions in discussing the meaning of sisterhood and the value of a college sorority.

Purpose

• To foster a dialogue on the meaning of sisterhood.

• To define or redefine sisterhood based on a shared experience of members.

• To create a personal commitment to the meaning of sisterhood among sisters.

• To encourage the practice of that sisterhood among the chapter.

Instructions

1. Instruct the sisters to find a partner.

2. Ask the sisters to face each other and join with other pairs so that the entire group has formed two concentric circles (an inner and an outer circle).

3. Read aloud the following:

(a) I will give you a question to discuss with your partner. First, one of you will speak for 30 seconds, and then the other one will get a chance to talk about the question. Respond to the question with whatever comes to mind and with what you are willing to share about the question.

(b) When I signal, the sisters in the inner circle will move one person to their right to find their new partner.

(c) I will give you another question and you will discuss the question as before. We will continue in this way for about 10 to 15 minutes.

4. After completing the concentric circle dialogue, ask all sisters to sit in one large circle and use this dialogue among the sisters to define or redefine the meaning of sisterhood for their chapter. Other issues may arise for future educational sessions, so keep a notepad handy to write down comments. Encourage the sisters to read their meaning of sisterhood publicly on occasion to remind one another throughout the year.

Possible Discussion Questions

1. How does one be a good sister?

2. What did you learn about sisterhood prior to joining a sorority? From your family and friends?

3. What words do people use to describe a sister?

4. What words do people use to describe a sorority?

5. What are some of the stereotypes about a sorority?

6. What traits or characteristics are unique about our sisterhood?

7. How do you show your sisterhood on a daily basis?

8. What values do you expect from another sister?

9. Why would somebody be excluded or kicked out of the sorority?

10. In what ways can a sister show she cares for another sister? Is she willing to help or be there for a sister in time of need?

11. What qualities create a healthy, strong sisterhood?

12. How do you show support to another sister?

13. Why do you think sororities may have a negative public image on a college campus or are stereotyped?

Sample Definition of Sisterhood

A common bond of friendship among women, a family. Those who have a love for their sorority and a sincere interest in the care of their sisters; a willingness to help or be there for a sister in time of need; and shared common values of love, loyalty, honesty, understanding, and respect.

Revised from *Out on Fraternity Row: Personal Accounts of Being Gay in a College Fraternity,* edited by Shane L. Windmeyer and Pamela W. Freeman, Alyson Publications, 1998.

Shane L. Windmeyer and Pamela W. Freeman, Lambda 10 Project.

How Homophobia
Hurts the College Sorority

Homophobia is defined as the fear and hatred of people who love and are sexually attracted to those of the same sex, and it includes prejudice and acts of discrimination resulting from that fear and hatred. Derived from the Greek *homos,* meaning "same," and *phobikos,* meaning "having a fear of and/or aversion for," the term *homophobia* was coined by George Weinberg in 1972 in his book *Society and the Healthy Homosexual.*[1]

Like other forms of oppression, homophobia not only oppresses members of the target or minority groups (gays, lesbians, bisexuals, and transgendered people) but also, on many levels, hurts members of the agent or dominant group (heterosexuals).[2] As a result, everyone eventually loses, and more specifically, the negative effect of homophobia remains alive.

Sororities, partially because they are made up of women, often are viewed as being less homophobic than male fraternities. The impact of homophobia on sisterhood, however, is still very real and does threaten sororities. Many times homophobia as well as sexism and other forms of prejudice, compounded by peer pressure, can result in harassment and violence. Many people do not see the connections between themselves and people different from them who may be similarly oppressed. Women in sororities can benefit from a view of the links of oppression. Issues such as sexism, racism, homophobia, classism, ableism, anti-Semitism, and ageism, are linked by a common origin—economic power and control.[3] Those who have such a view believe that in order to eliminate any one oppression successfully, all oppressions must be subsequently dealt with or else success will be limited and incomplete. Educational efforts among the Greek community need to reflect this theory of oppression to have an impact on the organizational culture.

Therefore, homophobic beliefs and actions not only pose potential harm to individuals of all sexual orientations but also jeopardize sisterhood itself. Despite this, most Greek educational efforts either fail to address homophobia altogether or raise it simply as an isolated "side issue" unrelated to the other issues and concerns. Such a practice will only continue to hurt Greek life. In actuality, homophobia harms all sisters and the goals of the college sorority.

The following list adapts the theory of Warren J. Blumenfeld, from his book *Homophobia: How We All Pay the Price,* to the college sorority and the female experience. It also mirrors ideas presented by Suzanne Pharr in the book *Homophobia: A Weapon of Sexism* to show the interrelated nature of the two forms of oppression for women. This information may be useful to foster an educational dialogue about how homophobia hurts the college sorority and to heighten awareness on issues of sexual orientation.

1. Homophobia jeopardizes sisterhood by inhibiting close, intimate friendships among sorority women and their ability to show affection toward other women for fear of being perceived as lesbian or bisexual.

2. Homophobia locks sorority women into rigid gender-based roles that inhibit self-expression and exploration of female identity. Because of this, women may shy away from activities that could be denoted as "tomboy" and occupations that might traditionally be associated with masculine behaviors. Such practices limit the choices of women and restrict the development of a positive female identity—straight, lesbian, or bisexual.

3. Homophobia creates a negative environment for sisterhood by compromising the integrity of heterosexual sorority women. Lesbian baiting may be a common practice among some women to pressure and harass other women through calling, or threatening to call them, lesbians. As such, homophobia is used as a way to keep potential lesbians or bisexual women from joining the sorority or to kick them out, or for heterosexuals to portray themselves as superior.

4. Homophobia can be used to stigmatize, silence, and target people who are perceived to be lesbian or bisexual, or labeled by others as lesbian or bisexual. Such an environment may be hostile to these sisters and lead to harms that are often associated with being lesbian or bisexual.

5. Homophobia creates an environment in which sorority sisters are sometimes pressured to conform to heterosexual norms of dating and the expectation to have sex. Women who do not conform to such heterosexual norms may have their sexuality questioned by others in a negative manner.

6. Homophobia breeds an attitude of sexual conquest among men that can have a negative impact on women in sororities. Fraternity men often feel pressure to "get laid" to prove their virility as heterosexual males. Such environments encourage men to use women as trophies of sexual conquest and lead to higher likelihood of rape, sexual objectification, and other forms of sexual abuse of women.

7. Homophobia is one cause of premature sexual involvement, which increases the chances of sexually transmitted diseases such as AIDS/HIV and pregnancy. Sorority women often may be pressured to prove their "heteronormalcy" by becoming sexually active. Such a perspective impairs educational efforts on safer sex and sexuality awareness in the college sorority.

8. Homophobia restricts communication among sorority sisters and diminishes the possibility of creating a true sense of sisterhood and community, especially when the sorority discovers another sister is lesbian or bisexual.

9. Homophobia prevents sorority chapters from receiving the benefits of friendship and leadership offered by lesbian or bisexual sisters. Chapters may blackball or kick out members who are suspected to be lesbian or bisexual. At other times, a lesbian or bisexual sister may leave the sorority because of harassment or fear of violence.

10. Homophobia remains the leading cause of suicide among youth.

11. Homophobia compromises the entire learning environment on a college campus for all students.

12. Homophobia inhibits the appreciation of diversity in a campus community and adds to the harassment of and violence toward all minority groups. Such an environment impairs the progress of educational efforts on multiculturalism and diversity by not recognizing gay students in the campus dialogue.

13. Homophobia saps energy from more constructive sorority projects. The time and energy could be better spent doing sisterhood activities or philanthropy.

Revised from *Out on Fraternity Row: Personal Accounts of Being Gay in a College Fraternity,* edited by Shane L. Windmeyer and Pamela W. Freeman, Alyson Publications, 1998.

NOTES

1. George Weinberg, *Society and the Healthy Homosexual* (New York: St. Martin's Press, 1972).

2. Warren J. Blumenfeld, *Homophobia: How We All Pay the Price* (Boston: Beacon Press, 1992).

3. Suzanne Pharr, *Homophobia: A Weapon of Sexism* (Inverness, CA: Chardon Press, 1988).

Shane L. Windmeyer and Pamela W. Freeman, Lambda 10 Project.

What Do You Do When You Learn a Sister Is Lesbian or Bisexual?

The assumption that sororities, when compared to fraternities, are more open and comfortable environments for someone coming out is not necessarily true. In many ways, sororities have avoided sexual orientation issues just as frequently as or more so than fraternities. Most sorority nondiscrimination policies and educational efforts neglect to discuss or mention sexual orientation. As a result, it's more than likely that many sorority sisters have never knowingly encountered someone who is lesbian or bisexual and may not know what to do when they learn a sister is lesbian or bisexual. Such lack of knowledge and preparation perpetuates the ignorance and fear surrounding homosexuality and jeopardizes sisterhood for both gay and straight sorority sisters. This list suggests ideas to keep in mind when a sorority sister learns that another sister is lesbian or bisexual.

A Sorority Sister Comes Out to You...
What to Do:
- Listen to what your sister has to say and try to keep an open mind.
- Understand the personal risk she took in telling you, and if you are confused, be honest about your feelings. Realize the trust she has in you.
- Realize your sister has not changed. You may be shocked, but remember that she is still the same person she was before she came out to you.
- Respect her choice to tell you by letting her know you will not tell anyone she is lesbian or bisexual. You realize she has to come out to the sorority chapter when she is ready.
- Do not shy away from your sister. Feel free to ask questions in an open manner to better understand her, such as:

* How long have you known that you were lesbian or bisexual?
* Do other sisters or friends know that you are lesbian or bisexual?
* Has it been hard for you to carry around this secret?
* How can I support you?

• "Actions speak louder than words," so offer your support and willingness to help her through her coming-out process. She may really need a sister to count on right now.

• Communicate support to your sister. She may feel isolated, as if she is the only one in this situation.

• Make sure you know what you are talking about by using resources on the college campus. Try to educate yourself and, if comfortable, be an ally on the issue.

• Most important, remember the meaning of sisterhood and be a good sister.

A Sorority Sister Is "Outed" to the Chapter...
What to Do:

• Approach the sister in private (if possible) and let her know you are willing to listen and be a sister.

• Calm the sister if she is upset by the outing and allow her to take the lead or speak about her feelings.

• Stand up for your sister as you would for any other sister.

• Attempt to resolve any conflict among other sisters who may not understand by asking them to give the sister some time to process her feelings.

• Seek expertise from campus officials or the national headquarters if you are concerned about the chapter's response and need help processing the experience.

• Let the sister know clearly that you value her as a sister and as a person, no matter what.

A Sorority Sister Is Suspected or Perceived to Be Lesbian or Bisexual...
What to Do:

• Try not to assume anything about your sister's sexual orientation.

• Remember that your sister may be lesbian or bisexual, but she may not be ready to acknowledge this to herself or others. She needs to come out when she is ready.

• Be supportive of your sister, possibly bringing up gay topics to communicate that you would be a person with whom she can talk.

• Understand that your sister may not be lesbian or bisexual.

Your Sister Is Lesbian or Bisexual...
What Not to Do:

• Do not think it is just a phase and you can help your sister find the "right" man.

• Do not be afraid to ask questions about being lesbian or bisexual or about her coming-out process.

• Do not assume that she finds you attractive.

• Do not try to change her. Accept her as being lesbian or bisexual.

• Do not ignore your sister or treat her differently after she has come out. Still invite her to go along with you wherever you go and, most important, do not change who you are.

• Do not be ashamed or fail to defend a sister who is lesbian or bisexual if she is otherwise a good sister.

• Do not be afraid to use the word "lesbian" or "bisexual," and do not ignore her when she brings up gay topics.

• Do not try to restrict the sister's freedom to share being lesbian or bisexual or to be a public role model. The Greek system and the campus at large need more out student leaders to identify with. Do not be surprised if more Greeks start to come out of the closet.

• Do not be worried about what other chapters think or the reputation of the chapter. Lead by example, and remember that there are lesbian and bisexual women in every house. Some are simply less fortunate and do not have an "open-minded" environment for sisters to come out.

• Do not assume that all her guests are her dates, and do not make a big deal if she brings a date to the house or a fraternity or sorority function. Treat her with respect, as you would any other person.

• Do not kick your sister out of the sorority for being lesbian or bisexual. Such an action may be in violation of university policy and definitely contradicts the ideals of sisterhood.

• Do not be afraid to approach a lesbian or bisexual sister if you think her actions are inappropriate. Hold a lesbian or bisexual sister to the same standards as all sisters.

• Do not treat the sister as if she is a public relations disaster for the chapter. Support your sister's openness and work together to communicate similar messages. She will always speak as a member of the sorority. Trust that your sister is going to represent your sorority proudly wherever she goes, as always.

• Do not feel let down if the sister decides to leave the house due to other members' actions or behavior. Be supportive and continue to be her friend.

Revised from *Out on Fraternity Row: Personal Accounts of Being Gay in a College Fraternity*, edited by Shane L. Windmeyer and Pamela W. Freeman, Alyson Publications, 1998.

Shane L. Windmeyer and Pamela W. Freeman, Lambda 10 Project.

Creating a Greek Safe Zone Ally Program
Contributed by Regina Young Hyatt

Safe Zone Ally programs have been in existence on college campuses for several years. Schools such as Emory University, Northern Illinois University, Emporia State University, Western Illinois University, the University of North Carolina at Charlotte, Duke University, and hundreds of others have implemented such programs. The Safe Zone Ally program fosters a welcoming and supportive campus environment for lesbian, gay, bisexual, and transgendered students, faculty, and staff by creating a visible network of allies. Safe Zone Allies act as resource people who can provide support and information while respecting privacy.[1]

Safe Zone Ally programs employ a visible network of people, including students, faculty, or staff members. People who have attended some training agree to post, wear, or display a symbol that indicates involvement with the program. The role of an ally varies, but by posting the symbol, the participant agrees to listen openly, confront homophobic jokes or comments, use inclusive language, keep shared information confidential, and educate himself or herself on issues related to gay, lesbian, bisexual, and transgender concerns.

Why the Safe Zone Ally Program Is Important to the Greek Community

In February 2000 a fraternity pledge was tied to a tree on the campus of the University of Florida. I AM A FAG was written on his face.[2] This was just one example of the homophobia that exists within the Greek system all across the United States. Other acts of intolerance and bigotry are exemplified, and the need for support is evident in the stories written by the women in this book, as well as in the stories of men in *Out on Fraternity Row: Personal Accounts of Being Gay in a College Fraternity.*[3]

Greek life is representative of American life in general—groups of people coming together with common interests and concerns. Many gay and lesbian people enter into Greek life with the same interests and concerns held by their brothers and sisters. The greatest goal of the Greek community is fostering brotherhood and sisterhood. A study by Douglas Case indicates that lesbian, gay, and bisexual students join fraternities and sororities for reasons similar to those of heterosexual students.[4] These reasons include friendship and camaraderie, a support group and sense of belonging, and social activities. Homophobia hurts brotherhood and sisterhood by inhibiting the development of close friendships. Of course, developing friendships is one of the central components of Greek life.

With possibly 10% of Greek students being gay, lesbian, or bisexual, it is becoming increasingly important for Greek communities to recognize and appreciate their GLB members. Creating a Safe Zone program is an excellent way to accomplish this goal and to create an environment free of homophobia.

As mentioned previously, many college campuses currently have Safe Zone programs, and your institution also may have one. The question is, "Have you or your sisters ever heard of it?" We hope the answer is yes, but chances are the answer is no. Creating a Greek Safe Zone Ally program can provide visibility to your group and other members of the Greek community. Visibility is the cornerstone of the Safe Zone Ally program. By creating a visible network of allies, we can create an atmosphere of support and love for our gay, lesbian, bisexual, and transgendered brothers and sisters. You may ask, "Why do we need a Greek Safe Zone Ally program if my institution already has a program?" A great question! We believe Greek communities can become a part of an existing program, but we also advocate creating something specific to Greek organizations. Such a strong negative image exists regarding Greeks and homophobia. Safe Zone is a visible, proactive way to combat this image and to show support for closeted members within the Greek system specifically.

Clearly, we are doing something incorrectly when it comes to the issues of support and love. In the survey by Douglas Case, more than 70% of those responding said they had encountered homophobic or heterosexist attitudes within their chapter. Also, of those students who were gay, lesbian, bisexual, or transgendered, only 12% came out to someone in their chapter.[5] This is not a welcoming environment, yet we would all like to believe that our chapters are open to diversity. Displaying the Safe Zone symbol, providing training to members of the Greek community, and educating ourselves on issues of sexual orientation form the path to creating a welcoming environment in the college Greek system.

How to Start a Greek Safe Zone Ally Program

• Assess the needs of the Greek community of which you are a part. Are there GLBT members of the Greek community at your institution? Chances are the answer will be yes, although many members may be closeted.

• Seek the support of a campus department or office. Your institution may already have a Safe Zone program. If so, enlist the help of its coordinators to help you get started. If not, try the student affairs or student services area. Someone there should be able to help. Talk to the Greek adviser as well.

• Do research. Many institutions have their Safe Zone information on the Web. Some well-placed phone calls to other institutions could help. The Lambda 10 Project also has developed a Greek Safe Zone Ally program with a set of resources specifically designed for college Greeks on any campus. Visit the Web site at www.lambda10.org for additional information.

• Decide on a method of delivery. At my institution we decided that no one could post the Safe Zone symbol until they went through some training. We offer two-hour sessions to faculty, staff, and students throughout the school year. Perhaps chapter meetings or an all-Greek educational event would be an appropriate time to do limited training.

• Develop handouts or a manual. It's important to provide allies with resources so they can be helpful to others when asked questions or for information. Manuals should include basic information about what it means to be GLBT, strategies for being an effective ally, and a bibliography of other resources.

• Develop a Greek Safe Zone logo. This is an important part of Safe Zone. Below you can see a sample logo created specifically from the Lambda 10 Project's Greek Safe Zone Ally program for college campuses nationwide. The Greek Safe Zone Ally symbol comes with a brief training manual for educating allies. You can purchase these logos for your program by visiting www.lambda10.org. But you may also choose to design your own for your Greek community.

• Create effective publicity and promotion for the program. I am a big advocate of the WIFM theory: What's in It for Me? As it is with any program, people need to know how they can benefit by participating. The answer is simple. An environment that is welcoming and supportive of *all* brothers and sisters benefits everyone, not just heterosexuals. Every bit of promotion you do for the program needs to send this message.

• Do not be discouraged if enthusiasm among Greek members is lacking. One or two Safe Zone Allies are better than none. Not every member of the Greek community is ready or willing to take on this role. You do not want to force anyone to become an ally.

GREEK
SAFE ZONE
ALLY

Benefits and Risks of Being a Greek Safe Zone Ally

To be an ally is to unite oneself with another to promote a common interest. People who are allies are not only helpers but also have a common interest with those whom they desire to help. In an alliance, both parties stand to benefit from the bond or connection they share.[6] An ally is a person who believes society is a better place when it practices inclusion of all people rather than the exclusion of some people. He or she educates himself or herself to develop an understanding of gay, lesbian, bisexual, and transgendered people.

The benefits of becoming a Safe Zone Ally are many. You have the opportunity to learn so much more about people who are GLBT and how your values and beliefs about sexual orientation affect your own life and the lives of others. You can impact the life of another person by being a role model and simply by caring enough to listen. This is what brotherhood and sisterhood are all about. The role of ally is also the role of an educator. Confronting derogatory language or jokes, teaching others what you have learned about GLBT issues, and speaking supportively about GLBT concerns are the cornerstone of what it means to be an ally. Your support or care for another person may be the only support and care that that person has in his or her life. Becoming an ally means you are empowering yourself to fight prejudice and bigotry in the world. You become strong!

I would be naïve if I let you believe being an ally was easy or without risk. As a vocal ally, I truly understand these risks. Others will speculate about your own sexual orientation, so you have to be comfortable with who you are. You will become the subject of gossip and rumors. In the Greek community this can be especially difficult. Morality and values often play a role in discussions about sexual orientation, so you must be comfortable with your morality and values.

The benefits of creating a Greek Safe Zone and becoming a Safe Zone Ally outweigh the risks. Such endeavors also help to meet the goal that is common to all Greek organizations—fostering an environment of brotherhood and sisterhood. What is in it for me, as an individual, is also important. The knowledge of the individual impact that allies can make is very significant. Knowing that you made a difference in the life of another person is powerful.

Conclusion

Safe Zone Ally programs do work. Students who have started such programs say that they feel Safe Zone helped them to improve the overall campus climate. It is comforting for students to know there is a safe place to discuss issues of sexual orientation and that there is education of the campus community regarding these issues.[7] A Greek Safe Zone Ally program will work for Greek communities as well. While Greeks are less likely to be a part of or know about campus Safe Zone programs, they need it most, for closeted members to feel safe and to create environments that are free from homophobia.

Creating a Safe Zone program specifically for Greek communities is paramount. Many times Greek organizations have visibility and power on college campuses that other student organizations do not have. Showing that the Greek community on your campus is supportive of GLBT people proves that Greeks believe in brotherhood and sisterhood for all people. Greek organizations were founded on the principles of challenging the status quo and embracing the rights of all people. Live up to this principle.

Regina Young Hyatt *is the assistant director of student activities at the University of North Carolina at Charlotte. She also volunteers as one of the facilitators for the campus-wide Safe Zone program, serves as coadviser to the gay student group PRIDE, and is a member of the Gay, Lesbian, Bisexual, and Transgender Faculty/Staff Concerns Committee.*

NOTES

1. "Opening Minds, Opening Doors, Opening Hearts" (training manual of the Northern Illinois University Safe Zone Ally program, DeKalb, 1999).

2. Matthew Boedy, "U. Florida's Phi Delt May Face Immediate Suspension," *Independent Florida Alligator,* March 27, 2000.

3. Shane L. Windmeyer and Pamela W. Freeman, *Out on Fraternity Row: Personal Accounts of Being Gay in a College Fraternity* (Los Angeles: Alyson Publications, 1998).

4. Douglas N. Case, "A Glimpse of the Invisible Membership," in "Perspectives," Newsletter of the Association of Fraternity Advisors 23, April-May 1996, 7–10.

5. Ibid.

6. See note 1.

7. Ronnie Sanlo, "College Safe Zone Programs: Does Practice Reflect Theory?" *Student Affairs Today,* June 1999.

Because the Bible Tells Me So...
Contributed by Rebecca Jimenez and Douglas Bauder

- *Our sorority ritual is based on the Bible and Christian teachings, so how can we accept gays into membership?*
- *Since I was raised a Christian, how can I be expected to give up my moral beliefs in order to accept someone who is gay?*
- *How can I support a lesbian sorority sister when the Bible says homosexuality is wrong?*

Well, that depends, in part, on how you read the Bible. Each of us comes to understand scripture (or any holy writing) based upon a variety of things, including the religious traditions out of which we come, the values of our families, our personal understanding of God, and our life experiences, to name a few.

Peter Gomes, chaplain at Harvard and author of a fascinating work, *The Good Book: Reading the Bible With Mind and Heart,*[1] has some suggestions about how we might approach this task. He spends considerable time looking at the ways the Bible has been used and abused over the centuries to justify racism, anti-Semitism, sexism, and finally, what he calls "the last prejudice," homophobia.

Is it possible that at the heart of the argument that blacks are inferior, that Jews are going to hell, and that women are "below" men is a particular way of reading the Bible? Unfortunately, it is! And Gomes and many other Christians and Jews believe that the Bible is still being used (abused) to keep gay men and lesbians second-class citizens. Some so-called "people of faith" have even used scripture as a means for advocating violence against those who identify as homosexual or bisexual.

There are others who believe, in effect, that the Bible says *nothing* about homosexuality as an orientation. Rather, those passages that refer to homosexual behavior are speaking not about loving, consensual relationships but about abusive and idolatrous behavior.[2]

While the controversies surrounding sexuality and spirituality probably cannot be resolved in the context of one simple exercise, we would like to invite you and your friends to consider the possibility of interpreting scripture in some new ways. In 1994 Chris Glaser, an ordained Presbyterian pastor and a gay man, wrote a devotional guide *The Word is OUT: The Bible Reclaimed For Lesbians and Gay Men,* a collection of 365 daily meditations.[3] We have chosen two to read and reflect on. We invite you to consider the questions following each meditation. You may answer them on your own or discuss them with others. As you do this, we encourage you to think of the Bible as a compass for your personal journey and not as a club with which to beat up on other people.

Meditation One

For it was you who formed my inward parts;
You knit me together in my mother's womb.
I praise you, for I am fearfully and wonderfully made.
—Psalm 139:13–14

God wove together our bodies. God wove together our gender and our sexuality. The tender intimacy of God's personal involvement in our embryonic creation is a cause for praise, awe, and wonder.

God must have conceived us the way we are: not the way we express ourselves—that is up to us—but who we are. If we are gay, God made us that way. If we are lesbian, God made us that way. If we are bisexual, God made us that way. If we are transgendered, God made us that way.

Our sexual differences have made us a target for blame, fear, and horror by those who don't understand. Rather, they should be a cause for praise, awe, and wonder that we exist. God is very creative and not committed to one formula of existence. God is not as dull or unimaginative as people seem to think!

1. What messages did you receive as you were growing up about your gender? List several. Were they positive, negative, or neutral?

2. What is one message that you would like to have heard?

3. How did you feel about yourself as a girl or a boy? How did you express those feelings?

4. What messages did you receive as you were growing up about people with different sexual orientations (homosexual or bisexual)? How did you feel about those messages?

5. Do you know someone, now, who is lesbian, gay, bisexual, or transgendered? Has knowing this person changed your feelings about issues related to homosexuality? In what way?

6. Think about your gender identity and sexual orientation and, then, reread Psalm 139:13–14. Is there something you need to do at this point in your life to affirm that you are "fearfully and wonderfully" made? What is it?

Thank you for intricately weaving me "in the depths of the earth," my mother's womb, Creator God.

Meditation Two

In everything do unto others as you would have them do to you; for this is the law and the prophets.
—Matthew 5:12

Jesus here turned into a positive what other teachers of this time had said in the negative: Do not do to others what you would not want them to do to you.

Until we love ourselves properly, as Martin Luther encouraged, we may try to "feel better about ourselves" by putting down other categories of people. One of my big disappointments when coming out as gay was discovering that the oppressed, who presumably would know better, easily fall into oppressive behavior. Though more sensitive to our own racism, for example, gay men and lesbians can behave as racist as the rest of the society. People of color, who might also know better, may be as homophobic. And all of us may be hesitant to share what little power we have.

Jesus transformed others' prohibition into positive action: "Do to others as you would have them do to you."

It's not enough to refrain from racism. If we want people of color to support our rights, then we must support theirs, whether or not they do so for us. The Golden Rule, expressed in most religions, does not make our behavior dependent on how others act. Rather, it's based on how we want to be treated.

1. Can you remember a time in your life when the Golden Rule first became real for you? What were the circumstances?

2. As you think about a particular individual or group of people, to whom do you have the most trouble applying this lesson? Why?

3. Imagine you are struggling with strong emotional or sexual feelings for a friend of the same gender. What would be helpful for you to hear someone say that would make you feel accepted?

4. Think of someone in your sorority or fraternity who might be lesbian or gay. In the context of your friendship, what would it look like to "do unto them as you would have them do unto you"?

Help me to do for others what I would like them to do for me.

Finally, we invite you to think of one of your sorority sisters who joined when you did and with whom you learned about the ideals and values of the sisterhood. Together you discussed your reasons for joining, discovered your common bonds, shared your dreams and visions, your joys and sorrows, your triumphs and disappointments. Suppose through this process you became close friends—truly sisters. And now, precisely because you are so close, because of your common experiences through the university and sorority, because your friend trusts and feels safe with you, because she embraces the same values you do, such as honesty and truth, she confides in you that she is lesbian. She finally must be honest and open, must unburden herself of the silence and fear of discovery with another person she can trust, and you are the person she chooses.

1. How do you respond? Can you suddenly change how you feel about your friend? Can you immediately forget the respect and affection you have held for your sister? In light of Psalm 139, can you honestly believe that either of you is *not* created in the image of God or is *not* a sacred, beloved child of God?

2. Consider again Matthew 5:12. The Golden Rule may be the most concise expression of the whole of the Bible and of Christianity. Indeed,

every one of the world's major religions bears this same foundational decree. Just as you want to be accorded dignity, spoken to in truth and honesty, treated with compassion and kindness, so too are you called to act accordingly in all of your relationships with others. Will you allow this calling to be extended to your sister now?

We have seen how interpretation of the Bible and Christian teachings are influenced by various factors, cultural and personal. Every day we interpret our life experiences under the influence of these same factors, based on usually unconscious assumptions. We invite you to engage the exercises on these pages to become more aware of those influences and assumptions. For example, how have these influences and assumptions colored Christian teachings? In what ways might some interpretations of the Bible come into conflict with its fundamental themes of justice and compassion? And, especially, we invite you to be intentional about putting into action the Christian values on which your sorority is founded. How will you express justice and compassion in your daily interactions? How will you seek wisdom and truth?

Ultimately, how we see ourselves and relate to others is deeply rooted in our spirituality, our understanding of God. It may well be that the issues we have raised, the approach to scripture we have suggested, and the questions we have posed have enabled you to look at yourself or your beliefs in some new ways. Perhaps in doing so you find yourself wanting to know more. Here are some resources, in addition to those already cited, that you may find helpful.

John E. Fortunato, *Embracing the Exile* (San Francisco: Harper, 1982).

Virginia Ramey Mollenkott, *Sensuous Spirituality* (New York: Crossroad, 1993).

Suzanne Pharr, *Homophobia: A Weapon of Sexism* (Inverness, CA: Chardon Press, 1997).

Letha Dawson Scanzoni and Virginia Ramey Mollencott, *Is The Homosexual My Neighbor?* (San Francisco: Harper, 1994).

Maurine C. Waun, *More Than Welcome* (St. Louis: Chalice Press, 1999).

Walter Wink, editor, *Homosexuality and Christian Faith: Questions of Conscience for the Churches* (Minneapolis: Fortress Press, 1999).

Rebecca Jimenez *is an ordained American Baptist minister and director of the Center for University Ministry, Indiana University, Bloomington.*

Douglas Bauder *is an ordained Moravian minister and coordinator of the Gay, Lesbian, Bisexual, Transgender Student Support Services Office, Indiana University, Bloomington.*

NOTES

1. Peter Gomes, *The Good Book: Reading the Bible With Mind and Heart* (New York: William Morrow, 1996).

2. Daniel Helminiak, *What the Bible REALLY Says About Homosexuality* (San Francisco: Alamo Square Press, 1994).

3. Chris Glaser, *The Word is OUT: The Bible Reclaimed for Lesbians and Gay Men* (San Francisco: Harper, 1994).

Dealing With Sororities and Sexual Orientation Issues
Contributed by Teresa L. Hall

Coming out in a sorority—how could there be a more comfortable environment in which to share information about ourselves? Certainly, organizations based on love and friendship have the potential to be warm, nurturing, and inclusive, especially to those who are experiencing personal turmoil or strife. Unfortunately, though, sororities do not always live up to the image of inclusiveness one might expect. Many factors make sororities distinct from other student organizations, one important difference being the emphasis on unity within the chapter. Explicitly as well as implicitly, there exists pressure to conform to the chapter culture. Members who violate the norms of the group are often considered outcasts, and rather than being valued for their individuality, they are often seen as threats to chapter cohesion. Women who reveal their lesbian or bisexual identity may be viewed as threats to the sanctity of the chapter. Sorority chapters are filled with complex relationships. Understanding the webs of relationships that exist within a chapter is critical to serving as an ally to a woman who is lesbian, bisexual or questioning her sexual identity.

As a Greek affairs professional for many years, I worried about the level of support that lesbians or women questioning their sexual identities felt within their chapters. I served as the primary university contact for fraternities and sororities on two very different campuses with strong Greek systems: Southeast Missouri State University and Indiana University, Bloomington. In my current position as director of student activities, the coordinator for Greek life reports to me, and I am responsible for adjudicating group violations of the code of student conduct. I am a longtime supporter of Greek systems, particularly sororities. I know I would not be the person I am today without my sorority experience.

The purpose of this resource is to explain the organizational structure of the sorority system, beginning with a description of sorority life from the individual perspective. Descriptions of the local chapter, campus system, alumnae, and national levels will follow. This information can serve as a helpful resource for those who are unfamiliar with the sorority system but wish to be of assistance to women who face difficulty because of their sexual orientation or because of homophobia in their organizations. Each section is introduced with a scenario to provide a context in which the reader can apply the information.

Individual

A private conversation between two sisters is overheard, leading to rumors in the chapter about their sexuality.

Joining a sorority is a special experience. A woman is not simply affiliating with an established group; she joins the chapter as part of a group—a new-member class. In many instances the closest of relationships develop out of her new member group. Women of a new-member class, aside from joining the chapter at the same time, are often at similar places in their educational careers. On most campuses, the majority of women who join sororities are first-year students. The size of new-member classes can range from a handful of women to as many as 50 or more. For many women, those from their new-member class are the friends and sisters with whom they share their entire college experience.

Another important relationship for women in sororities is between a new member and her "big sister." A big sister is assigned to a new member sometime during her new-member period. This process varies from organization to organization: In some it is a mutual selection process whereby both the big sister and new member indicate preferences, and in other cases big sisters are granted little sisters without input from new members. This relationship between an initiated, more seasoned member of the chapter and a new member is established in the hope that the older member can guide and teach the new member about the intricacies of chapter life. Often, families exist within chapters. Families, as designated by colors or special apparel, are the networks of little sisters connected to one big sister. The relationships extend further to show kinship between sisters matched to a big sister, and then when little sisters have little sisters—similar to siblings, children, and cousins.

Informal groups also develop within the chapter. These groups develop over similar interests, majors, backgrounds or even due to living arrangements. Informal groups often become the main source of fellowship for chapter members—they will eat, study, shop, etc. together in these groups.

So how can this information be useful when rumors spread about the sexual orientation of a sister or sisters? The significance of the big sister/little sister relationship can be important in such a scenario toward mentoring initiates to help them understand the principles of acceptance and inclusion, true sisterhood, and the concept of support for one another. The relationships among individuals also can be used to control rumors and provide factual and educational information.

Chapter

A date function is coming up, and a sister would like to bring the woman she is dating.

This complex web of relationships exists within a structured and hierarchical organizational environment. Each chapter has an executive board consisting of a variety of officers, but usually included are the following positions:

- president
- membership development officer
- recruitment officer
- new member development officer
- secretary
- treasurer
- other officers as dictated by local custom or need

In addition to an executive board, chapters often have standards or judicial boards that deal with alleged violations of chapter policy or conduct of behavior. It is important to know about these boards, because the existence of them affects the privacy of each member. A chapter member who has a personal problem or indiscretion would most likely have her situation discussed by one or both of these boards. While some groups of women are better at being discreet and keeping confidences than are others, chapter structure will affect privacy.

Most business is conducted at chapter meetings, which are held weekly. Some variation of *Robert's Rules of Order* are followed; the adherence to rules of order also is dictated by local custom or need. Issues pertaining to the whole chapter are discussed at chapter meetings. The efficacy of the executive board determines the extent to which personal or private matters are kept that way and not made the business of the entire chapter. Failure to discuss something at a chapter meeting may not necessarily mean the issue will not be discussed by other members of a chapter. Chapter members are highly aware of what is happening within the personal lives of their membership, and they sometimes involve themselves in issues that do not concern them.

Other forums for discussion of personal issues are gavel pass or candlelights, which are special meetings called when there are issues or controversies that may not be resolved through the regular business mechanisms. They provide members a free opportunity to express thoughts and feelings outside of the structure of meetings.

If a sister in a chapter that had never dealt with same-sex dating wanted to bring her female date to a chapter function, she may be well advised to take advantage of the organizational structure to prepare the membership. Having the support of the chapter's officers may help pave the way for acceptance and support for the sister and her date. Also, discussing such an upcoming function in a forum that has been established for the purpose of understanding the personal issues of sisters, such as a gavel pass, may empower the sister to share information about herself in a supportive setting.

Greek System

A chapter is being stereotyped as being lesbian; other groups are refusing to socialize or sponsor activities with the group.

A chapter exists within a Greek system, which consists of all social fraternities and sororities on campus. Most Greek systems have three governing boards:

- Panhellenic Council (for the traditionally white sororities)
- Interfraternity Council (for the traditionally white fraternities)
- Pan-Hellenic Council (for the historically black fraternities and sororities)

These three councils are local units of national governing boards. Their authority is drawn from that which the national fraternities and sororities have granted to the local councils through their respective national councils. The governing councils have established guidelines and procedures that determine how chapters and individuals should be treated. A reality within most Greek systems is a strong and speedy rumor mill. Information, both accurate and inaccurate, spreads quickly within the Greek system, so privacy within the chapter is not the only issue with which a woman will need to contend.

If a woman is concerned about her treatment in a chapter, the Panhellenic president could be a likely ally. In addition, if a chapter is being ostracized by the campus's entire Greek system, the IFC, Panhellenic, and Pan-Hellenic presidents could be allies in addressing the problem through their leadership within their respective councils.

Alumnae

An alumna adviser cancels an educational program that was to include a panel with lesbian, gay, bisexual, and heterosexual students.

Members of sororities interact with alumnae as visitors returning to the chapter for special occasions or as alumnae advisers. Undergraduate members are likely to be more liberal and progressive in their views than the alumnae. Alumnae view the current undergraduate experience through the frame of reference of their own experiences, and over time these perceptions and memories will have changed. Remembered accounts of what it was like when an alumna was in the chapter may not be entirely accurate.

Alumnae are the leadership of the national organization. Executive boards are elected, usually biennially, at the national conventions at which undergraduates are the primary voting members. The power and influence of undergraduates as well as that of alumnae members varies from one organization to another. As within the chapter, a structured organizational environment exists within the national organization. Beyond the elected executive board of the national organization exist many appointed volunteer positions within the organization. For example, alumnae advisers often report to a state, regional, or province officer who in turn reports to a national executive board officer. Organizations differ on the selection and appointment of an adviser. For most sororities or women's fraternities, the national organization confirms the appointment of advisers.

Capitalizing on the influence of the votes of undergraduate members can be helpful when an alumna adviser's views about acceptable programs conflict with the needs of a local chapter. While the authority structure appears to be "top-down," the national organizations pride themselves on being democratic in setting of policy. Staff members who help students develop leadership skills can help leaders on the local level learn to be assertive in communicating with advisers and alumnae. Such assertiveness can be necessary in confronting alumnae in constructive ways as the educational needs of the chapter undergo inevitable change, sometimes in a direction that is uncomfortable for the alumnae.

National Headquarters

The nondiscrimination clause of the national organization does not include sexual orientation, nor does the organization offer any resources regarding sexuality.

Each national organization has a headquarters with a paid staff, many of whom are initiated members of the organization. The size of the national staff is consistent with the size of the national organization; i.e., the more chapters and members an organization has, the more staff members it will have. Most national organizations have paid staff who travel to visit chapters. Titles for these positions vary from traveling consultant to educational leadership consultant. These staff members are often recent graduates who will spend a year or two working for the national organization by traveling to chapters to improve organizational development. These are well-intentioned individuals who do not carry much organizational clout.

If a national organization's nondiscrimination clause is not meeting the needs of the membership at the local level, one strategy is to use the traveling consultant as a communications link. Often, these staff members are recent enough graduates that they can relate especially well to the values and issues facing the local membership. Also on the local level, members in institutions with inclusive nondiscrimination clauses can point out to the national leaders the inconsistencies between campus and organizational policy. Finally, student affairs staff at the campus level can supplement resources on the national level by offering campus resources to local chapters and notifying national organizations and staff of their existence. Showing that sharing of resources does not always have to be from the national to the local level, but can be two-way, can help to bridge gaps between understanding of issues on the national level and the local level.

The complex web of relationships that makes up a sorority could work in support of a woman who is lesbian, bisexual, or questioning of her identity, or it could work against her. Understanding how Greek-letter organizations are structured is important to anyone who wants to be an ally for members of a sorority. Knowing the structure allows an ally to use it to the member's advantage when addressing personal issues.

Teresa L. Hall, Ph.D., *is the director of student activities at Towson University in Maryland. Her professional career includes work in Greek life at Southeast Missouri State University and Indiana University, Bloomington.*

Responding to a Tragedy of Homophobia
Contributed by Sonia ImMasche

Most campuses have procedures in place to address incidents, emergencies, and tragedies. Most national or international fraternities and sororities have similar procedures. When an incident of homophobia occurs in the Greek community, however, standard campus and national or international response procedures can be severely tested and may not be sufficient to address the challenges presented by such an incident.

Any Greek-related incident or tragedy has the potential to draw attention from other people on campus and those in the media. Regardless of whether the incident involves a few individuals or an entire chapter, it is difficult to keep others from hearing about it and speculating about it. When the incident involves homophobia, the response challenges can multiply exponentially.

Responding to an incident of homophobia in the Greek community is different from dealing with other incidents and tragedies. The general response model includes addressing concerns of chapter members, other chapters, parents, alumni, national or international headquarters, and the institution. Incidents of homophobia can generate emotional responses, which can be more intense and can affect more people than other types of Greek-related incidents. Homophobic incidents reinforce stereotypes of Greek-letter organizations as being bastions of intolerance that perpetuate the ignorance and fear surrounding homosexuality. While many types of incidents may not have a negative impact on the other Greek chapters on a campus, an incident of homophobia has a negative impact on all chapters and most (if not all) of the individual chapter members—especially those who are gay, lesbian, bisexual, or transgendered. Chapters and their members are more likely to respond with anger toward the individual(s) or chapter(s) responsible for the incident. The response most likely will be vocal and public as the other chapters attempt to express their outrage and their need to distance themselves from the offenders. Chapter members who also are a part of the GLBT community become vulnerable. Where these individuals may have felt comfortable or supported prior to the incident of homophobia, they now may feel exposed and unsupported. Members who have not yet come out or who are out only to chapter members may fear being outed to the entire campus. They may also fear being abandoned as chapters rush to disclaim their involvement in the incident. In chapters where one or more members are out and supported by the chapter, an incident of homophobia may place these members in the position of becoming the "gay token"—the gay Greek who is supposed to speak for the entire Greek community (both GLBT and straight). Chapters with gay members will be challenged to support their members, while addressing the potential of being labeled as the "gay chapter" by other Greeks, unaffiliated students, faculty, staff, and community members. By association, the host institution also comes under attack, because the perpetrators of the incident are involved in campus-recognized or -supported organizations. My institution is not the first to experience an incident of homophobia in our Greek community. Unfortunately, our institution probably will not be the last to experience an incident of this type. The insights we have gained may be of benefit to other institutions. It is this perspective that we have been asked to share.

Colorado State University and our Greek community were confronted with a significant incident of homophobia in October 1998. Homecoming that year occurred during the same time frame as the brutal attack on Matthew Shepard. The annual homecoming parade (an event jointly sponsored by the university, the public school district, and the city) had a *Wizard of Oz*–related theme, which prompted numerous entries with scarecrows. This particular year, we were celebrating the 125th anniversary of our city's official founding. The community homecoming steering committee decided to select "There's No Place Like Home!" as the parade theme—hence the numerous *Wizard of Oz* images on parade entries.

The parade is relatively large. In 1998 we had 176 entries, including all of the local schools, many youth groups, numerous junior and senior high school bands, many businesses, campus clubs, residence halls, departments, Greek organizations, and other student groups as well as entries from local government offices and service agencies. One sorority and fraternity jointly sponsored a float, which included a scarecrow that had been defaced with antigay graffiti. Five of the fraternity's new members (pledges) rode in the pickup truck that was pulling the float and displayed the scarecrow at random moments during the parade. By odd coincidence, however, the scarecrow was not in place whenever the float was in sight of parade officials.

The rescuers who found Matthew Shepard said they thought he was a scarecrow when they first saw him tied to the fence where his assailants left him for dead. The defaced parade scarecrow was immediately connected to Matthew Shepard when a parade story and a picture appeared in the campus newspaper on the Monday following the parade. At the same time, Matthew was in our local community hospital fighting for his life. What ordinarily would have been an extremely distasteful incident became international in scope. The *Denver Post* reported on October 13, 1998—one day after the float story first appeared in our campus newspaper:

Scarecrow Float Sparks Inquiry
By J. Sebastian Sinisi (Denver Post Staff Writer)

> *Colorado State University launched an investigation Monday into how a float carrying a scarecrow and antigay graffiti got into the homecoming parade this past weekend…. The graffiti's offensiveness was compounded by the fact that University of Wyoming student Matthew Shepard, victim of an apparent hate crime due to his sexual preference, was dying in Poudre Valley Hospital, only a few miles away. Shepard, who was severely beaten and tied to a fence like a scarecrow, died early Monday.*

The article goes on to describe the offense in detail, follows up with reactions to it by university officials, and paints a negative picture of the climate in Fort Collins and Colorado.

Response Plan

Our institution and Greek community have experience in responding to tragedy. The response plan we use is comprehensive and works extremely well. Even with a strong blueprint, however, our prior response experiences could not accurately predict the intense reaction created by this incident. Some responses were not immediately foreseeable. Therefore, we had to develop portions of our response strategy as we went along. Some of the perspectives gained from this experience might be helpful to other campuses.

Who Needs to Know

As soon as an incident occurs or becomes known, key individuals need to be notified and pulled together to form a response team. General procedures for Greek Life called for notification of the director of Greek life and the vice president for student affairs. This was done Saturday afternoon, as soon as the scarecrow incident came to light. In retrospect, however, contact procedures should have included the director of university public relations and the university president. Had this contact occurred, the response team could have met and developed a plan before the incident was reported in the campus newspaper and subsequently picked up by other media.

Forming the Response Team

An incident response team needs to include representation from a variety of institutional offices and organizations. The Colorado State team included: the President's Office; the Office of the Vice President for Student Affairs; Judicial Affairs; the student body president and vice president; university legal counsel; GLBT Student Services; the Office of Greek Life; the vice president of University Advancement (University Development and Alumni Relations); university director of public relations; and the campus police department. The response team met daily at 8 A.M. during the first week of the crisis. Less frequent contact was maintained following the first week.

Setting Response Priorities

If an incident occurs, it may be necessary to respond quickly. At its first meeting, the response team reported on initiatives, which had already begun. All team members were briefed on the incident and related concerns. Response priorities were identified and individuals or offices were assigned to take specific responsibility for portions of the response plan. Team members with intertwined responsibilities provided updated status reports as the initial response progressed. The response team identified the following as immediate needs:

• *Set up safe places for students to come to talk about their feelings and concerns. Seek support from university staff to be available to meet with students.* The GLBT Student Services Office (which was in the process of moving to a new location when the float incident occurred) set up a large discussion space in the foyer of the Student Center Theater. This area was staffed and heavily used by students during the first several weeks after the parade. Many student-friendly offices displayed LGB SAFE ZONE stickers and signs reading DIVERSITY WELCOMED HERE as an indication to students that the spaces were safe for them to use. The University Counseling Center made its staff available to speak with students who did not wish to use one of the more "public" areas. The counseling center also provided staff support to the members of the fraternity and sorority that sponsored the float—to help them work through the multitude of issues they were facing and the feelings members were having.

• *Identify one or more key institutional spokespeople to answer all media inquiries and public comments.* In our case, initial responses came primarily from the university president and the vice president for student affairs. The director of university public relations provided backup support. The director of public relations assumed more of the communication responsibilities as the disciplinary process (which was detailed) continued past the original one-week estimate.

• *Establish a means to notify all Greek chapters and their members of the details of the response plan and the need for them to support the plan.* Chapter presidents, Panhellenic and IFC executive council members, NPHC council members, Latino chapters, and chapter delegates were notified on Monday of a special meeting to be held on Tuesday afternoon in conjunction with the regularly scheduled meetings of Panhellenic and IFC. Initial contact with these groups requested that they refer all inquiries to the vice president's office or public relations. Chapter leaders also were asked to encourage their members to refrain from speculation about the incident and to wait until details were shared at the Tuesday meeting.

• *Contact appropriate national or international headquarters and alumni advisers to get them "on board" with the institutional response and to emphasize the need to work as a team as investigation and decision making proceed.* Do not be surprised if the responses differ from organization to organization. We experienced one response from the sorority involved. The fraternity had a different response, which initially surprised us. (The differences in these responses will be covered in another section.)

• *Designate one or more key institutional spokespeople to address concerns raised by donors and alumni.*

• *Establish a plan to further investigate the incident and to implement disciplinary procedures for any individual(s) or chapter(s) involved in the incident.* It is important that any disciplinary process be in response to violation of specific student codes of conduct, violation of event regulations, or violations of the law. (Several parade participation requirements were violated in this particular case, which enabled the disciplinary process.) While the initial stages of the investigation and response were in progress, the university was contacted several times by the American Civil Liberties Union. The ACLU contacts reiterated the response team's initial acknowledgment that all investigation and any subsequent disciplinary action needed to focus on conduct codes and event regulations. Be *very careful* to separate the disciplinary action and subsequent sanctions from First Amendment rights and free speech issues, which also are associated with the incident. Even though antigay speech or displays are abhorrent, free speech rights still allow them.

• *Determine the need for a campus or community gathering (such as a service, vigil, or speak-out) to address the crisis.* Make necessary arrangements for such an event if one is to be held.

• *Determine the emotional and experiential preparedness of designated staff people to work with the crisis.* Campuses that do not have a strong network of connections with the GLBT community (including staff and student relationships and support services), and front-line staff who do not have personal connections or experience in working with GLBT people can feel uncomfortable and overwhelmed when dealing with crisis issues created by the incident. Good advance training and personal relationships with GLBT staff and students are excellent resources when a crisis occurs. I am fortunate to have a strong relationship with a number of GLBT students. The float incident was extremely upsetting to me, and I was concerned that my relationship with these students would be severely damaged. I saw one of the students on Tuesday morning and felt compelled to apologize to him and ask him if he would ever speak to me again. This student was absolutely wonderful. He reached out, hugged me, and told me that the incident was not my fault and that we still were good friends. Even though he was in pain, he offered to provide any assistance he could to help us work through the crisis together. When the story began to circulate via E-mail and the wire services, I also received a call from a professional colleague who had been a good friend for many years. He told me he wanted to hear our side of the story before he made any judgments or comments in the media. His support was wonderful. Many times over the next several months, he referred media inquiries directly to us, telling the contact people that our university was working hard on the issue and that we needed to be able to tell the story ourselves. As the university worked through all of the follow-up, many other colleagues called or sent E-mail messages offering their support. All of these contacts were beneficial and much appreciated.

What Comes Next—Institutional and Educational Response

After immediate needs are taken care of, additional responses can be put in place.

• *Use the incident and reaction as a "teachable moment."* The immediacy of the incident can facilitate learning that otherwise could be resisted or not occur at all. In addition to any services, vigils, or speak-outs, schedule additional programs to address the incident and provide education. Speakers who can draw out stereotypes and explore myths in open dialogue with students are effective. The fraternity involved with the float brought the director of Equality Colorado, Sue Anderson, to campus after the first few days of the crisis. Sue spoke to a very large crowd of students and challenged the crowd to come up with all of the "gay" terms they had ever heard and to ask any questions they had ever had. The dialogue was open and spirited, and our students learned a lot. Speakers who are booked before an incident occurs and who speak after the incident need to be brought "up to speed" on the campus situation and encouraged to incorporate this material into their presentations. Our Greek community was very fortunate in this regard. We already had scheduled a new member program for the Friday following the parade and were bringing in Mike McCree to be the speaker. Mike was able to work the float incident into his presentation in a very effective manner. By coincidence, we also had scheduled Shane Windmeyer to bring his presentation "Truth and Brotherhood: Being Gay in a College Fraternity" to campus at the beginning of November. Our new director of campus activities had worked with Shane when both were at Indiana University. He suggested that Shane's program, related to *Out on Fraternity Row*, would be a good choice, as we planned to address the issue of homophobia and Greeks. Little did we know how much we would need this program.

• *Bring in additional resource programs and make use of those programs that already exist on your campus.* Include resource materials, reading lists, and discussion of homophobia in Greek leadership classes, round tables, and workshops. Shane donated several copies of *Out on Fraternity Row* to our Greek resource library. We have been able to use the book very effectively to generate class discussions and to provide support to students who are doing presentations or writing papers.

• *Create follow-up educational opportunities for subsequent academic terms.* Build bridges with the GLBT students' support office on campus (if none currently exist). Actively work to raise awareness and consciously combat homophobia in your Greek community and on your campus. We have learned over the years that there is very little about gay bashing that is covert. Education to combat homophobia needs to be on the agenda every year. As with other educational interventions that we as professionals must keep on the front burner (alcohol, sexual assault, hazing, diversity of all kinds, etc.), the topic of homophobia can be difficult to approach with students. The "been there, done that" attitude of some students and the rapid turnover in our undergraduate membership make ongoing education very important. The challenge, however, is to grab student interest so that the issues remain a priority for them. It is unfortunate that some students are more attracted to supporting antigay behavior than they are to learning about the ills of homophobia.

The incident on our campus attracted attention on the Internet and the World Wide Web. Before the crisis abated, the President's Office received thousands of E-mail messages. The need to respond was evident immediately. A staff person in the office was designated to reply to all of the messages, and an institutional response was written. This response was shared with every person and office receiving E-mail as a result of the incident.

• *Following the first days of the crisis, official institutional statements and responses had been written for a number of issues.* All of these documents where posted on the Web site for the President's Office. Callers and E-mail inquiries were directed to the Web site.

• *The office of Greek life sent a personal response to everyone who sent a personalized E-mail message to our office.* People who forwarded general listserv-generated E-mail messages were sent the general university response. Many of these people later replied with appreciation for having received a reply. Many also said that they appreciated everything that the university was doing in response to the incident. We also received a number of phone calls and voice mail messages. I returned phone calls when voice mail messages included a phone number. When I was able to reach the people who had called, they usually were willing to talk and appreciative of our interest in their concerns.

• *Our campus has other Greek chapters and student organizations with Greek letter names that are very similar to the names of the chapters responsible for the incident.* As E-mail networks spread the incident message around the world, these student organizations and chapters became inundated with E-mail messages and comments left on their Web sites. In many instances, it was necessary for these organizations to shut down their Web sites and E-mail addresses. They also came to Greek life and other front-line staff for assistance and to process the feelings their members were having—especially since none of these organizations were a party to the original incident. Even more distressing for the students and the university was the fact that some of these organizations have gay members. It was doubly hurtful for these groups and their members to receive negative messages and hate mail for an incident in which the group did not take part. Many of the messages also labeled the organizations and their individual members as being homophobic—a statement that is far from the truth.

• *Student staff members in Greek life were overwhelmed by phone calls.* The phone line was rerouted to a special voice mail message, which directed callers to the university Web site.

• *In many cases where students, organizations, or staff were becoming overwhelmed, we were able to call on our personal connections within the GLBT community to help us do a "reality check" and to respond in an appropriate manner.* In some instances, personal friends and colleagues assisted by responding to messages that had the potential to escalate tensions. One of our Christian groups received several messages that were inflammatory. The key student leader in this group is very close to a number of GLBT students who stepped in and responded to messages that were "loaded." In several cases, the GLBT students involved wrote back that they too found the messages offensive. They also clearly identified themselves as members of the GLBT community and set the record straight as to the nature of the incident and the university's response. The efforts of these students were extremely helpful and very much appreciated.

• *Key response persons and Greek life professional staff need to be prepared to share relevant information and to address criticisms and concerns.* The initial response of the sorority chapter was to assume collective responsibility for the float—even though few of their members had worked on it. Sorority representatives had told the fraternity several days before the parade that they was severing their relationship with the float project, because things were disorganized and out of hand. The sorority had already disciplined the member involved with the defacing of the scarecrow, and leaders assumed that they had covered all of their bases. When the float still displayed the sorority name and the scarecrow, the women felt they had "dropped the ball" by not showing up the morning of the parade and preventing the float from being in the parade. The sorority members, with the support of their national organization and their alumnae, voted to close the chapter and relinquish their charter. The chapter members moved out on Wednesday. The fraternity, on the other hand, took the position that the scarecrow was the act of a few people and did not directly involve the rest of the fraternity membership. The fraternity alumni and national organization did not concur with the undergraduate assessment of the incident but also did not support possible closure of the chapter. This difference in approach created a lot of anger and controversy. Members of the Greek community were especially concerned, because they felt the fraternity was dodging its responsibility. The residual feelings related to the fraternity response are an issue we still address.

• *As the disciplinary process progresses, it is important to differentiate between public and private information.* Individual students generally are protected by the Family Education and Right to Privacy Act. (I say "generally" because some of these rights to privacy have been modified in certain states as the result of court cases.) Greek chapters are not protected by FERPA. If the institution has a peer judicial board for the Greek community (which is the case at our institution), the integrity of this board and the board's role in institutional discipline must be protected and supported. Following the conclusion of the judicial board process, the students recommended that the university withdraw recognition for both organizations. Since the sorority already had closed, the board recommended a projected date for possible reinstatement of the sorority and recolonization of the group, should the campus climate support this effort. The fraternity recognition was withdrawn, and a number of stipulations were put in place regarding the possibility of reinstatement. The fraternity chapter already had been placed in "Alumni Receivership" by the national organization. One of the judicial board sanctions required full compliance with all of the provisions of the receivership before reinstatement would be considered. The university accepted and fully supported the decisions made by the judicial board.

• *Expect references to the incident to resurface over a significant period of time.* Announcement of disciplinary sanctions, educational programs, event anniversaries (in our case, the 1999 homecoming parade), reinstatement or recolonization of chapters involved in the incident, formation of new chapters to replace chapters that may have been closed as a result of the incident, and other factors can serve as catalysts to revisit the incident. When the fraternity involved in the incident regained university recognition more than a year after recognition had been withdrawn, reaction from the campus media was immediate and critical. The campus newspaper article neglected to include important information about the recognition process, which included probation and "one strike, you're out" provisions. The article also did not address the dramatic changes that had occurred in the composition of the fraternity's membership. Almost all of the old members had left the chapter. All of the other members joined after recognition was withdrawn and were part of the effort to reorganize the chapter and educate the membership. Ironically, the Greek life staff was off campus at a retreat center preparing for IMPACT Weekend for our Greek community when the article was published. Notified by our student staff, we were able to work with the public relations office and the office of the vice president for student affairs to get the city newspaper to carry the story with the "missing information" clearly included. More than 60 of our students came to IMPACT Weekend having read the article. Several representatives of the fraternity were a part of this group. Facilitators of IMPACT were briefed about the entire situation before the students arrived and were prepared to address the issue when it arose. The students, much to their credit, were able to confront the issue on their own and to discuss it positively as an integral part of our need to change the Greek culture on our campus.

• *Be prepared to highlight changes that have been made—especially when return references to an incident do not include current information.* The institution and Greek life will need to be prepared to provide this information. old pictures and old information were used in some cases and probably will continue to be used in the future. Our office experienced a lot of frustration because the media used old material with no alterations. Fortunately for us, the assistance we received from our local newspaper helped change a little bit of the information when other news media picked up the reinstatement story.

Looking Back...

Twenty/twenty hindsight makes it easy to second-guess decisions made during crisis management situations. Although there are a few things that we would change, the majority of our responses worked effectively and still provide support for us. Our institution and many of our students have learned a lot as a result of the events precipitated by the scarecrow incident. Although the learning environment is not one I would have chosen, the experience and insights we all have gained are invaluable.

What Could/Should We Have Done Differently?

I should have called the President's Office and public relations right away, in addition to the director of Greek life and the vice president for student affairs. We have followed this expanded protocol for every Greek-related situation which has occurred since the scarecrow incident first confronted us. This procedure is effective and allows us to prepare for worst-case scenarios.

During the months prior to the parade, the community homecoming steering committee discussed the need to change the parade staging location and the lineup staffing. Since these changes would require extensive discussions with city officials, police agencies, and parade organizers, all involved recommended that these discussions be delayed until after the October 1998 parade. In retrospect, we should not have tried to hang in one more year. If the changes had been made prior to the 1998 parade, we might have avoided most of the scarecrow incident. On the other hand, the scarecrow incident paved the way for lots of support for the changes that ultimately were made. Although the changes would have occurred one way or another, all parties were more willing to come to consensus and to develop some very creative ways of managing parade check-in and logistics. We also were able to move the staging and lineup areas and portions of the route to more desirable locations—changes that had been discussed for more than a decade but never deemed possible to implement.

The university general counsel's office worked with us to modify the parade entry application to make this document a more effective contract than the application formerly in use. The revised application creates a stronger obligation for entry sponsors to comply with all parade regulations. The new wording also holds organizations and individuals more accountable for their actions during the parade. Although the revisions did not come about due to any lapse on the part of the Community Homecoming Steering Committee, it would have been easier to prevent incidents and to complete any necessary disciplinary follow-up actions if the revisions had been in place before the 1998 parade.

The Human Side... What Has Happened to Our University and Community as a Result

The university's response to the scarecrow incident was quick and decisive. The fraternity has learned that the actions of their members were not acceptable, and the group has changed dramatically.

As a Greek community, we have learned firsthand how challenging it is to withdraw recognition from an organization and still have the organization continue to exist. Despite the challenge, the learning experiences outweigh the anger and frustration that accompanied the process.

The university lost some alumni and donor support as a result of the incident. Some were upset because the incident had occurred. Others withdrew support because they disapproved of the university investigation and disciplinary sanctions. Responses were polarized, indicating that personal "core values" were being challenged by the incident and its aftermath.

The differing reactions of the individuals and chapters involved raise the questions: "Why did these people think that the scarecrow was OK?" "Why did the sorority (as a group) respond by assuming collective responsibility for the incident, while the collective voice of the fraternity chose the opposite path?" It is inappropriate to speculate. However, this type of incident directly relates to many issues of human dignity and is the tip of the proverbial iceberg when we look at other individual and group behaviors that can play out with some of our students.

A communitywide candlelight vigil was held in the student center sculpture garden on Tuesday evening—the day after Matthew Shepard's death. One of the speakers expressed the hope that Matthew's death would not merely be a "10-day wonder," as so many significant deaths or events had been in the past. The huge crowd in attendance agreed with this sentiment, and many have kept this commitment. Others in our larger community, however, drifted away from this feeling as subsequent weeks went by. During this particular time, our larger community was debating an upcoming election ballot issue—whether to amend the city charter to extend equal rights to everyone in our community and to outlaw discrimination based on sexual orientation. Proponents of the measure felt that equal rights were being denied to the GLBT population. Opponents expressed the view that the proposal created "special rights," not equal rights. Had the election occurred during the week following Matthew Shepard's death, the proposed measure would have passed. When the election did occur approximately three weeks after the vigil, the ballot measure was defeated.

Although much of our community was affected by the scarecrow incident, the bulk of attention centered on the university. The city and the school district were spared.

Colorado State University also has had the opportunity to begin the healing process. The university was selected as the venue for the world premiere of the film *Journey to a Hate-Free Millennium*. A number of student organizations and university departments were able to work together to host this project. Our Greek community was among those invited to participate. Our students responded by cosponsoring the event. Opportunities of this type are one way to engage our students, while sending a signal that homophobia and abusive behavior are not OK.

Sonia ImMasche *has been a full-time Greek affairs professional at Colorado State University since 1974. She is a charter member of the Association of Fraternity Advisors and has been involved with AFA in a number of capacities. She served as a member of the AFA executive board from 1981 to 1990.*

Checklist for a Climate of Acceptance

Diversity educators advocate for setting a standard of acceptance and appreciation as a normal part of an institution's daily activities. This approach to fostering inclusiveness and respect calls for attention to diversity in all aspects of an organization's routine. One or two token diversity programs each year will not fulfill the need for education. Building a climate of acceptance in sororities requires a commitment at all levels, ranging from individual members to the national and international headquarters and including the university administration. The following checklist is suggested as a guide for creating a climate of acceptance in sororities—a climate where a sister who is lesbian or bisexual may feel a sense of safety and support among her sisters.

Individual members should...

_____1. Refrain from ridiculing people on the basis of sexual orientation, such as through jokes, name-calling, and display of demeaning images or messages.

_____2. Confront others who may ridicule or harass people on the basis of sexual orientation.

_____3. Be committed to learning about sexual orientation, as shown through participation in educational programs and personal study.

_____4. Assume responsibility for learning how to respond to a sister who is lesbian or bisexual and wants or needs to talk.

_____5. Insist that leaders of the chapter state their commitment to diversity, including that pertaining to sexual orientation.

_____6. Show compassion and support for a sister who has been victimized by harassment or sexual assault.

Chapters should...

_____1. Include expectations for appreciating diversity in training for pledges and actives.

_____2. Create a diversity statement, either from national headquarters or locally developed, that promotes respect for all people regardless of sexual orientation.

_____3. Display the diversity statement prominently in the house and/or in printed materials about the chapter.

_____4. Develop a procedure for addressing harassing behaviors, including those directed at people on the basis of their sexual orientation.

_____5. When incidents of harassment or sexual assault occur, cooperate with university officials in addressing the matter through provision of information, participation in hearings, and other actions.

_____6. When incidents of harassment or sexual assault occur, show support for a sister who has been victimized by assisting her in reporting the incident and participating in campus and legal procedures.

_____7. Contribute to the education of other chapters on campus, both fraternities and sororities, by modeling acceptance and appreciation of diverse memberships.

_____8. Support individual members who wish to state publicly their support for persons who are gay, lesbian, bisexual, or transgendered.

_____9. Sponsor and support events that contribute to understanding of sexual orientation issues; do not sponsor or support events that perpetuate homophobia.

_____10. Encourage sisters to be honest with one another by creating an atmosphere of support for differences. Remember: This leads to a stronger sense of sisterhood.

_____11. Have policies that apply to guests and alumnae, making it clear that it is not acceptable to use demeaning language or harass members on the basis of sexual orientation.

_____12. Periodically review traditions, such as songs and events, to be sure that language and actions are not demeaning to people who are gay, lesbian, bisexual, or transgendered.

National and international headquarters and professional sorority associations should...

_____1. Promote understanding about sexual orientation issues through educational materials that have been prepared at the national level and made readily available through publicity to chapters.

_____2. Publicize a strong statement about appreciation for diversity and respect that includes sexual orientation.

_____3. Provide resources to assist chapters with educational initiatives that are designed to increase understanding about sexual orientation. National chapter consultants who travel to various college campuses should be prepared to address problems and questions about sexual orientation issues.

_____4. State an expectation of zero tolerance for harassment and sexual assault of any kind on the basis of sexual orientation.

_____5. Establish procedures for holding chapters accountable if they condone or tolerate harassment or sexual assault based on sexual orientation.

_____6. Highlight the accomplishments of lesbian and bisexual sisters in national publications.

_____7. Review periodically any publications, rituals, and traditional events that include text or behaviors that ridicule or demean persons on the basis of sexual orientation and take steps to ensure that such text and behaviors will be discontinued.

_____8. Communicate with university personnel the commitment of the sorority to fostering an environment of inclusiveness, respect, and appreciation for diversity, and offer to work with the university personnel in responding to any incidents that may occur in the sorority that would contradict this commitment.

_____9. Provide strong leadership in working with other national headquarters toward encouraging a climate of respect and inclusiveness.

_____10. Support local chapters and individuals who wish to initiate educational efforts, especially at the local level.

University personnel should…

_____1. Communicate university standards and expectations in regard to diversity to all student organizations, including sororities.

_____2. Be available to sorority leaders to assist with planning educational efforts to increase understanding about diversity, including sexual orientation (i.e., develop a diversity peer education program).

_____3. Develop a procedure for responding to incidents of harassment and sexual assault based on sexual orientation and communicate to sorority members that such procedures are available.

_____4. Assert a position in support of diversity and individual rights when faced with political pressure to exclude gays, lesbians, bisexuals, and transgendered persons from regular university life, including jobs and benefits.

_____5. Provide educational sessions for house directors and housing corporation boards to explain the university's standards and expectations in support of diversity.

_____6. Review periodically all institutional publications and policies to ensure that language that ridicules, demeans, or excludes persons because of sexual orientation is eliminated.

_____7. Support establishment of a Lambda Delta Lambda (a national sorority for lesbian, bisexual, and progressive women) chapter on your campus.

_____8. Inform faculty and staff who present educational programs in sororities about human sexuality, sexually transmitted diseases, sexual assault, and related topics not to be heterosexist and not to assume that all members of sororities are heterosexual.

_____9. Ensure that staff in campus resource offices, such as counselors, health professionals, and advisers, are trained about sexual orientation issues (i.e., heterosexism).

_____10. Provide leadership for creating supportive campus environments for other institutions and policy makers.

Shane L. Windmeyer and Pamela W. Freeman, Lambda 10 Project.

Questions, Policy Statements, and Resolutions Affirming Diversity

In many cases, if you never ask a question, you will never get an answer. Likewise, many sorority members never ask questions regarding the policies and practices of national or international sororities on sexual orientation issues. Others may ask, but never get an answer. Either way, there are still a lot of questions to be asked and answers to be given on this topic.

We offer suggested questions for you and your sisters to ask your national or international sorority leaders about their position, practices, and policies pertaining to sexual orientation. We believe all sisters—straight, lesbian, or bisexual—must begin asking the questions and insisting that their sororities take a proactive stance to affirm diversity including sexual orientation. Sample policy statements and resources also are provided to assist with such efforts and to suggest potential methods to be inclusive in your particular sororities and within your college or university campuses. And remember, if at first you do not succeed, try and try again. Let your sorority leadership know how important this issue is to your chapter and to the ideals of sisterhood. The more people ask the same questions, the more the "right" answer will be given.

Sample Questions to Ask Your Sorority Leadership Until You Get the "Right" Answer

1. Does our sorority have any written organizational policies dealing with sexual orientation, such as membership policies, standards policies, position statements, personnel policies, and so forth? If not, why not?

2. Do we discuss the issue of sexual orientation and being lesbian or

bisexual in any of our educational programs and resources? Do we provide our chapter with any educational resources to help a sister who comes out? If not, what are we waiting for?

3. Do we include workshops or other educational programs on sexual orientation issues at conventions or national or regional leadership conferences? If so, what does the program entail? Are there speakers? Facilitators?

4. Do we include the issue of sexual orientation in training for staff (such as leadership consultants) or volunteer alumnae? If so, what types of things are covered in the training? If not, why not? Is the issue of sexual orientation addressed in any of our resource materials, such officer manuals, volunteer adviser manuals, and other materials? If not, why not?

5. Would we be open to including an article or resources about sexual orientation in our national magazine or other publications? Have we ever done this? If not, why not?

6. What type of advice would our national sorority leadership give in the following circumstances, and how do we expect our members to know appropriate ways to deal with these situations if we do not have any policies or resources on the topic?

(a) What should our sorority do if a sister comes out to the chapter?

(b) Can our sorority president kick out a member because she is a lesbian or bisexual but by all accounts is a good sister? Is this OK?

(c) What should we do if someone openly lesbian wants to rush our sorority? Can we exclude her from being a member for this sole reason?

(d) Can a member take a same-sex date to the sorority formal?

(e) How do we stop rumors that our chapter is a "lesbian sorority" just because we have an out lesbian sister? Should we care?

What are your questions to ask? Remember to be courteous, professional, and sisterly, but you have a right to get an answer. Feel free to share your responses with the Lambda 10 Project, so others can see the positive work of your sorority to be inclusive of all types of diversity.

Shane L. Windmeyer and Pamela W. Freeman, Lambda 10 Project.

Our Sorority—
Chapter Diversity Statement

Our Sorority is an all-inclusive society of sisters. It values differences in people and diversity within our organization, the campus community, and society at large. It recognizes the different perspectives and contributions an all-inclusive people can make toward improving the sisterhood of the sorority and humanity.

Our Sorority policy is to welcome and reach out to people of different ages, nationalities, ethnic groups, physical abilities and qualities, sexual orientations, health status, religions, backgrounds, and educational experiences as well as to any others who may experience discrimination or abuse.

Our Sorority does not discriminate against any group or individual. In fact, the sorority will actively oppose any and all forms of discrimination.

Our Sorority also desires to help the Greek community and society at large to develop similar policies and practices that support diversity and assist in making the world a better place for all to live.

Adapted from the diversity policy of the National Society of Performance and Instruction and revised from *Out on Fraternity Row: Personal Accounts of Being Gay in a College Fraternity*, edited by Shane L. Windmeyer and Pamela W. Freeman, Alyson Publications, 1998.

Shane L. Windmeyer and Pamela W. Freeman, Lambda 10 Project.

Inter/National Sorority Headquarters Policy Statement on Sexual Orientation

Inter/National Sorority does not judge its sisters on the basis of sexual orientation. Thus, if a sister declares that she is lesbian or bisexual, we recognize this to be her personal right, free of censure or coercion. Of course, no chapter is required to offer membership to anyone, but it should not use "sexual orientation" as a reason not to offer membership. It may not expel any sister on the basis of "sexual orientation."

Aside from the fact of "sexual orientation," a sister who is straight, lesbian, or bisexual may have a sexual lifestyle that may be unattractive to other sisters due to various reasons besides her sexual identity. This does not categorize either sister as "right" or "wrong," as long as they are respectful and fair-minded regarding one another's sexual orientation.

Inter/National Sorority does follow an ethical code when it comes to sexual conduct. Sexual conduct must always be consensual, not exploitative or coercive, and between equals. Regardless of an individual's sexual orientation, we encourage our chapters to process sexual ethical issues on both an informal and formal basis.

Inter/National Sorority does believe that sisterhood is incompatible with sexual conduct between members that in any way has a negative impact on the sisterhood of the chapter, and we encourage the chapter to have a respectful conversation about this belief.

The sorority's position is brief, simple and clear. Behavior, not sexual orientation, is the basis for evaluating the worth of a sister.

For those who disagree or who are concerned, the sorority's policy makes it clear that concerns, objections, even disagreement with the policy do not classify such a person as "right" or "wrong." Our policy states, however, that such concerns or disagreements do not empower a person to deny membership to other persons because their beliefs or sexual orientations are different or to remove a person from membership for similar reasons.

Our policy respects all sexual orientations as well as individuals who may disagree. It urges that chapters, with the assistance of professionals, talk about their feelings and concerns.

Adapted from the Statement of Sexual Orientation of Zeta Beta Tau Fraternity as stated in the Fraternity Code of Ethics, Section III and revised from *Out on Fraternity Row: Personal Accounts of Being Gay in a College Fraternity*, edited by Shane L. Windmeyer and Pamela W. Freeman, Alyson Publications, 1998.

Shane L. Windmeyer and Pamela W. Freeman, Lambda 10 Project.

Western Regional Greek Conference Resolution on Heterosexism Within the Campus Greek Communities

Whereas, the Greek community is a vital part of undergraduate campus life and seeks to promote and to engage students in an ongoing process of personal and group development, and to provide an understanding and appreciation of the diversity of the peoples on the campus; and

Whereas, heterosexism, behavior which makes individuals the target of oppression, harassment or discrimination based upon their homosexual or bisexual orientation, is directly counter to the ideals of the educational experience and shall not be tolerated or permitted; and

Whereas, the Western Regional Greek Conference has addressed these issues in its 1991 programming; therefore

Be it resolved, that the Western Regional Greek Conference member campuses, through their InterFraternity and Panhellenic Councils, be strongly encouraged to challenge all behaviors and attitudes which are heterosexist in nature; and

Be it further resolved, that Western Regional Greek Conference member campuses, through their InterFraternity and Panhellenic Councils, discourage and seek to ban from their campuses all activities, competitions, social events and themes, membership recruitment attractions and other practices which are heterosexist in nature; and

Be it further resolved, that the Western Regional Greek Conference strongly encourages its member campuses to develop and implement ongoing sexual orientation awareness, education, and sensitivity programs for the Greek communities; and

Be it further resolved, that the Western Regional Greek Conference member campuses be made aware of this resolution through the WRGC Newsletter.

Adopted at the 1991 Western Regional Greek Conference.

Association of Fraternity Advisors Resolution on Heterosexism Within the Greek Community

Whereas, an understanding and appreciation of the diversity of peoples of the campus and world community is one of the goals of the student development co-curriculum on the college campus; and

Whereas, the Greek community is a vital part of the student development co-curriculum and is maintained to promote and engage students in an ongoing process of personal and group development; and

Whereas, heterosexism, defined as behavior which makes individuals the target of oppression, harassment, or discrimination based upon their homosexual or bisexual orientation, is directly counter to the ideals of the educational experience and must not be tolerated or permitted; now therefore

Be it resolved, that the Association of Fraternity Advisors strongly encourages the campus Greek Affairs professional to implement sexual orientation awareness, education, and sensitivity programs for the Greek community; and

Be it further resolved, that the campus Greek Affairs professional, or the appropriate authority, be strongly encouraged to challenge Greek chapter or member behaviors or attitudes which are heterosexist in nature; and,

Be it further resolved, that each men's and women's fraternity and sorority be strongly encouraged to implement sexual orientation awareness, education, and sensitivity programs on all membership levels and to develop appropriate responses to heterosexist behaviors; and

Be it further resolved, that all Association members and an executive office officer of general fraternity and sorority be made aware of this resolution.

Adopted December 1, 1990, at the Annual Business Meeting, Association of Fraternity Advisors.

University Statement on Affirming Diversity

The [university name] is committed to celebrating the rich diversity of people in the campus community to include all students, faculty, staff, alumni, and guests of the university. We believe that our educational environments must foster freedom of thought and opinion in the spirit of mutual respect. All of our programs, activities, and interactions are enriched by accepting each other as we are and by celebrating our uniquenesses as well as our commonalities.

The diversity of the campus community takes many forms. It includes differences related to race, ethnicity, national origin, gender, sexual orientation, religion, age, and ability. We believe that any attempt to oppress any individual or group is a threat to everyone in the community. We are guided by the principle that celebrating diversity enriches and empowers the lives of all people.

Therefore, everyone who chooses this university must understand that we will not tolerate any form of bigotry, harassment, intimidation, threat, or abuse, whether verbal or written, physical or psychological, direct or implied. Alcohol or substance abuse, ignorance, or "it was just a joke" will not be accepted as an excuse. Such behavior will be dealt with appropriately through the disciplinary process.

Our campus community is a rich, alive, and dynamic academic environment that is designed to enable all individuals to stretch and grow to their full potential. Only by understanding and celebrating our diversities can we create a safe learning environment where innovation, individuality, and creativity are maintained. We pledge ourselves to this end.

Adapted from the Statement on Diversity from the Indiana University Division of Residential Programs and Services.

Indiana University Code of Student Rights, Responsibilities, and Conduct

Non-Discrimination and Harassment Based on Sexual Orientation Policies

Under this policy, the university will not exclude any person from participation in its programs or activities on the basis of arbitrary considerations of such characteristics as age, color, disability, ethnicity, gender, marital status, national origin, race, religion, sexual orientation, or veteran status.

Harassment Based on Sexual Orientation

a. Students are responsible to respect each other's personal dignity regardless of sexual orientation.

b. A student has the right to be free from harassment based on sexual orientation.

(1) A student has the right to be free from harassment based on sexual orientation in any building or at any location on any university property.

(2) A student has the right to be free from harassment based on sexual orientation that occurs in a building or on property that is not university property if the harassment arises from university activities that are being conducted off the university campus, or if the harassment compromises the security of the university community or the integrity of the educational process.

c. Harassment includes any behavior, physical or verbal, that victimizes or stigmatizes an individual on the basis of sexual orientation and involves any of the following:

(1) The use of physical force or violence to restrict the freedom of action or movement of another person or to endanger the health or safety of another person;

(2) Physical or verbal behavior that involves an express or implied threat to interfere with an individual's personal safety, academic efforts, employment, or participation in university sponsored extracurricular activities and causes the person to have a reasonable apprehension that such harm is about to occur;

(3) Physical behavior that has the purpose or reasonably foreseeable effect of interfering with an individual's personal safety, academic efforts, employment, or participation in university sponsored extracurricular activities and causes the person to have a reasonable apprehension that such harm is about to occur.

(4) The conduct has the effect of unreasonably interfering with an individual's work or academic performance or creating an intimidating, hostile, or offensive working or learning environment.

d. Indiana University administrators are responsible for publicizing and implementing the university's harassment policy in their respective jurisdictions.

e. Students who believe that they are victims of harassment based on sexual orientation may obtain information concerning the university's policy and complaint procedures at the office of the campus Affirmative Action Officer or the Dean of Students.

Excerpted from Indiana University's Code of Student Rights, Responsibilities, and Conduct, "Part I: Student Rights and Responsibilities," 1997.

Out & Online: Being Gay and Greek Resources (URL: www.lambda10.org)

Technology has created a place for everyone; gay Greeks are not any different. The Lambda 10 Project has invested significant resources into creating an online community for gay, lesbian, and bisexual men and women and their allies in the college Greek system—a place where out and proud Greeks can be who they are. Where a closeted sister or brother can meet other gay Greeks anonymously and find support from them. Where a straight brother or sister can ask questions on what to do if a member comes out to the chapter.

Similar in purpose to this book and our first book, *Out on Fraternity Row: Personal Accounts of Being Gay in a College Fraternity,* such online communities are important places to create visibility, support, and education in an ongoing manner. Lambda 10 Online provides this place for the college Greek community on issues of sexual orientation and provides the most current updates, news, resources, and initiatives to create a stronger Greek system free of homophobia.

Highlights include the following:

Who's Out? An initiative where out men and women list their names, college/university attended, and their Greek affiliation to create more visibility and to show that there are indeed gay men and women in every college fraternity/sorority. E-mail links also are given to contact these members. The list continues to grow.

Out in Front A special section devoted to showcase international fraternities and sororities that have implemented programs, policies, and practices on issues of sexual orientation. Section also features gay-positive efforts by local fraternity and sorority chapters.

Chat & Bulletin Board Regularly scheduled chat room discussions on timely topics with special guests and a bulletin board to post messages for other members. A great place to meet other gay men and women in a fraternity or sorority.

Greek Safe Zone Allies A place to learn how to be an ally and how to start a Greek Safe Zone on your campus. Also, a forum for straight allies to post comments about issues of sexual orientation and what it is like to have a gay brother or sister. Comments can range from serious concerns to humorous anecdotes.

News & Personal Features Up-to-date alerts on news in the media regarding sexual orientation and Greek life as well as special, in-depth features written by men and women who have come out to their brothers and sisters.

Online Clearinghouse of Resources & Links A select listing of educational materials, Web site links, and programs to assist in efforts to create change in the Greek system on issues of sexual orientation. An excellent place to find information on speakers, national organizations, and newly created educational initiatives and efforts.

Shane L. Windmeyer and Pamela W. Freeman, Lambda 10 Project.

It's All Gay and Greek to Me: Definitions of Commonly Used Gay and Greek Terminology

Active: a fully initiated member of a sorority/fraternity.

Alumnus/Alumna: an initiated member who is no longer an undergraduate.

Ally: refers to heterosexual individuals who are accepting and supportive of people who are lesbian, gay, and bisexual and who work to reflect support in their personal beliefs, language, and behaviors. Allies also take action to combat homophobia and heterosexism within themselves and others, and in societal institutions.

Bid: a formal invitation to join a sorority/fraternity.

Bisexual: refers to persons who are capable of feeling attracted to and engaging in relationships with people of both sexes.

Blackballed: denotes that a bid has been denied or membership terminated.

Chapter: a local group of a national or international fraternal organization.

Coming out: shortened version of the phrase "coming out of the closet," which is a metaphor for disclosing one's sexual orientation to others.

Closeted or in the closet: hiding one's sexual orientation.

Dyke: predominantly used to refer negatively to lesbians or to stereotype them as masculine. Some lesbians have reclaimed the term as a symbol of pride in their strength and independence.

Faggot: predominantly used to refer to gay men in a derogatory fashion, implying weakness and lack of masculinity. Derived from the Latin word meaning a "bundle of sticks" that was used to burn witches at the stake. Some gay men have reclaimed this term for use within their own community.

Formal: the period set aside for structured rushing.

Gay: used to refer to homosexual men, although some homosexual women use it also to define who they are. Often used as a shorthand reference to all homosexuals. With *homosexual* frequently perceived as referring to the sexuality of being gay, it often is preferable to use *gay* for men and *lesbian* for women rather than *homosexual.*

Gender identity: an individual's self-perception as male or female. Gender identity is distinct from sexual orientation (which refers to whom an individual is attracted to).

GLB-sensitive fraternity: a term recently used to categorize Delta Lambda Phi National Fraternity, Alpha Lambda Tau National Fraternity, and Lambda Delta Lambda National Sorority. These fraternal organizations are founded on the premise of supporting gay, lesbian, bisexual, and transgender needs and issues. Membership is exclusively male (for fraternity) or female (for sorority) and is open to anyone regardless of sexual orientation. Straight members are welcome and must be allies to the gay community.

Hell Week: slang term used by some Greek members to describe activities the week leading up to initiation.

Initiation: the formal ceremony/traditional ritual which brings the pledge or associate into full membership of a sorority or fraternity.

Interfraternity Council: the programming body of collegiate fraternities.

Kinsey Scale: a 0-6 Likert-type scale used to understand the complexity of sexual diversity as depicted by the late, well-known sex researcher Alfred Kinsey. The scale represents on the 0 side heterosexuality, point 3 in the middle being bisexuality, and on the 6 side homosexuality. Kinsey's research shows that sexual identity falls naturally somewhere on this continuum between 0 to 6 and paved the way for educated dialogue on the concepts of sexual identity and sexual orientation. The scale bearing his name garnered worldwide attention and is still used today as a model to explain the complexity of sexuality.

Lambda: the eleventh letter of the Greek alphabet, which was chosen in 1970 by the Gay Activists Alliance in New York as a symbol of liberation. In 1974 the first International Gay Rights Conference adopted the lambda as an international symbol for gay and lesbian liberation. It was originally used in jewelry and art for homosexuals to reveal their identity to each other secretly. Spartan platoons made up solely of homosexual men are said to have had this symbol emblazoned on their shields. The lambda represents synergy, the concept that the whole is greater than its independent parts.

Legacy: a rushee who is a granddaughter/grandson, daughter/son, or sister/brother of a member of a particular sorority/fraternity.

Lesbian: refers to homosexual women. Derived from the name of the Greek Island of Lesbos, where the poet Sappho ran a school for women in 400 B.C. Due to homosexual referring to mainly the sexuality of what it means to be lesbian, many times the preferred words to use over the word *homosexual* is *gay* for men or *lesbian* for women.

Line: the new members of a National Pan-Hellenic Council sorority/fraternity.

Multicultural Greeks: usually the representation of Latino/a, Asian, Native American sororities/fraternities. Sometimes GLB-sensitive fraternities/sororities are also included in this category.

National Pan-Hellenic Council or Black Greek Council: the governing body of collegiate sororities/fraternities that are historically African-American.

Outing: the act of revealing another individual's sexual orientation, usually without permission.

Panhellenic Conference: the central programming body of collegiate sororities.

Pink triangle: thousands of gay men and men perceived to be gay were condemned in World War II to Nazi concentration camps and labeled with pink triangles, similar to the way in which Jews were forced to wear yellow stars. Displayed with the point down, the pink triangle has been reclaimed as a symbol of remembrance and pride.

Pledge/Associate member: a new member who has not been initiated.

Pledgeship: the time when new members learn the history, traditions, and goals of the sorority/fraternity.

Queer: predominantly a derogatory term used to refer to gay men, lesbians, and bisexuals, implying that they are unnatural, unusual, or freakish. Some gay men, lesbians, and bisexuals have reclaimed this term as a source of empowerment and pride in being different from the norm.

Rainbow flag: displayed with the red strip at the top, the rainbow flag was designed by Gilbert Baker in San Francisco in 1979 to celebrate the diversity of the lesbian and gay community. The colors are in the order of the rainbow (red, orange, yellow, green, blue, and violet) and show that sexual orientation crosses all ethnic, religious, economic, political, and social sections of society. The symbol is now recognized by the International Congress of Flag Makers as a symbol of gay and lesbian pride.

Rush: the social activity in which mutual choice and selection occurs to seek and determine new sorority/fraternity membership.

Rushee: person interested in becoming a member of a sorority/fraternity.

Secret sister: often a sisterhood bonding activity designed for new and older members of the sorority to get to know each other. The secret sister is a mystery, and nobody knows who her secret sister is. A secret sister may leave notes and homemade gifts for a new sister until a predetermined time when the new sister is able to guess who is her secret sister or when the secret sister is revealed to the new sister. The notes and gifts are often clues about the secret sister (i.e. hometown, likes/dislikes, hobbies, sorority customs, etc.) Such a practice may also be associated with "Big Sis and Little Sis" and similar activities.

Sexual orientation: the direction of an individual's emotional, physical, and/or sexual attraction to others, which may be toward the same sex (homosexual), the opposite sex (heterosexual), or both sexes (bisexual). Research has shown that sexual orientation exists on a continuum, rather than a set of distinct categories. The term *sexual preference* is not synonymous with sexual orientation and is not considered to be an accurate term to define one's sexual identity, due to the limited scope of sexuality implied by the word. Sexual orientation represents the varied and complex nature of sexuality and defining one's sexual identity.

Sexual behavior: refers to an individual's sexual activities or actions (what a person does), which may or may not be congruent with an individual's sexual identity (how a person identifies her or his sexual orientation). Sexual identity (who we are) is distinct from sexual behavior (what we do).

Stonewall: the Stonewall Inn is a gay bar on Christopher Street in the Greenwich Village area of New York City. A June 27, 1969, police raid on the Stonewall sparked a three-day riot which has become a symbol of gay and lesbian resistance to societal oppression. The Stonewall riots are often said to be the birthplace of the modern gay and lesbian rights movement.

Straight: a term used to refer to people who are heterosexual.

Compiled from definitions in the "Opening Minds, Opening Doors, Opening Hearts" SAFE ZONE Manual at Northern Illinois University, 1999.

Updated and adapted from "It's All Greek to Me…" published in *Out on Fraternity Row: Personal Accounts of Being Gay in a College Fraternity*, edited by Shane L. Windmeyer and Pamela W. Freeman, Alyson Publications, 1998.

About the Editors

Shane L. Windmeyer is one of the foremost commentators on issues of sexual orientation and Greek life on college campuses and is also coeditor of the book *Out on Fraternity Row: Personal Accounts of Being Gay in a College Fraternity.* He joined Phi Delta Theta Fraternity in spring 1992 while attending Emporia State University and recalls coming out to his brothers as one of his most rewarding undergraduate experiences. As a result, he created the Lambda 10 Project National Clearinghouse for Gay, Lesbian, & Bisexual Greek Issues in 1995 to help support gay fraternity men and women and to educate others about issues of homophobia within the college Greek system. Windmeyer graduated from Emporia State University with a bachelor's degree in communication and received his master's degree in higher education and student affairs administration from Indiana University. He currently works as Assistant Director of Student Activities at the University of North Carolina at Charlotte.

Pamela W. Freeman is associate dean of students and director of the Office of Student Ethics and Antiharassment Programs at Indiana University. She cochairs the Gay, Lesbian, Bisexual Antiharassment Team and the Racial Incidents Team, which have been nationally recognized as having "best practices" in addressing bias-motivated incidents on college campuses. A coeditor of the book *Out on Fraternity Row: Personal Accounts of Being Gay in a College Fraternity,* she also codirects the Lambda 10 Project National Clearinghouse for Gay, Lesbian, & Bisexual Greek Issues. Freeman is a member of the Indiana Civil Rights Commission's Hate Crimes Advisory Panel; has chaired the Indiana University Commission on Multicultural Understanding since 1991 and served on the campus's Educational Task Force on Gay, Lesbian, Bisexual Concerns; and supervises the Gay, Lesbian, Bisexual Student Support Services Office. She received her bachelor's and master's degrees from Purdue University and her doctorate from the University of Tennessee, Knoxville.